Progress Asses
Support System

HOLT

WORLD HISTORY

Human Legacy

HOLT, RINEHART AND WINSTON

A Harcourt Education Company

Orlando • Austin • New York • San Diego • London

Printed in the United States of America

ISBN- 978-0-03-093782-8
ISBN 0-03-093782-5

3 4 5 6 7 8 9 912 12 11 10 09 08 07

Contents

The Progress Assessment Support System (PASS) consists of the following elements:

- Diagnostic Test
- Test-Taking Tips
- Section Quizzes
- Chapter Tests
- Unit Tests
- End-of-Year Test
- Answer Key

Each element is designed to help you assess your students' progress in mastering the concepts and information in the textbook. You will be able to determine which students need additional assistance and which ones are progressing satisfactorily.

The Diagnostic Test covers the major concepts and facts that you will teach during the year. This test assesses what students know about the subject on their first day.

The Test-Taking Tips are suggestions to students about how to be more successful on tests. You may want to photocopy these tips and give them to each student. Review the tips with students occasionally, especially before a major test. The tips may help relieve some of the anxiety that affects some students when they have to take a test.

Each Section Quiz assesses students' knowledge of the material in that section. These quizzes do not duplicate the questions asked in the textbook. Similarly, the Chapter Tests assess students' knowledge of the material in the entire chapter. These tests are different from the assessment material in the textbook.

The Unit Tests take the assessment process to the next level: students are assessed on what they have learned in the chapters that make up a unit. Units are usually three or four chapters long.

The End-of-Year Test repeats the questions in the Diagnostic Test. This repetition of content will allow you to compare a student's results on both tests and determine the progress that student has made over the course of the year.

The Answer Key provides answers to each test.

1. Master the question

Have you ever said, "I knew the answer, but I thought the question asked something else"? Be very sure that you know what a question is asking. Read the question at least twice before reading the answer choices. Approach it as you would a mystery story or a riddle. Look for clues. Watch especially for words like not and except—they tell you to look for the choice that is false or different from the other choices or opposite in some way.

2. Track your time

Use all the time you are given to take a test in order to avoid making errors. Here are some checkpoints to help you monitor your time.

- How many questions should be completed when one quarter of the time is gone? When half the time is gone?
- What should the clock read when you are halfway through the questions?
- If you find yourself behind your checkpoints, you can speed up.
- If you are ahead, you can—and should—slow down.

3. Study the directions

In order to follow the directions you have to know what the directions are! Read through the directions once. Then read the directions again. Study the answer sheet. How is it laid out? What about the answer choices? Are they arranged

A B
C D or A B C D

Be very sure you know exactly what to do and how to do it before you make your first mark.

4. Take it all in

When you finally hear the words "You may begin," briefly preview the test to get a mental map of your tasks.

- Know how many questions you have to complete.
- Know where to stop.
- Set your time checkpoints.
- Do the easy sections first; easy questions can be worth just as many points as hard ones.

5. Negatives do not fit

Be sure to watch for negative words in the questions such as *never*, *unless*, *not*, and *except*. When a question contains one of these negative words, look for the answer that does not fit with the other answers.

6. Jot it down
You might have made a special effort to memorize some information for the test. If you are worried you will forget as soon as the testing period begins, jot it down on the back of your test or on your scratch paper as soon as the teacher begins the test. Then go on and work on the test itself.

7. Anticipate the answers
Before you read the answer choices, answer the question yourself. Then read the choices. If the answer you gave is among the choices listed, it is probably correct.

8. How much do I write?
If a writing question contains the following terms, you will need several sentences for a complete answer:

- describe
- write
- justify
- why
- explain

9. Significant details
You will often be asked to recall details from reading a passage. Read the question before you read the passage. Underline the details as you read. But remember that the correct answers do not always match the wording of the passage precisely.

10. In your own words
Sometimes the wording of a passage might be a bit different than the language you are used to using. Read the question and restate the question in your own words to make sure you are very comfortable with what is being asked.

11. Go with your gut
Your first impulse is most often correct. Be careful about changing your answers on multiple choice or true/false questions. If you do decide to change your answer, be totally confident in making the change.

12. Master the reading comprehension question
If you are taking a reading comprehension test, read the selection, master all the questions, and then re-read the selection. The answers will be likely to pop out the second time around. Remember: A test isn't trying to trick you; it's trying to test your knowledge and your ability to think clearly.

13. Spot those numbers

Have you ever said, "I got off by one and spent all my time trying to fix my answer sheet"? Make it a habit to

- match the number of each question to the numbered space on the answer sheet every time.
- leave the answer blank if you skip a question.
- keep a list of your blank spaces on scratch paper or somewhere else—but not on your answer sheet. The less you have to erase, the better.

14. Rely on 50/50

"I . . . have . . . no . . . clue." It is time to make an educated guess—not a wild guess, but an educated guess. Always read every choice carefully.

- Watch out for distracters—choices that may be true, but are too broad, to narrow, or not relevant to the question.
- Eliminate the least likely choice.
- Then, eliminate the next least likely choice, and so on until you find the best answer.
- If two choices seem equally correct, look to see if "All of the above" is an option.
- If it is, that might be your choice.
- If no choice seems correct, look for "None of the above."

15. Try. Try. Try.

Keep at it. Don't give up. This sounds obvious, so why say it? You might be surprised by how many students do give up. Remember: The last question is worth just as much as the first question, and the questions don't get harder as you go. If the question you just finished was really hard, an easier one is probably coming up soon. Take a deep breath, and keep on slogging. Give it your all, all the way to the finish.

16. Find the main idea

The main goal of a reading comprehension section is to test your understanding of a reading passage. Be sure to keep these suggestions in mind when you read a selection on a test:

- Read the passage once to get a general overview of the topic.
- If you don't understand the passage at first, keep reading. Try to find the main idea.
- Then, read the questions so that you'll know what information to look for when you re-read the passage.

17. I'm stuck!

If you come across a question that stumps you, don't get frustrated or worried. First, master the question to make sure you understand what is being asked. Then work through many of the strategies you have previously learned. If you are still stuck, circle the question and go on to others. Come back to the problem question later. What if you still have no idea? Practice the 50/50 strategy and then take your best educated guess.

18. Minutes to go

If you become short on time, quickly scan the unanswered questions to see which might be easier to answer. Quickly go with your instinctive answer on those questions in order to complete as many questions as possible.

19. Search for skips and smudges

To avoid losing points on a machine-graded test make sure you

- did not skip any answers.
- gave one answer for each question.
- made the marks heavy and dark and within the lines.
- get rid of smudges.

Make sure there are no stray pencil marks on your answer sheet. Cleanly erase those places where you changed your mind. Check for little stray marks from pencil tapping. Check everything. You are the only person who can!

20. I'm done!

When you think you are finished with your test you still need to check it. First, take a look at the clock and see how much time you have left. Go back and review your answers for any careless mistakes you may have made such as leaving a question blank or putting two answers to one question. Be sure to erase any stray marks, review the hardest questions you answered, and turn the test in at the end of the time period. There is nothing to be gained from finishing first—or last, for that matter.

Name ______________________________ Class __________________ Date ___________________

Diagnostic Test

MULTIPLE CHOICE For each of the following, write the letter of the best choice in the space provided.

_____ 1. Early humans living during the Stone Age most likely
a. lived in small groups and moved to new areas as food became scarce.
b. settled in permanent villages for common defense.
c. were uninterested in art or music.
d. worshipped one god.

_____ 2. What was an important development for early people of the Stone Age?
a. the use of tools
b. calendars
c. writing
d. cave art

_____ 3. The Neolithic Revolution marked the
a. end of Homo habilis.
b. creation of man-made fire.
c. beginning of agricultural societies.
d. introduction of stone tools.

_____ 4. Hammurabi's Code was an
a. early method of communication.
b. early written code of law.
c. effort to tax the Babylonians.
d. ethical code for waging war.

_____ 5 The world's first civilization arose
a. in China.
b. along the Nile River.
c. in Mesopotamia.
d. in the Indus Valley.

_____ 6. Many scholars believe that Judaism
a. developed under Julius Caesar.
b. died out in 1000 BC.
c. was founded by David, Israel's greatest king.
d. was the world's first monotheistic religion.

_____ 7. During the Old Kingdom, Egyptians built pyramids because of their belief in
a. archaeology.
b. reincarnation.
c. the afterlife.
d. medical studies.

_____ 8. The experience of Hyksos rule led pharaohs in the New Kingdom to
a. create Egypt's first permanent army.
b. pass laws forbidding weapons in Egypt.
c. organize teams of archers to protect the pyramids.
d. rely on geographical barriers for protection.

_____ 9. The Rosetta Stone helped historians to
a. understand the purpose of the pyramids.
b. understand Egyptian writing.
c. decipher Linear A.
d. find the source of the Nile.

Name ______________________ Class ______________ Date ______________

Diagnostic Test

_____ 10. The early Indus settlements of Harappa and Mohenjo Daro can best be described as
a. disorganized units.
b. small villages.
c. well planned and carefully laid out.
d. lacking clean water and sanitary conditions.

_____ 11. The *Vedas*, *Upanishads*, and *Mahabharata* are some of the sacred texts of
a. Islam.
b. Dualism.
c. Hinduism.
d. Buddhism.

_____ 12. What Zhou idea was used to explain the dynastic cycle?
a. Yin and Yang
b. Enlightenment
c. the Middle Road
d. Mandate of Heaven

_____ 13. The Mycenaean states formed
a. an early Greek civilization.
b. the first industrial empire.
c. an early African trading kingdom.
d. the first matriarchal society.

_____ 14. The world's first democracy existed in
a. Athens.
b. Sparta.
c. Knossos.
d. Carthage.

_____ 15. Which of the following Greeks is known for a method of learning through questions?
a. Plato
b. Socrates
c. Aristotle
d. Sophocles

_____ 16. Which of the following phrases describes the government of the Roman Republic?
a. unrestricted use of military rule
b. network of local governments
c. use of clergy to write and enforce laws
d. system of checks and balances

_____ 17. Law and order, a stable government, and widespread trade were characteristics of
a. the Pax Romana.
b. the Early Republic.
c. the Late Republic.
d. the Age of Constantine.

_____ 18. Caesar, Pompey, and Crassus are known as the
a. Good Emperors.
b. Julio-Claudians.
c. First Triumvirate.
d. Second Triumvirate.

_____ 19. The Hohokum people of North America adapted to desert farming by
a. using terraces.
b. planting crops in riverbeds.
c. using slash-and-burn techniques.
d. digging irrigation canals.

_____ 20. Mesoamerica is the region that includes
a. South America and Central America.
b. North America and Central America.
c. southern Mexico and northern Central America.
d. northern Mexico and the Mid-West.

_____ 21. The Olmec culture is called the "mother culture" of Mesoamerica
a. because all Mesoamericans descend from one Olmec female.
b. because the Olmec gave rise to all later civilizations in the area.
c. because the Olmec were worshipped.
d. and the Maya culture is called the "father culture."

_____ 22. During the Qin dynasty, strict laws and harsh penalties were the result of a political philosophy called
a. Daoism.
b. Legalism.
c. Imperialism.
d. Confucianism.

_____ 23. The Mauryan Empire was the first empire to
a. unite much of India.
b. allow elected officials.
c. encourage private businesses.
d. expand through peaceful means.

_____ 24. A characteristic of the Gupta golden age was
a. great works of art and architecture.
b. equal distribution of wealth.
c. the introduction of democracy.
d. the end of the caste system.

_____ 25. Sharia, the Muslim legal system,
a. regulated trade.
b. is made up of opinions and writings over several centuries.
c. was written by Muhammad.
d. only applies to Muslim men.

_____ 26. The conflict over the successor to Muhammad
a. was negotiated peacefully.
b. was confined to Mecca.
c. never divided the followers of Islam.
d. led to the Sunni-Shia division.

_____ 27. The actions of the Umayyad dynasty conflicted with the Muslim belief in equality when
a. they used military power to grow.
b. they converted to Sufism.
c. Arab Muslims became a ruling class.
d. they split into Shia and Sunni groups.

_____ 28. The African kingdom of Aksum thrived
a. due to a monopoly on salt.
b. because of its location along the Mediterranean.
c. due to advanced iron technology.
d. because its location on the Red Sea was ideal for controlling trade.

_____ 29. Ghana became a wealthy kingdom
a. by conducting silent auctions.
b. by taxing ships in Ghana's ports.
c. through sales of camels to Bedouins.
d. by controlling the gold and salt trade.

_____ 30. Islam was introduced to West Africa
a. by Muhammad.
b. by Muslim traders.
c. by Sunni Ali.
d. after the Jesuits arrived in Timbuktu.

_____ 31. In China, under Song rule, the civil service exam system tested a person's
a. ability to add and subtract large sums.
b. skills as a diplomat.
c. knowledge of Confucianism.
d. knowledge of Chinese history.

_____ 32. One result of Mongol rule in China was
a. foreign trade increased.
b. increased violence.
c. that the Mongol culture died out over time.
d. that the country was closed to all foreigners.

_____ 33. What factor allowed Japan to limit contact with other cultures?
a. climate
b. religion
c. language
d. geography

_____ 34. The Eastern Roman Empire
a. fell to Germanic tribes called Vandals.
b. became known as the Byzantine Empire.
c. relocated to Damascus.
d. rejected all forms of Christianity.

_____ 35. Who were the Rus?
a. three brothers from Rome who set up a trading post in Moscow
b. northern Europeans, perhaps Vikings, who united the Slavs and formed a state called Kievan Rus
c. three sisters who liberated the Slavs to form a state called Kievan Rus
d. monks who migrated from Constantinople to Moscow

_____ 36. Charlemagne, who created an empire in Western Europe in the late 700s, is also known for
a. allowing the Muslims to build the city of Tours.
b. his opposition to Christianity and missionaries.
c. his interest in education and religion.
d. his interest in exploration of the New World.

_____ 37. The Vikings were successful raiders because
a. they lived in dense forests across Europe.
b. they were skilled riders with fast horses.
c. their nomadic lifestyle made them difficult to find and capture.
d. they built fast moving ships that allowed for surprise attacks.

_____ 38. In the Middle Ages, the feudal system was the political and social system, while the manorial system was the
a. legal system.
b. educational system.
c. religious system.
d. economic system.

_____ 39. The document known as the Magna Carta
a. limited the king's power.
b. favored the monarchy.
c. abolished the monarchy.
d. gave commoners the vote.

_____ 40. The goal of the Crusades was
a. to reclaim the Holy Land.
b. to show allegiance to the patriarch.
c. to convert Muslims to Christianity.
d. to preserve the Byzantine Empire.

_____ 41. In the High Middle Ages, new farming technology required fewer people to produce food and enabled more people to
a. move to towns.
b. buy their own farms.
c. become knights.
d. live on manors.

_____ 42. Scholasticism is the
a. belief in public education.
b. translation of Greek texts into Arabic.
c. use of intellect and logic to bring together opposing ideas.
d. systematic approach to cultural diffusion.

_____ 43. Which of the following statements describes humanism?
a. The purpose of all human work is to glorify God.
b. The potential of the human mind is almost limitless.
c. A spiritual focus leads to personal fulfillment.
d. A person's potential is reached through meeting the needs of others.

_____ 44. One of the causes of the Renaissance was
a. limited trade following the Crusades.
b. increased interest in spiritual matters.
c. the growth of large, wealthy city-states in Italy.
d. decreased interest in scientific and technical knowledge.

_____ 45. The concern that the church was moving from its spiritual roots led to the
a. Edict of Worms.
b. Protestant Reformation.
c. Age of Reason.
d. start of the church court.

_____ 46. How did the compass and the astrolabe aid the Age of Exploration?
a. Explorers went in search of new technology.
b. Explorers hoped to trade these items to the Chinese.
c. Marco Polo took these items to Kublai Khan.
d. They enabled sailors to plot courses and sail long distances.

_____ 47. The primary cause for the drastic drop in the Native American population of the Americas in the 1500s was
a. massive migration.
b. harsh climatic events.
c. the introduction of guns.
d. the introduction of diseases.

_____ 48. Mercantile nations established colonies in order to
a. trade with other colonies.
b. control sources of raw materials and provide markets for manufactured goods.
c. increase imports of manufactured goods to the home country.
d. more easily trade with other mercantile nations.

_____ 49. One section of the Atlantic Slave Trade network was called the
a. Middle Passage.
b. Columbian Exchange.
c. Encomienda System.
d. Mississippi Waterway.

_____ 50. The Mughal Empire was the
a. first civilization in India.
b. first Muslim empire in India.
c. only governing republic in India.
d. only civilization without religion.

_____ 51. The purpose of the Great Wall of China was
a. as an observatory for Asian astronomers.
b. to protect China from invasions from the north.
c. to limit trade with India.
d. as a memorial to Chinese emperors.

_____ 52. Ming emperors isolated China because
a. they thought European weapons might cause the peasants to rebel.
b. they were disappointed with the tribute gained from Zheng He's voyages.
c. they did not want to divert attention from building the Great Wall.
d. they disliked European influence and sought to preserve China's traditions.

_____ 53. The Spanish Armada revealed
a. England's growing military power.
b. Spain's invincible naval forces.
c. Spain's opposition to the Catholic Church.
d. Charles V's goal of a Catholic Europe.

_____ 54. Restoration was the name given to the
a. the growing gold trade in the Netherlands.
b. return to a monarchy in England.
c. establishment of Puritanism.
d. reign of Oliver Cromwell in England.

_____ 55. For what is Peter the Great best known?
a. as the cause of the Time of Troubles
b. for abdicating the throne
c. for the westernization of Russia
d. for the death of Ivan the Terrible

_____ 56. The Enlightenment was the
a. idea that all physical objects exert force.
b. belief that the earth is the center of the universe.
c. emphasis on using reason to understand truth.
d. five basic steps used to form and test a hypothesis.

_____ 57. Enlightenment thought had a profound influence on
a. Louis XIV.
b. the Carlsbad Decrees.
c. Otto von Bismarck.
d. the U.S. Constitution.

_____ 58. What was a major cause of the French Revolution?
a. strong leadership
b. ambitious generals
c. inequalities in society
d. foreign intervention

_____ 59. The chaos following the Reign of Terror
a. allowed Napoleon to rise to power.
b. forced the United States to intervene.
c. positioned the Catholic Church to take over.
d. allowed Horatio Nelson to rule France.

_____ 60. The purpose of the Napoleonic Wars was to
a. unite the French people.
b. defend France's borders.
c. establish Napoleon as king.
d. expand the French Empire.

_____ 61. The Industrial Revolution was
a. the formation of cottage industry guilds.
b. the conflict between cottage and factory workers.
c. a race between Great Britain and the United States for higher production rates.
d. a shift to power driven machinery and factory production.

_____ 62. Factory working conditions in Britain improved as a result of
a. labor strikes.
b. American unions.
c. the Luddite Movement.
d. new education laws.

_____ 63. A characteristic of socialism is
a. corporate empires.
b. increased mercantilism.
c. privately owned property.
d. that society controls industry.

_____ 64. Industry was transformed in the late 1800s due to the availability of
a. coal.
b. electric power.
c. steam power.
d. water power.

_____ 65. The construction of vast railroad systems was made possible
a. because of electric engines.
b. by the Bessemer process.
c. through the use of assembly lines.
d. through improved communication.

_____ 66. Which aspect of city life made migration to the suburbs possible?
a. city green spaces
b. skilled factory jobs
c. public transportation
d. multistoried buildings

_____ 67. In Great Britain, the goal of Chartism was
a. voting rights for all men.
b. voting rights for all women.
c. protection for child workers.
d. standardized factory wages and hours.

_____ 68. In 1804, Haiti became
a. the final resting place of Napoleon.
b. the first Latin American colony in the Caribbean.
c. the first Latin American territory to break its ties with Europe.
d. the first Latin American colony to obtain independence through peaceful means.

_____ 69. The U.S. Civil War was about
a. voting rights for African Americans.
b. Reconstruction.
c. taxation without representation.
d. states' rights and the issue of slavery.

_____ 70. Key figures in the unification of Italy were
a. Napoleon, Victor Emmanuel, and the Medici.
b. the Medici, Garibaldi, and Cavour.
c. Garibaldi, Mazzini, and Cavour.
d. the Medici, Mazzini, and Metternich.

_____ 71. Bismarck hoped realpolitik would help him achieve his goal of
a. ruling Germany.
b. unifying Germany.
c. spreading idealism.
d. overthrowing the king.

_____ 72. In the early 1900s, unrest in Russia
a. caused Lenin to call for the overthrow of the czar.
b. ultimately increased the power of the czar.
c. triggered World War II.
d. improved the status of Russian Jews.

_____ 73. The Sepoy Mutiny in India resulted in
a. India gaining self-rule.
b. India becoming two nations.
c. the East India Company taking control of India.
d. the British government taking direct control of India.

_____ 74. The British took control of Egypt in 1882 to
a. slow the spread of Islam.
b. control the diamond mines.
c. ensure the security of the Suez Canal.
d. remove the French imperialists.

_____ 75. The Spanish-American War
a. gained more colonies for Spain.
b. resulted in the Philippines becoming an American colony.
c. forced Cuba to become a monarchy.
d. was a victory for Spain.

_____ 76. The four factors that led to World War I were militarism, imperialism, nationalism, and
a. socialism.
b. isolationism.
c. nuclear power.
d. alliances.

_____ 77. Russia entered World War I because Czar Nicholas
a. wanted to expand the empire.
b. took advice from Grigory Rasputin.
c. hoped the cause would unite his country.
d. feared an attack from Great Britain.

Diagnostic Test

_____ 78. One reason the United States entered World War I was
a. Germany's policy of unrestricted submarine warfare.
b. the hope it would stabilize the United States economy.
c. the belief it would bring a quick end to the war.
d. to get backing for the League of Nations.

_____ 79. The peace agreement ending World War I was called the
a. Call to Power.
b. Zimmerman Note.
c. Treaty of Versailles.
d. New Economic Policy.

_____ 80. The Stock Market Crash of 1929 signaled the beginning of
a. the New Deal.
b. World War II.
c. the Great Depression.
d. an economic rebound.

_____ 81. Mussolini, Stalin, and Hitler
a. were benevolent dictators.
b. ran totalitarian governments.
c. headed democratic nations.
d. led anarchist movements.

_____ 82. The goal of the Nuremberg Laws was to
a. guarantee Hitler's absolute power in Germany.
b. exclude Jews from mainstream German life.
c. end the reign of violence spreading through Germany.
d. form an alliance between Germany, Italy, and Japan.

_____ 83. Control of the Atlantic was critical in World War II because
a. Axis powers dominated on land.
b. Japan controlled all shipping routes on the Pacific.
c. it protected the United States from direct attack.
d. it was the supply route to Britain and the Soviet Union.

_____ 84. The Nazi campaign to systematically kill Jews, Poles, Slavs, Gypsies, homosexuals, and disabled people is known today as the
a. Sitzkreig.
b. Holocaust.
c. Blitzkreig.
d. Higher Order.

_____ 85. In World War II, fighting with Japan ended
a. with an Allied victory in Iwo Jima.
b. after the Battle of Midway.
c. with MacArthur's victory in the Battle of the Bulge.
d. after the United States dropped atomic bombs on Japan.

_____ 86. The purpose of the Marshall Plan was to
a. provide support for the Warsaw Pact.
b. maintain political stability in Europe.
c. gain control over Eastern Europe.
d. rebuild European military power.

_____ 87. The goal of the North Koreans in 1950 was to
a. unite their divided nation under a communist government.
b. participate in the space race.
c. make Asia a communist continent.
d. isolate Korea from communist influence.

_____ 88. The Cold War ended when the
a. Solidarity Movement failed.
b. Soviet Union collapsed.
c. United States won the arms race.
d. Soviet Union held a democratic election.

_____ 89. The Berlin Wall was built to
a. end the spread of communism.
b. block supplies to the west.
c. prevent an invasion from Great Britain.
d. stop migration from East to West Germany.

_____ 90. The "Quit India" campaign became violent when
a. Indira Gandhi was elected prime minister.
b. the British informed India it was not required to fight for the Allies in World War II.
c. the British imprisoned Gandhi and thousands of others.
d. Pakistan was created.

_____ 91. The United States supported South Vietnam because of U.S. concerns about
a. another war.
b. the spread of communism.
c. Vietnam's economy.
d. French imperialism.

_____ 92. The Tet Offensive in 1968 resulted in
a. the end of the Vietnam War.
b. the surrender of North Vietnam.
c. the destruction of the Ho Chi Minh Trail.
d. increased American opposition to the war.

_____ 93. President Nixon's visit to China ended
a. the Cultural Revolution.
b. communism in China.
c. China's isolation from the world.
d. the Tiananmen Square Massacre.

_____ 94. Democracy spread through African nations in the 1990s in part because
a. public education grew.
b. the Cold War ended.
c. the United Nations forced out the dictatorships.
d. missionaries introduced ideas of democracy.

_____ 95. An independent Jewish state was achieved through
a. the Peel Commission.
b. Arab-Israeli negotiations.
c. a United Nations proposal.
d. the Haganah military power.

_____ 96. The United States led a multinational force in the Persian Gulf War in 1990 to
a. free Kuwait.
b. find the Taliban.
c. block trade routes.
d. empower the Kurds.

_____ 97. Castro's goals for Cuba included
a. restoring the free press.
b. redistribution of wealth.
c. establishing a Marxist regime.
d. friendly relations with the United States.

_____ 98. For more than seventy years, Mexico's government was not a true democracy because
a. it was run by dictatorships.
b. the church ruled Mexico.
c. it was a one-party system.
d. the militia was in control.

_____ 99. Economic interdependence occurs when
a. transportation creates a demand for new goods.
b. cultural diffusion is a goal of developing nations.
c. developed nations control all aspects of life in developing nations.
d. countries can't provide all of the raw materials and finished goods they need.

_____ 100. The purpose of the green revolution is to
a. stop pesticide use on plants.
b. decrease water pollution.
c. help build developing economies.
d. increase the world's food supply.

Name ______________________ Class ______________ Date ______________

The Beginnings of Civilization

Section Quiz

Section 1

MATCHING In the space provided, write the letter of the term or place that matches each description. Some answers will not be used.

_____ 1. Preserved remains or imprints of living things

_____ 2. The first part of the Stone Age

_____ 3. People who hunt animals and gather wild plants, seeds, fruits, and nuts to survive

_____ 4. Early humans named for their upright posture

_____ 5. The time before the invention of writing

_____ 6. Scientists who dig into ancient settlements to find objects used by early people

_____ 7. "Wise man"

_____ 8. A community of people who share a common culture

_____ 9. Early humanlike beings and humans

_____ 10. Scientists who study fossils to learn about human origins

a. society

b. anthropologists

c. hominids

d. fossil

e. Homo sapiens

f. archaeologists

g. prehistory

h. Paleolithic Era

i. artifacts

j. Neanderthal

k. Homo erectus

l. hunter-gatherers

m. absolute dating

Name ______________________ Class ______________ Date ______________

The Beginnings of Civilization

Section Quiz

Section 2

MULTIPLE CHOICE For each of the following, write the letter of the best choice in the space provided.

_____ 1. The shift from hunting and gathering to farming is called the
- a. Bronze Age.
- b. Iron Age.
- c. Ice Age.
- d. Neolithic Revolution.

_____ 2. Which factor most influenced the types of crops grown?
- a. animals
- b. language
- c. geography
- d. tools

_____ 3. Domestication meant that early humans could
- a. live in covered dwellings.
- b. produce their own food.
- c. predict climate changes.
- d. build more efficient tools.

_____ 4. Which group was more likely to contain people of different social status?
- a. hunter-gatherers
- b. Neanderthals
- c. settled people
- d. Paleolithic hominids

_____ 5. Technological advances, social ranking, and trade developed once people
- a. were not worried about basic survival.
- b. discovered Çatal Hüyük.
- c. were able to navigate mountains and deserts.
- d. learned to polish stones.

MATCHING In the space provided, write the letter of the term or place that matches each description. Some answers will not be used.

_____ 6. Animal-based disease

_____ 7. One of the oldest farming sites discovered

_____ 8. Used for cooking, storing water, grains, and oils

_____ 9. Period of history when people learned to use metal

_____ 10. First animal to be domesticated

- a. dog
- b. measles
- c. Bronze Age
- d. pottery
- e. Çatal Hüyük
- f. horse

The Beginnings of Civilization

Section Quiz

Section 3

FILL IN THE BLANK For each of the following statements, fill in the blank with the appropriate word, phrase, or name.

1. In early farming villages, a(n) ________________________ economy was utilized.

2. A ________________________ is a complex culture that includes cities, government, religion, record keeping, specialized jobs, social classes, and arts and architecture.

3. A division of ________________________ came from increased wealth.

4. Skilled craft workers, or ________________________, devoted their time to carpentry, metal work, basketry, weaving, or pottery.

5. Over time, writing evolved from using picture symbols or pictographs to using more ________________________ symbols.

TRUE/FALSE Mark each statement **T** if it is true or **F** if it is false. If false explain why.

_____ 6. The earliest civilizations grew up in dry, desolate valleys.

____

____

_____ 7. Flooding enriched the soil and helped produce enough food.

____

____

_____ 8. Early civilization developed formal religious institutions.

____

____

_____ 9. Priests rarely became powerful figures or leaders.

____

____

_____ 10. Cultural diffusion brought advances in farming, writing, and art.

____

____

Name ______________________ Class ______________ Date ______________

The Beginnings of Civilization

Chapter Test

Form A

MULTIPLE CHOICE For each of the following, write the letter of the best choice in the space provided.

_____ 1. How did ice ages affect worldwide migration patterns?
   a. As ocean levels rose during the ice ages, societies were isolated on continents.
   b. Land bridges connecting continents were exposed, aiding migration.
   c. Many roads became impassable, halting migration.
   d. Disruption in agriculture forced people in previously settled communities to become nomadic migrants.

_____ 2. Early humans living during the Stone Age most likely
   a. lived in small groups and moved to new areas as food became scarce.
   b. settled in permanent villages for common defense.
   c. were uninterested in art or music.
   d. worshipped one common god.

_____ 3. What was an important development of early Stone Age culture?
   a. domestication of animals
   b. farming
   c. the wheel
   d. language

_____ 4. The shift from hunting and gathering to farming is called the Neolithic Revolution because it
   a. coincided with the development of wooden tools.
   b. changed life dramatically.
   c. began the process of global warming.
   d. began a long period of warfare in the Fertile Crescent.

_____ 5. Agriculture emerged
   a. after a warming trend resulted in new plants and animals.
   b. as glaciers moved toward the equator bringing water.
   c. when religious leaders forced some people to become farmers.
   d. in the Paleolithic Era.

_____ 6. What led to the building of permanent settlements?
   a. migration to the Americas
   b. development of simple governments
   c. the development of agriculture
   d. the end of bloody warfare

_____ 7. One characteristic of civilization is
   a. a university.
   b. fertile river valleys.
   c. developed cities.
   d. industry.

Name ______________________ Class ______________ Date ______________

The Beginnings of Civilization

Chapter Test

Form A

_____ 8. The earliest record keeping was used to
a. record births and deaths.
b. record history for future generations.
c. keep track of economic transactions.
d. express abstract ideas.

_____ 9. Cultural diffusion may have affected an early civilization
a. by making it more difficult to control trade.
b. by encouraging the preservation of distinct characteristics.
c. when people adopted new customs, skills, and technologies.
d. by lowering the standards for entry into a craft guild.

PRACTICING SOCIAL STUDIES SKILLS Study the visual below and answer the question that follows.

Early Human Migration

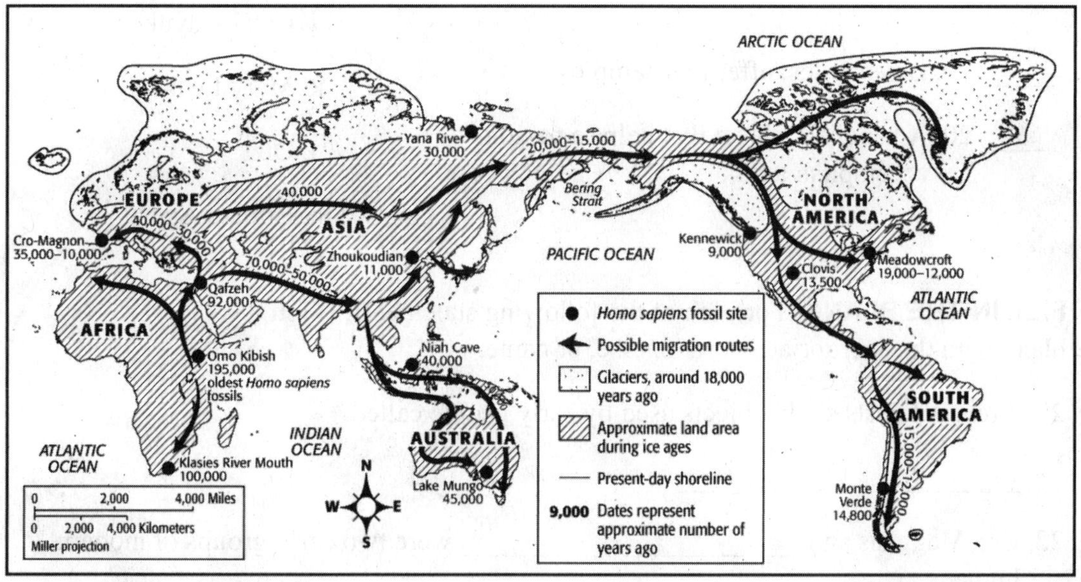

_____ 10. According to the map, what part of the world did humans reach last?
a. Africa
b. Europe
c. the Americas
d. Australia

Name ______________________ Class ______________ Date ______________

The Beginnings of Civilization — Chapter Test

Form A

MATCHING In the space provided, write the letter of the term, person, or place that matches each description. Some answers will not be used.

_____ 11. A preserved Neolithic man

_____ 12. Introduction of items made from copper and tin

_____ 13. The raising and adapting of wild plants and animals for human use

_____ 14. Skilled crafts workers

_____ 15. An early Neolithic settlement

_____ 16. An early hominid

_____ 17. Time before written records

_____ 18. Developed to organize and regulate cities and civilizations

_____ 19. Ceremonies, offerings, temples

_____ 20. A handheld object that helps a person accomplish a task

a. domestication

b. smallpox

c. Australopithecus

d. government

e. tool

f. artisans

g. traditional economy

h. religion

i. prehistory

j. Çatal Hüyük

k. Mary Leakey

l. Ötzi

m. Bronze Age

FILL IN THE BLANK For each of the following statements, fill in the blank with the appropriate word, phrase, or name.

21. Archaeologists study objects used by early people called ______________________.

22. Cro-Magnons and ______________________ were two early groups of modern humans.

23. As their way of life began to change, people developed new ______________________ such as hoes, to make life easier.

24. Farming villages that produced a ______________________ could support craftspeople and priests.

25. The buying and selling of food, raw materials, and finished products between regions is called ______________________.

The Beginnings of Civilization

Chapter Test

Form B

SHORT ANSWER On a separate sheet of paper, answer each of the following questions in complete sentences. Remember to use specific examples to support your answers.

1. How do scholars learn about prehistoric humans? Discuss two different specialties, and how those scholars uncover the history of peoples who lived before the invention of writing.

2. How did the roles of men and women differ in hunter-gatherer societies?

3. What social changes occurred as a result of the development of agriculture?

4. How did cities differ from farming villages?

5. What is cultural diffusion, and what were its effects on early societies?

PRACTICING SOCIAL STUDIES SKILLS Study the map below and, on a separate sheet of paper, answer the question that follows in complete sentences.

Early Human Migration

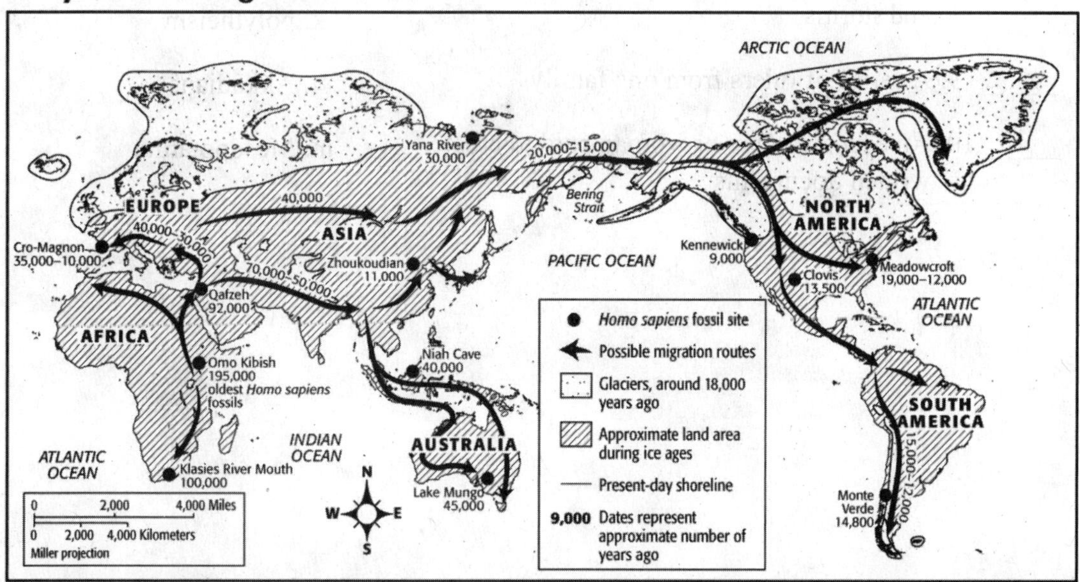

6. How were humans able to migrate from Asia to the Americas? What tools or technologies may have been needed to make the journey?

Name ______________________ Class ______________ Date ______________

The Ancient Near East

Section Quiz

Section 1

MATCHING In the space provided, write the letter of the term, person, or place that matches each description. Some answers will not be used.

_____ 1. Area whose name means, "between the rivers," the site of the world's first known civilization

_____ 2. The worship of many gods

_____ 3. People who developed the first known civilization

_____ 4. An early system of writing

_____ 5. Babylonian king known for a written code of law

_____ 6. Group of people ruled by Sargon I

_____ 7. A pyramid-shaped temple

_____ 8. The Sumerian god believed to rule the air and storms

_____ 9. A series of rulers from one family

_____ 10. An educated man or woman paid to create written documents

a. geometry

b. Enlil

c. scribe

d. ziggurat

e. Sumerians

f. Tigris

g. cuneiform

h. Hammurabi

i. city-state

j. dynasty

k. polytheism

l. Akkadians

m. Mesopotamia

Name ______________________ Class ______________ Date ______________

The Ancient Near East

Section Quiz

Section 2

TRUE/FALSE Mark each statement **T** if it is true or **F** if it is false. If false explain why.

_____ 1. The Hittites were a warlike Indo-European tribe that settled in the region known as Asia Minor around 2000 BC.

____

____

_____ 2. The Hittites refused to learn from others or to blend elements of different cultures into their own.

____

____

_____ 3. The Assyrians' power rested in their ability to negotiate peace with neighboring countries.

____

____

_____ 4. Under the Assyrian system of government, kings ruled through local leaders, each of whom governed a small area of the empire.

____

____

_____ 5. Because farming was difficult and resources were limited, the Phoenicians relied on trade and the sea for their livelihood.

____

____

Name ______________________ Class ______________ Date ______________

The Ancient Near East

Section Quiz

Section 3

FILL IN THE BLANK For each of the following statements, fill in the blank with the appropriate word, phrase, or name.

1. The Hebrew religion is known as ______________________.
2. Accounts of the Hebrews' early history appear in five sacred books called the ______________________.
3. In a journey known as the ______________________ the Hebrews made their way out of Egypt, where they had been held as slaves.
4. According to Hebrew history, Moses was chosen by God to receive a collection of moral laws known as the ______________________.
5. The Hebrew people made a ______________________, or a solemn agreement, to follow God's law.
6. The Hebrews believed the land of ______________________ was promised to them by God. This land was described as "flowing with milk and honey."
7. Israel's first king was a man named ______________________, chosen for his military leadership.
8. Shortly after the death of King Solomon, Israel's Twelve Tribes formed two kingdoms. One was called Israel and the other was called ______________________.
9. Unlike most other ancient peoples, the Hebrews practiced ______________________, the belief in only one god.
10. Written by early Jewish scholars, the ______________________ contains explanations and interpretations of the other sacred texts.

Name ______________________________ Class ________________ Date ________________

The Ancient Near East

Section Quiz

Section 4

TRUE/FALSE Mark each statement **T** if it is true or **F** if it is false. If false explain why.

_____ 1. For centuries, the Persians were ruled by the Medes, who had conquered them.

____

____

_____ 2. When Cyrus the Great rose to power, he abolished the Persian army and signed a peace treaty with the Medes.

____

____

_____ 3. At the time of his death in 530 BC, Cyrus ruled the largest empire in the world.

____

____

_____ 4. Zoroastrianism was one of the first religions to teach dualism, the belief that the world is controlled by two opposing forces.

____

____

_____ 5. During the reign of Xerxes, Persian culture reached a high point.

____

____

Name ______________________ Class ______________ Date ______________

The Ancient Near East

Chapter Test

Form A

MULTIPLE CHOICE For each of the following, write the letter of the best choice in the space provided.

_____ 1. The geography of Mesopotamia led people to
a. migrate to the Sinai Peninsula.
b. adopt hunting and gathering as a way of life.
c. develop methods to control water.
d. build cities along the Mediterranean coastline.

_____ 2. Sumerians developed a large trading network because
a. they wanted slaves to build ziggurats.
b. the empire included many different kingdoms.
c. their army was not powerful.
d. they lacked raw materials such as wood and metal.

_____ 3. Which of the following groups was the most brutal in dealing with opposition and dissent?
a. the Hittites
b. the Phoenicians
c. the Chaldeans
d. the Assyrians

_____ 4. One thing the Chaldeans and Hittites had in common was
a. they used terror to control their huge empires.
b. they adopted aspects of Sumerian culture.
c. their empires did not fall.
d. they worshipped one god.

_____ 5. Who was the first king of Israel?
a. Saul
b. David
c. Solomon
d. Nebuchadnezzar II

_____ 6. A Jew who eats kosher food is following
a. the Diaspora.
b. Mosaic law.
c. Hammurabi's Code.
d. the Psalms.

_____ 7. Which Persian king was widely admired for his tolerance of the customs of peoples he conquered?
a. Cyrus the Great
b. Cambyses II
c. Darius
d. Zoroaster

_____ 8. The Royal Road was built in order to
a. discourage far-flung trading networks.
b. foster communication between distant parts of the empire.
c. conquer additional territory.
d. encourage tourism.

Name ______________________ Class ______________ Date ______________

The Ancient Near East

Chapter Test

Form A

PRACTICING SOCIAL STUDIES SKILLS Study the visuals below and answer the questions that follow.

The Assyrian Empire

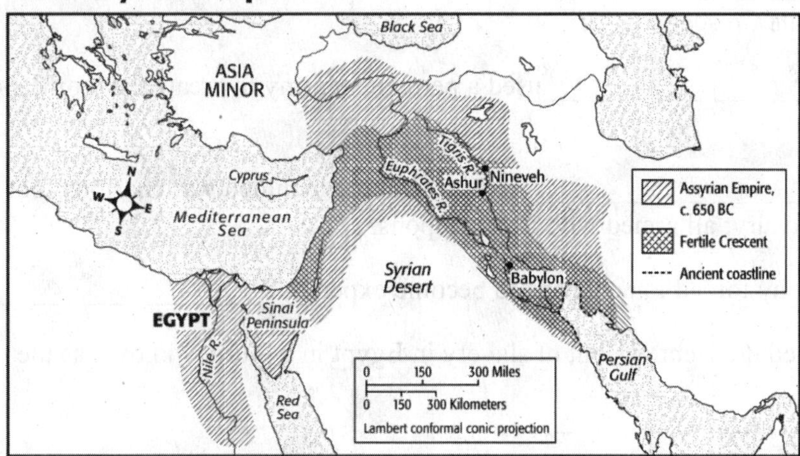

_____ 9. According to the map above, the Assyrians conquered territory mainly
a. bordering the Persian Gulf.
b. in the Syrian Desert.
c. in the Fertile Crescent and Nile river valley.
d. to gain access to the Black Sea.

> **196. If a man put out the eye of another man, his eye shall be put out.**
> **197. If he breaks another man's bone, his bone shall be broken.**
> **198. If he put out the eye of a freed man, or break the bone of a freed man, he shall pay one gold mina**
> **199. If he put out the eye of a man's slave, or break the bones of a man's slave, he shall pay one-half of its value.**
> **200. If a man knock out the teeth of his equal, his teeth shall be knocked out.**
> **201. If he knock out the teeth of a freed man, he shall pay one-third of a gold mina.**
>
> **—from Hammurabi's Code**

_____ 10. Based on this passage from Hammurabi's Code, in Babylonian society
a. all people were treated equally.
b. no one owned slaves.
c. slaves were less valuable than freed men.
d. women had the same rights as men.

Name ______________________ Class ______________ Date ______________

The Ancient Near East

Chapter Test

Form A

FILL IN THE BLANK For each of the following statements, fill in the blank with the appropriate word, phrase, or name.

11. ______________________ is the area between the Tigris and Euphrates rivers in the Fertile Crescent.

12. ______________________ used a permanent army to create the world's first empire.

13. The ______________________ war machine included war chariots, foot soldiers, and a cavalry; all armed with iron weapons.

14. Geography forced Phoenicians to become expert ______________________.

15. Moses led the Hebrews out of slavery in Egypt in a journey known as the ______________________.

16. The most important belief of Judaism is called ______________________.

17. The ______________________ were a group of highly trained soldiers at the heart of the Persian army.

18. ______________________ were Persian government officials who helped keep control over the huge empire.

TRUE/FALSE Indicate whether each statement below is true or false by writing **T** or **F** in the space provided.

_____ 19. The Sumerians practiced polytheism.

_____ 20. The development of cuneiform marked the transition from prehistory to the historical age.

_____ 21. Hittite military advantages included iron weapons and war chariots.

_____ 22. The Phoenicians most significant achievement was the development of cuneiform.

_____ 23. Western civilization's laws and values have been greatly influenced by the Ten Commandments.

_____ 24. The Talmud is the most sacred text of Judaism.

_____ 25. Zoroastrianism was a monotheistic religion that taught that good and evil controlled the world.

The Ancient Near East

SHORT ANSWER On a separate sheet of paper, answer each of the following questions in complete sentences. Remember to use specific examples to support your answers.

1. Describe the government of Sumer and how it changed over time.

2. What were the distinct roles of men and women in Sumer?

3. What two military advantages helped the Hittites build a strong empire?

4. Describe how Judaism has influenced the laws and values of western civilization.

5. Why was Darius's reign the high point of Persian culture? Explain using examples from the text.

PRACTICING SOCIAL STUDIES SKILLS Study the map below and, on a separate sheet of paper, answer the questions that follow in complete sentences.

The Assyrian Empire

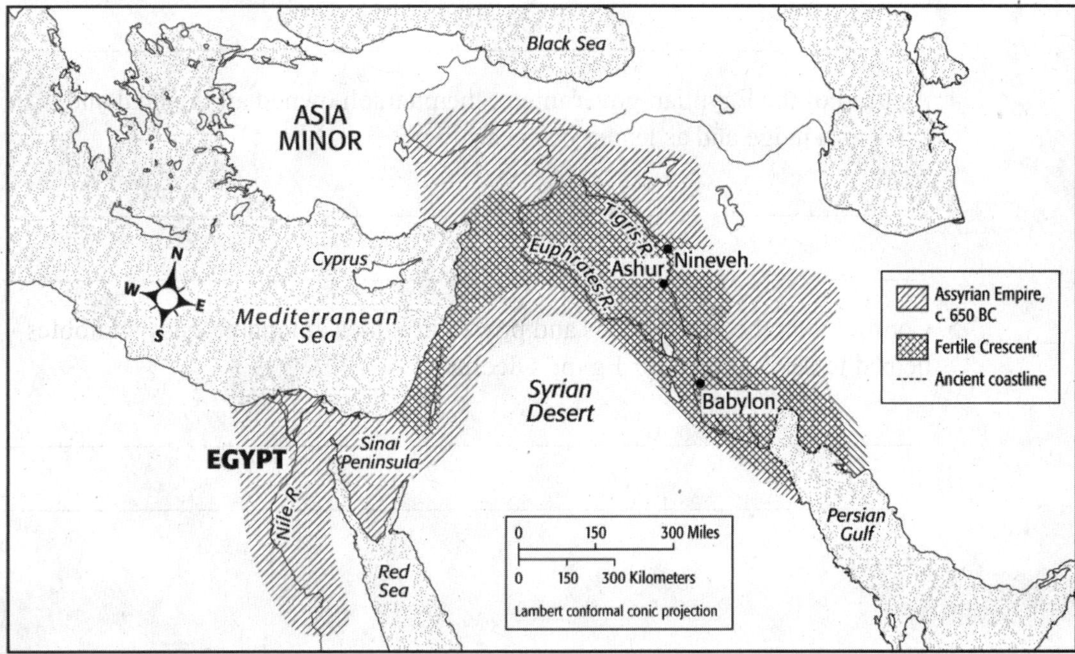

6. Many people sought to control the area covered by the Assyrian empire. Based on the map and information from the chapter, explain why this region was valuable.

7. Based on the map and information from the chapter what factors may have prevented the Assyrians from extending their empire?

Name ______________________ Class ______________ Date ______________

Nile Civilizations

Section Quiz

Section 1

TRUE/FALSE Mark each statement **T** if it is true or **F** if it is false. If false explain why.

_____ 1. The Nile River and the Sahara Desert were important natural barriers that kept the Egyptian people safe from invaders.

____

____

_____ 2. Around 3100 BC Egypt was divided into two separate kingdoms by a ruler named Menes.

____

____

_____ 3. The pyramids were built as temples to the Egyptian gods so all Egyptians could worship together.

____

____

_____ 4. As head of the Egyptian government, the pharaoh owned all the land and acted as a judge and as leader of the army.

____

____

_____ 5. Conflict with the Sea Peoples and power struggles among priests and nobles helped to set the stage for Egypt's decline.

____

____

Name ______________________ Class ______________ Date ______________

Nile Civilizations

Section Quiz

Section 2

MATCHING In the space provided, write the letter of the term, person, or place that matches each description. Some answers will not be used.

_____ 1. Process that prevented the breakdown of a dead body

_____ 2. Someone who copied texts or kept public records

_____ 3. Granite slab used by historians to decode Egyptian writing

_____ 4. Egyptian god of the sun

_____ 5. Egyptian writing system

_____ 6. A god credited with introducing civilization to Egypt

_____ 7. Famous stone statue of a creature with the body of a lion and the head of a person

_____ 8. Tall, thin pillar with a pyramid-shaped top

_____ 9. Reedy plant growing along the Nile

_____ 10. A life force, or an individual's personality separated from the body

a. Amon-Re
b. Osiris
c. Thoth
d. mummification
e. scribe
f. Great Sphinx
g. Rosetta Stone
h. papyrus
i. hieroglyphics
j. obelisk
k. Horus
l. *ka*
m. quarry

Name ______________ Class ______________ Date ______________

Nile Civilizations

Section Quiz

Section 3

MULTIPLE CHOICE For each of the following, write the letter of the best choice in the space provided.

_____ 1. Which is a true statement about the kingdom of Nubia?
- a. Nubia had few natural resources.
- b. Nubia conquered Egypt during the Egyptian Middle Kingdom.
- c. The Nubian people were expert traders, archers, and pottery makers.
- d. The Nubians rejected all Egyptian influences in religion and culture.

_____ 2. Farming was almost impossible in Nubia because
- a. the rocky landscape made agriculture difficult.
- b. the Nile did not flow in Nubia.
- c. farming tools and technology were not available.
- d. the wrong type of soil existed there.

_____ 3. The kingdom of Kush became wealthy as a result of
- a. increased trade with Egypt.
- b. an improved irrigation system.
- c. cutting all ties with the Hyksos people.
- d. an increasingly educated population.

_____ 4. The most valuable resource in the Meroitic kingdom was
- a. diamonds.
- b. iron.
- c. salt.
- d. llamas.

_____ 5. Which of the following led to the decline of the Meroitic kingdom?
- a. an invasion by the Egyptians
- b. the demand for new technology
- c. a dramatic change in climate
- d. a decline in trade

Name ______________________________ Class ________________ Date ________________

Nile Civilizations

Chapter Test

Form A

MULTIPLE CHOICE For each of the following, write the letter of the best choice in the space provided.

_____ 1. Why did pharaohs have absolute power in Egypt?
   a. Pharaohs ruled the country using terror.
   b. Egyptians believed the pharaoh was a god in human form.
   c. The kingdom was small enough for one man to exercise complete control.
   d. Egyptians believed the pharaoh received instructions directly from the vizier.

_____ 2. What important change occurred in Egypt when Akhenaton became pharaoh?
   a. Most Egyptians worshipped the Hittite gods.
   b. Egypt became monotheistic.
   c. Most Egyptians converted to Judaism.
   d. Egypt became polytheistic.

_____ 3. Egyptians practiced mummification in order to
   a. keep the *ka* from vanishing.
   b. preserve the body for resurrection.
   c. show their respect to pharaohs.
   d. find cures for common diseases.

_____ 4. Objects were buried with Egyptian mummies in order to
   a. buy the person's entry into heaven.
   b. keep the gods happy.
   c. display wealth.
   d. serve the *ka*.

_____ 5. An Egyptian scribe quickly producing business documents would most likely use which form of writing?
   a. hieroglyphics
   b. demotic
   c. cuneiform
   d. hieratic

_____ 6. Egypt's history as an independent kingdom ended in the 330s BC when
   a. an earthquake destroyed Alexandria.
   b. the Assyrians plundered the tombs of the pharaohs.
   c. Ramses surrendered to the Nubians.
   d. it was conquered by Greek armies under Alexander the Great.

_____ 7. What were key differences between the Meroitic kingdom and earlier Kushite culture?
   a. Rulers of the Meroitic kingdom abandoned many aspects of Egyptian culture the earlier Kushites had adopted.
   b. Pyramids were no longer built in the Meroitic kingdom.
   c. The Meroitic kingdom was monotheistic; earlier Kushite culture was not.
   d. Women in earlier Kushite culture enjoyed a higher status than they did in the Meroitic kingdom.

Name ______________________ Class ______________ Date ______________

Nile Civilizations

Chapter Test

Form A

PRACTICING SOCIAL STUDIES SKILLS Study the map below and answer the question that follows.

New Kingdom Egypt

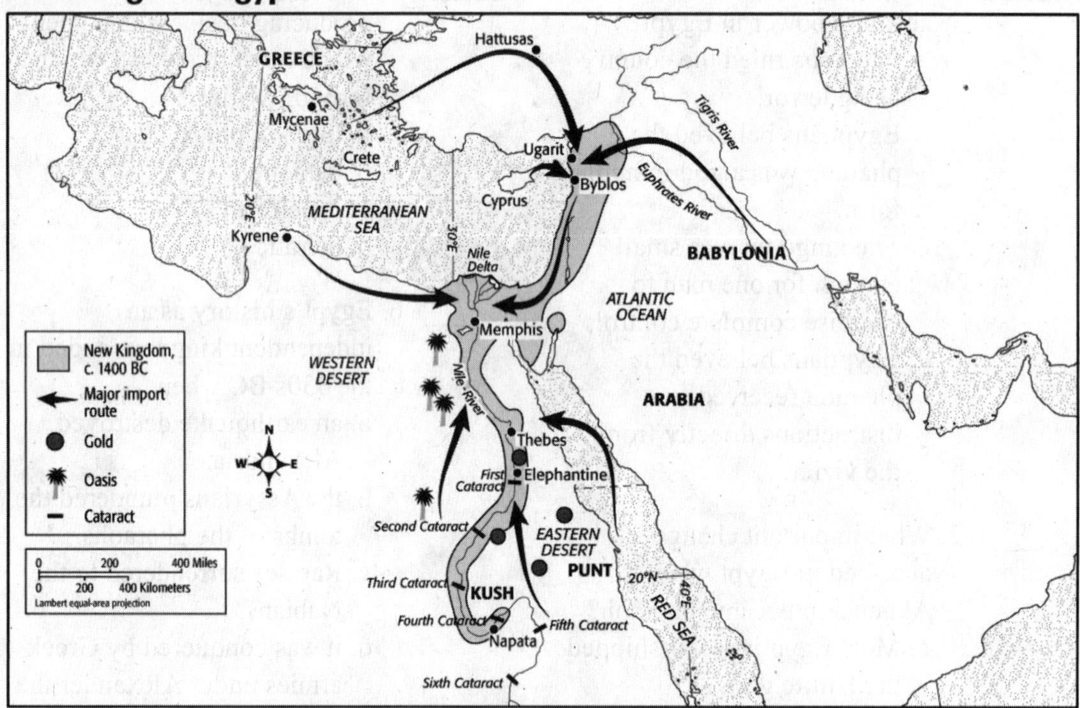

_____ 8. How would traders ship goods from Punt to Thebes?

a. using an overland route through the Sahara Desert
b. by ship on the Nile
c. by ship through the Red Sea
d. by ship through the Mediterranean Sea

Nile Civilizations

Chapter Test
Form A

MATCHING In the space provided, write the letter of the term, person, or place that matches each description. Some answers will not be used.

_____ 9. The sun god

_____ 10. A state ruled by religious figures

_____ 11. Helped historians to decode Egyptian writing

_____ 12. Defeated the Hittites and led a great empire

_____ 13. Goddess of nature

_____ 14. Area at the mouth of a river made up of fertile silt deposits

_____ 15. Founded Egypt's first dynasty

_____ 16. Rocky stretches of the Nile with rapid currents and waterfalls

_____ 17. Used to make paper-like sheets for writing

_____ 18. Kushite ruler who conquered all of Egypt

a. Osiris
b. bureaucracy
c. Menes
d. Nubia
e. cataracts
f. papyrus
g. Re
h. delta
i. Isis
j. Piankhi
k. Ramses II
l. Rosetta Stone
m. theocracy

FILL IN THE BLANK For each of the following statements, fill in the blank with the appropriate word, phrase, or name.

19. The ________________________ that surrounded Egypt helped protect the country from invasion.

20. ________________________, huge structures built as tombs for Egypt's rulers, are the most famous symbols of the Old Kingdom.

21. An Egyptian who wanted to quickly gain social status might become a(n) ________________________.

22. The main Egyptian writing system was ________________________.

23. The largest part of Egyptian society, about 90 percent of the population, was made up of ________________________.

24. Egyptian rulers sometimes hired Nubians as police and soldiers because they were such skilled ______________________.

25. Kushite culture changed substantially after the capital's move to ______________________.

Nile Civilizations

Chapter Test

Form B

SHORT ANSWER On a separate sheet of paper, answer each of the following questions in complete sentences. Remember to use specific examples to support your answers.

1. Why do you think Hatshepsut dressed like a man?
2. Describe the rights and duties of Egyptian women. How did they compare to the rights and duties of women in other ancient societies?
3. If you were visiting an art museum, how would you recognize a painting as one done in ancient Egypt?
4. Compare and contrast the economies of Egypt and Nubia.

PRACTICING SOCIAL STUDIES SKILLS Study the map below and, on a separate sheet of paper, answer the questions that follow in complete sentences.

New Kingdom Egypt

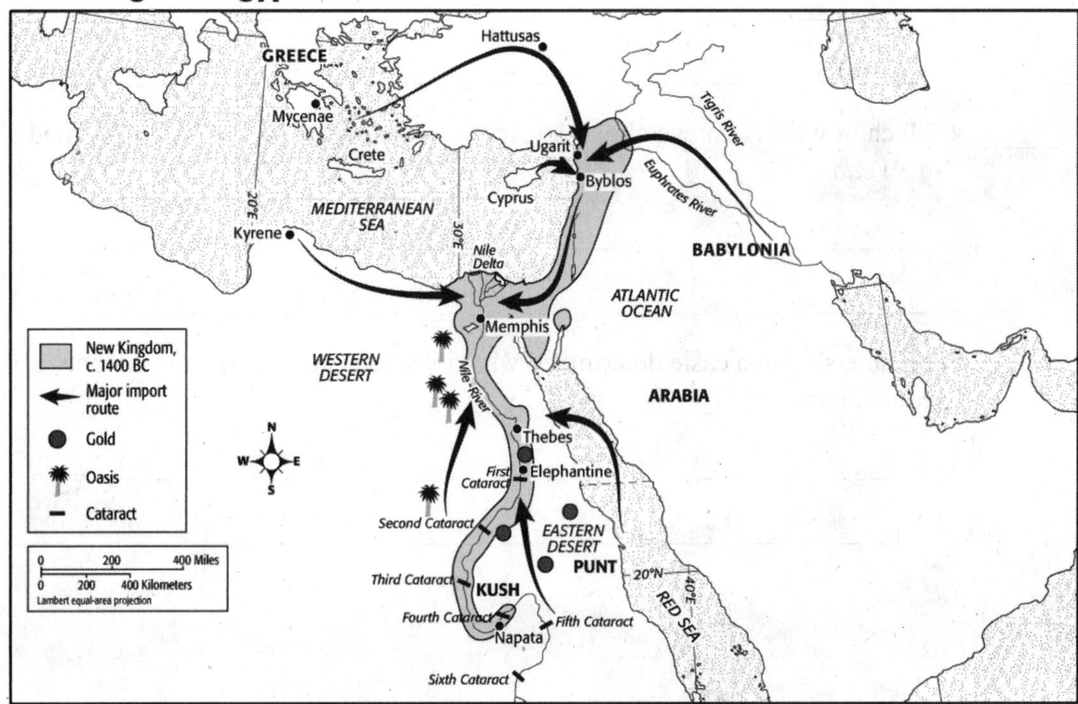

5. Describe one of the routes traders could use to ship gold to Memphis.
6. What geographic factors influenced the shape of the New Kingdom of Egypt?

Name ______________________ Class ______________ Date ______________

Ancient India and China

Section Quiz

Section 1

TRUE/FALSE Mark each statement **T** if it is true or **F** if it is false. If false explain why.

_____ 1. Harappa and Mohenjo Daro were two cities from the Indus Valley civilization.

____

____

_____ 2. Seasonal winds called monsoons influence India's climate by bringing heavy rains during the summer and cool, dry air in the winter.

____

____

_____ 3. The lack of uniformity and planning among Indus Valley cities suggests that there was no central authority over the civilization.

____

____

_____ 4. Much of what is known about the Aryans comes from sacred writings called the *Vedas*.

____

____

_____ 5. Membership in a caste determined what jobs one could hold and who one could marry.

____

____

Name ______________________ Class ______________ Date ______________

Ancient India and China

Section Quiz

Section 2

MULTIPLE CHOICE For each of the following, write the letter of the best choice in the space provided.

_____ 1. A basic tenet of Hinduism is the belief that
- a. *devas* cannot be portrayed in art.
- b. it is impossible to achieve *moksha.*
- c. the founder of Hinduism is Vishnu.
- d. everything in the world is an aspect of Brahman.

_____ 2. The concept of karma is best described as
- a. the sum effect of one's actions during life.
- b. being reborn into another life.
- c. the relationship between Rama and Sita.
- d. the continuous pattern of life and death.

_____ 3. In Hinduism, a person's dharma, or set of spiritual duties and obligations is based on
- a. their class and station in life.
- b. *devas.*
- c. bad karma.
- d. dedication to a deity.

_____ 4. The sacred texts of Hinduism include the *Vedas*, *Upanishads* and
- a. the Ganges.
- b. Ganesha.
- c. *Bhagavad Gita.*
- d. the Harappa.

_____ 5. Because *ahimsa* is so important to Jains
- a. they follow elaborate rituals.
- b. most Jains pursue military careers.
- c. many Jains collect valuable art and sculpture.
- d. many Jains are vegetarians.

Name ______________________________ Class ________________ Date ______________

Ancient India and China

Section Quiz

Section 3

MATCHING In the space provided, write the letter of the term, person, or place that matches each description. Some answers will not be used.

_____ 1. Where the founder of Buddhism sat and meditated

_____ 2. Central truths of Buddhism

_____ 3. A series of steps that lead to enlightenment and salvation

_____ 4. Founder of Buddhism

_____ 5. Enlightened people who remain on Earth to help others

_____ 6. State of perfect peace in which the soul is free from suffering

_____ 7. Indian leader who promoted the spread of Buddhism

_____ 8. The leading religion in all of East and Southeast Asia by AD 500

_____ 9. Buddhist sect whose title means, "Way of the Elders"

_____ 10. To live in moderation

a. Siddhartha Gautama

b. Buddhism

c. Bodh Gaya

d. Middle Way

e. nirvana

f. Zen

g. Korea

h. Four Noble Truths

i. Eightfold Path

j. bodhisattvas

k. Ashoka

l. Theravada

m. Mahayana

Name ______________________________ Class ________________ Date ________________

Ancient India and China

Section Quiz

Section 4

FILL IN THE BLANK For each of the following statements, fill in the blank with the appropriate word, phrase, or name.

1. Historians believe Chinese civilization began in the ___________________ valley where people started growing crops about 9,000 years ago.

2. Fine dusty soil called ___________________ in the valley of Huang He contributed to fertile farming conditions in China.

3. The ___________________, the world's tallest mountains, separate China from India and from the rest of southern Asia.

4. The ___________________, a vast desert, provided protection from enemies who would invade China from the west.

5. Most historians date the beginning of early Chinese civilization to the rise of the ___________________ dynasty.

6. The use of ___________________ bones to ask questions of one's ancestors led to the development of Chinese writing.

7. The Zhou introduced the idea called the ___________________ to explain why the Shang were overthrown.

8. It was ___________________ who said that a leader should be advised by qualified, well-informed people, which led Chinese emperors to select advisors based on merit rather than on birth.

9. Confucian thoughts on how to improve society were later colleced in a book called the ___________________.

10. The philosopher ___________________ wrote an influential book about Daoist beliefs called the *Dao De Jing*.

Ancient India and China

Chapter Test

Form A

MULTIPLE CHOICE For each of the following, write the letter of the best choice in the space provided.

_____ 1. The people of India's first civilization depended on monsoon rains to bring water for crops
a. which only happened every other year.
b. and to loosen rocks used for building.
c. and to cause flooding which deposited fertile soil.
d. and wash away accumulated debris from city streets.

_____ 2. Archaeologists have found two, large, well planned Indus Valley cities—Harappa and
a. Mohenjo Daro.
b. Sudra.
c. Brahmaputra.
d. Ganges.

_____ 3. The Buddha taught
a. following your desires leads to enlightenment.
b. suffering is not part of human life.
c. it is best to avoid meditation.
d. those who follow the Eightfold Path can attain nirvana.

_____ 4. During the Vedic period members of each *varna*
a. married into a higher *varna*.
b. followed the Middle Way.
c. played specific roles in society.
d. changed castes frequently.

_____ 5. Most Jains are vegetarians because
a. strict dietary laws in the *Mahabharata* forbid eating meat.
b. they are careful to not harm any living creature.
c. they dislike the religious rituals surrounding the butchering of animals.
d. they cannot eat anything that requires cooking.

_____ 6. Confucius responded to the chaos in China during the late Zhou period by
a. withdrawing from the world and becoming a monk.
b. teaching that people should love and respect one another through traditional manners and rituals.
c. teaching about the dynastic cycle to encourage people to rise up against corrupt rulers.
d. encouraging people to retreat from the laws of society.

Name ______________________ Class ______________ Date ______________

Ancient India and China

Chapter Test
Form A

PRACTICING SOCIAL STUDIES SKILLS Study the map and the passage below and answer the questions that follow.

Spread of Buddhism

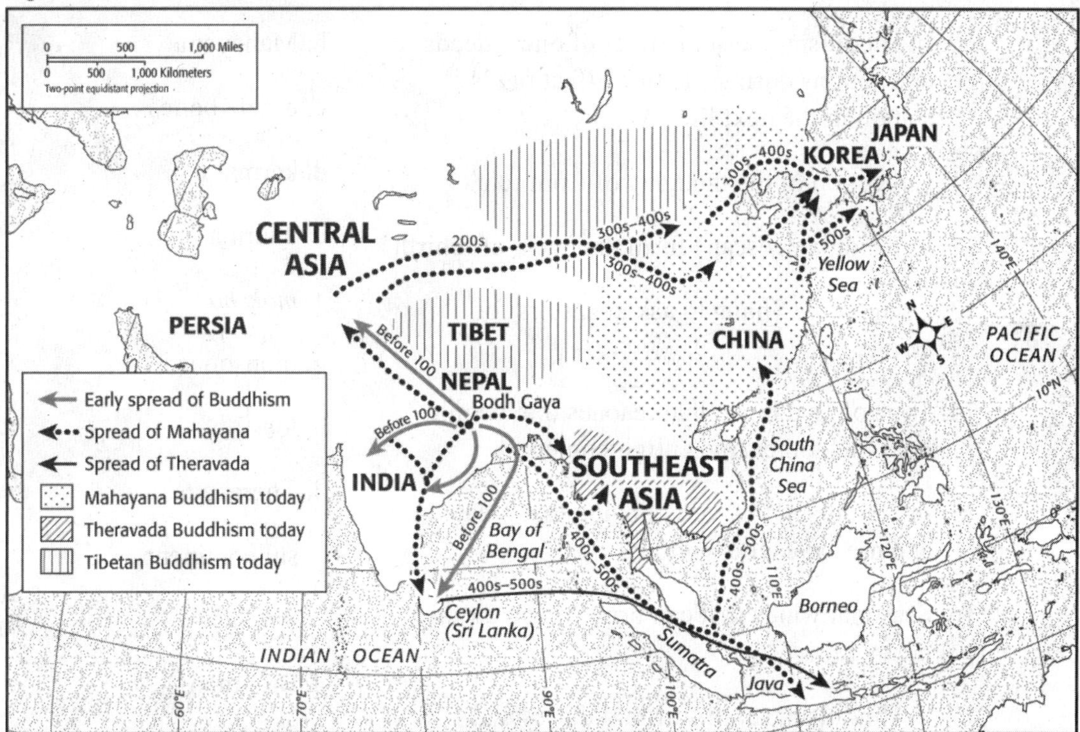

_____ 7. Where did Theravada Buddhism spread from?
- a. India
- b. Ceylon
- c. Tibet
- d. Southeast Asia

> **"The Brahmin was his mouth, of both his arms was the Rajanya [Kshariya] made. His thighs became the Vaisya, from his feet the Sudra was produced."**
>
> **—*Rigveda*, 10.90**

_____ 8. This passage refers to the creation of the
- a. *varnas*.
- b. Aryans.
- c. rajas.
- d. *Vedas*.

Name ______________________ Class ______________ Date ______________

Ancient India and China

Chapter Test

Form A

MATCHING In the space provided, write the letter of the term or place that matches each description. Some answers will not be used.

_____ 9. Type of soil picked up by the Huang He river

_____ 10. In Hinduism, the sum effect of one's deeds and actions during life that affect one's station in the next life

_____ 11. Collection of the thoughts of Confucius

_____ 12. In Hinduism, escape from the cycle of rebirth

_____ 13. Used by the Shang to ask ancestors for advice

_____ 14. Type of Buddhism that teaches that people help each other find enlightenment

_____ 15. In Hinduism, the eternal being that created and preserves the world

_____ 16. Seasonal winds that can bring warm air and heavy rains

_____ 17. In Hinduism, set of spiritual duties and obligations

_____ 18. Teaches that the best way to attain nirvana is to become a monk or nun

a. *Analects*
b. Mahayana
c. oracle bones
d. karma
e. dharma
f. *moksha*
g. monsoons
h. loess
i. Theravada
j. subcontinent
k. Aryans
l. Brahman
m. court

FILL IN THE BLANK For each of the following statements, fill in the blank with the appropriate word, phrase, or name.

19. Sacred writings called the ______________________ include many details about Aryan history and society.

20. Hindus believe that the *atman* is released from the body at death and later reborn in another body in a process called ______________________.

21. Some Hindus practice a series of physical and mental exercises called ______________________ to focus their bodies and minds and aid meditation.

22. Right attitude, right effort, and right mindfulness are all part of the ______________________.

23. Buddhism spread from India through missionary work and

    ________________________.

24. The principle of the ________________________ was introduced by the Zhou to gain acceptance for their rule.

25. ______________________ teaches that all things in nature are connected. By finding one's place in nature it is possible for a person to achieve harmony with the universe.

Name ______________________ Class ______________ Date ______________

Ancient India and China

Chapter Test Form B

SHORT ANSWER On a separate sheet of paper, answer each of the following questions in complete sentences. Remember to use specific examples to support your answers.

1. What factors suggest that the Indus civilization was a single society and not a collection of independent city-states?
2. How does Jainism differ from Hinduism?
3. How did Buddhism change after the Buddha's death?
4. Describe three advances made by the Shang.
5. Explain the Mandate of Heaven.

PRACTICING SOCIAL STUDIES SKILLS Study the map below and, on a separate sheet of paper, answer the question that follows in complete sentences.

Spread of Buddhism

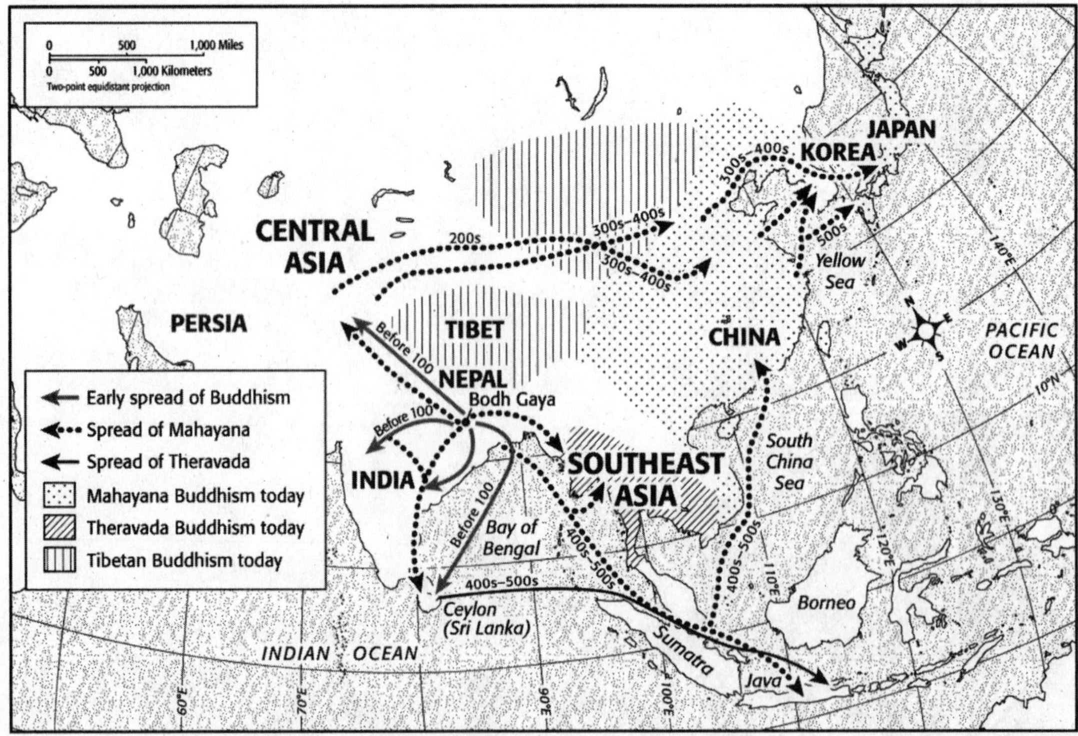

6. Use the map to explain why people in Japan practice the same form of Buddhism as people in China.

Name ______________________________ Class ___________________ Date ___________________

The Dawn of Civilization

Unit Test

Form A

MATCHING In the space provided, write the letter of the term or place that matches each description. Some answers will not be used.

_____ 1. The first part of the Stone Age

_____ 2. The shift from hunting and gathering to farming

_____ 3. Objects found by archaeologists such as coins, tools, and pottery

_____ 4. Spread of ideas, beliefs, and customs from one culture to another

_____ 5. Region between the Mediterranean Sea and the Persian Gulf

_____ 6. Worship of many gods

_____ 7. Babylonian laws

_____ 8. A state ruled by religious leaders

_____ 9. Ancient writing on a granite slab

_____ 10. In Hinduism, a set of spiritual duties and obligations

a. cultural diffusion

b. Hammurabi's Code

c. Rosetta Stone

d. satraps

e. Paleolithic Era

f. dharma

g. Fertile Crescent

h. theocracy

i. Neolithic Revolution

j. Zoroastrianism

k. polytheism

l. artifacts

m. bureaucracy

n. *moksha*

FILL IN THE BLANK For each of the following statements, fill in the blank with the appropriate word, phrase, or name.

11. Scientists learn about prehistory by studying preserved remains called ________________________, artifacts, and cultures.

12. As prehistoric people developed more sophisticated tools, the Paleolithic Era gave way to the ________________________ Era.

13. The first people to develop a civilization in Mesopotamia were the ________________________.

14. The ________________________ were known for their sea trade, alphabet, purple dye, and glassblowing.

Name ______________________ Class ______________ Date ______________

The Dawn of Civilization

Unit Test

Form A

15. The belief that set ancient Hebrews apart from other ancient peoples was the belief in

    ______________________.

16. Cyrus, Darius, and Xerxes were rulers of ______________________.

17. The geographic features that had the greatest influence on the development of Egypt were the desert and ______________________.

18. Central to Egyptian religion was the belief in a(n) ______________________.

19. The first civilization in India, called ______________________, was named after its river valley location.

20. Historians' knowledge of early Aryan society comes from studying the sacred writings called ______________________.

TRUE/FALSE Indicate whether each statement below is true of false by writing **T** or **F** in the space provided.

_____ 21. Cities with well-developed social and economic institutions are the basis of all civilizations.

_____ 22. Ötzi the Iceman, discovered in the Alps, was not found with any personal belongings.

_____ 23. The Neolithic Revolution did not radically change how people lived.

_____ 24. All early civilizations have several characteristics in common.

_____ 25. Abraham was Israel's first king.

_____ 26. Zoroastrianism, which began in Persia, was one of the first religions to teach dualism.

_____ 27. Egyptians did not believe pharaohs were gods; instead they believed the pharaohs controlled the gods.

_____ 28. Pyramids in the Old Kingdom were used as tombs for kings.

_____ 29. Egyptians built temples to house and honor their gods.

_____ 30. A group of people broke away from Buddhism and formed a new religion called Jainism.

The Dawn of Civilization

Unit Test
Form A

MULTIPLE CHOICE For each of the following, write the letter of the best choice in the space provided.

_____ 31. The earliest hominid fossils were found in
a. Africa.
b. Europe.
c. land bridges.
d. Asia.

_____ 32. Two early groups of Homo sapiens were Cro-Magnon and
a. Australopithecine.
b. Homo habilis.
c. Neanderthal.
d. "upright man."

_____ 33. Domestication of plants and animals makes them
a. susceptible to disease.
b. more useful to humans.
c. more easily found in the wild.
d. adaptable to all environments.

_____ 34. Social classes began to develop based on occupation, wealth, and
a. ability to write.
b. knowledge of history.
c. influence.
d. ability to locate copper.

_____ 35. One way Homo erectus differed from earlier hominids
a. was the inability to make tools.
b. was brain size.
c. was the ability to use language.
d. was that they never migrated out of Africa.

_____ 36. The best-known work of Sumerian literature, the *Epic of Gilgamesh*, was written in
a. cuneiform.
b. the Phoenician alphabet.
c. pictographs.
d. AD 1000.

_____ 37. The first people in Near Eastern culture to master ironworking were the
a. Amorites.
b. Babylonians.
c. Hittites.
d. Sumerians.

_____ 38. Israel split into two kingdoms
a. after the death of Solomon.
b. before Saul was named king.
c. when the Philistines entered Israel.
d. after Israel became part of Persia.

_____ 39. Darius I created
a. Zoroastrianism.
b. a united Greek empire.
c. a strong Hittite government.
d. a permanent army of paid soldiers.

_____ 40. New Kingdom pharaohs built a powerful military to
a. obtain fertile farmlands.
b. punish the Sumerians.
c. strengthen Egypt's trade economy.
d. prevent foreign control of Egypt.

_____ 41. The pharaoh Akhenaten is best known for
a. introducing monotheism.
b. being a woman.
c. defeating Ramses the Great.
d. forging an alliance with Sargon.

_____ 42. Because Egyptians were masters of human anatomy, their greatest scientific advances were in
a. medicine.
b. papyrus scrolls.
c. astronomy.
d. the study of ka.

_____ 43. When the Middle Kingdom collapsed, Kush expanded to rule all of
a. Arabia.
b. Egypt.
c. Nubia.
d. Sahara.

_____ 44. The most valuable product of Meroë was
a. wheat.
b. copper.
c. silver
d. iron.

_____ 45. Hindus call the eternal being that created and preserves the world
a. Siva.
b. Vishnu.
c. Krishna.
d. Brahman.

_____ 46. The *Bhagavad Gita* is found in the
a. *devas*.
b. *Mahabharata*.
c. *Upanishads*.
d. *Vedas*.

_____ 47. Over time, Buddhism developed three main traditions called Theravada, Mahayana, and
a. Tibetan.
b. Jainism.
c. Bodh Gaya.
d. Bodhisattvas.

_____ 48. China's first civilization developed
a. in the Gobi.
b. on high mountains.
c. next to mining centers.
d. in river valleys.

_____ 49. According to the Mandate of Heaven
a. the Shang should never have accepted Zhou rule.
b. the gods will only support a powerful ruler.
c. the gods favored the Shang over the Zhou.
d. the gods would not allow corrupt rulers to hold power.

Name ______________________ Class ______________ Date ______________

PRACTICING SOCIAL STUDIES SKILLS Study the map below and answer the question that follows.

Early Human Migration

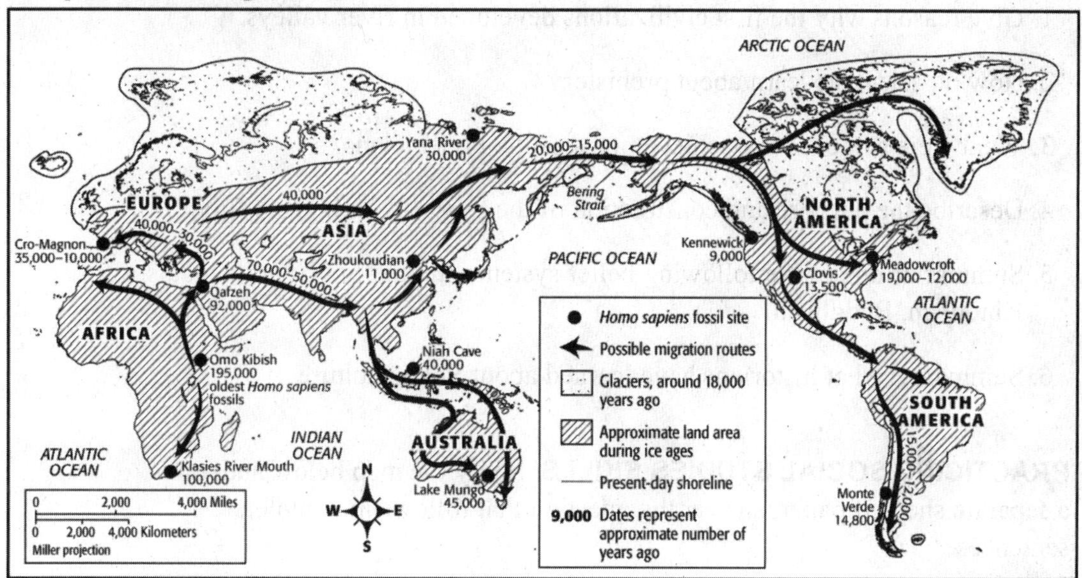

_____ 50. According to the map, on which continent did early humans originate?
- a. Asia
- b. Africa
- c. South America
- d. Europe

SHORT ANSWER On a separate sheet of paper, answer each of the following questions in complete sentences. Remember to use specific examples to support your answers.

1. Give reasons why the first civilizations developed in river valleys.

2. How do scientists learn about prehistory?

3. What were some lasting achievements of the Phoenicians?

4. Describe the purpose and construction of the pyramids in ancient Egypt.

5. Summarize one of the following belief systems studied in this unit: Judaism, Hinduism, Buddhism.

6. Summarize what historians have learned about Shang culture.

PRACTICING SOCIAL STUDIES SKILLS Study the map below and, on a separate sheet of paper, answer the question that follows in complete sentences.

New Kingdom Egypt

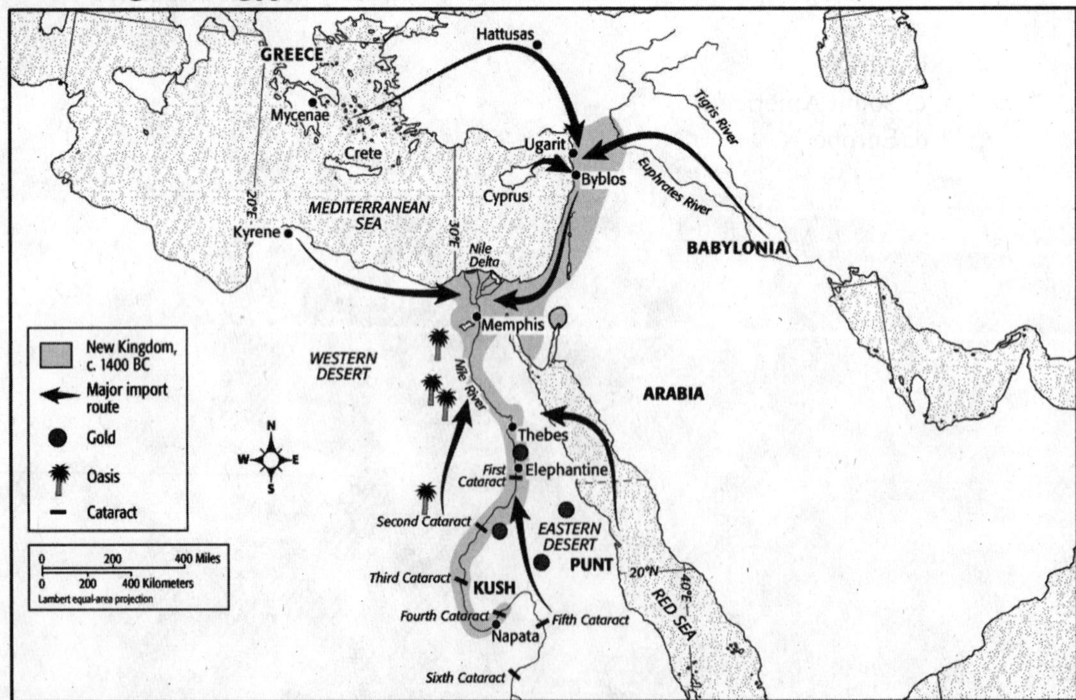

7. Explain how geographic features influenced New Kingdom trade.

Name ______________________ Class ______________ Date ______________

Classical Greece

Section Quiz

Section 1

TRUE/FALSE Mark each statement **T** if it is true or **F** if it is false. If false explain why.

_____ 1. The Minoan civilization developed on Crete after the Mycenaean civilization collapsed.

____

____

_____ 2. Mycenaean society was dominated by intense competition, frequent warfare, and powerful kings.

____

____

_____ 3. In a typical Greek city-state, a polis was built around a high area called the agora.

____

____

_____ 4. The Spartans developed a military lifestyle in order to prevent rebellions by helots, or state slaves.

____

____

_____ 5. Although the Greeks believed in hundreds of gods and goddesses, the 12 Olympian gods were the most influential.

____

____

FILL IN THE BLANK For each of the following statements, fill in the blank with the appropriate word, phrase, or name.

1. The government of ______________________ was the world's first democracy.

2. A democracy is a form of government run by the ______________________.

3. ______________________ thought he could end unrest in Athens through harsh punishment.

4. A lawmaker, ______________________, took a step toward real democracy by allowing all men in Athens to take part in an assembly that governed the city and to serve on juries.

5. A ______________________ is a leader who seizes power by force and claims to rule for the good of the people.

6. Putting aside their rivalry, Athens and Sparta worked together to defeat the ______________________.

7. The ______________________ League was headed by Sparta.

8. ______________________ commissioned the building of the Parthenon, as he wanted Athens to be the most glorious city in Greece.

9. During the early years of the Peloponnesian War, Sparta and its allies dominated on land, while Athens and it allies dominated the ______________________.

10. After a long cycle of warfare, ______________________ took control of all of Greece in the 340s BC.

Name ______________________ Class ______________ Date ______________

Classical Greece **Section Quiz**

Section 3

MATCHING In the space provided, write the letter of the term, person, or place that matches each description. Some answers will not be used.

_____ 1. The love of wisdom

_____ 2. Thought the basic nature of life could be discovered by working through a series of questions

_____ 3. Argued that only philosophers were qualified to lead

_____ 4. Philosopher who tried to apply philosophical principles to every kind of knowledge

_____ 5. Clear and ordered thinking

_____ 6. The process of making inferences

_____ 7. Tells the story of the last year of the Trojan War

_____ 8. Story of Odysseus's long journey home after the Trojan War

_____ 9. First major writer of history in Greece

_____ 10. Drama that focuses on hardships faced by Greek heroes

a. reason

b. *philosophia*

c. Aristotle

d. the *Odyssey*

e. Socrates

f. Herodotus

g. logic

h. Hesiod

i. tragedy

j. Achilles

k. the *Iliad*

l. Sappho

m. Plato

Classical Greece

Section Quiz

Section 4

TRUE/FALSE Mark each statement **T** if it is true or **F** if it is false. If false explain why.

_____ 1. The Hellenistic culture create blended Greek civilization with ideas from Persia, Egypt, and Central Asia.

____

____

_____ 2. In the Hellenistic world, the biggest change was that the Greek city-state became the main political unit.

____

____

_____ 3. During the Hellenistic period, some women gained the right to receive an education and the right to own property.

____

____

_____ 4. The Hellenistic period witnessed tremendous achievements in arts, but saw a decline in science and technology.

____

____

_____ 5. Eratosthenes was best known for calculating the size of the world, coming remarkably close to the actual circumference of the globe.

____

____

Name ______________________ Class ______________ Date ______________

Classical Greece

Chapter Test

Form A

MULTIPLE CHOICE For each of the following, write the letter of the best choice in the space provided.

_____ 1. Spartan society revolved around training for war because
- a. warfare was their favorite activity.
- b. Spartans feared helot rebellions.
- c. Spartans wanted to dominate the entire Mediterranean world.
- d. Spartans believed they could not achieve immortality without proving their bravery in battle.

_____ 2. Which of the following gods or goddesses was the deity of wisdom?
- a. Athena
- b. Apollo
- c. Hera
- d. Ares

_____ 3. Which of the following is the correct sequence of influential men in the development of democracy in Athens, from first to last?
- a. Draco, Solon, Peisistratus, Cleisthenes
- b. Cleisthenes, Pericles, Draco, Solon
- c. Solon, Peisistratus, Cleisthenes, Alexander
- d. Solon, Draco, Cleisthenes, Peisistratus

_____ 4. Why did the Persian emperor Darius attack the Greek mainland?
- a. to gain control of Greece's vast natural resources
- b. to exact revenge for the Athenians' victory at Marathon
- c. to kidnap Helen, the beautiful queen of Athens
- d. to punish Athens for aiding the Ionians in their revolt against Persian rule

_____ 5. Macedonia was able to take control of all of Greece in the 340s BC because
- a. the Persian Empire had soundly defeated Athens and Sparta.
- b. a terrible plague had weakened Athens and Sparta.
- c. a long cycle of warfare left all of Greece vulnerable to attack.
- d. Xerxes was a brilliant commander of the Macedonian army.

_____ 6. Some of the earliest examples of Greek epic poetry were
- a. written by Aristophanes.
- b. the *Iliad* and the *Odyssey*.
- c. written by women.
- d. written for the festival of Dionysus.

Name ______________________ Class ______________ Date ______________

Classical Greece

Chapter Test

Form A

PRACTICING SOCIAL STUDIES SKILLS Study the map below and answer the question that follows.

The Peloponnesian War

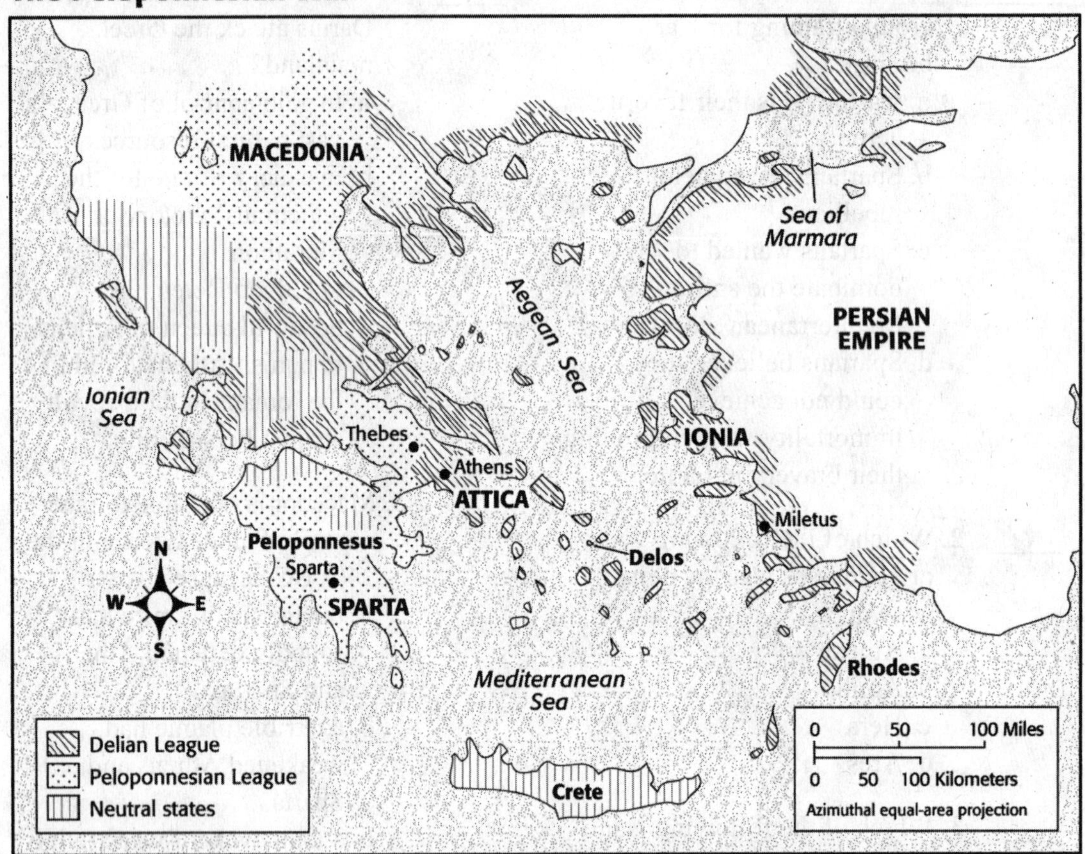

_____ 7. What statement about the Peloponnesian War is best supported by the map?

a. Athens and Sparta were both members of the Delian League.
b. The Persian Empire sent a navy to aid Athens.
c. Athens needed ships to communicate with its allies.
d. Ionia refused to enter the Delian League.

Name ______________________________ Class ________________ Date __________________

Classical Greece

Chapter Test

Form A

MATCHING In the space provided, write the letter of the term, person, or place that matches each description. Some answers will not be used.

_____ 8. Method of learning through questions

_____ 9. Argued that people should use reason to help them learn about the world

_____ 10. Calculated the circumference of the globe

_____ 11. Foot soldiers

_____ 12. Philosophers who equated pleasure with good

_____ 13. Made tribes, not families or social groups, the basis for elections

_____ 14. Emphasize reason, self-discipline, emotional control, and personal morality

_____ 15. An alliance of several Greek city-states led by Athens

_____ 16. Basic political unit in Greece

_____ 17. Greek poet

a. Epicureans

b. Peloponnesian League

c. Eratosthenes

d. Delian League

e. Socratic method

f. Plato

g. polis

h. Aristotle

i. Stoics

j. Sappho

k. hoplites

l. Zeus

m. Cleisthenes

FILL IN THE BLANK For each of the following statements, fill in the blank with the appropriate word, phrase, or name.

18. Historians consider the ________________________ to be the first Greeks.

19. A typical Greek city-state included a(n) ________________________ where people shopped, did business, gossiped, and discussed politics.

20. The assembly in Athens, in which all people eligible to take part in government voted directly on an issue, was an example of ________________________.

21. In the ________________________, Athens surrendered to Sparta in 404 BC.

22. Since ________________________ believed that only philosophers should lead governments, he did not support Athenian democracy.

23. Aeschylus, Sophocles, and ________________________ were three great writers of tragedy who lived in Athens.

24. The Macedonian king ____________________ conquered every major city-state in Greece except Sparta before his assassination.

25. The artists of the ____________________ period learned to convey emotion and movement in their works, especially sculpture.

Name ____________________ Class ______________ Date ______________

Classical Greece

Chapter Test

Form B

SHORT ANSWER On a separate sheet of paper, answer each of the following questions in complete sentences. Remember to use specific examples to support your answers.

1. Compare and contrast the Minoan and Mycenaean civilizations.
2. What circumstances led to a golden age in Athens?
3. Describe the nature of democracy in Athens.
4. In what ways did the *Iliad* and the *Odyssey* contribute to Greek culture?
5. How did Alexander encourage the blending of cultures in his empire?

PRACTICING SOCIAL STUDIES SKILLS Study the map below and, on a separate sheet of paper, answer the question that follows in complete sentences.

The Peloponnesian War

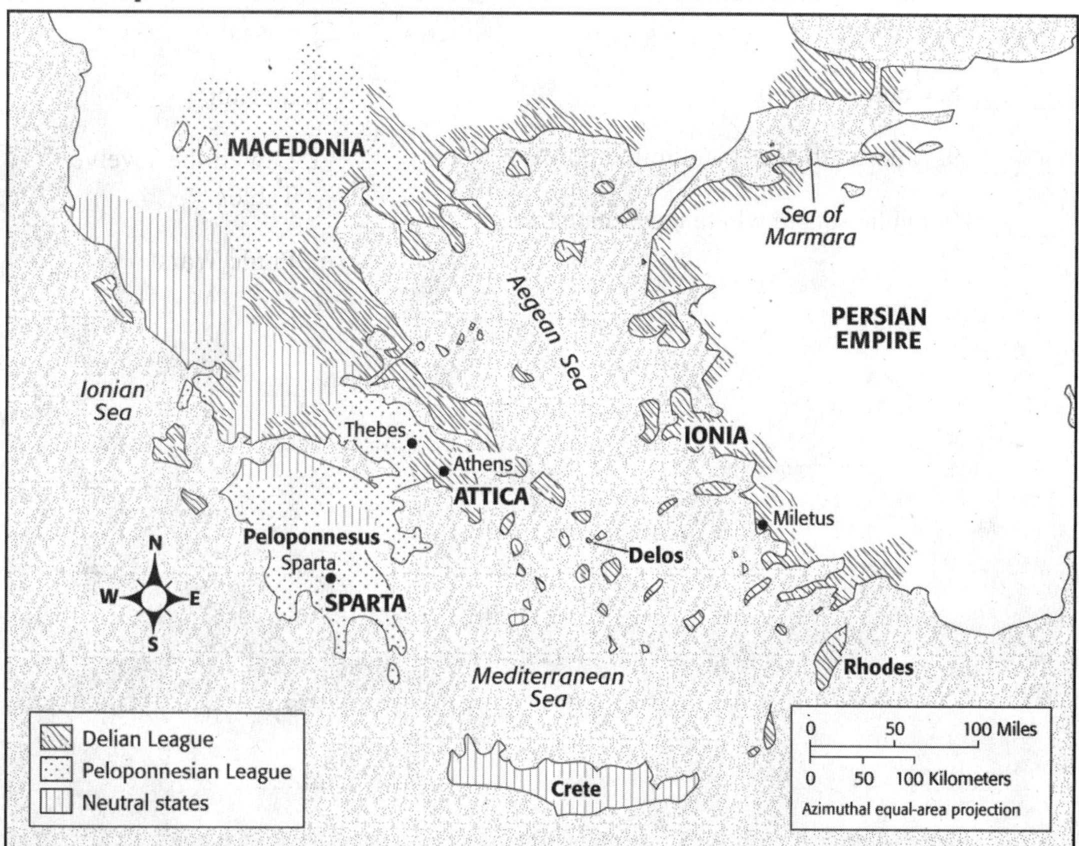

6. Use the map to explain how geography impacted the Peloponnesian War.

Rome and Early Christianity

Section Quiz

Section 1

MATCHING In the space provided, write the letter of the term or place that matches each description. Some answers will not be used.

_____ 1. Member of an aristocratic family

_____ 2. Conflict between Carthage and Rome

_____ 3. One of two chief executives of the Roman Republic

_____ 4. Type of government in which elected officials govern the state

_____ 5. Acted as advisors, controlled public finances, and handled foreign relations

_____ 6. Official who was elected by, and responsible for, protecting plebeians

_____ 7. Hill on which Rome's wealthiest citizens lived

_____ 8. Common people

_____ 9. Ruler with nearly unlimited power

_____ 10. Public square where the Senate met

a. republic
b. patrician
c. plebeians
d. tribune
e. Forum
f. constitution
g. Senate
h. Capitoline
i. Palatine
j. consul
k. dictator
l. Law of the Twelve Tables
m. Punic Wars

Name ______________________ Class ______________ Date ____________

Rome and Early Christianity

Section Quiz

Section 2

TRUE/FALSE Mark each statement **T** if it is true or **F** if it is false. If false explain why.

_____ 1. When Gaius Marius eliminated property restrictions, poor people joined the army hoping to acquire plunder and land at the end of a war.

____

____

_____ 2. The murder of Julius Caesar in 44 BC represented an attempt to dismantle the Republic and return governing power to the monarchy.

____

____

_____ 3. During his rule, Augustus expanded the borders of the empire, created a police force in Rome, presided over religious reforms, and undertook a vast building program.

____

____

_____ 4. Stable government, a strong legal system, widespread trade, and peace contributed to expansion and stability during the period known as the Pax Romana.

____

____

_____ 5. Any Roman citizen in the provinces could appeal any unfair treatment directly to the emperor.

____

____

Name ______________________ Class ______________ Date ______________

Rome and Early Christianity

Section Quiz

Section 3

MULTIPLE CHOICE For each of the following, write the letter of the best choice in the space provided.

_____ 1. Some common elements shared by nearly all members of Roman society were religion, education, entertainment, and
a. adoption.
b. health.
c. public office.
d. Greek language.

_____ 2. In Roman society, the head of the family was typically
a. the family's oldest living male.
b. the woman who had the most children.
c. the man whose age was nearest to 21.
d. the family's oldest living female.

_____ 3. Priests known as augurs were important members of Roman society because
a. they were responsible for collecting taxes.
b. they were teachers as well as priests.
c. they were consulted before any important decisions were made.
d. they worked with the Senate in making laws.

_____ 4. The Roman engineering achievement that made large public structures possible was
a. the development of advanced math concepts.
b. the development of measuring devices.
c. the development of concrete.
d. the development of organized labor.

_____ 5. The language of ancient Rome—Latin—lives on in
a. the Germanic languages.
b. the Romance languages.
c. Homer's *Iliad*.
d. modern drama.

Name ______________________ Class ______________ Date ______________

Rome and Early Christianity — Section Quiz

Section 4

TRUE/FALSE Mark each statement **T** if it is true or **F** if it is false. If false explain why.

_____ 1. The teachings of Jesus are rooted in Judaism.

____

____

_____ 2. The Zealots made up a branch of Judaism that supported cooperation with Roman conquerors.

____

____

_____ 3. Paul of Tarsus is credited with establishing Christian churches throughout the eastern Mediterranean.

____

____

_____ 4. Over time, bishops in Rome felt that the Roman bishop, or pope, should be recognized as the head of the entire church.

____

____

_____ 5. Christianity was finally outlawed in the Roman Empire when Constantine issued the Edict of Milan in 313.

____

____

Name ______________________ Class ______________ Date ______________

Rome and Early Christianity

Section Quiz

Section 5

TRUE/FALSE Mark each statement **T** if it is true or **F** if it is false. If false explain why.

_____ 1. After the rule of the Good Emperors, civil wars and invasions by tribal peoples threatened the stability of the Roman Empire.

____

____

_____ 2. To maintain the money supply, emperors minted new coins with copper and lead, increasing the face value of the coins.

____

____

_____ 3. When Diocletian took the throne in 284, he divided the empire in two, to improve efficiency.

____

____

_____ 4. Attacks by the Huns forced tribes such as the Vandals and Visigoths into the territory of the Roman Empire.

____

____

_____ 5. In 476, Odoacer's victory over the last Roman emperor in the west marked the end of the Western Roman Empire.

____

____

Name ______________________ Class ______________ Date ______________

Rome and Early Christianity

Chapter Test

Form A

MULTIPLE CHOICE For each of the following, write the letter of the best choice in the space provided.

_____ 1. Electing tribunes and displaying the Law of the Twelve Tables
   a. benefited patricians.
   b. showed the influence of the Etruscans.
   c. protected plebeians against unjust treatment by patricians.
   d. violated the constitution hammered out by patricians and plebeians.

_____ 2. What caused the Third Punic War?
   a. the Romans' desire to destroy Carthage
   b. the Romans' need for more land as its population grew
   c. Hannibal's desire to conquer rural northern Italy
   d. the Carthaginians' fear that Roman expansion would interfere with trade and commerce

_____ 3. Why did Octavian adopt the title "first citizen"?
   a. to emphasize that he had more power than other magistrates
   b. to illustrate the duties of citizens in a republic
   c. to show that he was retiring from politics
   d. to avoid the title of king or emperor

_____ 4. Wealthy Romans dominated politics during the Pax Romana because
   a. only patricians were allowed to hold office.
   b. public officials were not paid so only the wealthy could participate.
   c. most citizens were uninterested in politics.
   d. the Roman masses cared only about bread and circuses.

_____ 5. Roman audiences enjoyed public entertainment
   a. in the Forum on Capitoline Hill.
   b. in temples and at the Forum.
   c. on the Palatine and Pont du Gard.
   d. in the Colosseum or at Circus Maximus.

_____ 6. As a conquered people in the Roman Empire
   a. the Jews were forced to convert to Christianity.
   b. the Jews did not abandon monotheism.
   c. Jews were denied religious freedom.
   d. all Jews cooperated with Roman rule.

_____ 7. Paul of Tarsus helped to attract non-Jews to Christianity by
a. dispensing with some Jewish customs.
b. following Jewish food laws.
c. actively opposing the teaching that Jesus was the Messiah.
d. remaining in Rome.

_____ 8. Which of the following describes the government of Diocletian?
a. a democratic, open society where debate was encouraged
b. a corrupt republican government
c. a government that regulated every aspect of life
d. an unstable military dictatorship

_____ 9. What caused inflation after the last of the Good Emperors died?
a. the minting of new coins containing copper and lead in order to maintain the money supply
b. the layoff of thousands of soldiers to save money
c. the tax cut implemented to spur the Roman economy
d. the flood of foreign currency into Rome as a result of increased trade

Name ______________________ Class ______________ Date ______________

Rome and Early Christianity

Chapter Test

Form A

PRACTICING SOCIAL STUDIES SKILLS Study the chart below and answer the question that follows.

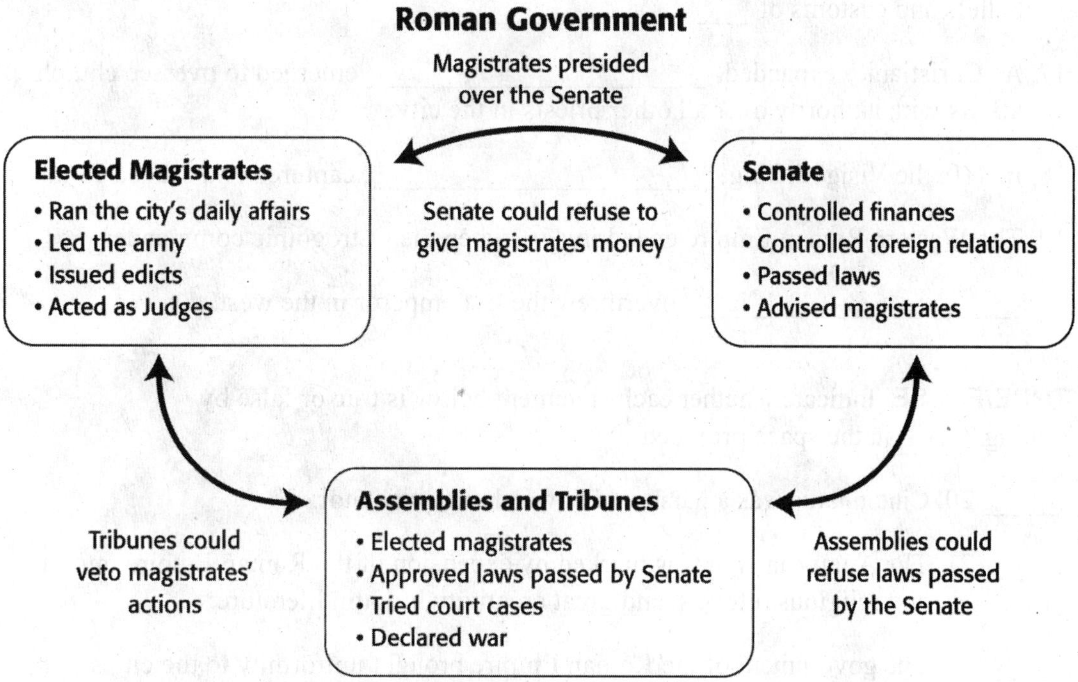

Roman Government

Magistrates presided over the Senate

Elected Magistrates
- Ran the city's daily affairs
- Led the army
- Issued edicts
- Acted as Judges

Senate could refuse to give magistrates money

Senate
- Controlled finances
- Controlled foreign relations
- Passed laws
- Advised magistrates

Tribunes could veto magistrates' actions

Assemblies and Tribunes
- Elected magistrates
- Approved laws passed by Senate
- Tried court cases
- Declared war

Assemblies could refuse laws passed by the Senate

_____ 10. In what way could tribunes check the power of the elected magistrates?
   a. by vetoing laws
   b. by vetoing the actions of the magistrates
   c. by controlling the magistrates' budget
   d. by passing laws

FILL IN THE BLANK For each of the following statements, fill in the blank with the appropriate word, phrase, or name.

11. Plebeians elected officials called ______________________, whose job was to protect them from unfair treatment by patricians.

12. The ______________________ hoped to help the soldier-farmers of Rome by redistributing public land to small farmers.

13. The period from the beginning of Augustus's reign until the death of the last Good Emperor is known as the ______________________.

14. The Roman family was led by the ______________________, who had extensive powers over other members of the family.

15. ______________________ was the language of Rome.

Name ______________________ Class ______________ Date ______________

Rome and Early Christianity

Chapter Test

Form A

16. The new religion that emerged in the Roman world, Christianity, was rooted in the beliefs and customs of ______________.

17. As Christianity expanded, ______________ emerged to oversee church affairs with authority over all other priests in the city.

18. In 410, the Visigoth king, ______________, captured and sacked Rome.

19. The Western Roman Empire ended in 476, when the Ostrogothic commander ______________ overthrew the last emperor in the west.

TRUE/FALSE Indicate whether each statement below is true or false by writing **T** or **F** in the space provided.

_____ 20. Cincinnatus was a harsh and power-hungry dictator.

_____ 21. The Augustan Age was marked by expansion of the Roman Empire, moral and religious reforms, and great creativity in Latin literature.

_____ 22. The government of the Roman Empire brought uniformity to the cities of the Mediterranean world.

_____ 23. After the Pax Romana, weak leaders and economic troubles hurt the Roman Empire.

_____ 24. The emperor Constantine helped to spread Christianity when he became a Christian.

_____ 25. Constantine built a new capital city in the village of Byzantium because the eastern half of the Roman Empire was richer and better defended.

Name ______________________ Class ______________ Date ______________

Rome and Early Christianity

Chapter Test

Form B

SHORT ANSWER On a separate sheet of paper, answer each of the following questions in complete sentences. Remember to use specific examples to support your answers.

1. How did Italy's geography contribute to making Rome a great empire?
2. How did the Roman Empire differ from the Roman Republic?
3. What did the Roman poet mean when he said that only two things interested the Roman masses—bread and circuses?
4. What was appealing about Christianity to people in the Roman world?
5. In what significant ways did Diocletian change the Roman Empire?

PRACTICING SOCIAL STUDIES SKILLS Study the chart below and, on a separate sheet of paper, answer the questions that follow in complete sentences.

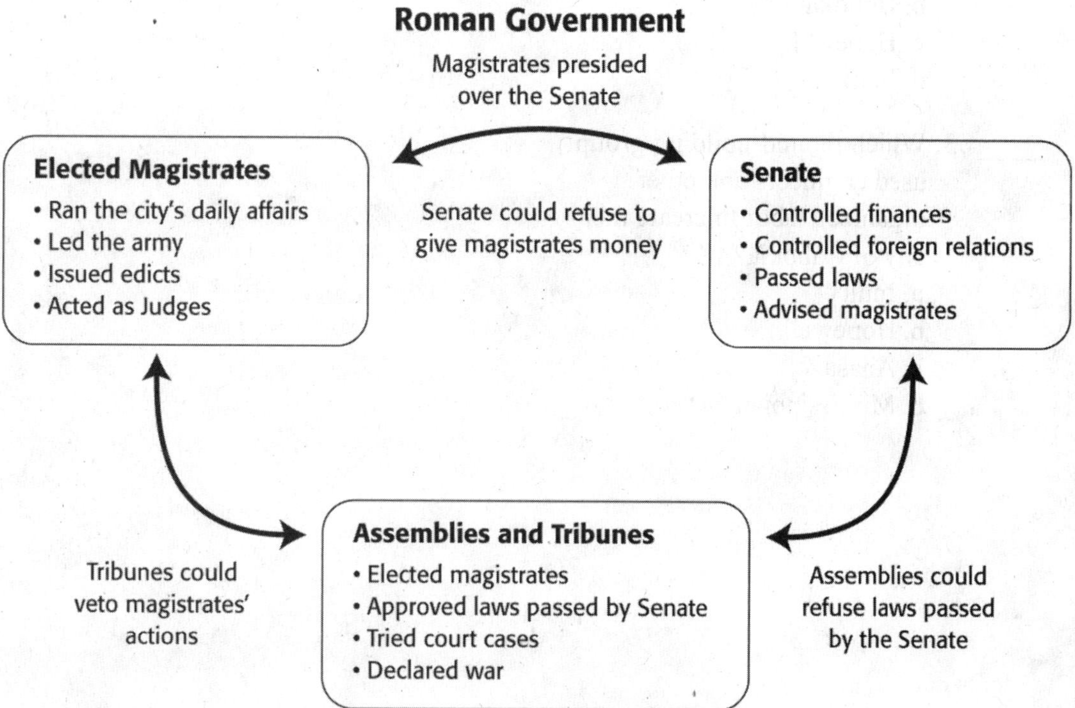

6. How did the Senate check the power of the magistrates?
7. How did assemblies and tribunes check the power of the Senate?

Name ________________ Class ____________ Date ____________

The Americas

Section Quiz

Section 1

MULTIPLE CHOICE For each of the following, write the letter of the best choice in the space provided.

_____ 1. Which North American farming group in the Desert West created an irrigation system incorporating shallow canals and dams?
a. Anasazi
b. Hohokam
c. Plains Indians
d. Mississippian

_____ 2. Which cliff-dwelling group developed pueblos, often including underground rooms called kivas?
a. Anasazi
b. Hohokam
c. Hopewell
d. Inuit

_____ 3. Which mound-building group used engineers and other organized labor to create the city of Cahokia?
a. Inuit
b. Hopewell
c. Anasazi
d. Mississippian

_____ 4. Which group lived in the Arctic regions of North America?
a. Inuit
b. Hopewell
c. Anasazi
d. Mississippian

_____ 5. Which group used elm bark to create dwellings called longhouses?
a. Plains Indians
b. Hopewell
c. Iroquois
d. Mississippian

Name ______________________ Class ______________ Date ______________

The Americas

Section Quiz

Section 2

TRUE/FALSE Mark each statement **T** if it is true or **F** if it is false. If false explain why.

_____ 1. The first farming settlements in the Americas were in Mesoamerica, the region including southern Mexico and northern Central America.

____

____

_____ 2. The Zapotec were the first group to build large towns in Mesoamerica.

____

____

_____ 3. The Maya made significant advances in astronomy, math, and writing, and were among the first people to use the concept of zero.

____

____

_____ 4. The Aztec Empire became strong and wealthy through trade and by taxing the people they conquered.

____

____

_____ 5. The Aztecs created a unified kingdom by establishing only one social class.

____

____

Name ______________________ Class ______________ Date ______________

The Americas

Section Quiz

Section 3

MATCHING In the space provided, write the letter of the term, person, or place that matches each description. Some answers will not be used.

_____ 1. Capital of the Inca Empire

_____ 2. Set of colored and knotted cords used by the Inca to track the movement of goods

_____ 3. Group who lived in the highlands of Peru from about 800 to 400 BC

_____ 4. Labor tax that the common people of the Inca Empire were required to pay

_____ 5. Inca leader who used alliances and military might to expand the empire

_____ 6. Group who lived in the coastal desert of Peru from about 400 BC to AD 600

_____ 7. Population data

_____ 8. Cooperative community in the Inca Empire

_____ 9. Second-highest mountain range in the world

_____ 10. Desert people known for huge designs made on the desert floor

a. Chavín

b. Moche

c. Nazca

d. geoglyphs

e. Pachacuti

f. census

g. elite

h. ayllu

i. Cuzco

j. quipu

k. Andes

l. Chavín de Huantar

m. mita

Name ______________________ Class ______________ Date ______________

The Americas

Chapter Test

Form A

MULTIPLE CHOICE For each of the following, write the letter of the best choice in the space provided.

_____ 1. Cultures of the Desert West included
   a. the Hopewell and the Mississippian.
   b. the Hohokam and the Anasazi.
   c. the Mound Builders.
   d. the Inuit and the Iroquois.

_____ 2. Which of the following provide useful clues about Hopewell society?
   a. paintings found on the walls of cliff dwellings
   b. their early written records
   c. carvings made from walnut tusks
   d. objects buried inside large stone and earth mounds

_____ 3. How did the lives of Plains Indians change after European contact?
   a. They abandoned farming and began to use horses to follow the buffalo herds.
   b. They stopped traveling in small groups and instead settled in European-style villages.
   c. They learned European agricultural techniques and began to farm the fertile grassland for the first time.
   d. They learned how to domesticate animals and became dependent on farm products for food.

_____ 4. What types of buildings and structures were in Olmec towns?
   a. massive burial mounds and apartment houses
   b. longhouses
   c. elaborate tombs and giant stone heads
   d. igloos and larger residential buildings

_____ 5. Scholars believe the Olmec influenced other Mesoamerican civilizations because
   a. there is no evidence of the Olmec after their mysterious decline.
   b. they were a relatively recent civilization.
   c. their agricultural practices were widely copied by later civilizations.
   d. the influence of their calendar, written language, and artistic designs can be seen in many other civilizations.

_____ 6. What did the Zapotec, Toltec, and Maya cultures have in common?
   a. All practiced human sacrifice.
   b. All used their strong militaries to dominate a large region for hundreds of years.
   c. All were based in farming villages.
   d. All were in Mesoamerica.

The Americas

Chapter Test

Form A

_____ 7. The Aztec Empire grew wealthy through
a. rich farmland and control of excellent hunting ground.
b. rich natural resources.
c. tribute and trade.
d. the sale of slaves.

_____ 8. What led to the downfall of both the Inca Empire and the Aztec Empire?
a. the arrival of Spanish explorers
b. a massive meteor that caused catastrophic damage
c. climate change
d. internal warfare between city-states

_____ 9. Which of the following were especially skilled builders of temples, forts, and roads?
a. the Aztecs
b. the Inca
c. the Maya
d. the Olmec

_____ 10. Which of the following was true about Inca society?
a. All lived with the fear of being sacrificed to the gods.
b. People were allowed to worship only the sun god.
c. Families were grouped in cooperative communities.
d. Individual achievements were highly valued and richly rewarded.

TRUE/FALSE Indicate whether each statement below is true or false by writing **T** or **F** in the space provided.

_____ 11. The Hohokam were able to farm in the desert because they developed an irrigation system.

_____ 12. The Iroquois League provided a model for the United States government.

_____ 13. Slash-and-burn agriculture was used by the Maya to clear land for farming maize, beans, and squash.

_____ 14. Priests and priestesses were at the top of the Aztec social order.

_____ 15. The strict Aztec social order did not allow individuals such as farmers or warriors to move into higher social classes.

_____ 16. The Moche are best known for their skilled metalwork and for their pottery, which depicted scenes of daily life.

_____ 17. Because the Inca did not have a written language, they were unable to develop a system of record keeping.

PRACTICING SOCIAL STUDIES SKILLS Study the map below and answer the question that follows.

North American Cultures

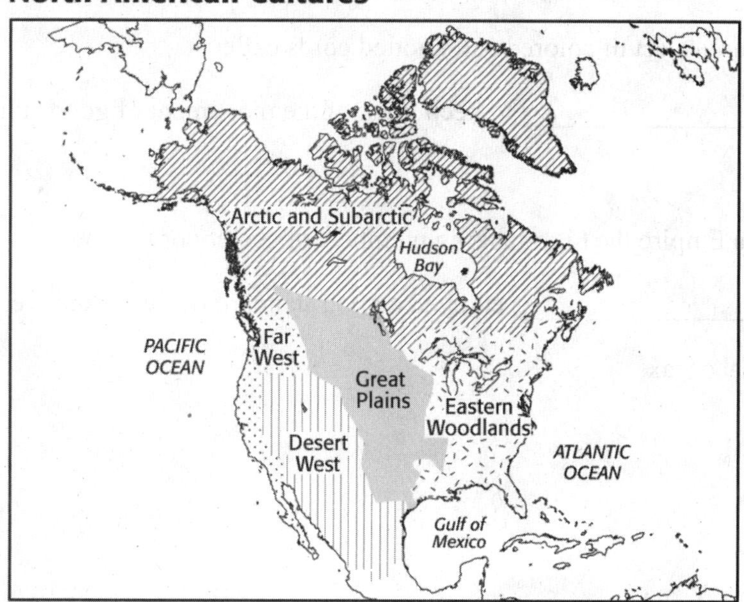

_____ 18. Based on the map, which of the culture groups below would be most likely to build log homes?
a. the Desert West
b. the Eastern Woodlands
c. the Great Plains
d. the Arctic and Subarctic

FILL IN THE BLANK For each of the following statements, fill in the blank with the appropriate word, phrase, or name.

19. Pueblos, built by the Anasazi, resembled modern apartment buildings. Those built in caves high up on canyon walls are called ______________________.

20. The ______________________ of the Eastern Woodlands built some of the earliest cities in North America, including the large city of Cahokia.

21. The complex writing system used by the Maya for record keeping included symbols called ______________________.

22. The city that served as the center of the Aztec Empire was called ______________________.

23. The Nazca created huge designs including geometric shapes and the outlines of animals on the ______________________.

24. The Inca used a set of colored and knotted cords called a ______________________ to keep track of the movement of goods throughout the empire.

25. In the Inca Empire the high-ranking members of society or ______________________, enjoyed a good standard of living and were exempt from the labor tax.

Name ______________ Class ______________ Date ______________

Form B

SHORT ANSWER On a separate sheet of paper, answer each of the following questions in complete sentences. Remember to use specific examples to support your answers.

1. Where is Mesoamerica, and why was it the site of the first farming settlements in America?

2. Describe the city of Tenochtitlán.

3. Compare and contrast the religious practices of the Maya and Aztec civilizations.

4. Describe the economy of the Inca.

PRACTICING SOCIAL STUDIES SKILLS Study the map below and, on a separate sheet of paper, answer the questions that follow in complete sentences.

North American Cultures

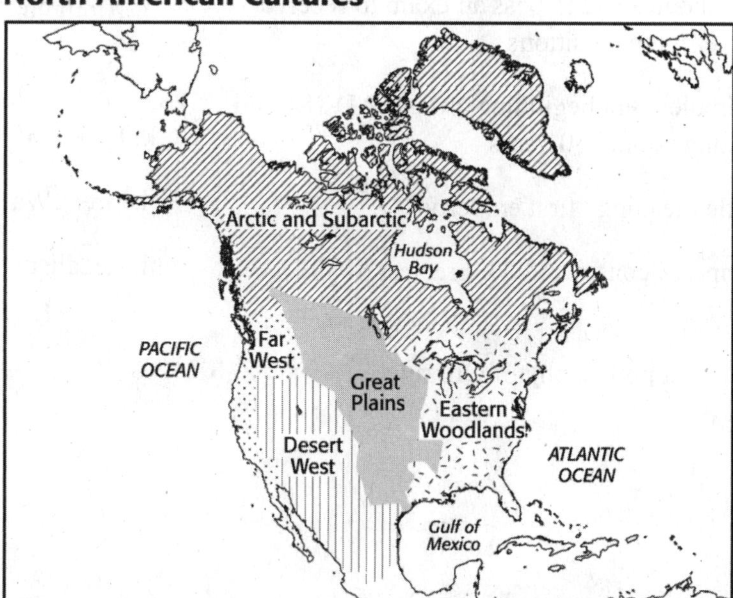

5. Describe the cultural traits shared by the peoples living in one of the regions on the map above.

6. Which region do you think was most heavily populated? Which do you think was least populated? Explain your answer.

Name _______________ Class _______________ Date _______________

Empires of China and India

Section Quiz

Section 1

MATCHING In the space provided, write the letter of the term, person, or place that matches each description. Some answers will not be used.

_____ 1. Emperor who began the Han dynasty and appointed Confucian scholars to advise him

_____ 2. Nomads who lived in the grasslands north of China

_____ 3. Daoist sect that promoted unrest during the Han dynasty

_____ 4. Period during which the Qin states rose to power

_____ 5. A structure made from defensive walls in northern China

_____ 6. Candidates had to pass an exam to receive government positions

_____ 7. Turbulent era beginning around AD 184 and lasting about 350 years

_____ 8. Title meaning "first emperor"

_____ 9. Emperor considered the greatest of all Han rulers

_____ 10. Political philosophy of Qin rule

a. Warring States period

b. Zhou dynasty

c. Shi Huangdi

d. civil service system

e. Liu Bang

f. Empress Lü

g. Emperor Wudi

h. civil service

i. Xiongnu

j. Yellow Turbans

k. Period of Division

l. Great Wall

m. Legalism

Name _______________ Class _______________ Date _______________

Empires of China and India

Section Quiz

Section 2

TRUE/FALSE Mark each statement **T** if it is true or **F** if it is false. If false explain why.

_____ 1. During China's Han dynasty, women and men were treated equally and had the same educational opportunities and social status.

____

____

_____ 2. According to Confucian teachings, the well-being of the state was dependent on strong family ties.

____

____

_____ 3. During the Han dynasty, peasants grew wealthy as a result of government efforts to limit the wealth of landowners and merchants.

____

____

_____ 4. The items traded on the Silk Road were small, valuable, and highly profitable luxury items.

____

____

_____ 5. Buddhism gained popularity in China by AD 200, largely because people found its message more hopeful than that of Daoism or Confucianism.

____

____

Empires of China and India

Section Quiz

Section 3

TRUE/FALSE Mark each statement **T** if it is true or **F** if it is false. If false explain why.

_____ 1. In 326 BC, Alexander the Great and his invading army were defeated by an Indian force including 200 war elephants.

____

____

_____ 2. The Mauryan empire began around 321 BC, when Chandragupta Maurya seized the throne of Magadha, a kingdom along the Ganges River.

____

____

_____ 3. Chandragupta's grandson, Ashoka, was a weak ruler who did little to improve the lives of his people.

____

____

_____ 4. An active sea trade enabled the Tamil kingdoms to gain wealth and develop a sophisticated culture, including poetry.

____

____

_____ 5. Instead of Buddhism, the Gupta kings promoted Hinduism, building Hindu temples and creating the setting for a revival of Hindu writing.

____

____

Name ______________________ Class ______________ Date ______________

Empires of China and India

Section Quiz

Section 4

FILL IN THE BLANK For each of the following statements, fill in the blank with the appropriate word, phrase, or name.

1. Social roles in Gupta India were largely shaped by ______________________, legal codes, and gender.
2. Many of the finest paintings of ancient India are found in Buddhist and Hindu ______________________.
3. A Hindu legal code, called ______________________, helped define people's roles in Gupta India.
4. Trade played a key role in spreading Indian art, architecture, and religions such as ______________________ and Buddhism to Southeast Asia.
5. The most spectacular Hindu and Buddhist temples were covered with detailed ______________________.
6. During the Gupta era, ______________________ became the language of literature.
7. One of the greatest writers of the age, ______________________, wrote beautiful poems and plays including one about a king who falls in love.
8. During the Gupta period, India was linked by the ______________________ to markets in the Mediterranean and China.
9. The Chinese traveler ______________________ is a source of information about the Gupta period.
10. The Indian astronomer Aryabhata knew that ______________________ was a shere and calculated its circumference.

Name ______________________ Class ______________ Date ______________

Empires of China and India

Chapter Test

Form A

MULTIPLE CHOICE For each of the following, write the letter of the best choice in the space provided.

_____ 1. Which of the following would a follower of Legalism most likely have supported as a punishment for a scholar who criticized the government?
a. firing him from his university position
b. torture and death
c. a weekend prison sentence
d. forced labor on massive building projects

_____ 2. Why did the Han develop a civil service system?
a. to reward soldiers for military service
b. to encourage higher education among the nation's youth
c. to obtain officials who held Confucian values
d. to solidify the dynasty's power by offering rivals government jobs

_____ 3. Buddhism became popular in China because
a. the emperor became a Buddhist in AD 200.
b. civil service exams were based on Buddhist principles.
c. Zhang Qian introduced Buddhism when he returned from Central Asia.
d. its message of rebirth and escape from suffering offered more hope than did Confucianism.

_____ 4. Chandragupta divided his empire
a. among his four sons.
b. into two districts, each governed by one of his wives.
c. into districts and appointed relatives and generals to rule them.
d. among his fellow Jainist monks.

_____ 5. Which of the following promoted Buddhism in India?
a. Kautilya
b. Ashoka
c. Chandragupta
d. the Tamils

Name ______________________ Class ______________ Date ______________

Empires of China and India

Chapter Test
Form A

PRACTICING SOCIAL STUDIES SKILLS Study the map and passage below and answer the questions that follow.

The Silk Roads

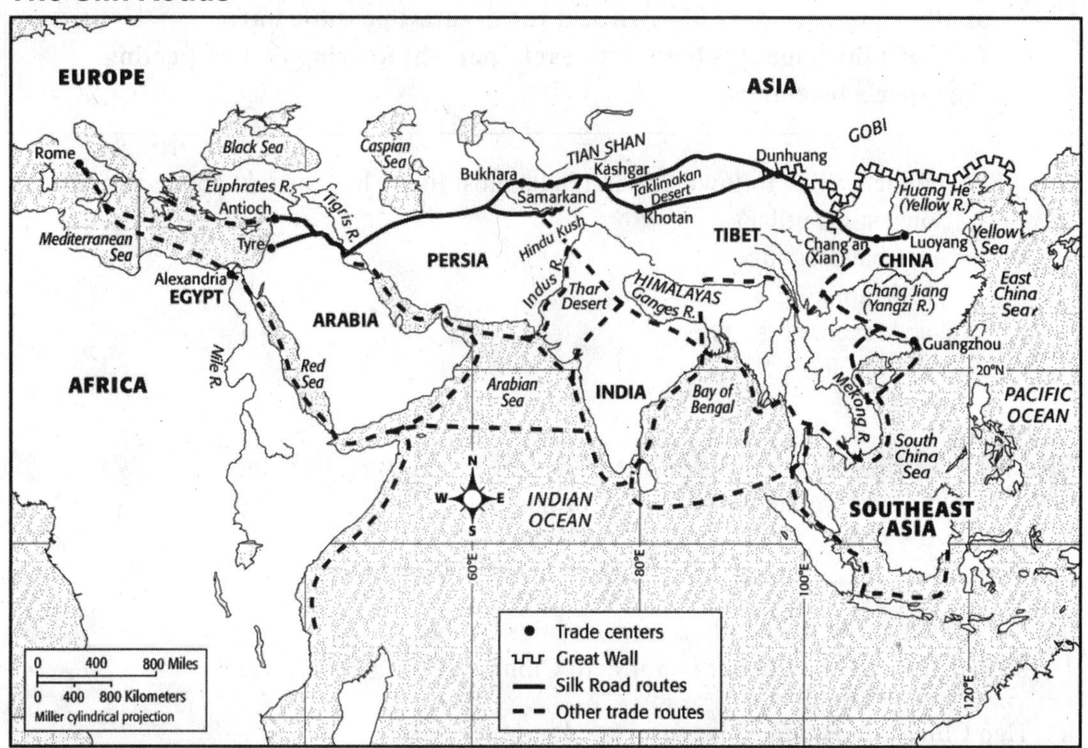

_____ 6. Which of the following represented one trade route upon which silk could travel to Rome?

a. over the Silk Roads from Guangzhou to Tyre, then by boat through the Mediterranean Sea to Rome
b. by an overland route from Guangzhou to Chang'an, connecting to the Silk Roads, then to Antioch, and then by boat through the Mediterranean Sea to Rome
c. by boat down the Nile to Alexandria and then through the Mediterranean Sea to Rome
d. by boat from Guangzhou to Khotan and on to Rome

_____ 7. Which of the following best explains why Buddhism spread from India to China?

a. China and India share a common border.
b. Both countries traded with nomads beyond the Great Wall.
c. China and India were linked by trade routes.
d. Indian traders sailed west to China.

Empires of China and India

Chapter Test

Form A

> **"The Beloved of the Gods… honors members of all sects [religions]… Whoever honors his own sect and disparages [speaks poorly about] another man's… does his own sect the greatest possible harm. Concord [harmony] is best, with each [person] hearing and respecting the other's teachings."**

___ 8. Which of the following individuals most likely had the text above inscribed on a stone pillar?
a. Chandragupta
b. Ashoka
c. Alexander the Great
d. Confucius

FILL IN THE BLANK For each of the following statements, fill in the blank with the appropriate word, phrase, or name.

9. The ____________________ dynasty unified China in 221 BC.

10. The Han dynasty frequently dealt with raids by the ____________________ on settled areas on the frontier in northern China.

11. Han China's most prized manufactured product was ____________________.

12. ____________________ was a Han historian who wrote *Records of the Grand Historian*.

13. The Gupta Empire reached its height under Emperor ____________________, who expanded the territory of the empire and ruled during a time of prosperity and cultural achievement.

14. ____________________ played a key role in spreading Buddhism and Hinduism from India to Southeast Asia.

15. Plays and poems written during the Gupta period were usually written in ____________________.

16. We know a great deal about life in Indian society due to the writings of the Chinese Buddhist monk named ____________________.

Empires of China and India

Chapter Test

Form A

TRUE/FALSE Indicate whether each statement below is true or false by writing **T** or **F** in the space provided.

_____ 17. The Han dynasty reached its height under Emperor Liu Bang.

_____ 18. The Period of Division followed a stable and prosperous period under the Later Han dynasty.

_____ 19. In Han China, all children received a free public education.

_____ 20. The Han dynasty raised taxes, causing some peasants to lose their land.

_____ 21. Buddhism was brutally repressed in China during the Later Han.

_____ 22. The first Mauryan emperor gave up his throne to become a Jainist monk.

_____ 23. Indian civilization flourished during the period of the Gupta Empire.

_____ 24. Indian doctors were unable to perform surgery, repair broken bones, or treat wounds.

_____ 25. Historians consider the Maurya period to be a golden age in ancient India.

Name _______________ Class _______________ Date _______________

Empires of China and India

Chapter Test
Form B

SHORT ANSWER On a separate sheet of paper, answer each of the following questions in complete sentences. Remember to use specific examples to support your answers.

1. Evaluate Shi Huangdi's boast that his dynasty would last "unto one thousand and ten thousand generations."

2. Imagine you lived in Han society. What would your family life be like? What would you expect your future family life to be like?

3. How did Ashoka try to improve the lives of people in his empire after his conversion to Buddhism?

4. Describe why the Gupta period in India is considered a golden age.

PRACTICING SOCIAL STUDIES SKILLS Study the map below and, on a separate sheet of paper, answer the questions that follow in complete sentences.

The Silk Roads

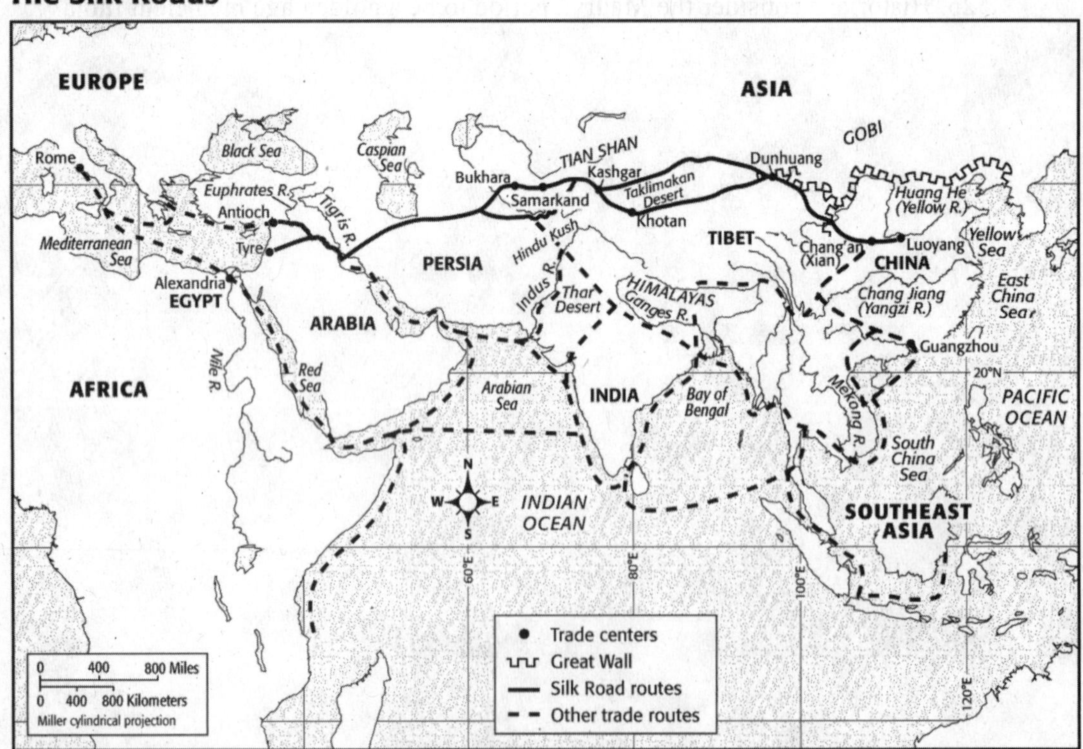

5. Describe two trade routes that could have been used to transport silk to Antioch.

6. Why do you think the Silk Roads became famous trade routes?

Name ______________________ Class ______________ Date ____________

The Growth of Civilizations

Unit Test

Form A

MATCHING In the space provided, write the letter of the person that matches each description. Some answers will not be used.

_____ 1. Allowed all men in Athens to take part in the assembly

_____ 2. Named Roman dictator for life

_____ 3. Divided Athens into 10 tribes

_____ 4. Led Carthage's army in the Second Punic War

_____ 5. Philosopher who emphasized reason and logic

_____ 6. Persian emperor who planned an attack on the Greek mainland

_____ 7. Influential leader who helped rebuild Athens

_____ 8. The greatest Han ruler, made Confucianism China's official government philosophy

_____ 9. Philosopher who asked a long series of questions to discover basic nature of life

_____ 10. Leader of Macedonia who built the largest empire the world had seen

a. Alexander the Great

b. Solon

c. Cleisthenes

d. Socrates

e. Darius

f. Pericles

g. Wudi

h. Julius Caesar

i. Plato

j. Hannibal

k. Aristotle

l. Maurya

m. Shi Huangdi

FILL IN THE BLANK For each of the following statements, fill in the blank with the appropriate word, phrase, or name.

11. Historians consider the ______________________ the first Greeks because they spoke a form of the Greek language.

12. The twelve most influential Greek gods were the ______________________ gods.

13. ______________________ was the world's first democracy.

14. The ______________________ was Rome's body of members who advised officials, controlled public finances, and handled foreign relations.

15. The Pax Romana began under the reign of ______________________.

16. The ______________________ League was made up of the Cayuga, Mohawk, Oneida, Onondaga, and Seneca nations.

Name ______________________ Class ______________ Date ______________

The Growth of Civilizations

Unit Test

Form A

17. The Maya and Aztec lived in Mesoamerica; the Inca lived in

    ____________________.

18. The political philosophy of the Qin Dynasty, ____________________, taught that a powerful and efficient state was the key to control and order.

19. Buddhism spread from India to China over the ____________________.

20. During the Gupta period, ____________________again became the main religion of India.

TRUE/FALSE Indicate whether each statement below is true of false by writing **T** or **F** in the space provided.

_____ 21. The Minoan civilization grew through a series of conquests.

_____ 22. Sparta was one of the mightiest city-states in Greece.

_____ 23. As leader of the Delian League, Athens was the richest, mightiest polis in Greece.

_____ 24. One characteristic of the Pax Romana was stable government.

_____ 25. The Romans did not have a written code of law.

_____ 26. Paul of Tarsus helped make Christianity a broader religion, attracting many new followers.

_____ 27. The Maya developed a complex writing system called cuneiform.

_____ 28. Lui Bang's defeat of the Qin ruler showed that he had the mandate of heaven.

_____ 29. The fall of the Later Han dynasty was partly the result of peasants being burdened with high taxes and heavy debt.

_____ 30. Ashoka abandoned his policy of conquest and worked to improve the lives of the people in the empire after converting to Hinduism.

MULTIPLE CHOICE For each of the following, write the letter of the best choice in the space provided.

_____ 31. By the 800s BC, the basic political unit in Greece was the
a. polis.
b. army.
c. senate.
d. assembly.

_____ 32. In the direct democracy of Athens, eligible people
a. served on trial juries.
b. voted on issues.
c. participated in writing the laws.
d. voted for representatives.

_____ 33. The Greek cities in Ionia were conquered by
a. Persians.
b. Athenians.
c. Spartans.
d. Mycenaeans.

_____ 34. Athens and Sparta were bitter enemies who worked together
a. to build an empire.
b. to protect Marathon.
c. to fight the Persians.
d. to govern the mainland.

_____ 35. The Battle of Salamis changed the nature of the wars by
a. removing Xerxes from control of the Persian navy.
b. changing the war from a foot battle to a naval war.
c. giving the Spartan army a foothold in Persia.
d. stranding the Persian army in Greece.

_____ 36. The Hellenistic world differed from the Hellenic world in its
a. warlike attitudes.
b. form of government.
c. lack of technological advances.
d. poor treatment of philosophers.

_____ 37. The Punic Wars began because
a. the Romans declared war on Sicily.
b. the Romans built a powerful navy.
c. Carthage and Rome came into direct conflict.
d. Carthage wanted to expand and control large areas of farmland.

Name ______________ Class ______________ Date ______________

PRACTICING SOCIAL STUDIES SKILLS Study the visual below and answer the questions that follow.

The Peloponnesian War

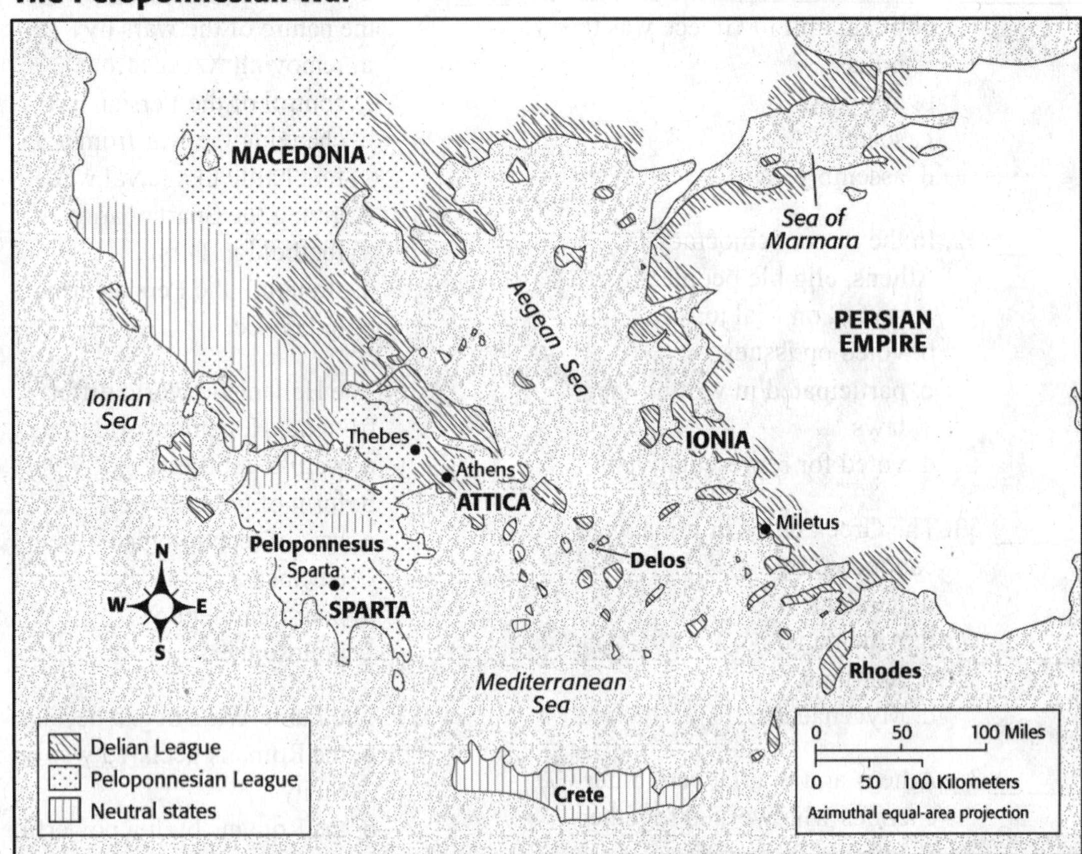

_____ 38. The Delian League controlled mostly
- a. the Persian Empire.
- b. large inland areas.
- c. Macedonia.
- d. islands and coastal areas.

_____ 39. One state that remained neutral was
- a. Crete.
- b. Macedonia.
- c. Ionia.
- d. Rhodes.

Name ______________________ Class ______________ Date ______________

The Growth of Civilizations

Unit Test

Form A

MULTIPLE CHOICE For each of the following, write the letter of the best choice in the space provided.

_____ 40. The primary reason for political and social revolution in the late republic of Rome was
a. widespread famine.
b. outside military threats.
c. Roman intolerance of other religions.
d. growing tensions between the social classes.

_____ 41. The Great Plains Indians left their farming settlements
a. after their crops were destroyed.
b. because they wanted to unite with other tribes.
c. after Europeans introduced horses to the area.
d. because the Hopewell tribes forced them to migrate.

_____ 42. The Zapotec people
a. grew wealthy from trade with the Toltecs.
b. built the first true city in Mesoamerica.
c. expanded after conquering the Olmecs.
d. were the first people to construct pyramids.

_____ 43. The Aztec Empire gained strength through trade and
a. the tribute system.
b. selling goods to Europeans.
c. surplus farming.
d. sale of gold and silver.

_____ 44. How did the mita system affect Inca society?
a. Merchants rose to upperclass status.
b. Unemployment spread across the classes.
c. A reward system was an incentive to workers and production increased.
d. The elderly and sick received the food and supplies they needed.

_____ 45. How did the Moche and Nazca people adapt to their South American environment?
a. They built irrigation canals.
b. They used terrace farming.
c. They lived as hunter gatherers.
d. They practiced slash-and-burn agriculture.

_____ 46. Though internal conflict had weakened the Inca Empire, its end is marked by which event?
a. the arrival of the Spanish in Peru
b. an invasion by the Aztec
c. a famine that killed many
d. the overthrow of Pachacuti

_____ 47. India was first united by the
a. Tamil Empire.
b. Gupta Empire.
c. Pandya Empire.
d. Mauryan Empire.

The Growth of Civilizations

_____ 48. Chandragupta Maurya controlled his empire through
- a. a rotating group of military advisors.
- b. independent rulers who had total control of their area.
- c. a strong centralized government.
- d. a government modeled on that of Athens.

_____ 49. The first power to create a unified Chinese empire was
- a. the Qin dynasty.
- b. the Han dynasty.
- c. the Zhou dynasty.
- d. the Mauryan dynasty.

_____ 50. Empress Lü gained control of the Han dynasty because
- a. she overthrew the emperor.
- b. her son was too young to rule.
- c. she was the first wife of Liu Bang.
- d. she had a clear mandate from heaven.

Name ______________________ Class ______________ Date ______________

The Growth of Civilizations

Unit Test

Form B

SHORT ANSWER On a separate sheet of paper, answer each of the following questions in complete sentences. Remember to use specific examples to support your answers.

1. Describe Athenian democracy.

2. Describe life during the Pax Romana.

3. Compare and contrast the Aztec and Maya civilizations.

4. Describe the influence of either Hinduism or Buddhism on Indian society.

PRACTICING SOCIAL STUDIES SKILLS Study the map below and, on a separate sheet of paper, answer the question that follows in complete sentences.

The Silk Roads

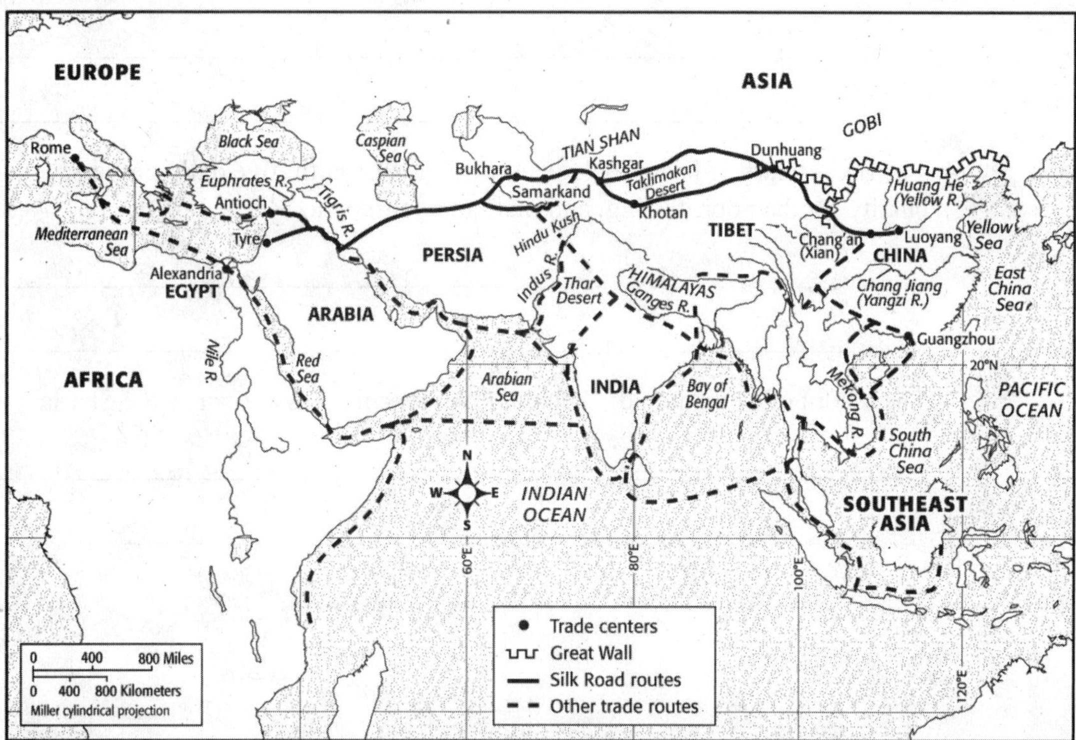

5. What role did the Silk Roads play in the diffusion of ideas? Use information from the chapter as well as details from the map to support your answer.

Name ______________________ Class ______________ Date ______________

Muslim Civilization Section Quiz

Section 1

TRUE/FALSE Mark each statement **T** if it is true or **F** if it is false. If false explain why.

_____ 1. Muhammad was raised by his uncle and grew up to become a merchant in the city of Mecca.

____

____

_____ 2. Muhammad reported that the angel told him that Allah was the one and only true and all-powerful God.

____

____

_____ 3. From the beginning, all people in Mecca shared Muhammad's beliefs.

____

____

_____ 4. The Five Pillars of Islam include a profession of faith, five daily prayers, charity for the poor, fasting, and making a journey to Mecca.

____

____

_____ 5. The record of Muhammad's behavior and teachings is known as the Sharia.

____

____

Name _______________ Class _______________ Date _______________

Muslim Civilization

Section Quiz

Section 2

MULTIPLE CHOICE For each of the following, write the letter of the best choice in the space provided.

_____ 1. In the first years after the death of Muhammad, the Muslim community was ruled by
a. Muhammad's sons.
b. Muhammad's wife.
c. the Persians.
d. caliphs.

_____ 2. Only 10 years after Muhammad's death
a. Islam spread to Europe.
b. the Seljuk Turks were in power.
c. Medina and Mecca revolted.
d. his followers had created an empire.

_____ 3. Under Muslim rule, Christians and Jews were allowed to
a. practice their own religions.
b. live without restrictions.
c. become Islamic leaders.
d. become caliphs.

_____ 4. The word "caliph" means
a. enemy.
b. Muhammad.
c. successor.
d. Islam.

_____ 5. The Shia were members of
a. the Sunni.
b. Ali's descendants.
c. Yazid's family.
d. the Umayyad.

_____ 6. The Abbasid dynasty moved the capital of the caliphate to
a. Spain.
b. Tours.
c. Medina.
d. Baghdad.

_____ 7. The Umayyads established Arabic as the official language and
a. lost Constantinople in 707.
b. extended the caliphate's borders.
c. were victors at the Battle of Tours.
d. strengthened Shia rule.

_____ 8. Under the Abbasids
a. Islam remained confined to the Arabian Peninsula.
b. education was not considered important.
c. Islam attracted people of many cultures.
d. trade was not allowed.

_____ 9. The spread of Islam to West Africa and Southeast Asia was due to
a. trade.
b. literature.
c. art.
d. conquests.

_____ 10. Muslim mystics who seek a mystical and personal connection to Allah are known
a. as Shia.
b. as Sunnis.
c. as Sharias.
d. as Sufis.

Muslim Civilization

Section Quiz

Section 3

MATCHING In the space provided, write the letter of the term, person, or place that matches each description. Some answers will not be used.

_____ 1. Famous medical scholar

_____ 2. Beautifully styled writing

_____ 3. Wrote a history of the world

_____ 4. Number system that went from India to Europe

_____ 5. Tall towers from which the faithful are called to prayer

_____ 6. Baghdad academy

_____ 7. An instrument for determining the position of stars and planets

_____ 8. Wrote commentaries on Aristotle and explored the relationship between reason and faith

_____ 9. Arrangement of floral images in an intricate, interwoven geometric design

_____ 10. Most significant written work in Islam

a. the House of Wisdom
b. algebra
c. Ibn Sina
d. arabesque
e. Whirling Dervishes
f. calligraphy
g. astrolabe
h. Ibn Khaldun
i. minarets
j. Qur'an
k. Omar Khayyam
l. Ibn Rushd
m. Arabic numerals

Muslim Civilization

Chapter Test

Form A

MULTIPLE CHOICE For each of the following, write the letter of the best choice in the space provided.

_____ 1. At the time of Muhammad's birth, what brought religious pilgrims to Mecca?
a. deep harbors on the Red Sea
b. the Kaaba
c. the Dome of the Rock
d. the variety of mosques

_____ 2. Some Meccans did not accept Muhammad's teachings because
a. his followers argued publicly.
b. he told the Meccans that their idol worship was sinful.
c. he refused to share the angel's message.
d. he chose to live in Yathrib.

_____ 3. Islam spread to places such as West Africa and Southeast Asia because
a. escaped Umayyad princes set up dynasties there.
b. Muslims sent missionaries there.
c. the Abbasids conquered those lands.
d. Muslim traders traveled there.

_____ 4. Rulers in the Umayyad dynasty were
a. secular.
b. Sunnis.
c. Shia.
d. Sufis.

_____ 5. Some were unhappy with Umayyad rule when
a. they extended privileges to non-Muslims.
b. they favored the Shia.
c. they did not extend the empire.
d. they ruled contrary to the Muslim ideal of equality.

_____ 6. What was the result of Muslim scholars translating Greek texts into Arabic?
a. It kept the information from Europeans.
b. It limited what Muslim scholars studied.
c. The texts were then translated into Latin and used in European universities.
d. Everyone under Muslim rule was required to learn Greek and Arabic.

_____ 7. There are no human figures in Islamic art because Muslims believe that
a. portraying people might tempt some to worship the images.
b. people are inherently sinful and not worthy of representation.
c. calligraphy is the only acceptable artistic style.
d. art should focus solely on religious topics.

PRACTICING SOCIAL STUDIES SKILLS Study the passage and map below and answer the questions that follow.

> **"Do not argue with the followers of earlier revelation otherwise than in a most kindly manner—unless it be such of them as are bent on evil-doing—and say: 'We believe in that which has been bestowed from on high upon us, as well as that which has been bestowed upon you; for our God and your God is one and the same..."**
>
> **—Qur'an 29:46**

_____ 8. The "followers of earlier revelation" are Jews and Christians, illustrating that Muslims believe that

a. there is more than one true God.
b. Jews and Christians worship idols.
c. Jews, Christians, and Muslims worship the same God.
d. Jews and Christians worship a different God than Allah.

Expansion of Islam, 632–760

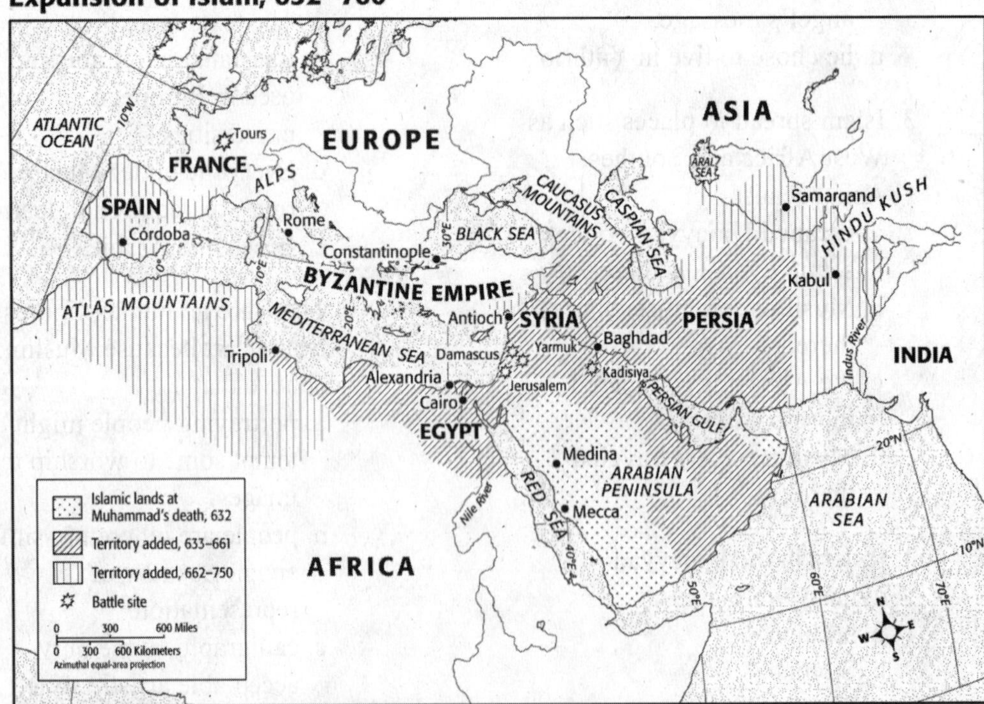

_____ 9. By AD 661, Islamic lands encompassed

a. only the area around Media and Mecca.
b. most of Egypt, the Arabian Peninsula, and Persia.
c. approximately half the Arabian Peninsula.
d. all of northern Africa, Spain, Persia, and the Arabian Peninsula.

Muslim Civilization

Chapter Test
Form A

MATCHING In the space provided, write the letter of the term, person, or place that matches each description. Some answers will not be used.

_____ 10. Legal system of rules

_____ 11. Acts of worship central to Islam

_____ 12. Finds the position of stars and planets

_____ 13. Individual report in the Sunna on Muhammad's actions

_____ 14. Made a lasting scholarly contribution with his commentaries on Aristotle

_____ 15. "Struggle for the faith"

_____ 16. Muslim mystics

_____ 17. Muhammad's journey from Mecca to Medina

a. astronomy
b. hadith
c. Ibn Rushd
d. the hegira
e. astrolabe
f. Sharia
g. Sufis
h. Ibn Sina
i. Five Pillars of Islam
j. jihad

FILL IN THE BLANK For each of the following statements, fill in the blank with the appropriate word, phrase, or name.

18. The sacred text of Islam is called the ______________________.

19. Followers of Islam are known as ______________________.

20. The ______________________, a record of Muhammad's behavior and teachings, provides Muslims with guidance in daily life.

21. For the ______________________, only imams can interpret the Qur'an.

22. The ______________________, supported by the Shia and others, overthrew the Umayyad dynasty.

23. Beautifully styled writing called ______________________ is a distinctive feature of Islamic art.

24. The Muslim faithful are called to prayer from tall towers in mosques called ______________________.

25. ______________________ wrote *The Rubaiyat*, a collection of poems that show a man pondering deep questions about God, life after death, and other serious topics.

Name ____________________ Class ____________ Date ____________

Muslim Civilization

Chapter Test

Form B

SHORT ANSWER On a separate sheet of paper, answer each of the following questions in complete sentences. Remember to use specific examples to support your answers.

1. Why did Muhammad leave Mecca?

2. Describe the Five Pillars of Islam.

3. How did Muslims treat non-Muslims in lands they conquered?

4. According to Islamic texts, what were the rightful roles of family members?

5. Describe some of the scholarly and scientific advances made by Muslims.

PRACTICING SOCIAL STUDIES SKILLS Study the map below and, on a separate sheet of paper, answer the questions that follow in complete sentences.

Expansion of Islam, 632–760

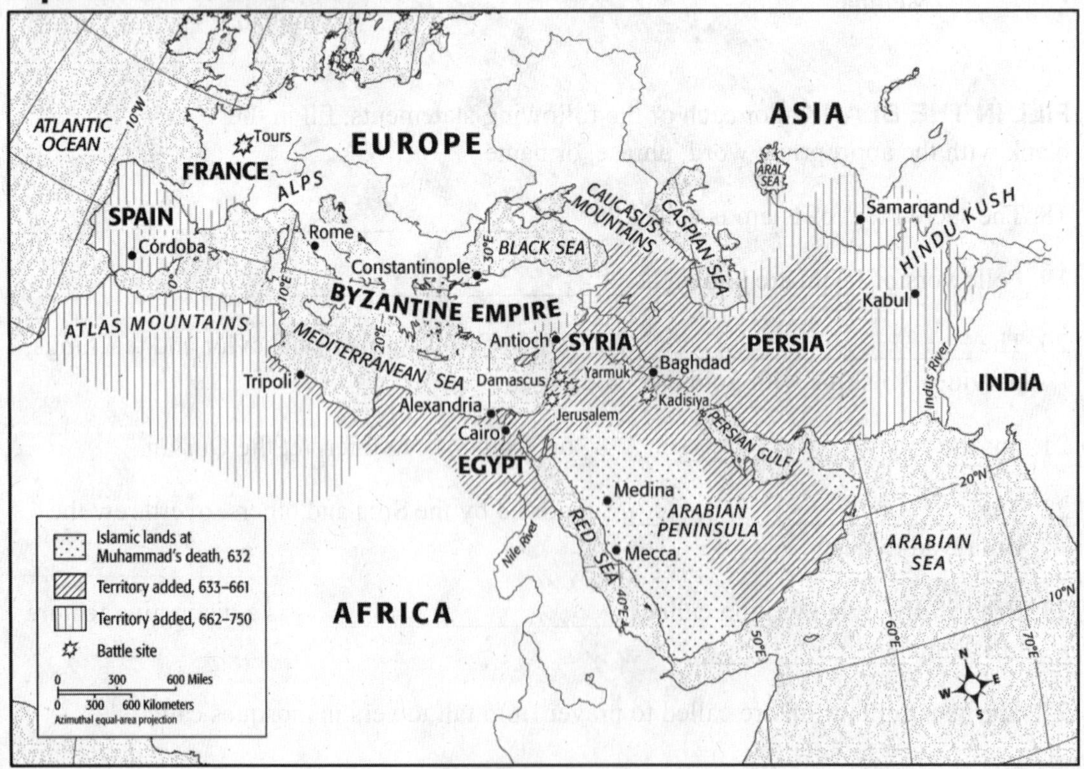

6. What territory was added between 662 and 750?

7. By 750, Islamic territory touched three continents. Identify the three continents.

Name ______________________ Class ______________ Date ______________

African Kingdoms

Section Quiz

Section 1

FILL IN THE BLANK For each of the following statements, fill in the blank with the appropriate word, phrase, or name.

1. Africa is more than ______________________ times the size of the United States.

2. The ______________________ is the world's largest desert.

3. The region of Africa south of the Sahara that divides the desert from wetter areas is called the ______________________.

4. A band of ______________________, or open grassland, extends east from Central Africa before wrapping back toward the south.

5. Certain ______________________, or small organisms, thrive in African's tropical areas.

6. In some parts of Africa, people raised herd animals. This practice is called ______________________.

7. In some areas, people of the same gender who had been born within a few years of each other formed groups called ______________________.

8. The task of remembering and passing on oral traditions was entrusted to ______________________.

9. ______________________ tools enabled Africans to live in places where they could not before.

10. In most ______________________ societies, cattle were an important food source and often determined one's status.

Name ______________________________ Class ________________ Date ____________________

African Kingdoms

Section Quiz

Section 2

MATCHING In the space provided, write the letter of the term, person, or place that matches each description. Some answers will not be used.

_____ 1. King of Aksum in about 320

_____ 2. Aksum's official religion

_____ 3. Large stone monument

_____ 4. One of the first written languages in Africa

_____ 5. During the 600s and 700s, these invaders came to Africa, conquering parts of East and North Africa

_____ 6. Most famous of the Zagwe kings

_____ 7. The dynasty that claimed to be descendants of King Solomon and the Queen of Sheba

_____ 8. Seasonal winds that influenced trade on Africa's East coast

_____ 9. Language that developed from blending a Bantu language and Arab words

_____ 10. The kingdom located between the Limpopo and Zambezi rivers

a. Christianity
b. Ge'ez
c. Aksum
d. Lalibela
e. Islam
f. monsoons
g. Solomonid
h. Swahili
i. Ezana
j. Great Zimbabwe
k. Muslims
l. Shona
m. stelae

Name ______________________ Class ______________ Date ______________

African Kingdoms

Section Quiz

Section 3

TRUE/FALSE Mark each statement **T** if it is true or **F** if it is false. If false explain why.

_____ 1. North African traders used camels to carry supplies across the Sahara.

____

____

_____ 2. The wealthy kings of Ghana ensured that gold prices stayed high by making a law that only kings were allowed to own large gold nuggets.

____

____

_____ 3. Mansa Musa's generosity brought Mali to the attention of the people of Europe, and Mali began to appear on European maps for the first time.

____

____

_____ 4. By the 1460s the rulers of Ghana had become strong and rich enough to take control of the former empire of Mali.

____

____

_____ 5. Askia Muhammad was a strong leader who is credited with being the first Christian ruler of Songhai.

____

____

Name ______________________ Class ______________ Date ______________

African Kingdoms

Chapter Test

Form A

MULTIPLE CHOICE For each of the following, write the letter of the best choice in the space provided.

_____ 1. Why did pastoralists leave the Sahara about 5,000 years ago?
   a. Parasites made the area dangerous to live in.
   b. The Sahara became drier and more land became desert.
   c. Ironworkers began to outnumber pastoralists.
   d. People wanted to trade their animals for supplies.

_____ 2. What common feature did many African societies share?
   a. They claimed to be descendants of the Queen of Sheba.
   b. They were village-based cultures made up of extended families and age-set groups.
   c. They originated in sub-Saharan Africa.
   d. They were forced to pay tribute to stronger groups that lived in the area.

_____ 3. Under King Ezana, Aksum became
   a. a Muslim kingdom that was soon taken over by Kush.
   b. an isolated society based on agriculture and led by a landowning class.
   c. a small society centered on seafaring and trade.
   d. a wealthy kingdom with a wide trading network and a written language.

_____ 4. While many other peoples in East Africa were Muslim,
   a. all of Ethiopia was inhabited by Jews called Beta Israel.
   b. the people of Ethiopia worshipped the descendants of Aksum.
   c. most people in Ethiopia were Christian.
   d. the leaders of Ethiopia rejected all forms of religion.

_____ 5. North African traders crossed the Sahara to trade salt for
   a. gold.
   b. food.
   c. spices.
   d. ivory.

_____ 6. How did Sunni Ali make revolts among conquered people less likely?
   a. by bribing the Tuareg
   b. by replacing local leaders with his own followers
   c. by practicing religious tolerance
   d. by allowing local leaders to remain in place

Name ______________________________ Class ________________ Date ________________

African Kingdoms

Chapter Test

Form A

PRACTICING SOCIAL STUDIES SKILLS Study the map and passage below and answer the questions that follow.

West African Kingdoms

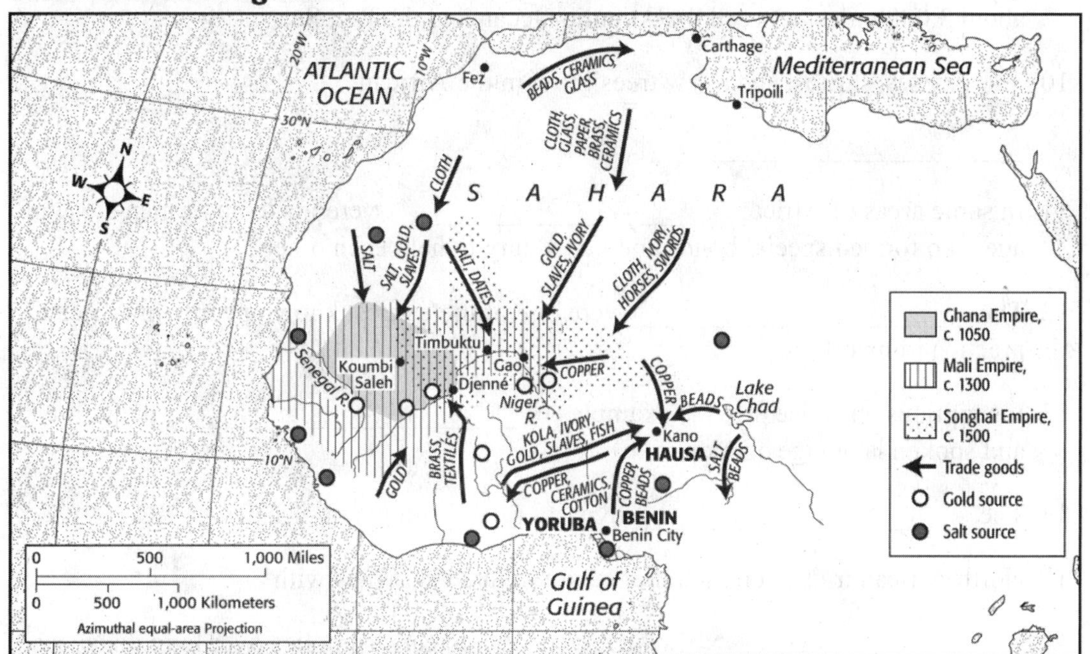

_____ 7. Where was the Songhai Empire located?
   a. on the Atlantic Ocean
   b. the Senegal River
   c. on the banks of Lake Chad
   d. in the area surrounding the Niger River

> **"He sits in a pavilion around which stand ten pages holding shields and gold-mounted swords: and on his right hand are the sons of the princes of the empire, splendidly clad and with gold plaited into their hair."**
>
> **—al Bakri, *The Book of Routes and Kingdoms*, c. 1067**

_____ 8. Based on the quote above, what do you think impressed al Bakri about the king of Ghana?
   a. the king's ability to farm
   b. the king's ability to read
   c. the king's wealth
   d. the king's hospitality

Name ______________________ Class ______________ Date ______________

African Kingdoms

Chapter Test

Form A

FILL IN THE BLANK For each of the following statements, fill in the blank with the appropriate word, phrase, or name.

9. Northern Africa is dominated by the ______________________, which stretches about 3,000 miles between the Atlantic Ocean and the Red Sea.

10. Tall grasses, shrubs, and a few trees grow in the African ______________________.

11. In some areas of Africa, ______________________ were made up of men close in age who formed special bonds and had a duty to help each other.

12. The ______________________ were one of the earliest known people in Africa to practice ironworking.

13. Inscriptions on stelae provide examples of ______________________, the written and spoken language of Aksum.

14. The ______________________ dynasty ruled Ethiopia until 1974.

15. North African traders crossed the Sahara in large caravans with ______________________, which were able to carry supplies over long distances.

16. Under the leadership of ______________________, Mali became a wealthy and sophisticated empire.

17. Songhai's first Muslim ruler was ______________________.

TRUE/FALSE Indicate whether each statement below is true or false by writing **T** or **F** in the space provided.

_____ 18. Africa has a wide variety of climates and vegetation.

_____ 19. It was the responsibility of children in African families to pass on oral traditions and local history.

_____ 20. Aksum was notable for its early conversion to Islam.

_____ 21. Kush declined when its port city was destroyed and the kingdom was cut off from trade.

_____ 22. King Lalibela built stone Christian churches that showed the skill and technological knowledge of Ethiopians.

_____ 23. Along East Africa's coast, Arab influences began to shape the local culture.

_____ 24. Sundiata's pilgrimage to Mecca eventually led Europeans to search West Africa for the source of Mali's riches.

_____ 25. The people of the Yoruba kingdoms were widely admired for their brass sculptures.

Name ______________________ Class ______________ Date ______________

African Kingdoms

Chapter Test Form B

SHORT ANSWER On a separate sheet of paper, answer each of the following questions in complete sentences. Remember to use specific examples to support your answers.

1. Describe the location and climate of Africa's rain forests.
2. Describe the duties of men and women in a typical West African family.
3. What have stelae been able to tell us about Aksum communication?
4. Suppose that you are a sailor from a coastal town of East Africa in April, AD 1100. You have a ship loaded with ivory and coconut oil and want to trade it for rice and bananas. What do you do?
5. How did Mansa Musa's pilgrimage to Mecca change Mali?

PRACTICING SOCIAL STUDIES SKILLS Study the map below and, on a separate sheet of paper, answer the questions that follow in complete sentences.

West African Kingdoms

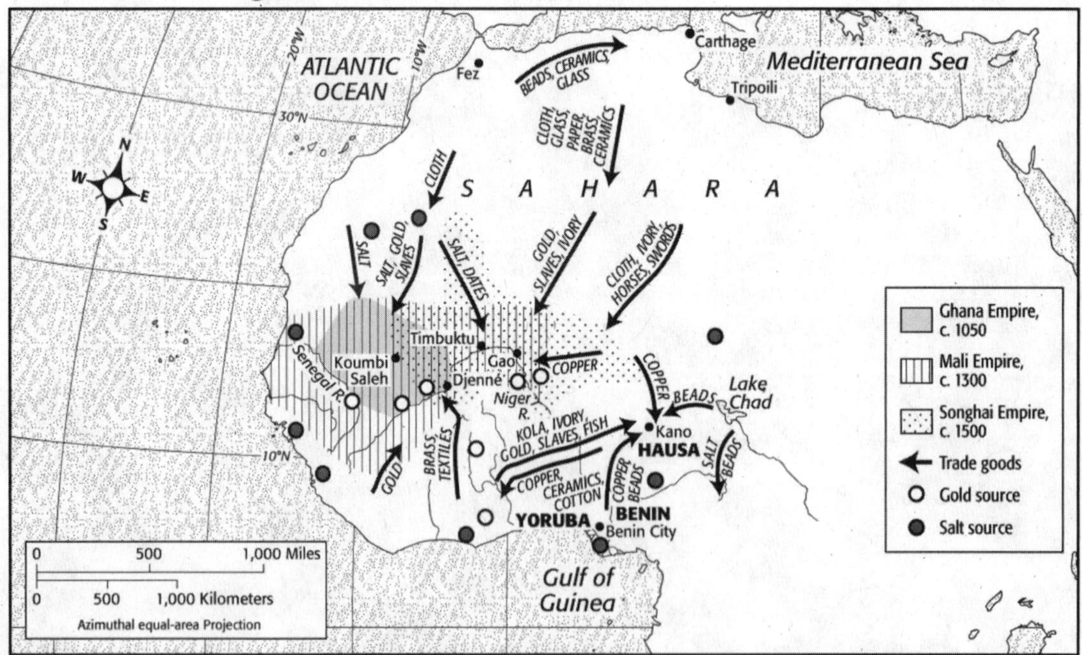

6. What goods were brought across the Sahara desert to be traded in Ghana?
7. Why do you think the Ghana, Mali, and Songhai empires arose in similar locations?

Name ______________________ Class ______________ Date ______________

Cultures of East Asia

Section Quiz

Section 1

FILL IN THE BLANK For each of the following statements, fill in the blank with the appropriate word, phrase, or name.

1. The completion of the ______________________, which connected northern and southern China, was the greatest accomplishment of the Sui dynasty.

2. The ______________________ ruled China between the Sui and the Song dynasties.

3. The only woman to hold the title of emperor in Chinese history was ______________________.

4. Under the Song, a new form of Confucianism called ______________________ gained favor.

5. During the Tang period the Chinese developed woodblock printing. The Song created another form of printing called ______________________.

6. Increased food production during the Tang and Song periods led to ______________________ growth.

7. Du Fu and Li Bo were two of the greatest ______________________ of the Tang period.

8. As trade created a strong, prosperous economy, ______________________ became more important members of Song society.

9. ______________________ trade increased when overland trade routes were lost during the Tang dynasty.

10. As the power of the aristocratic families declined a new class, called the gentry, developed. However, most people in China were ______________________.

Name _______________ Class _______________ Date _______________

Cultures of East Asia

Section Quiz

Section 2

TRUE/FALSE Mark each statement **T** if it is true or **F** if it is false. If false explain why.

_____ 1. In 1206 Temujin united the Mongol clans and took the title Genghis Khan, which means "Universal Ruler."

____

____

_____ 2. The Mongols were such brutal and terrifying warriors that some people surrendered to them without a fight.

____

____

_____ 3. Genghis Khan defeated the Chinese and founded a new dynasty in China called the Yuan.

____

____

_____ 4. Yuan rulers promoted foreign trade by welcoming foreign merchants and offering some traders special privileges.

____

____

_____ 5. Kublai Khan successfully invaded Japan and brought the Japanese under Mongol rule.

____

____

Name ______________________ Class ______________ Date ______________

Cultures of East Asia

Section Quiz

Section 3

MATCHING In the space provided, write the letter of the term, person, or place that matches each description. Some answers will not be used.

_____ 1. Groups based on extended family ties

_____ 2. Religion based on "way of the kami"

_____ 3. Family group from which emperors claim descent

_____ 4. Wrote the *The Tale of Genji*

_____ 5. Regent who sent young scholars to China

_____ 6. Family who controlled Japan during most of the Heian period

_____ 7. Period known for elegance and style of court life

_____ 8. One of three rival kingdoms that wanted control of Korea

_____ 9. Korean pottery with a blue-green glaze

_____ 10. Overthrew Koryo dynasty

a. Shinto

b. Yamato

c. Fujiwara

d. Lady Murasaki Shikibu

e. Silla

f. Heian

g. clans

h. Confucianism

i. monogatari

j. Mongols

k. archipelago

l. Prince Shotoku

m. celadon

Name ______________________ Class ______________ Date ______________

Cultures of East Asia

Section Quiz

Section 4

MULTIPLE CHOICE For each of the following, write the letter of the best choice in the space provided.

_____ 1. Different cultures developed on mainland Southeast Asia because contact among people in the area was limited by
a. vast deserts.
b. fertile plains.
c. law.
d. mountains.

_____ 2. Mainland Southeast Asia is made up of Cambodia, Laos, Thailand, Myanmar, Vietnam, as well as
a. parts of Malaysia.
b. Sumatra.
c. Java.
d. East Timor.

_____ 3. The two most important trade routes were the Sunda Strait and
a. the Malacca Strait.
b. the Java Strait.
c. the Malay Strait.
d. the Borneo Strait.

_____ 4. Hinduism, Buddhism, and Islam spread in Southeast Asia through
a. Mongol conquests.
b. trade and missionaries.
c. the work of Marco Polo.
d. forced conversions.

_____ 5. The Chinese were briefly defeated in Vietnam by two
a. kings.
b. farmers.
c. sisters.
d. soldiers.

Name ______________________________ Class ________________ Date ________________

Cultures of East Asia

Chapter Test

Form A

MULTIPLE CHOICE For each of the following, write the letter of the best choice in the space provided.

_____ 1. Which Chinese dynasty ended the Period of Disunion?
a. the Tang
b. the Han
c. the Sui
d. the Song

_____ 2. Most of the expansion of the Tang dynasty occurred during the reign of
a. Yangdi.
b. Taizong.
c. Wendi.
d. Wu Zhao.

_____ 3. Kublai Khan adopted many Chinese practices
a. yet Mongols were forbidden to marry Chinese.
b. but he was not able to rule China.
c. and the Chinese adored him.
d. and encouraged friendship between the Mongols and the Chinese.

_____ 4. What was the Pax Mongolia?
a. It was the trade route between the Mongol Empire and Rome.
b. It was the period when the Mongol Empire established peace and stability across Asia.
c. It was the Chinese alphabet adapted for Mongol use.
d. It was the title given to Kublai Khan by the Chinese.

_____ 5. Which geographic feature had the most influence on the development of culture in Japan?
a. the Ring of Fire
b. typhoon
c. the island of Hokkaido
d. the sea

_____ 6. Which countries had the greatest cultural influence on Japan?
a. Korea and China
b. Vietnam and Myanmar
c. Southeast Asia and China
d. Korea and Southeast Asia

_____ 7. Indians traders and missionaries influenced Southeast Asia by bringing Hinduism, Buddhism and
a. monsoons.
b. Sanskrit.
c. rice.
d. Tang rule.

Name ______________ Class ______________ Date ______________

Cultures of East Asia

Chapter Test

Form A

FILL IN THE BLANK For each of the following statements, fill in the blank with the appropriate word, phrase, or name.

8. ______________ was the only woman in Chinese history to hold the title of emperor.

9. Buddhism became so important in China from about 400 to 845 that the period is known as the ______________.

10. After Temujin united the Mongol tribes, he took the title ______________.

11. An Italian trader named ______________ visited the Yuan court in China and later published a popular book about his experiences.

12. Japanese clans worshipped nature spirits called ______________.

13. All Japan's emperors claim descent from the ______________ clan.

14. The Japanese adopted fashion, food, art, tea, music, and ______________ ideas about family from the Chinese.

15. The capital city of the Khmer Empire was ______________.

16. ______________ was Pagan's first great king.

Cultures of East Asia

Chapter Test

Form A

PRACTICING SOCIAL STUDIES SKILLS Study the map below and answer the question that follows.

Southeast Asian Kingdoms, 600–1350

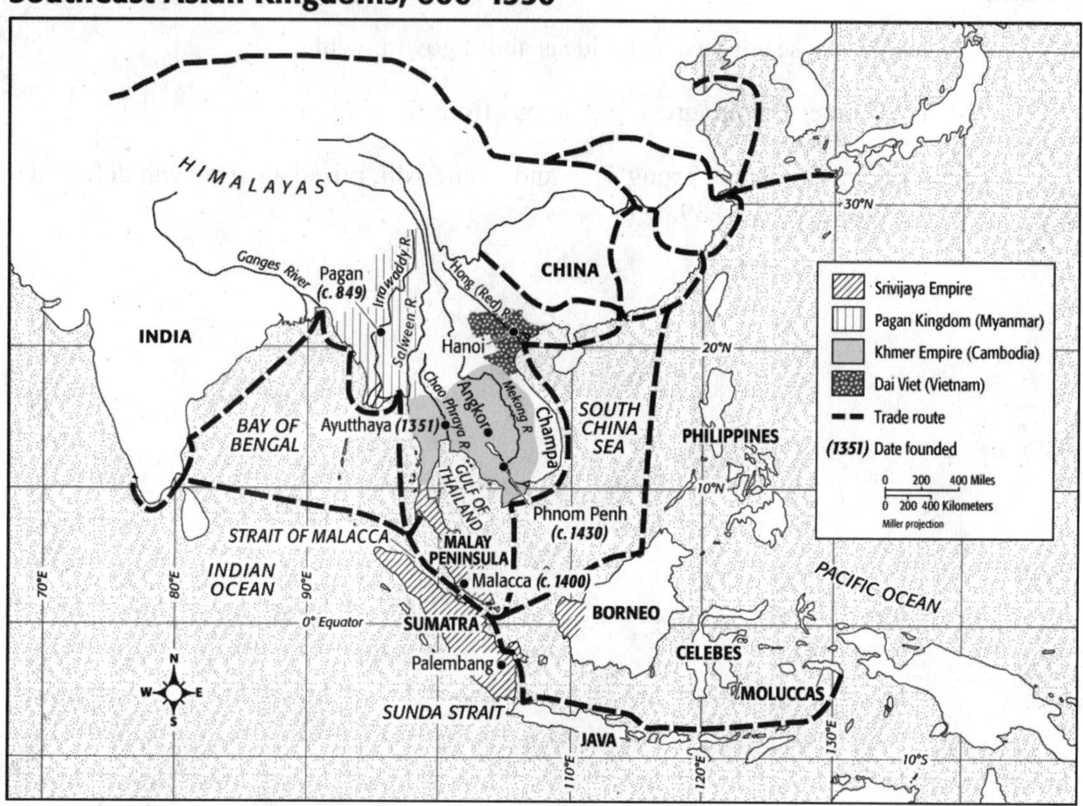

_____ 17. According to the map, trade between India and China passed through which of the following?
a. the Himalayas
b. the Philippines
c. the island of Celebes
d. the Strait of Malacca

TRUE/FALSE Indicate whether each statement below is true or false by writing **T** or **F** in the space provided.

_____ 18. The Tang period produced some of China's greatest poets.

_____ 19. The Tang period is known for its pottery figurines, many made to go into tombs.

_____ 20. Song rulers made the custom of footbinding illegal.

Cultures of East Asia

Chapter Test

Form A

_____ 21. The Pax Mongolia was a time of destructive warfare throughout Asia during which the Mongols fought for control of the continent.

_____ 22. The Chinese economy benefited from Mongol rule because trade expanded.

_____ 23. The Japanese adopted Tang ideas about government.

_____ 24. The Khmer Empire grew prosperous from farming rice.

_____ 25. Vietnamese sisters, Trung Trac and Trung Nhi, raised an army and defeated the Chinese in AD 39.

Name ______________________ Class ______________ Date ______________

Cultures of East Asia

Chapter Test

Form B

SHORT ANSWER On a separate sheet of paper, answer each of the following questions in complete sentences. Remember to use specific examples to support your answers.

1. Describe changes to Chinese society that occurred during the Song dynasty.

2. Describe two innovations developed during the Tang or Song dynasties.

3. What happened when the Mongols attempted to conquer Japan?

4. How did the sea shape the development of Japan?

5. Describe Japanese government and society during the Heian period.

PRACTICING SOCIAL STUDIES SKILLS Study the map below and, on a separate sheet of paper, answer the question that follows in complete sentences.

Southeast Asian Kingdoms, 600–1350

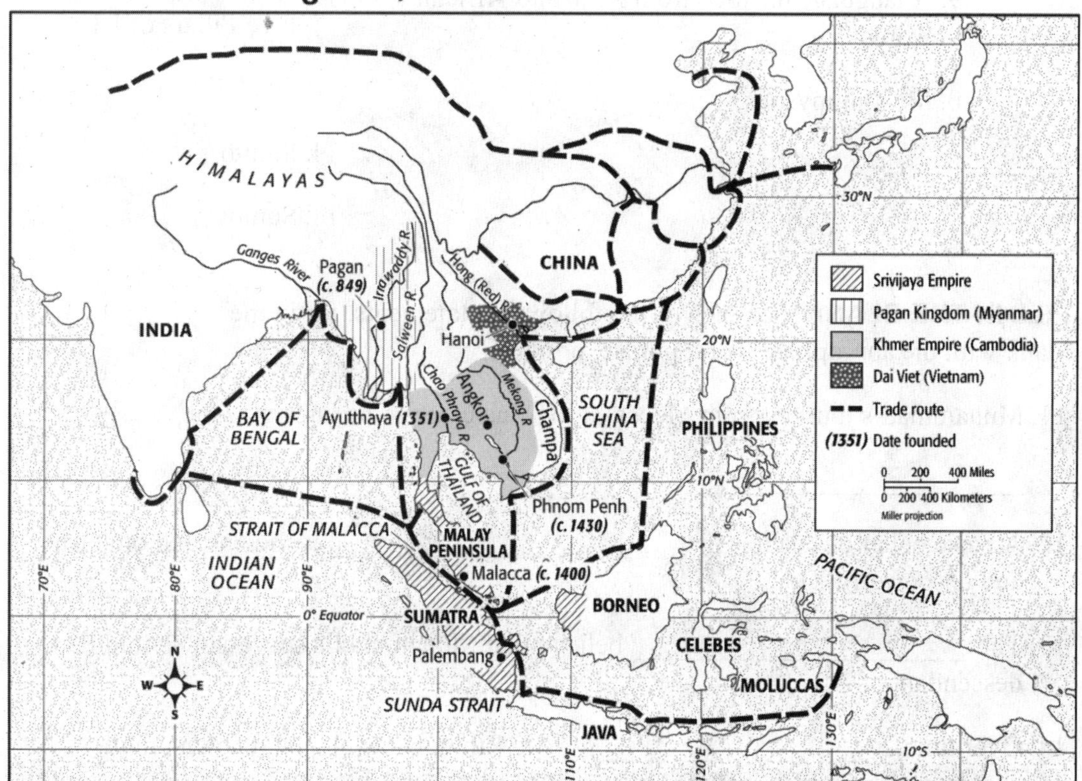

6. Which of the Southeast Asian kingdoms on the map are mainland kingdoms?

7. Describe the location of the Srivijaya Empire.

Name ______________________ Class ______________ Date ______________

Cultures in Contact

Unit Test

Form A

MATCHING In the space provided, write the letter of the term that matches each description. Some answers will not be used.

_____ 1. Direct revelations to Muhammad were written down as this

_____ 2. Basic acts of worship central to Islam

_____ 3. The written and spoken language of Aksum

_____ 4. Religion developed from belief in kami

_____ 5. Multistoried temple

_____ 6. Southeast Asian trade route

_____ 7. Sacred building in Mecca

_____ 8. In the Sunna, a report on Muhammad's life

_____ 9. A language blended from Arab and African words

_____ 10. Muslim mystics

a. Malacca Strait

b. Ge'ez

c. pagoda

d. hadith

e. griot

f. astrolabe

g. Qur'an

h. Kaaba

i. Sufis

j. Five Pillars of Islam

k. Swahili

l. Shinto

m. Sunnis

FILL IN THE BLANK For each of the following statements, fill in the blank with the appropriate word, phrase, or name.

11. Muhammad's journey from Mecca to Medina came to be known as the ______________________.

12. A basic belief of Islam is that ______________________ is the one and only true and all-powerful God.

13. The ______________________ believe that Muhammad's successor should be a descendant of Ali.

14. Over time, ______________________ in Ethiopia developed its own unique characteristics, which included elements of local customs.

15. Arab traders used ______________________ winds to visit the port towns on the East African coast.

16. Loyalty to family and ______________________ helped early African villagers work together.

17. Aksum's location on the Red Sea made it ideal for ______________________.

18. During the Sui dynasty, transportation improved with the completion of the ______________________.

19. The islands of Japan form a large island chain or ______________________.

20. Korea introduced Chinese writing and the religion of ______________________ to Japan.

TRUE/FALSE Indicate whether each statement below is true or false by writing **T** or **F** in the space provided.

_____ 21. Muhammad died without naming a successor and there was no clear candidate for the position.

_____ 22. Islamic religious art features images of human and animal figures.

_____ 23. Minarets are a common architectural feature of Muslim mosques.

_____ 24. Early African farmers were pastoralists of the Sahara.

_____ 25. About 5000 years ago, migration from the Sahara was caused by military threats.

_____ 26. Muslim invasions contributed to the decline of Aksum, although Aksum itself was never conquered.

_____ 27. The first inhabitants of Africa had to adapt to the continent's varied climates and geographical features.

_____ 28. During the Tang dynasty, Buddhism became so important that the years from 400 to 845 are known as the Age of Buddhism.

_____ 29. The use of paper money became popular under the Song dynasty.

_____ 30. Sea trade was not important during the Tang and Song dynasties.

Name ______________________ Class ______________ Date ______________

Cultures in Contact

Unit Test

Form A

MULTIPLE CHOICE For each of the following, write the letter of the best choice in the space provided.

_____ 31. According to Islam, women
a. are equal to men before Allah.
b. are equal to men before the law.
c. are eligible for the position of caliph.
d. are ineligible to own property.

_____ 32. Islam allowed People of the Book to
a. buy their freedom and leave.
b. practice their religion.
c. become caliphs.
d. live without paying taxes.

_____ 33. The main cause of division between Shia and Sunni Muslims was
a. basic religious beliefs.
b. succession of leadership.
c. the practice of rituals in Mecca.
d. treatment of the People of the Book.

_____ 34. Muslim society changed during the Umayyad dynasty
a. when women were forbidden to practice Islam.
b. when the rift between Shia and Sunni Muslims lessened.
c. when Arab Muslims became a ruling class.
d. when expansion was limited to peaceful means.

_____ 35. By translating the work of ancient Greek thinkers into Arabic, Muslims
a. established Arabic as a world language.
b. built a public university system.
c. established a long term alliance with Greece.
d. made available much of the science and philosophy taught in European universities.

_____ 36. How did the Abbasids gain support?
a. by promising everyone an equal say in government
b. by dividing and destroying the Umayyad opponents
c. by aligning themselves with the Umayyads
d. by appearing to represent many different causes

_____ 37. The Abbasids moved the capital of the caliphate to
a. Morocco.
b. Antioch.
c. Mecca.
d. Baghdad.

_____ 38. The kingdom of Ethiopia was formed by the descendants of
a. Ghana.
b. Mali.
c. Aksum.
d. Zimbabwe.

_____ 39. The Ghana economy grew in part from the Berber contribution of
a. secure ports.
b. gold.
c. water.
d. salt.

_____ 40. Mansa Musa's pilgrimage
a. increased the value of gold in Egypt.
b. brought Mali to the attention of Europeans.
c. resulted in the deaths of 60,000 people.
d. bankrupted his kingdom.

_____ 41. Songhai power increased
a. before Mansa Musa traveled to Mecca.
b. as Ghana's power declined.
c. by selling the gifts from Mansa Musa.
d. as Mali's power declined.

_____ 42. Askia Muhammad
a. was Songhai's first Muslim ruler.
b. ruled during Songhai's decline.
c. did not consider trade an important part of the economy.
d. ruled the Christian state of Songhai.

_____ 43. During the Heian period in Japan,
a. Japanese culture flowered.
b. nobles lived with commoners.
c. men were forbidden to read.
d. Japan was a Korean colony.

_____ 44. Early Korean society was mainly influenced by
a. African culture.
b. Japanese culture.
c. Chinese culture.
d. Vietnamese culture.

_____ 45. Two factors contributing to the rise of kingdoms in Southeast Asia were
a. farming and trade.
b. weather and science.
c. war and philosophy.
d. religion and technology.

_____ 46. The Pagan kingdom lost power
a. under Anawrahta.
b. by focusing on rice production.
c. when the Mongols crushed the Pagan armies.
d. by failing to develop a trade network.

_____ 47. The Khmer Empire grew prosperous
a. through trade.
b. through industry.
c. through tribute.
d. through rice farming.

_____ 48. What prevented the Mongols from invading Western Europe?
a. superior European armies
b. the death of the Great Khan
c. a wasting disease that afflicted Mongol ponies
d. the Pax Mongolia

Name ______________________ Class ______________ Date ______________

PRACTICING SOCIAL STUDIES SKILLS Study the visual below and answer the questions that follow

West African Kingdoms

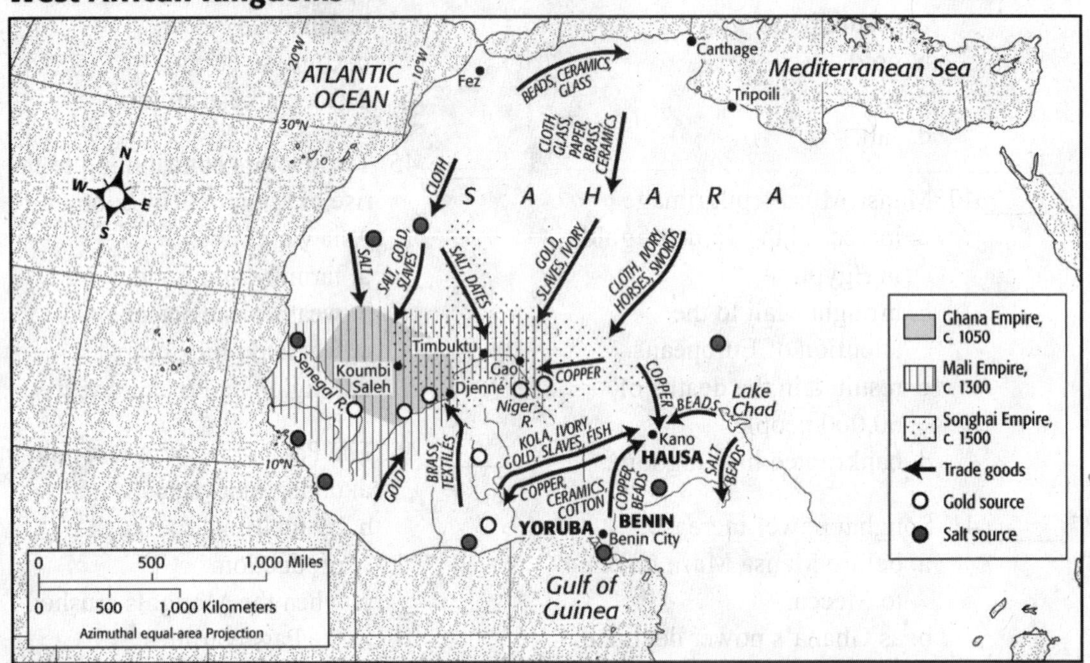

_____ 49. Which is the correct chronological order of the West African kingdoms?
a. Mali Empire, Songhai Empire, Ghana Empire
b. Songhai Empire, Mali Empire, Ghana Empire
c. Ghana Empire, Mali Empire, Songhai Empire
d. Mali Empire, Ghana Empire, Songhai Empire

_____ 50. What natural resource was located along the Niger River?
a. salt
b. gold
c. textiles
d. beads

Name ______________________ Class ______________ Date ______________

Cultures in Contact

Unit Test

Form B

SHORT ANSWER On a separate sheet of paper, answer each of the following questions in complete sentences. Remember to use specific examples to support your answers.

1. Describe the Five Pillars of Islam.

2. Name two accomplishments of the Abbasid dynasty.

3. Describe early African social structures.

4. What were the Bantu migrations?

5. What were some of the characteristics of Mongol rule in China?

PRACTICING SOCIAL STUDIES SKILLS Study the map below and, on a separate sheet of paper, answer the question that follows in complete sentences.

Japan, 1300

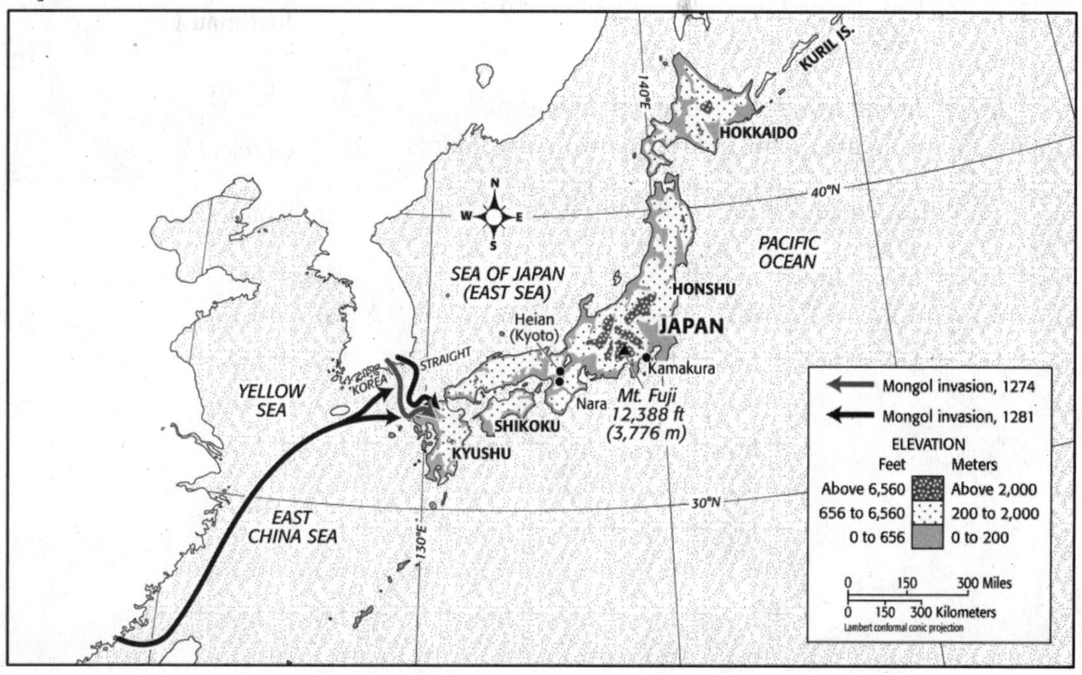

6. Use the map to describe the geography of Japan.

Name ______________________ Class ______________ Date ______________

Kingdoms and Christianity

Section Quiz

Section 1

MATCHING In the space provided, write the letter of the term, person, or place that matches each description. Some answers will not be used.

_____ 1. The capital of the Byzantine Empire

_____ 2. Eastern emperor who set up a commission to codify Roman law

_____ 3. Name for the church in the east after 1054

_____ 4. Justinian's top general

_____ 5. A church built during the reign of Justinian, known for its domes and arches

_____ 6. A rebellion by the Blues and Greens, groups named for colors worn by chariot teams

_____ 7. Co-ruler with Justinian

_____ 8. Tiny colored tiles fitted together and cemented in place

_____ 9. People who believed that paintings and sculptures could lead to the worship of idols

_____ 10. Language that replaced Latin in the eastern empire

a. Orthodox Church

b. Theodora

c. Hagia Sophia

d. Byzantium

e. Body of Civil Laws

f. Belisarius

g. mosaics

h. Nika Revolt

i. Constantinople

j. Justinian I

k. Roman

l. Greek

m. iconoclasts

Name ______________________ Class ______________ Date ____________

Kingdoms and Christianity Section Quiz

Section 2

TRUE/FALSE Mark each statement **T** if it is true or **F** if it is false. If false explain why.

_____ 1. Under Yaroslav the Wise, Kievan Rus reached the height of its power and prestige.

____

____

_____ 2. Christianity spread to Russia from the Byzantine Empire.

____

____

_____ 3. Cyril and Methodius developed a written alphabet in order to translate religious texts into the Slavonic language.

____

____

_____ 4. In 1241 Mongols from Asia established a Mongol state in southern Russia.

____

____

_____ 5. Alexander Nevsky was a very poor military leader.

____

____

Name ______________________ Class ______________ Date ______________

Kingdoms and Christianity

Section Quiz

Section 3

FILL IN THE BLANK For each of the following statements, fill in the blank with the appropriate word, phrase, or name.

1. The Angles and Saxons once lived in Germany, but had migrated to ______________________ in the 400s.

2. Anglo-Saxons were forced to unite in order to fight the ______________________.

3. One of Alfred the Great's greatest achievements was to establish a system of schools that educated ______________________ as well as children.

4. The period known as the Middle Ages is also called ______________________ times.

5. As pope, ______________________ promoted reforms that strengthened the papacy and made the pope one of the most influential figures in Europe.

6. The *City of God* was written by ______________________ after the sack of Rome.

7. Two forms of monasticism developed in Europe in the early Middle Ages—Celtic and ______________________.

8. Many ______________________ became centers of wealth and power because kings and nobles donated money or gifts in exchange for prayers said on their behalf.

9. Ireland did not have large cities, so instead of turning to bishops for spiritual guidance, people looked to the ______________________ of local monasteries.

10. Many Celtic monks were scholars who ran schools. Others were ______________________ who worked to spread Christianity to the people of the British Isles.

Name ______________________ Class ______________ Date ______________

Kingdoms and Christianity

Chapter Test

Form A

MULTIPLE CHOICE For each of the following, write the letter of the best choice in the space provided.

_____ 1. The Eastern Roman Empire
   a. fell to Germanic tribes called the Vandals.
   b. became known as the Byzantine Empire.
   c. relocated the capital to Antioch.
   d. rejected all forms of Christianity.

_____ 2. Although the people of Constantinople referred to themselves as Romans
   a. the eastern emperors were not interested in restoring the original Roman Empire.
   b. they were actually descendants of Germanic tribes.
   c. the emperor made Latin the official language instead of Greek.
   d. Greek cultural influences grew stronger over time.

_____ 3. Who were the Rus?
   a. three brothers from Constantinople who set up a trading post in Kiev
   b. northern Europeans, perhaps Vikings, who united the Slavs along the Dnieper River and formed a state called Kievan Rus
   c. Slavs who were imprisoned by the Khazars
   d. three sisters who fought the Khazars to liberate Slavic tribes from Kievan Rus

_____ 4. Because Cyril and Methodius were Greek monks
   a. they only spoke Greek while celebrating the mass in Moravia.
   b. it was the Byzantine version of Christianity that spread to Russia.
   c. they returned to Rome after converting the Moravians.
   d. they only spoke Latin and were rejected by speakers of the Slavonic language.

_____ 5. Why was the Cyrillic alphabet developed?
   a. to enable historians to record the history of the Rus
   b. to write the sacred text of the Slavic pagan religion
   c. to translate the religious texts of Byzantine Christianity for the Slavs
   d. to provide traders and merchants a way to record economic transactions

_____ 6. Which group ended the period of Kievan Rus dominance?
   a. the Nevskys
   b. the Teutonic Knights
   c. the Mongols
   d. the Slavs

_____ 7. Which of the following was instrumental in spreading Christianity to Ireland?
a. Augustine
b. Peter
c. Jerome
d. Patrick

_____ 8. Through the work of missionaries, a Christian society formed that included most of western Europe. Historians call that society
a. the Roman Catholic Church.
b. Christendom
c. monasticism.
d. the City of God.

PRACTICING SOCIAL STUDIES SKILLS Study the visual below and answer the question that follows.

© Adam Woolfitt/CORBIS

_____ 9. The mosaic above is typical of Byzantine art because it
a. pictures one of the Olympian gods.
b. has a non-religious subject.
c. was painted in watercolors.
d. is a religious subject created with colored tiles.

Name ______________________ Class ______________ Date ______________

Kingdoms and Christianity

Chapter Test

Form A

FILL IN THE BLANK For each of the following statements, fill in the blank with the appropriate word, phrase, or name.

10. ______________________ resulted from the emperor's efforts to systematically arrange the empire's existing laws and include new laws.

11. Justinian's top general, ______________________, recaptured many lost lands that had made up the Western Roman Empire.

12. Byzantine art included ______________________, images created with tiny colored tiles fitted together and cemented in place.

13. Cyril and ______________________ were Greek monks sent to Moravia to convert the Slavs to Christianity.

14. The first great king of the Anglo-Saxons was ______________________.

15. One of the most striking examples of Byzantine architecture is the

______________________.

16. In the *City of God*, written by ______________________, the author stated that people should pay less attention to the material world than they do to God's plan for the world.

17. Some Christians objected to icons. These people were called

______________________.

TRUE/FALSE Indicate whether each statement below is true or false by writing **T** or **F** in the space provided.

_____ 18. Justinian and his wife served as co-rulers of the Eastern Roman Empire.

_____ 19. Over time theological differences divided the eastern and western churches.

_____ 20. The Ottoman Turks attacked the city of Constantinople and renamed it Istanbul.

_____ 21. Christianity spread to Russia after the Rus attacked and defeated the Byzantines.

_____ 22. In 988 Grand Duke Vladimir made paganism the state religion of Kievan Rus.

_____ 23. The king of the Franks, Clovis, adopted Christianity when he won a difficult battle.

_____ 24. Augustine of Hippo strengthened the papacy and made the pope one of the most influential figures in Europe.

_____ 25. The conversion of people such as the Anglo-Saxons and the Franks helped to make western Europe largely a Christian society.

Name ______________________ Class ______________ Date ______________

Kingdoms and Christianity

Chapter Test

Form B

SHORT ANSWER On a separate sheet of paper, answer each of the following questions in complete sentences. Remember to use specific examples to support your answers.

1. What factors allowed the Eastern Roman Empire to thrive even after the Western Roman Empire was conquered?
2. Explain how religion influenced Byzantine art and architecture.
3. Summarize how Christianity spread in Russia.
4. How did Prince Alexander of Novgorod prevent the Mongols from destroying Russia?
5. Who were Alfred the Great and Clovis?
6. What contributions did monasticism make to Europe?

PRACTICING SOCIAL STUDIES SKILLS Study the visual below and, on a separate sheet of paper, answer the question that follows in complete sentences.

© Adam Woolfitt/CORBIS

7. What elements of this mosaic of Jesus would you lead you to conclude that it is an example of Byzantine art?

Name ______________________ Class ______________ Date ______________

The Early Middle Ages

Section Quiz

Section 1

MATCHING In the space provided, write the letter of the term, person, or place that matches each description. Some answers will not be used.

_____ 1. By 800, they ruled much of western and central Europe

_____ 2. Charlemagne invited them to teach and copy ancient texts

_____ 3. Officials who ruled parts of the empire in Charlemagne's name

_____ 4. Family to which Charlemagne belonged

_____ 5. The permanent capital city established by Charlemagne

_____ 6. The group Charlemagne conquered at Pope Leo III's request

_____ 7. Charlemagne's father

_____ 8. King of the Franks, and Emperor of the Roman People

_____ 9. They rewarded counts who did their jobs well and punished those who did not

_____ 10. A region in central Italy ruled by the pope

a. Papal States

b. Pippin

c. Charlemagne

d. the Lombards

e. Aachen

f. Carolingians

g. religion

h. counts

i. inspectors

j. law

k. the Franks

l. education

m. scholars

Name ______________________ Class ______________ Date ______________

The Early Middle Ages

Section Quiz

Section 2

TRUE/FALSE Mark each statement **T** if it is true or **F** if it is false. If false explain why.

_____ 1. The peace Charlemagne brought to western Europe has lasted until the present time.

____

____

_____ 2. The Viking raids started because the Vikings had trouble feeding their growing population in Scandinavia.

____

____

_____ 3. Among the places the Vikings settled were Iceland, Greenland, and North America.

____

____

_____ 4. The Magyars were the ancestors of the present-day Norwegians and were peaceful.

____

____

_____ 5. The Magyar army raided and destroyed churches in Rome, including Saint Peter's Basilica.

____

____

The Early Middle Ages

Section Quiz

Section 3

MULTIPLE CHOICE For each of the following, write the letter of the best choice in the space provided.

_____ 1. Land given to a knight for his services was called a
a. vassal.
b. fealty.
c. fief.
d. serf.

_____ 2. The feudal system developed
a. in response to invasions.
b. to grow more crops.
c. to provide manors for lords.
d. to protect the Church.

_____ 3. A typical manor would include
a. a church.
b. a grinding mill.
c. a blacksmith.
d. all of the above

_____ 4. Early castles were built for
a. comfort.
b. beauty.
c. defense.
d. animals.

FILL IN THE BLANK For each of the following statements, fill in the blank with the appropriate word, phrase, or name.

5. Skilled soldiers, called ______________________, fought for local nobles to defend their land.

6. The system of exchanging land for service was called ______________________.

7. The promise a knight made to protect his lord and remain loyal was called a(n) ______________________.

8. In medieval Europe the system that governed economics was called the ______________________ system.

9. In exchange for labor and a portion of the crops they grew, workers received a place to live and ______________________ from invaders.

10. It was the goal of every manor lord to make his manor ______________________, or able to produce everything people there needed to live.

Name ______________________ Class ____________ Date ____________

The Early Middle Ages

Section Quiz

Section 4

MATCHING In the space provided, write the letter of the term, person, or place that matches each description. Some answers will not be used.

_____ 1. Drove the Vikings to the Danelaw

_____ 2. Wife of Henry II, with her husband ruled all of England and about half of France

_____ 3. The governing body of England

_____ 4. Called Moors by the Christians

_____ 5. The victor of the Battle of Hastings

_____ 6. Created by union of Aragon and Castile

_____ 7. A document containing many provisions that restricted the king's power

_____ 8. Survey used to create a central tax system

_____ 9. Extended the power of the monarchy throughout France

_____ 10. Emperor of the Holy Roman Empire in the mid-900s

a. William the Conqueror

b. Domesday Book

c. Spain

d. Alfred the Great

e. Reconquista

f. Parliament

g. Capetians

h. Magna Carta

i. Otto the Great

j. Muslims

k. The Holy Roman Empire

l. Iberian Peninsula

m. Eleanor of Aquitaine

Name ______________________ Class ______________ Date ______________

The Early Middle Ages

Section Quiz

Section 5

FILL IN THE BLANK For each of the following statements, fill in the blank with the appropriate word, phrase, or name.

1. The majority of people in Europe were ______________________ and religion touched almost every aspect of their lives.

2. ______________________ is a person's level of devotion to their religion.

3. In the mid-1000s a pope with high ideals named ______________________ wanted to rid the church of corrupt practices such as buying and selling offices.

4. After the pope in Rome excommunicated the bishop of Constantinople, the Christian Church split in two: Roman Catholics and ______________________.

5. The papal term in office is called the ______________________.

6. Pope ______________________ stood up to the Holy Roman emperor Henry IV.

7. Holy Roman emperor Henry IV believed that he and other rulers should have the authority to name ______________________ to serve in their lands.

8. When someone is cast out of a church it is called ______________________.

9. The monastery at ______________________ became the core of a network of monasteries stretched across Western Europe.

10. One result of the conflict between pope and king was that the______________________ became one of the strongest figures in Europe.

Name ______________________ Class ______________ Date ______________

The Early Middle Ages

Chapter Test

Form A

MULTIPLE CHOICE For each of the following, write the letter of the best choice in the space provided.

_____ 1. Why did the pope name Charlemagne Emperor of the Roman People?

a. to ensure Charlemagne would not attack the Papal States
b. to thank Charlemagne for keeping him in power
c. to reward the Lombards of Italy for faithful service to the church
d. because Charlemagne refused to support the pope's authority unless he was crowned emperor

_____ 2. Which of the following statements correctly represents Charlemagne's views about education?

a. Education should only include military training and agricultural skills.
b. All leaders should learn to read and write.
c. Scholars are useless in an empire.
d. Only upper-class women need to receive an education.

_____ 3. Which king drove the Vikings north of London?

a. William
b. Henry
c. Harold
d. Alfred

_____ 4. Why was King Otto finally able to defeat the Magyars in the mid-900s?

a. The Magyars had settled into a permanent home.
b. The Germans had discovered gunpowder.
c. Careful animal husbandry had enabled Europeans to breed a faster horse.
d. A plague had weakened the Magyar army.

_____ 5. Europe became a feudal society because

a. the rarity of cash required land to be used as a payment for services.
b. Europeans needed to defend themselves against constant raids and invasions.
c. overpopulation required that a more efficient agricultural system be developed.
d. skilled craftspeople had emerged as farming techniques improved.

_____ 6. Christians drove the Moors out of the Iberian Peninsula during the

a. First Crusade.
b. sagas.
c. Reconquista.
d. Battle of Hastings.

Name ______________________ Class ______________ Date ______________

The Early Middle Ages

Chapter Test

Form A

_____ 7. The pope's influence in the Middle Ages resulted from
a. the fact that nearly everyone in Europe was Christian.
b. the economic influence of the Papal States.
c. the powerful army he headed under General Charlemagne.
d. his appointment by the Roman Emperor.

_____ 8. What led to the split in the Christian Church in 1054?
a. the defeat of the Papal States by Otto the Great
b. the desire of Henry IV for a divorce from his wife
c. a pacifist group's opposition to the Crusades
d. the refusal of the patriarch of Constantinople to recognize the pope's authority

PRACTICING SOCIAL STUDIES SKILLS Study the map below and answer the question that follows.

Vikings, Magyars, and Muslims, 800–1000

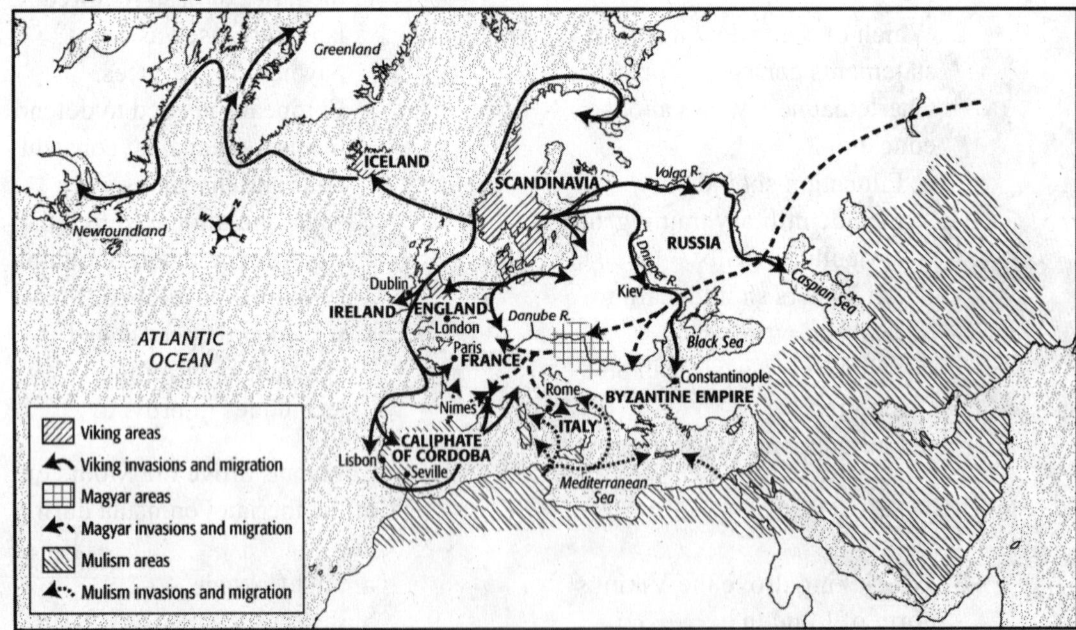

_____ 9. Based on the map above and what you know from the chapter, what was one result of the invasions and migrations depicted on the map?
a. Muslim scouting parties went to Scandinavia.
b. Some invaders settled in Europe.
c. The invaders had little influence in Europe.
d. All invaders ignored southern Europe.

The Early Middle Ages

Chapter Test Form A

MATCHING In the space provided, write the letter of the term, person, or place that matches each description. Some answers will not be used.

_____ 10. Survey taken of English residents and their possessions

_____ 11. Vikings

_____ 12. Observed strictly by monks of Cluny

_____ 13. Loyalty

_____ 14. Included Charles, Pippin, and Charlemagne

_____ 15. Church leader who wanted to purify the Christian Church

_____ 16. The land given to a knight for his service to a lord

_____ 17. Began to extend the power of the monarchy throughout France

_____ 18. Region in central Italy ruled by the pope

_____ 19. A person who owed service to his lord

a. fealty

b. Carolingians

c. Magna Carta

d. fief

e. Cistercian Order

f. Domesday Book

g. vassal

h. Benedictine Rule

i. sagas

j. Papal States

k. Leo IX

l. Norsemen

m. Hugh Capet

FILL IN THE BLANK For each of the following statements, fill in the blank with the appropriate word, phrase, or name.

20. Charlemagne chose officials called ______________________ to rule parts of the empire in his name.

21. Viking skills at ______________________ allowed them to cross the ocean in search of targets to raid.

22. A Viking explorer named ______________________ led an expedition to North America.

23. Although they were not slaves, ______________________ were legally tied to the manor on which they worked and could not leave without permission.

24. ______________________ is the governing body that makes England's laws.

25. The term in office of a pope is called a ______________________.

Name ______________________ Class ______________ Date ______________

The Early Middle Ages

Chapter Test

Form B

SHORT ANSWER On a separate sheet of paper, answer each of the following questions in complete sentences. Remember to use specific examples to support your answers.

1. Charlemagne made sweeping changes to many areas of Frankish society, including politics, education, religion, and law. In which area do you think Charlemagne had the greatest impact? Why?

2. Compare and contrast the raids launched by the Vikings and those launched by the Muslims.

3. Describe the duties a knight had to his lord and the duties a lord had to his knights.

4. What was the significance of the Magna Carta?

5. Why do you think the Cistercian Order was the most popular of the new monastic orders in the Middle Ages?

PRACTICING SOCIAL STUDIES SKILLS Study the map below and, on a separate sheet of paper, answer the question that follows in complete sentences.

Vikings, Magyars, and Muslims, 800–1000

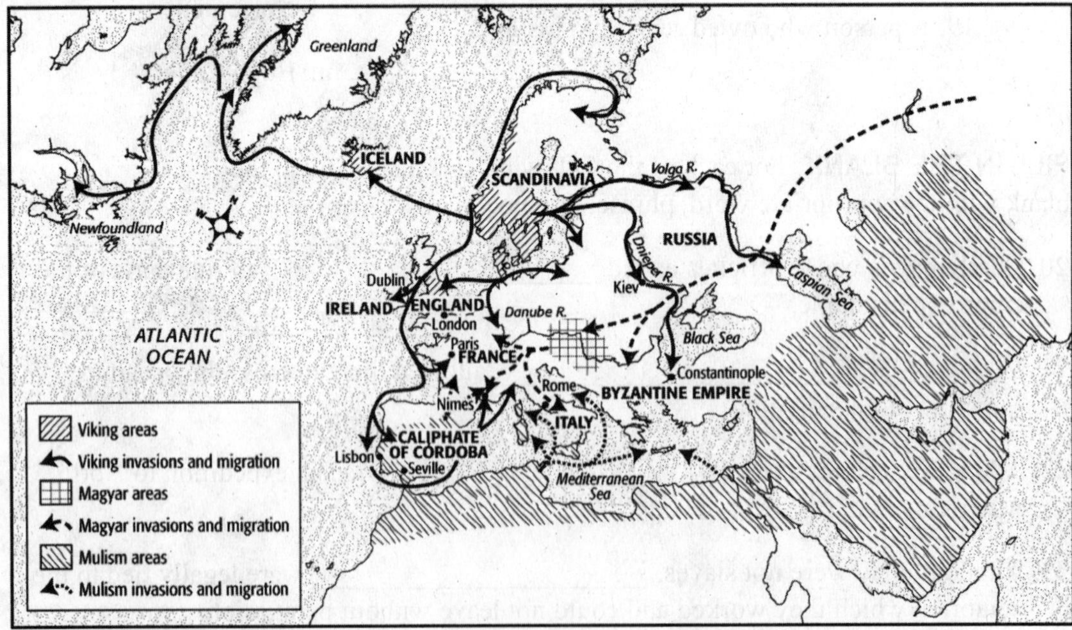

6. Which groups of raiders sometimes attacked northern France? If you lived in northern France in AD 900, which group would you be most afraid of? Why?

The High Middle Ages

Section Quiz

Section 1

TRUE/FALSE Mark each statement **T** if it is true or **F** if it is false. If false explain why.

_____ 1. During the Third Crusade, King Richard the Lion-hearted of England, set out to free Paris from the control of Saladin.

____

____

_____ 2. The Crusades were a series of religious wars fought to reclaim Jerusalem and the Holy Land.

____

____

_____ 3. Even though they were at war, Richard the Lion-hearted and Saladin had great respect for each other.

____

____

_____ 4. As a result of the Crusades, trade in Europe decreased.

____

____

_____ 5. Relations between religious groups changed as a result of the Crusades; many Europeans became more intolerant.

____

____

Name ______________________ Class ______________ Date ______________

The High Middle Ages

Section Quiz

Section 2

MATCHING In the space provided, write the letter of the term or place that matches each description. Some answers will not be used.

_____ 1. Some of the earliest people to get involved in medieval trade

_____ 2. A group of cities and towns in northern Germany that worked together to promote and protect trade

_____ 3. Where merchants and customers met to trade

_____ 4. The promise of a later payment

_____ 5. Trade organizations

_____ 6. A young person who has started to learn a craft

_____ 7. An apprentice who has learned the basics of his or her craft

_____ 8. Allowed merchants, instead of feudal lords, to run towns as they wanted

_____ 9. A tool that increased the size of the harvest farmers could grow on their land

_____ 10. Used the power of nature to grind wheat into flour

a. Parisians

b. Hanseatic League

c. apprentice

d. water mill

e. journeyman

f. Italians

g. coins

h. taxes

i. trade fair

j. heavy plow

k. guilds

l. charters

m. credit

Name ______________________ Class ______________ Date ______________

The High Middle Ages

Section Quiz

Section 3

MULTIPLE CHOICE For each of the following, write the letter of the best choice in the space provided.

_____ 1. The most important engineering advance in Gothic architecture was
   a. the gargoyle.
   b. illumination.
   c. stained glass.
   d. the flying buttress.

_____ 2. Thomas Aquinas combined Christian faith and rational thought in a system known as
   a. Divine Comedy.
   b. guilds.
   c. Scholasticism.
   d. chivalry.

_____ 3. Alchemy is
   a. an early form of science.
   b. a style of writing.
   c. a philosophy.
   d. a belief system.

_____ 4. Early in the Middle Ages few people other than monks or priests could read or write, therefore a popular topic for writers was
   a. the lives of saints.
   b. alchemy.
   c. death and dying.
   d. architecture.

_____ 5. Epic poems and romances were performed by wandering singers called troubadors and were intended as
   a. political commentary.
   b. entertainment.
   c. religious plays.
   d. social commentary.

Name ______________________ Class ______________ Date ______________

The High Middle Ages

Section Quiz

Section 4

FILL IN THE BLANK For each of the following statements, fill in the blank with the appropriate word, phrase, or name.

1. Beliefs that oppose official Church teachings are called ______________________.

2. The confusion that resulted from having more than one ______________________ weakened the influence of the Catholic Church.

3. ______________________ were members of new religious orders who, unlike monks, lived among the townspeople and preached.

4. The Hundred Years' War began as a dispute over the throne of ______________________.

5. In 1429 a young peasant girl helped change the course of the Hundred Years' War. Her name was ______________________.

6. Ultimately, the ______________________ were the winners of the Hundred Years' War.

7. Two families, the Lancasters and the Yorks, embarked on a war over the English throne. This war was known as the ______________________.

8. A devastating plague, brought to Europe by merchant sailors from Genoa, swept across the continent between 1347 and 1351 and was called the ______________________.

9. ______________________ million, or one third of Europe's population, died during the years of plague.

10. As a result of the plague, fewer people were available to work on farms. The people who were left demanded wages for their work, which led to the end of the medieval ______________________ system.

Name ______________________ Class ______________ Date ______________

The High Middle Ages

Chapter Test

Form A

MULTIPLE CHOICE For each of the following, write the letter of the best choice in the space provided.

_____ 1. The goal of the First Crusade was to
a. convert Muslims to Christianity.
b. take Jerusalem and the Holy Land away from the Byzantines.
c. take Jerusalem and the Holy Land away from the Muslims.
d. conquer Constantinople.

_____ 2. Which of the following was an effect of the Crusades?
a. Roman Catholics became more tolerant of Eastern Orthodoxy and Judaism.
b. Knights gained political power.
c. Important trade routes were destroyed.
d. European kings gained more political power.

_____ 3. Merchants asked the king for special charters for towns because
a. the merchants did not want to pay fees to feudal lords.
b. the Crusades made Europe less safe, so rural people banded together for protection.
c. they wanted to keep women out of guilds.
d. they wanted charters granting religious freedom.

_____ 4. Why were many of the written works created during the early Middle Ages religious texts?
a. Most people did not enjoy reading epics or romances.
b. Church law required it.
c. Few people outside of the clergy could read and write.
d. Few people were very religious.

_____ 5. Some medieval scholars disagreed with the ideas of Thomas Aquinas because he
a. was uneducated.
b. believed the ideas of non-Christians were worth consideration and study.
c. practiced alchemy despite Church laws forbidding it.
d. did not believe in the existence of God.

_____ 6. What was the end result of the War of the Roses?
a. The French drove the English out of their country.
b. The Lancasters won the throne.
c. The plague was spread by soldiers.
d. A Tudor nobleman took the throne, beginning a new era in English history.

_____ 7. The Black Death led to

a. massive witch hunts throughout Europe.
b. the collapse of the medieval manor system.
c. greater religious tolerance in Western Europe.
d. the end of the Hundred Years' War.

PRACTICING SOCIAL STUDIES SKILLS Study the visuals below and answer the questions that follow.

THE FIRST CRUSADES, 1095–1204

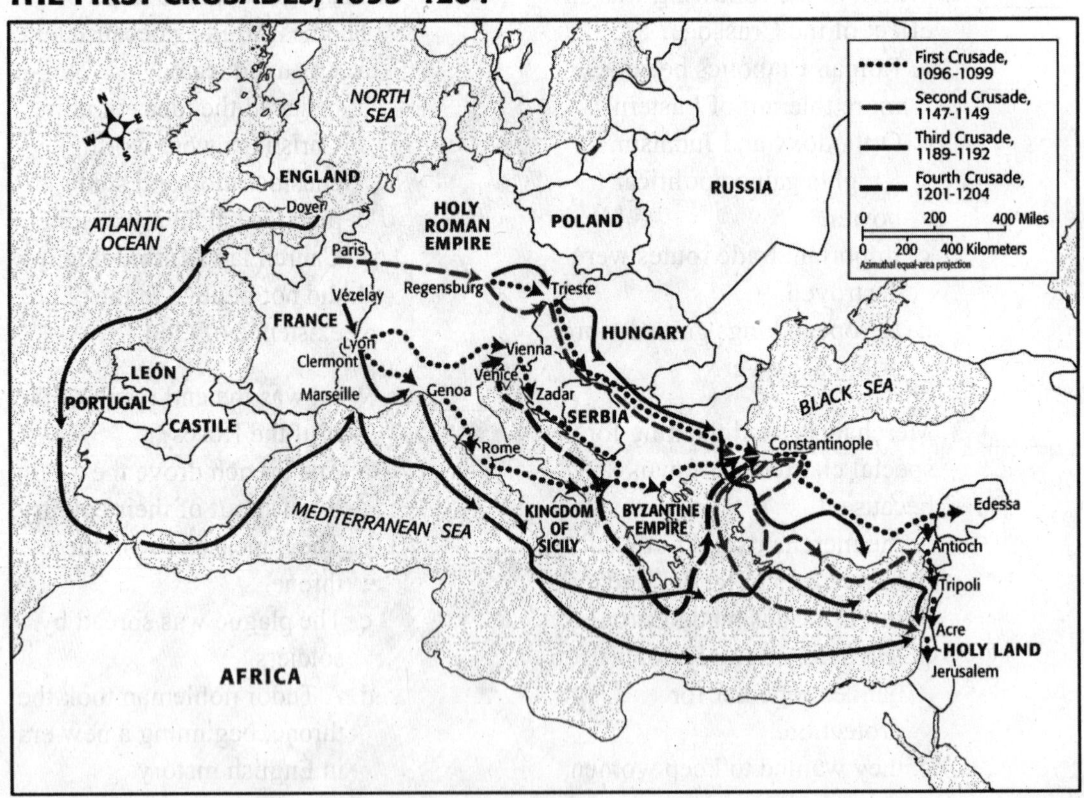

_____ 8. Crusaders from England on the Third Crusade primarily traveled to the Holy Land by

a. horse.
b. boat.
c. foot.
d. wagon train.

Name ______________________ Class ______________ Date ______________

The High Middle Ages

Chapter Test

Form A

© Peter Willi/SuperStock

_____ 9. The picture above shows an example of
  a. a medieval manor.
  b. illumination.
  c. a medieval guild.
  d. Gothic architecture.

FILL IN THE BLANK For each of the following statements, fill in the blank with the appropriate word, phrase, or name.

10. The ______________________ Crusade was the only one in which the Crusaders achieved their goal.

11. The most important early trading city in Italy was ______________________.

12. Europe's first banks were created as the use of currency and ______________________ increased, especially at trade fairs.

13. The process of decorating a written manuscript with pictures or designs was called

______________________.

14. King Arthur and his knights of the Round Table adhered to the code of

______________________.

15. The ______________________ was a devastating plague that killed as many as one in three people in Europe.

MATCHING In the space provided, write the letter of the term, person, or place that matches each description. Some answers will not be used.

_____ 16. Large woven wall hanging

_____ 17. A person who had mastered the basics of a craft

_____ 18. Muslim leader of the Holy Land during the Third Crusade

_____ 19. Used by merchants to get consumer goods to customers

_____ 20. A group of cities and towns in Germany that worked together to promote and protect trade

_____ 21. Legal procedures supervised by special judges to try suspected heretics

_____ 22. Wrote the *Divine Comedy*

_____ 23. Called the Council of Clermont to ask knights and nobles to help the Byzantines against the Turks

_____ 24. Changed the course of the Hundred Years' War

_____ 25. A person learning a trade with a skilled crafter

a. Geoffrey Chaucer

b. Joan of Arc

c. Richard the Lion-hearted

d. trade fairs

e. journeyman

f. Pope Urban II

g. vernacular

h. the Inquisitions

i. apprentice

j. tapestry

k. Dante Alighieri

l. Saladin

m. Hanseatic League

Name ______________________ Class ______________ Date ______________

The High Middle Ages

Chapter Test

Form B

SHORT ANSWER On a separate sheet of paper, answer each of the following questions in complete sentences. Remember to use specific examples to support your answers.

1. What profound social changes occurred as a result of the Crusades?
2. How do you think guilds helped people protect their own interests?
3. Describe what it might have been like to live in a European city during the Middle Ages.
4. Summarize the causes and effects of the plague.

PRACTICING SOCIAL STUDIES SKILLS Study the visual below and, on a separate sheet of paper, answer the question that follows in complete sentences.

© Peter Willi/SuperStock

5. What characteristics of Gothic architecture are visible in this photograph?

Name ______________________ Class ______________ Date ______________

Medieval Europe

Unit Test

Form A

MATCHING In the space provided, write the letter of the person that matches each description. Some answers will not be used.

_____ 1. Co-ruler with Theodora

_____ 2. Byzantine general who reconquered territory in northern Africa for the Roman Empire

_____ 3. Ruler at the height of Kievan Rus' power

_____ 4. United the Anglo-Saxons to fight the Danes

_____ 5. Viking who led an expedition to North America

_____ 6. Forced to accept the Magna Carta

_____ 7. Pope who excommunicated Henry IV

_____ 8. Muslim leader who succeeded in taking back the Crusader states

_____ 9. Nun who was also a famous medieval poet

_____ 10. Influential scholar who taught at the University of Paris

a. King John
b. Nestor
c. Hildegard of Bingen
d. Alfred the Great
e. Justinian
f. Charles Martel
g. Yaroslav the Wise
h. Saladin
i. Henry IV
j. Thomas Aquinas
k. Gregory VII
l. Belisarius
m. Leif Eriksson

FILL IN THE BLANK For each of the following statements, fill in the blank with the appropriate word, phrase, or name.

11. In Europe, the period following the fall of Rome is known as the Middle Ages or ______________________ times.

12. Religious themes were commonly found in ______________________ art such as mosaics and icons.

13. Constantinople's location on the Bosporus put it in a position to control ______________________ between Asia and Europe.

14. As the Vikings were terrorizing northern and western Europe, the ______________________ were invading from the east.

15. Vikings often attacked ______________________ because they were generally easy to plunder and held fine treasures.

Medieval Europe

Unit Test

Form A

16. Artisans and craftsmen formed ____________________ to protect their own interests.

17. ____________________, king of England, fought Saladin for control of Jerusalem.

18. A group of Northern German cities and towns that worked together to promote and protect trade was called the ____________________.

19. A ____________________ drew people from all over Europe to purchase a variety of goods.

20. The use of intellect and logic to bring together opposing ideas became known as ____________________.

TRUE/FALSE Indicate whether each statement below is true or false by writing **T** or **F** in the space provided.

_____ 21. Constantinople's location made it a major agricultural center.

_____ 22. The Justinian Code systematically arranged existing laws, legal opinions, and new laws.

_____ 23. As a result of the long conflict between Pope Gregory VII and Henry IV, the pope became one of Europe's strongest figures.

_____ 24. Serfs were legally tied to the manor on which they worked.

_____ 25. Beginning in the 1100s the Holy Roman Emperor was elected by a group of dukes and archbishops.

_____ 26. Leo IX was the first of a series of popes dedicated to reforming the papacy.

_____ 27. Cistercian monks lived in villages among the people they helped.

_____ 28. One result of the Crusades was an increase in trade in Europe.

_____ 29. The teaching of friars was believed to be a great weapon against heresy.

_____ 30. The Black Death was a plague that caused the death of about one third of the population in Europe.

Name ______________________ Class ______________ Date ______________

Medieval Europe

Unit Test

Form A

MULTIPLE CHOICE For each of the following, write the letter of the best choice in the space provided.

_____ 31. Alexander, Prince of Novgorod, encouraged the Russians to respond to the Mongols by
a. waging war against them.
b. not rebelling against them.
c. increasing trade with them.
d. converting them to Christianity.

_____ 32. Gregory the Great saw the role of pope as being the successor to the apostle Peter and
a. the Emperor of Rome.
b. immune to canon law.
c. supreme patriarch of the church.
d. advisor to the Eastern Church.

_____ 33. When the pope named Charlemagne Emperor of the Roman People it suggested
a. that Charlemagne should move the capital to Rome.
b. that pope wanted Charlemagne to succeed him.
c. that Charlemagne was also emperor of the Eastern Roman Empire.
d. that Charlemagne had restored greatness and had the backing of the church.

_____ 34. Charlemagne opened schools because he wanted leaders in his empire to be able to
a. lead an army.
b. pay him tribute.
c. read and write.
d. compose music.

_____ 35. The Vikings were successful warriors because they
a. were skilled riders with fast horses.
b. built fast ships enabling surprise raids.
c. had the largest trained army in Europe.
d. were descended from the Magyar warriors.

_____ 36. In a feudal society, a knight's chief responsibility was to
a. provide military service.
b. protect the peasants.
c. show allegiance to one noble.
d. farm the land for his lord.

_____ 37. The economic system of the Middle Ages was the
a. nobility system.
b. feudal system.
c. manorial system.
d. tribute system.

_____ 38. The Magna Carta
a. divided England.
b. created taxes.
c. declared war on France.
d. limited the king's power.

_____ 39. The wars between two families over the English throne were called the
a. Wars of Lancaster.
b. York Wars.
c. Wars of the English.
d. Wars of the Roses.

_____ 40. The Christian states' campaign to retake the Iberian Peninsula is called the
a. Reconquista.
b. Crusades.
c. Iberian Civil Wars.
d. War of Castile.

_____ 41. The feudal system in Europe was a system
a. of exchanging land for service.
b. to rid the church of corrupt bishops.
c. to free peasants and serfs.
d. of providing charters for towns.

_____ 42. The goal of the Crusades was
a. to take the Holy Land from Muslim control.
b. to regain Constantinople.
c. to force the Turks into Jerusalem.
d. to show the pope's political power.

_____ 43. When Crusaders attacked the city of Zara, held by the Christian king of Hungary, the pope
a. shifted his support to the Turks.
b. organized the Council of Clermont.
c. sent more troops to support the city.
d. excommunicated the Crusaders.

_____ 44. The increased use of money and credit led to
a. inflation.
b. an equal, classless society.
c. the creation of Europe's first banks.
d. religious laws banning the use of currency.

_____ 45. New farming technology increased crops and decreased
a. urban populations.
b. the need for workers in trade and industry.
c. unemployment.
d. the number of people needed to work on farms.

_____ 46. Historians study Chaucer's *Canterbury Tales* to learn more about
a. the French spoken in the Middle Ages.
b. what life was like in the Middle Ages.
c. Dante's view of the afterlife.
d. military techniques.

_____ 47. Epics and romances were intended as entertainment, so they were usually written and performed
a. in Greek.
b. in Latin.
c. in the vernacular.
d. by monks.

_____ 48. A dispute over the throne of France in 1328, led to the
a. Crusades.
b. Inquisition.
c. Wars of the Roses.
d. Hundred Years' War.

Name ______________________ Class ______________ Date ______________

PRACTICING SOCIAL STUDIES SKILLS Study the map below and answer the questions that follow.

Crusader States

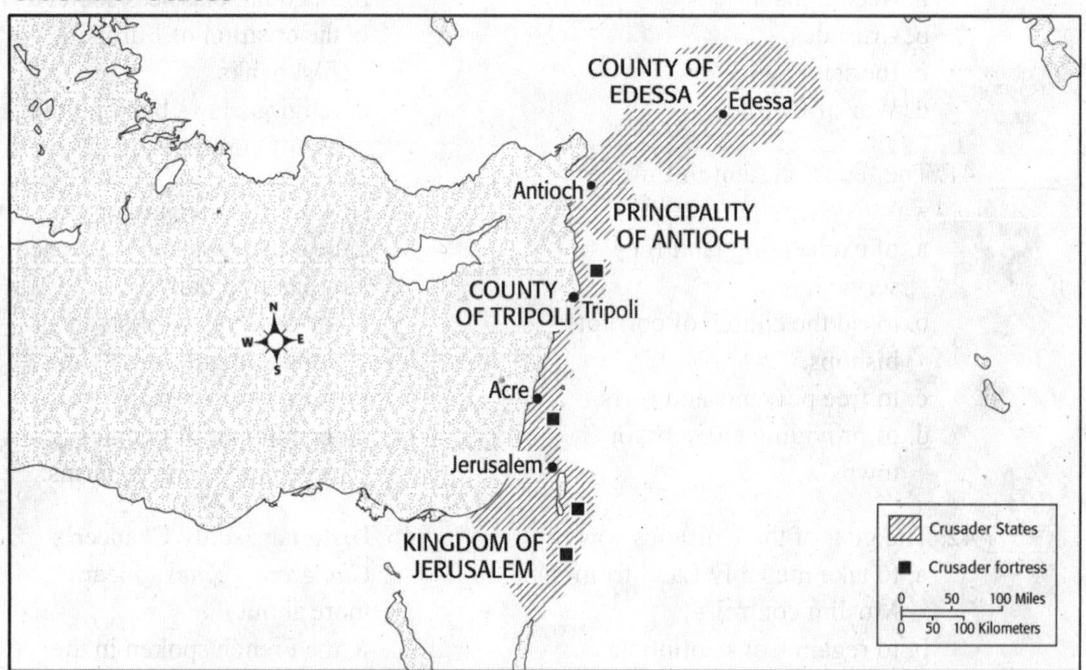

_____ 49. During the First Crusade, Crusaders established four states in the Holy Land named for the cities of

a. Jerusalem, Edessa, Antioch, and Tripoli.
b. Jerusalem, Acre, Antioch, and Tripoli.
c. Acre, Edessa, Antioch, and Tripoli.
d. Jerusalem, Edessa, Antioch, and Acre.

_____ 50. Most likely, the Muslims retook the city of Edessa first, because

a. it contained the greatest supply of natural resources.
b. a Crusader fortress was not located there.
c. it was the region furthest from Constantinople.
d. the Crusaders failed to establish a state there.

Medieval Europe Unit Test

Form B

SHORT ANSWER On a separate sheet of paper, answer each of the following questions in complete sentences. Remember to use specific examples to support your answers.

1. Summarize the issues that divided the eastern and western churches.
2. Explain how Cyril and Methodius helped spread Christianity throughout Russia.
3. Summarize Charlemagne's achievements.
4. What was the purpose of feudalism? Explain how it worked.
5. Describe life on a medieval manor.
6. What were the causes and effects of the Crusades?

PRACTICING SOCIAL STUDIES SKILLS Study the map below and, on a separate sheet of paper, answer the question that follows in complete sentences.

Crusader States

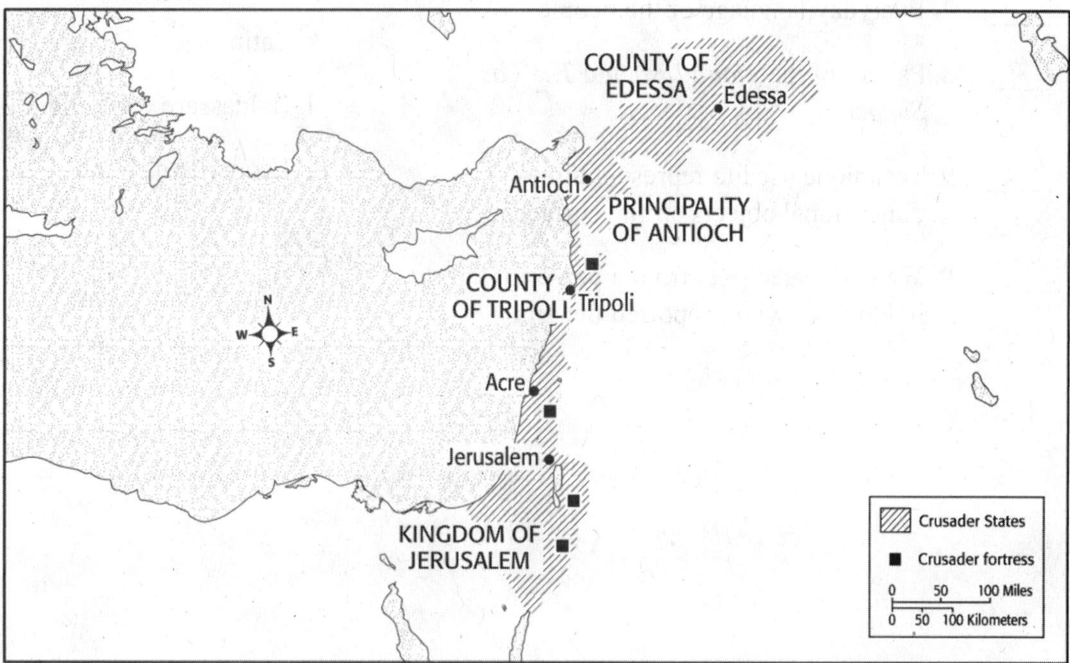

7. Most of the land surrounding the Crusader states was under Muslim control. Study the map and explain how this and other factors made it difficult for the Crusaders to maintain possession of the Holy Land.

Name ______________________ Class ______________ Date ______________

Renaissance and Reformation

Section Quiz

Section 1

MATCHING In the space provided, write the letter of the term, person, or place that matches each description. Some answers will not be used.

_____ 1. Movement that emphasized individual accomplishment

_____ 2. Sculpted the statue of *David*, and painted the ceiling of the Sistine Chapel in Rome

_____ 3. Political philosopher and statesman who advised rulers to separate morals from politics

_____ 4. Having a worldly rather than a spiritual focus

_____ 5. A sustained period of renewed interest and remarkable development in art, literature, science, and learning

_____ 6. Polish astronomer who suggested that the Sun sat at the center of the universe

_____ 7. Everyday language of the people

_____ 8. Painter of the *Mona Lisa* and *The Last Supper*

_____ 9. Technique used to represent three-dimensional objects on flat surfaces

_____ 10. Well-educated poet from a powerful family in Florence who supported the arts

a. secular

b. Lorenzo de Medici

c. Renaissance

d. Niccolò Machiavelli

e. humanism

f. perspective

g. Raphael

h. Michelangelo Buonarroti

i. Nicholas Copernicus

j. vernacular

k. Latin

l. Baldassare Castiglione

m. Leonardo da Vinci

Name ______________________ Class ______________ Date ______________

Renaissance and Reformation

Section Quiz

Section 2

FILL IN THE BLANK For each of the following statements, fill in the blank with the appropriate word, phrase, or name.

1. In Northern Europe, the ______________________ protected its members from pirates and made shipping safer by building lighthouses and training ship captains.

2. After spending time in Italy, the German artist ______________________ began to use the Italian techniques of realism and perspective in his own works.

3. ______________________ is traditionally given credit for inventing movable type.

4. Artists and scholars traveling to and from Italy helped Renaissance ideas spread, but it was easier access to ______________________ that quickly spread Renaissance ideas.

5. ______________________ was the leading Christian humanist. He wrote about the need for a pure and simple Christian life, and advised readers on such subjects as educating children.

6. The book *Utopia* was widely read across Europe. It was written by the English humanist and statesman ______________________.

7. English playwright ______________________ expressed a wide knowledge of natural science, humanist topics, and a deep understanding of human nature in plays that focused on the lives of realistic characters.

8. ______________________, who supported herself and her children by writing, championed the causes of equality and education for women.

9. Painter ______________________ perfected the oil painting technique that gave the Flemish School its distinctive style.

10. Flemish artist Pieter Brueghel the Elder used Italian techniques, but unlike the Italian paintings, his paintings showed scenes of ______________________.

Name ________________ Class ________________ Date ________________

Renaissance and Reformation Section Quiz

Section 3

TRUE/FALSE Mark each statement **T** if it is true or **F** if it is false. If false explain why.

_____ 1. By the early 1500s, concerns about the Roman Catholic Church developed into a reform movement that came to be called the Protestant Reformation.

____

____

_____ 2. Martin Luther believed it was helpful to the Church and its members to purchase indulgences.

____

____

_____ 3. A theocracy is a government in which church and state are joined and whose officials are considered to be divinely inspired.

____

____

_____ 4. King Henry VIII of England asked the pope to annul his marriage to Catherine of Aragon because she was not a Catholic.

____

____

_____ 5. Queen Mary returned England to the authority of the pope, but when she died, the new queen, Elizabeth, split England once again from Rome.

____

____

Section 4

MATCHING In the space provided, write the letter of the term, person, or place that matches each description. Some answers will not be used.

_____ 1. The movement by Catholics to reform the church itself

_____ 2. Founded by the Basque nobleman Ignatius of Loyola

_____ 3. Archbishop of Milan who built a new school for the education of priests

_____ 4. Worked to regain the district of Savoy which had turned to Calvinism

_____ 5. Church court of Rome that heard cases of people accused of being Protestant, or of breaking church law

_____ 6. Group of delegates who met and clarified Catholic teaching on important points

_____ 7. Protestant minority in France

_____ 8. Nun who reformed the Carmelite order

_____ 9. Agreement that allowed each German prince to choose either Catholicism or Lutheranism as the religion his subjects would practice

_____ 10. Conflict credited with expanding the Italian Renaissance throughout Europe

a. Charles Borromeo

b. Teresa of Avila

c. Huguenots

d. Council of Trent

e. Italian Wars

f. Francis of Sales

g. Pope Paul IV

h. Protestants

i. Anabaptists

j. Peace of Augsburg

k. Counter-Reformation

l. Roman Inquisition

m. Jesuits

Name ______________________ Class ______________ Date ______________

Renaissance and Reformation

Chapter Test

Form A

MULTIPLE CHOICE For each of the following, write the letter of the best choice in the space provided.

_____ 1. The church's scholastic education gave way to the subjects known as humanities and inspired the movement known as
- a. humanism.
- b. secularism.
- c. the Protestant Reformation.
- d. the vernacular.

_____ 2. Which of the following people advanced the idea that "the end justifies the means"?
- a. Sofonisba Anguissola
- b. Baldassare Castiglione
- c. Niccolò Machiavelli
- d. Donato Bramante

_____ 3. Johannes Gutenberg's invention has been described as revolutionary because
- a. with easier access to books, more people learned to read and more books were printed.
- b. with oil paints, Renaissance artists could paint much more detail than they could with watercolors.
- c. coupled with a large pool of unemployed workers, it led to early industrialization in parts of Central Europe.
- d. until guilds were created, craftspeople were unable to control the goods they produced.

_____ 4. How did the work of the Flemish School differ from Italian Renaissance painting?
- a. Flemish painters used watercolors, while Italian painters used oils.
- b. Flemish painters focused on religious symbolism, while Italian painters focused on secular themes.
- c. Italian painters focused on the details of everyday life, while Flemish painters tackled grand themes.
- d. Flemish painters focused on the details of everyday life, while Italian painters often showed mythological scenes.

_____ 5. Desiderius Erasmus's works were censored in Paris and condemned by the Church because he
- a. had become a Protestant.
- b. fanned the flames of discontent with the Church.
- c. was convicted of witchcraft.
- d. advocated a return to the ideals of ancient Greece and Rome.

_____ 6. What did the Edict of Worms decree about Martin Luther?
- a. It named him leader of the Catholic Church.
- b. It made him an outlaw and condemned his writings.
- c. It named him king of Germany.
- d. It excommunicated him.

_____ 7. Ulrich Zwingli founded a church in Switzerland that had which of these at its base?
a. democracy
b. theocracy
c. humanism
d. secularism

_____ 8. The Council of Trent
a. redefined Church doctrine to state that faith alone was needed to achieve salvation.
b. began a Holy War in Central Europe.
c. excommunicated Luther and sentenced him to death.
d. addressed corruption, and argued for the role of the church in salvation.

FILL IN THE BLANK For each of the following statements, fill in the blank with the appropriate word, phrase, or name.

9. _________________________ was a highly talented painter, writer, inventor, architect, engineer, mathematician, musician, and philosopher.

10. In contrast with Church teachings that individuality and achievement were relatively unimportant, _________________________ emphasized individual accomplishment.

11. _________________________ wrote theses in which he denied the power of indulgences to remit sin and criticized the power of the pope and the wealth of the church.

12. The doctrine of _________________________ holds that God knows who will be saved and therefore guides the lives of those destined for salvation.

13. In response to the spread of Protestantism, the Church began a series of reforms known as the _________________________.

14. The church court of Rome, known as the _________________________, tried people who were accused of being Protestant.

Name ______________________ Class ______________ Date ______________

Renaissance and Reformation — Chapter Test Form A

PRACTICING SOCIAL STUDIES SKILLS Study the map below and answer the question that follows.

Spread of Protestantism

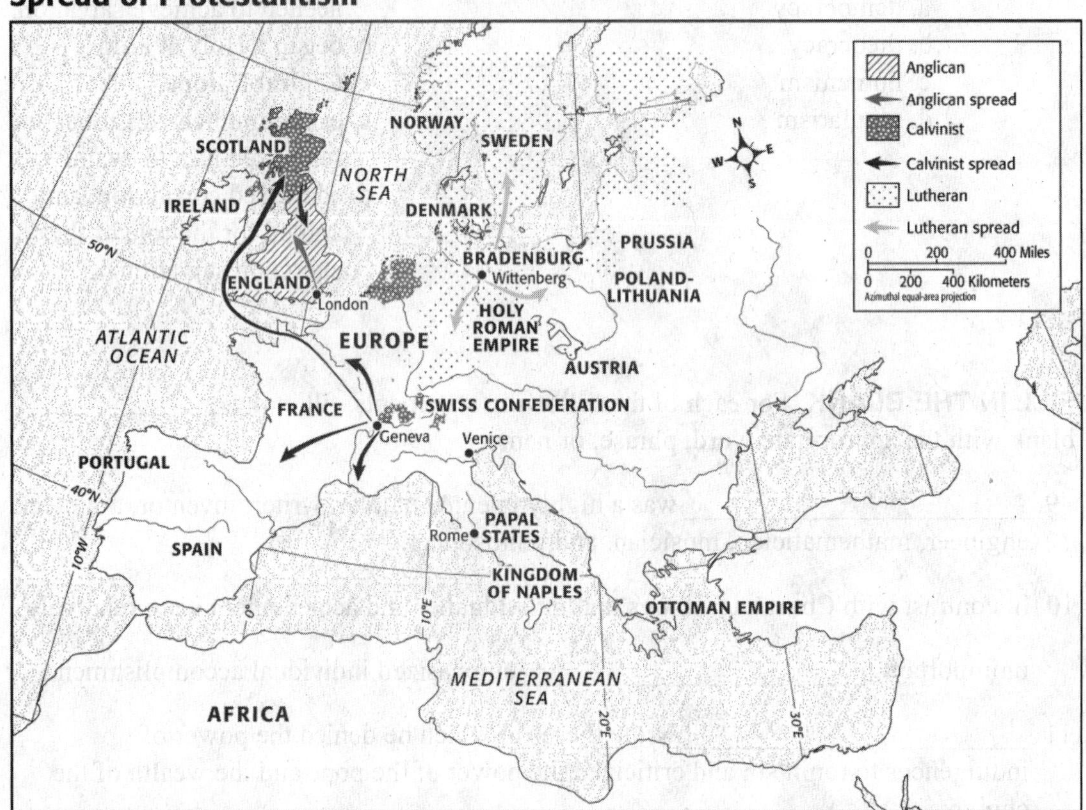

_____ 15. Which of the following statements is best supported by the map?

a. From Geneva, Anglicanism spread to England.

b. Protestantism did not spread into Rome or the Papal States.

c. Norway, Denmark, and Sweden remained Catholic.

d. Scotland, England, and Ireland shared the same faith.

Name ______________________ Class ______________ Date ______________

Renaissance and Reformation

Chapter Test

Form A

MATCHING In the space provided, write the letter of the term, person, or place that matches each description. Some answers will not be used.

_____ 16. Well-educated poet from a powerful family in Florence who supported the arts

_____ 17. Playwright believed by many to be the greatest Renaissance writer

_____ 18. Period of renewed interest and remarkable development in art, literature, science, and learning

_____ 19. Having a worldly rather than a spiritual focus

_____ 20. Wrote *Utopia*

_____ 21. Founded the Jesuits in 1534

_____ 22. Everyday language of the people

_____ 23. Nun who reformed the Carmelite order

_____ 24. Diplomat whose book *The Courtier* gave nobles new rules for refined behavior in a humanist society

_____ 25. Famous for the statue of *David* and the ceiling of the Sistine Chapel

a. Pieter Brueghel

b. Renaissance

c. Michelangelo Buonarroti

d. Jan van Eyck

e. Sir Thomas More

f. Baldassare Castiglione

g. Lorenzo di Medici

h. Frances of Sales

i. secular

j. Ignatius of Loyola

k. William Shakespeare

l. vernacular

m. Teresa of Avila

Name ______________________ Class ______________ Date ______________

Renaissance and Reformation Chapter Test

Form B

SHORT ANSWER On a separate sheet of paper, answer each of the following questions in complete sentences. Remember to use specific examples to support your answers.

1. How did the city-states such as Venice, Milan, and Florence contribute to the Renaissance?

2. How did humanism change the way people thought?

3. Describe three ways that the ideas of the Italian Renaissance spread to the north.

4. Describe how the Council of Trent impacted Catholicism.

5. Compare and contrast the ideals of Girolamo Savonarola and Ignatius of Loyola.

PRACTICING SOCIAL STUDIES SKILLS Study the painting below and, on a separate sheet of paper, answer the question that follows in complete sentences.

Return of the Hunters by Pieter Brueghel the Elder © Bridgeman Art Library, London/SuperStock

6. Does this painting seem to be the work of an Italian painter or one from Northern Europe? Explain.

Name ______________________ Class ______________ Date ______________

Exploration and Expansion

Section Quiz

Section 1

MULTIPLE CHOICE For each of the following, write the letter of the best choice in the space provided.

_____ 1. The period between the 1400s and 1500s in Europe is sometimes called the
a. Reformation.
b. Age of Exploration.
c. Dark Ages.
d. Age of Expansion.

_____ 2. Explorers who set out from Europe were looking for
a. fame.
b. wealth.
c. converts.
d. all of the above

_____ 3. Like Columbus, many Europeans in the 1400s thought the world
a. had no boundaries.
b. was flat.
c. centered around Europe.
d. was round.

_____ 4. The astrolabe allowed sailors
a. to spot land at a distance.
b. to sail into a headwind.
c. to have healthier diets.
d. to calculate their location.

_____ 5. Sea captains were aided by a new type of ship called the
a. caravel.
b. compass.
c. ducado.
d. lateen.

_____ 6. Who created a court for explorers in Portugal?
a. King John I
b. Prince Henry
c. Bartolomeu Dias
d. Queen Isabella

_____ 7. When the English realized they had reached a previously unknown land
a. English rulers refused to fund any more voyages.
b. the English queen sent Sir Francis Drake around the tip of South America.
c. English rulers sent John Cabot in search of a Northeast Passage.
d. English explorers led an expedition across the Isthmus of Panama.

_____ 8. On a voyage that began in 1497, Portuguese explorer Vasco da Gama reached
a. Brazil.
b. India.
c. San Salvador.
d. the Pacific Ocean.

_____ 9. An early European explorer who sailed for the English and the Dutch was
a. Henry Hudson.
b. Jacques Cartier.
c. Sir Francis Drake.
d. Vasco Núñez de Balboa.

_____ 10. Because of its location, which European country was the first to launch large-scale exploration voyages?
a. France
b. the Netherlands
c. Portugal
d. England

Name ____________________ Class ______________ Date ______________

Exploration and Expansion

Section Quiz

Section 2

FILL IN THE BLANK For each of the following statements, fill in the blank with the appropriate word, phrase, or name.

1. Native Americans died in large numbers because they had no resistance to European ____________________.

2. ____________________ led an expedition to the area that today is known as Mexico.

3. When the Spanish conquered Moctezuma II, it marked the end of the ____________________ Empire.

4. ____________________ was the home of the powerful Inca Empire.

5. Men who led the Spanish conquest of the Americas in the 16th century were known as ____________________.

6. In the ____________________ system, a colonist was given land and a number of Native Americans to work the land for him.

7. A document called the ____________________ divided the Americas between Spain and Portugal.

8. The Dutch established the colony of ____________________ along the Hudson River.

9. The reformer Bartolomé de Las Casas was a Spanish ____________________ who protested the unjust treatment of Native Americans.

10. The first English colony was established at ____________________ in present-day Virginia in 1607.

Exploration and Expansion

Section Quiz

Section 3

TRUE/FALSE Mark each statement **T** if it is true or **F** if it is false. If false explain why.

_____ 1. The Columbian Exchange was the exchange of plants, animals, people, and disease between Colombia and North America.

____

____

_____ 2. Before contact between Europe and the Americas, Europeans had never known of potatoes, corn, sweet potatoes, or turkeys.

____

____

_____ 3. The North American Indian population fell from around 2 million in 1492 to 500,000 by 1900.

____

____

_____ 4. The system of capitalism is based on government organization of most economic activities.

____

____

_____ 5. In joint-stock companies, investors bought shares of stock in a company and earned a portion of any profits the company made.

____

____

Name ______________ Class ______________ Date ______________

Section Quiz

Section 4

MULTIPLE CHOICE For each of the following, write the letter of the best choice in the space provided.

_____ 1. The Atlantic slave trade began in order to
a. supply workers for cotton plantations.
b. ease overpopulation in Africa.
c. remedy a shortage of labor in the Americas.
d. spread Christianity.

_____ 2. By the end of the 1600s, the slave trade was dominated by
a. the Spanish.
b. the French.
c. the English.
d. the Dutch.

_____ 3. The spread of people of African descent throughout the Americas and Western Europe is called the
a. African Diaspora.
b. Middle Passage.
c. triangular trade.
d. Columbian Exchange.

_____ 4. Keeping their cultural traditions alive was a way for some enslaved people to
a. resist the harsh conditions of slavery.
b. become free.
c. demonstrate indifference to the slave system.
d. win privileges from slaveholders.

_____ 5. The effects of the slave trade included
a. capturing the future leaders of African societies.
b. depriving millions of people of their freedom.
c. dividing Africans from one another as some rulers waged wars to gain captives.
d. all of the above

Name ______________________ Class ______________ Date ______________

Exploration and Expansion

Chapter Test

Form A

MULTIPLE CHOICE For each of the following, write the letter of the best choice in the space provided.

_____ 1. Mercantilists would advocate that a nation do which of the following?
   a. Import more goods than it exports.
   b. Sell more goods than it buys from foreign countries.
   c. Invest heavily in arts and education.
   d. Remove all barriers to free trade.

_____ 2. Some Native Americans helped Cortés because they
   a. resented paying tribute to Emperor Atahualpa.
   b. had intermarried with Spanish explorers.
   c. resented paying tribute to Moctezuma II.
   d. had been converted to Christianity.

_____ 3. Who of the following was a conquistador?
   a. Malinche
   b. Prince Henry
   c. Christopher Columbus
   d. Francisco Pizarro

_____ 4. Planters in the Americas began to use African slaves for labor because
   a. Aztecs refused to work on plantations.
   b. they believed Native Americans were not human.
   c. disease had killed millions of Native Americans.
   d. African slaves were cheaper than Native American slaves.

_____ 5. How did the Renaissance contribute to the Age of Exploration?
   a. by emphasizing the importance of converting people to Christianity
   b. by awakening a spirit of discovery and innovation in Europe
   c. by fostering a belief in the importance of working as a group
   d. by persuading Europeans that the pursuit of wealth was all-important

_____ 6. What was an effect of the Columbian Exchange?
   a. Native American diseases destroyed European populations.
   b. The exchange of foods and animals had a dramatic impact on later societies.
   c. Llamas began to be used as beasts of burden.
   d. The triangular trade became less profitable.

_____ 7. French settlers in Canada were mainly
   a. traders.
   b. conquistadors.
   c. farmers.
   d. slaveholders.

PRACTICING SOCIAL STUDIES SKILLS Study the map below and answer the question that follows.

The Slave Trade

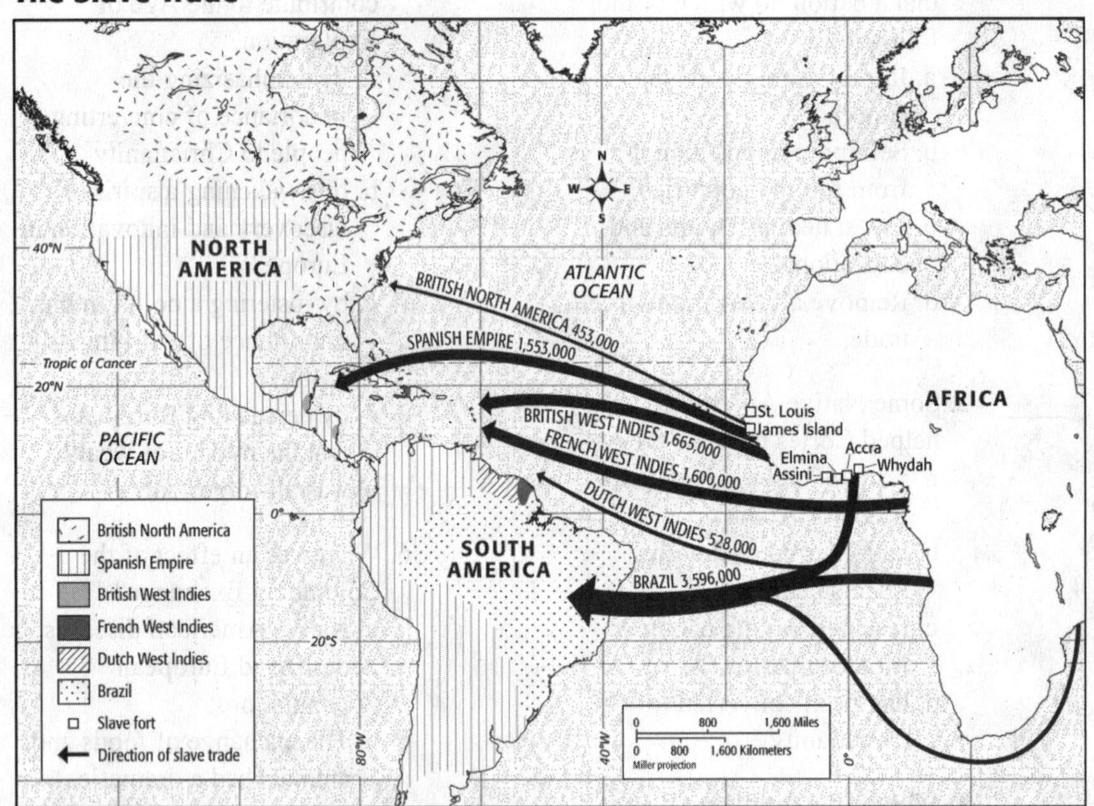

_____ 8. According to the map, the greatest number of African slaves were taken to
a. British North America.
b. Brazil.
c. the British West Indies.
d. the French West Indies.

FILL IN THE BLANK For each of the following statements, fill in the blank with the appropriate word, phrase, or name.

9. A new type of ship that was light and fast and highly maneuverable was known as the ______________________.

10. ______________________ of Portugal established a court for navigators and others interested in exploration.

11. The explorer ______________________ claimed Brazil for Portugal.

12. ______________________ were people who worked for a set period in exchange for passage to the Americas.

13. The ______________________ colony in Virginia was settled by people intending to make their fortunes by finding gold and silver.

14. Huge estates in the Americas called ______________________ grew cash crops such as sugar and tobacco.

15. The economic theory of ______________________ held that a nation's strength depended on its wealth.

MATCHING In the space provided, write the letter of the term, person, or place that matches each description. Some answers will not be used.

_____ 16. English colony started by the Pilgrims

_____ 17. Sailed around Africa to India

_____ 18. African who wrote about the horrific conditions on a slave ship

_____ 19. Conquered the Incas

_____ 20. A disease to which Native Americans had no resistance

_____ 21. Founded Quebec

_____ 22. Spread risk and profit among many investors

_____ 23. Helped explorers navigate using the positions of stars and planets

_____ 24. A terrifying ordeal for captive Africans en route to the Americas

_____ 25. First European to sail around the southernmost tip of Africa

a. smallpox
b. Samuel de Champlain
c. joint-stock companies
d. Middle Passage
e. astrolabe
f. Plymouth
g. Bartolomeu Dias
h. Olaudah Equiano
i. Francisco Pizarro
j. compass
k. Jamestown
l. capitalism
m. Vasco da Gama

Name ______________________ Class ______________ Date ______________

Exploration and Expansion

Chapter Test

Form B

SHORT ANSWER On a separate sheet of paper, answer each of the following questions in complete sentences. Remember to use specific examples to support your answers.

1. Name three reasons explorers set out from Europe in the 1400s and 1500s.

2. Write a description of your life as if you were a Native American living on an *encomienda* in the 16th century.

3. How did exploration of North America benefit France?

4. What were some positive effects of the Columbian Exchange?

5. In what ways did enslaved Africans resist their captivity?

PRACTICING SOCIAL STUDIES SKILLS Study the map below and, on a separate sheet of paper, answer the question that follows in complete sentences.

The Slave Trade

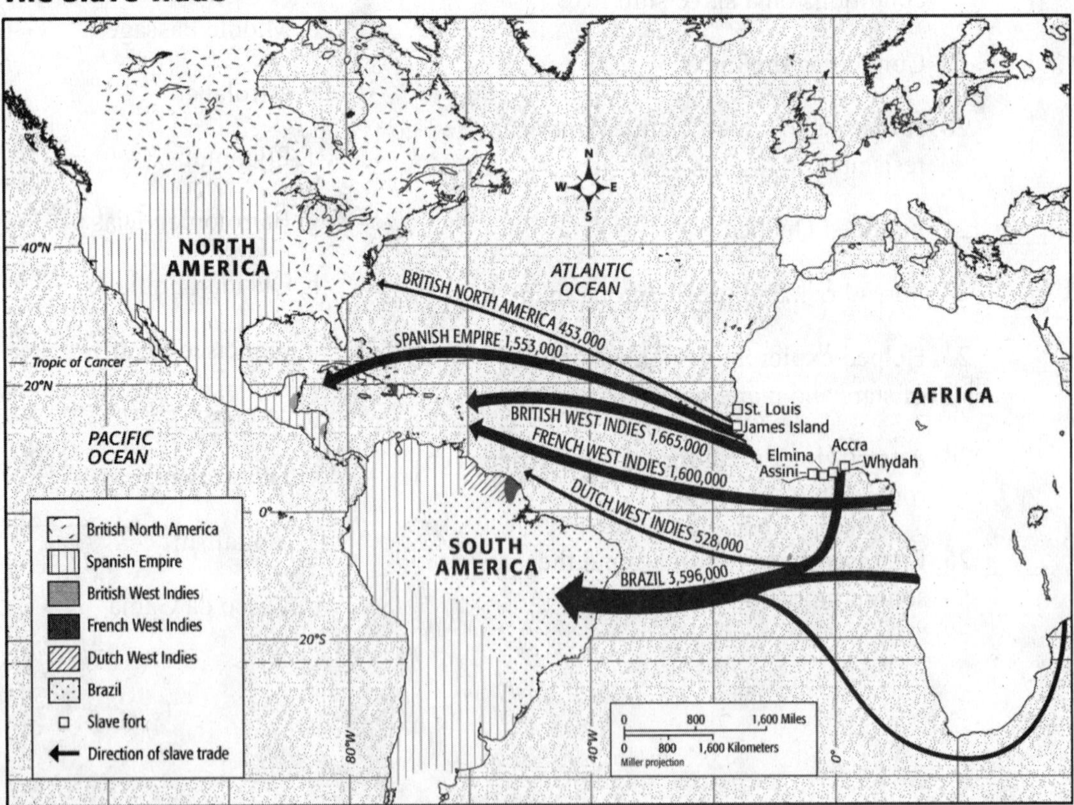

6. Describe the area from which most enslaved Africans came.

Name ______________________ Class ______________ Date ______________

New Asian Empires

Section Quiz

Section 1

TRUE/FALSE Mark each statement **T** if it is true or **F** if it is false. If false explain why.

_____ 1. The Ottoman Empire began in Anatolia in the 1300s and lasted until the early 1900s.

____

____

_____ 2. Orhan I led the siege that resulted in the fall of Constantinople in 1453.

____

____

_____ 3. Suleyman I became known as "the Lawgiver" as a result of improvements he made to the court system and legal code, and the new laws he issued to reduce corruption.

____

____

_____ 4. The Safavids and Ottomans were allies because the rulers of each empire practiced Islam.

____

____

_____ 5. 'Abbas's achievements produced a golden age in Safavid culture.

____

____

Name ______________ Class ______________ Date ______________

New Asian Empires

Section Quiz

Section 2

MULTIPLE CHOICE For each of the following, write the letter of the best choice in the space provided.

_____ 1. By the 1200s, most of northern India was under the control of
a. the Urdu consulate.
b. the Taj Mahal.
c. the Delhi sultanate.
d. the Gupta Empire.

_____ 2. The Mughal ruler Akbar worked to unify his diverse empire by
a. promoting religious tolerance.
b. creating an large network of schools and businesses.
c. enacting a policy of lifelong education for all citizens.
d. enacting harsh penalties for all criminal activity.

_____ 3. The religion of the Sikhs, known as Sikhism, blends
a. Sunni and Shia beliefs.
b. elements of Hinduism and Buddhism.
c. elements of Islam and Confucianism.
d. elements of Hinduism and Islam.

_____ 4. Which of the following best describes Shah Jahan?
a. He was a demanding ruler who, at the same time, supported art and literature.
b. He was tolerant of other religions and promoted the spread of Christianity and Hinduism.
c. He believed no one in India should live in luxury if others had to struggle just to feed themselves.
d. He brought lasting peace to India and its neighboring nations.

_____ 5. One example of the Mughal Empire's golden age
a. is the Delhi sultanate.
b. is the quality of Indian cloth.
c. is the Agra prison.
d. is the Taj Mahal.

Name ______________________ Class ______________ Date ______________

New Asian Empires

Section Quiz
Section 3

FILL IN THE BLANK For each of the following statements, fill in the blank with the appropriate word, phrase, or name.

1. After the death of Mongol leader ______________________ in 1294, the Yuan dynasty weakened.

2. In 1368, a peasant named Zhu Yuanzhang took the ruling name of ______________________ and founded the Ming dynasty.

3. Ming China was one of the most stable and prosperous times in China's history. The dynasty lasted nearly ______________________ years.

4. Emperor Yonglo made ______________________ the new capital of China.

5. The voyages of ______________________ demonstrated Ming China's growing sea power.

6. One reason for the Ming emperors' decision to ______________________ China was the arrival of European traders and Christian missionaries in the 1500s.

7. Although the Ming limited outside contacts, the Italian Jesuit priest ______________________ was highly respected at the Ming court.

8. As Ming China weakened, the Manchu swept in and took power. They called their dynasty ______________________.

9. After the Dutch began trading with China, ______________________ became the main Chinese export to Europe.

10. The beauty and superb quality of Ming ______________________ made it a valuable trade item, especially in Europe.

Name ______________________ Class ______________ Date ______________

New Asian Empires

Section Quiz

Section 4

MATCHING In the space provided, write the letter of the term, person, or place that matches each description. Some answers will not be used.

_____ 1. "The way of the warrior"

_____ 2. Leader who became shogun in 1603

_____ 3. Trained, professional warriors

_____ 4. Stressed discipline and meditation to focus the mind and gain wisdom

_____ 5. Form of poetry made up of three lines and 17 syllables

_____ 6. "Divine wind"

_____ 7. Supreme military leader of Japan

_____ 8. Type of play in which actors sang, dance, and interacted with the audience

_____ 9. Powerful warlords that held large estates

_____ 10. Quiet fishing village that is now the city of Tokyo

a. samurai

b. shogun

c. daimyo

d. Kamakura

e. *kamikaze*

f. Bushido

g. Zen Buddhism

h. haiku

i. Tokugawa Ieyasu

j. Edo

k. Minamoto Yoritomo

l. kabuki

m. Noh

Name _______________ Class _______________ Date _______________

New Asian Empires

Chapter Test

Form A

MULTIPLE CHOICE For each of the following, write the letter of the best choice in the space provided.

_____ 1. What enabled the Ottomans to expand beyond Anatolia?
   a. Christianity's decline in the Byzantine Empire
   b. a powerful military and gunpowder weapons
   c. the assistance of Serbs in the Balkans
   d. their tolerance of other cultures and religions

_____ 2. Janissaries contributed to the success of the Ottoman Empire because they
   a. were part of a highly organized and effective bureaucracy that ran the empire.
   b. converted people to Islam, giving Ottomans a shared religious background.
   c. were elite soldiers loyal only to the sultan.
   d. spied on the Byzantine army and passed on important strategic information.

_____ 3. Akbar created unity through much of India by
   a. forcing conquered people to convert to Islam.
   b. allowing local governors complete autonomy in governing diverse regions.
   c. stationing military units at strategic points throughout the empire.
   d. promoting religious tolerance and abolishing taxes on non-Muslims.

_____ 4. Which of the following Mughal leaders came into conflict with the Sikhs?
   a. Jahangir
   b. Akbar
   c. Babur
   d. Shah Jahan

_____ 5. Hongwu expanded his power as emperor by
   a. relaxing religious restrictions, creating rituals around his leadership, and moving the capital to Beijing.
   b. getting rid of high-level positions in the government, and killing his rivals.
   c. building the Forbidden City and adding high-level officials.
   d. destroying Beijing, the seat of Mongol power.

_____ 6. Why did Ming emperors decide to isolate China?
   a. They thought European weapons might cause the peasants to rebel.
   b. They were disappointed with the tribute gained from Zheng He's voyages.
   c. They did not want to divert people's attention from building the Great Wall.
   d. They disliked the influence of the Europeans and sought to preserve China's traditions.

_____ 7. During the Tokugawa period the role of the samurai changed because
a. feudalism disappeared.
b. the emperor gained power.
c. peace put the samurai out of work.
d. Confucianism gained in popularity.

_____ 8. The dynasty that ruled Korea from the late 14th century to the early 20th century was the
a. Turtle.
b. Choson.
c. Tokugawa.
d. Confucian.

PRACTICING SOCIAL STUDIES SKILLS Study the visual below and answer the question that follows.

akg-images, London/National Palace Museum, Taipei

_____ 9. Which dynasty was known for producing this type of porcelain?
a. the Qing
b. the Ottoman
c. the Ming
d. the Mughal

Name ______________________ Class ______________ Date ______________

New Asian Empires

Chapter Test

Form A

MATCHING In the space provided, write the letter of the term, person, or place that matches each description. Some answers will not be used.

_____ 10. Founder of the Ming Dynasty

_____ 11. Elite soldiers who were loyal only to the sultan

_____ 12. A professional warrior in feudal Japan

_____ 13. First Muslim government established in northern India

_____ 14. Protected northern China from Mongol threat

_____ 15. Became shogun in 1603

_____ 16. Religion that blended elements of Islam and Hinduism

_____ 17. Descendents of Osman I

_____ 18. Mughal ruler who built a new capital at Delhi

_____ 19. Strict code of ethics for warriors

a. Istanbul

b. Tokugawa Ieyasu

c. Shah Jahan

d. Sikhism

e. Janissaries

f. Great Wall

g. samurai

h. Ottomans

i. shogunates

j. Hongwu

k. the Qing

l. Delhi sultanate

m. Bushido

FILL IN THE BLANK For each of the following statements, fill in the blank with the appropriate word, phrase, or name.

20. Rulers of the Ottoman Empire were called ______________________.

21. The Ottoman Empire reached its height of power and cultural achievement under the leadership of ______________________.

22. ______________________ founded the Mughal Empire in 1526.

23. The ______________________, the greatest example of Mughal architecture, was built during the empire's cultural golden age.

24. The Ming emperor ______________________ sponsored overseas voyages to extend China's influence.

25. The supreme military leader of Japan, called the ______________________, ruled in the emperor's name.

Name ______________ Class ______________ Date ______________

New Asian Empires

Chapter Test

Form B

SHORT ANSWER On a separate sheet of paper, answer each of the following questions in complete sentences. Remember to use specific examples to support your answers.

1. Describe the Ottoman Empire under Suleyman I.

2. What are the elements of the golden age in Safavid culture?

3. What contributed to the decline of the Mughal Empire?

4. Describe the agricultural innovations that took place in Ming China and how they changed society.

5. Describe the feudal structure of Japan.

PRACTICING SOCIAL STUDIES SKILLS Study the image below and, on a separate sheet of paper, answer the question that follows in complete sentences.

akg-images, London/National Palace Museum, Taipei

6. Use your knowledge of the chapter to identify the vase pictured here and the role of porcelain in the country's economy.

Name ______________________ Class ______________ Date ______________

New Ideas, New Empires

Unit Test

Form A

MATCHING In the space provided, write the letter of the person that matches each description. Some answers will not be used.

_____ 1. A highly talented painter who was also a writer, inventor, architect, engineer, mathematician, musician, and philosopher

_____ 2. Credited with inventing movable type

_____ 3. Wrote theses that criticized the church, particularly the sale of indulgences

_____ 4. Established a church in Switzerland based on theocracy

_____ 5. Protestant reformer who preached the doctrine of predestination

_____ 6. Led an expedition to Mexico that ended with the conquest of the Aztec Empire

_____ 7. Priest who sought to protect Native Americans by replacing them as laborers with African slaves

_____ 8. Adventurer whose men were the first to circumnavigate the world

_____ 9. Ottoman leader who seized Constantinople and renamed it Istanbul

_____ 10. Emperor who ruled the Ottoman Empire at its height

a. John Calvin
b. Hernán Cortés
c. Ulrich Zwingli
d. Leonardo da Vinci
e. Ferdinand Magellan
f. Sir Francis Drake
g. Lorenzo de Medici
h. Bartolomé de Las Casas
i. Johannes Gutenberg
j. Martin Luther
k. Mehmed II
l. Suleyman I
m. Johann Tetzel

FILL IN THE BLANK For each of the following statements, fill in the blank with the appropriate word, phrase, or name.

11. Oil paints suited Northern Renaissance painters' love of ______________________.

12. ______________________ emphasized individual accomplishment and believed that the human mind was almost limitless.

13. Pope Paul III convened the ______________________ to examine the criticisms made by Protestants about Catholic teachings.

14. In the ______________________ system, a colonist was given a certain amount of land and a number of Native Americans to work the land for him.

New Ideas, New Empires

Unit Test

Form A

15. The first English colony in North America was at ____________________.

16. The transfer of plants, animals, and disease that resulted from large-scale contact between the societies of Europe and the Americas is called the ____________________.

17. Because overseas business ventures were costly, investors began to pool their money together into ____________________ companies to fund larger businesses.

18. The trading network in which European goods, captured Africans, and American products traveled across the Atlantic is called ____________________.

19. In Japan, samurai were expected to follow a strict code of ethics known as ____________________.

20. The ____________________ Empire was India's first Muslim empire.

TRUE/FALSE Indicate whether each statement below is true or false by writing **T** or **F** in the space provided.

_____ 21. The pope would not agree to an annulment for Henry VIII because Catherine and her nephew, Holy Roman Emperor Charles V, opposed it.

_____ 22. Martin Luther contradicted basic Catholic beliefs when he insisted that God's grace cannot be won by good works.

_____ 23. All African rulers were opposed to the slave trade.

_____ 24. The African Diaspora resulted from the slave trade.

_____ 25. The only goal of European exploration in the 1400s and 1500s was to find new, faster routes to Asia.

_____ 26. Unlike the Spanish and the Portuguese, the French did not enslave Native Americans.

_____ 27. The Safavid Empire never included Persia.

_____ 28. The Great Wall of China was built to honor the voyages of Zheng He.

_____ 29. When Hongwu did away with high-level positions to strengthen his own authority, the result was more powerful Ming emperors.

_____ 30. In the Japanese feudal system, all samurai received land from lords.

New Ideas, New Empires

Unit Test
Form A

MULTIPLE CHOICE For each of the following, write the letter of the best choice in the space provided.

_____ 31. The three influential city-states in northern Italy were Venice, Milan, and
a. Medici.
b. Naples.
c. Florence.
d. Rome.

_____ 32. One cause of the Renaissance
a. was the desire to end poverty.
b. was the printing press.
c. increased trade due to the Crusades.
d. mild weather that increased crop yields.

_____ 33. Something that is secular focuses on what is
a. worldly.
b. ancient.
c. glorifying to God.
d. important to the king.

_____ 34. Concern that the church had drifted too far from its spiritual roots led to
a. Christian humanism.
b. the theocracy movement.
c. the closing of monasteries.
d. the Protestant Reformation.

_____ 35. The Roman Inquisition was established to
a. spread humanism.
b. fight Protestantism.
c. take over the government.
d. clarify Church teachings.

_____ 36. What was the Edict of Worms?
a. a decree declaring Luther an outlaw
b. Luther's public declaration of his faith
c. Luther's public denial of the Catholic Church
d. Germany's request for religious freedom

_____ 37. The Jesuits formed to
a. unite the Catholic and Protestant faiths.
b. protest the church's growing influence on society.
c. monitor the churches' sale of gold to help the poor.
d. use education to combat the Protestant Reformation.

_____ 38. Exploration was fueled by a desire for money and
a. fame.
b. culture.
c. open space.
d. new technology.

_____ 39. The invention of the caravel was an advance in
a. mining technology.
b. farming.
c. shipbuilding.
d. industrial production.

_____ 40. Which country was the first to launch large-scale voyages of exploration?
a. Spain
b. Portugal
c. England
d. France

New Ideas, New Empires

_____ 41. European diseases were deadly to Native Americans because
a. the diseases destroyed crops.
b. they had no natural resistance.
c. they did not understand instructions to prevent disease.
d. they depended on Europeans for food.

_____ 42. One way a country can achieve a favorable trade balance is to
a. sell more goods than it buys.
b. demand payment in gold.
c. place taxes on exports.
d. grant independence to colonies.

_____ 43. The key to the Ottomans' success was their
a. ability to speak Persian and Arabic.
b. royal marriages.
c. trade agreements.
d. military force.

_____ 44. In the Ottoman Empire, non-Muslims
a. faced restrictions.
b. had to convert to Islam.
c. had to serve in the military.
d. had the same rights and privileges as Muslims.

_____ 45. The Mughal Empire began to decline during the reign of
a. Jahangir.
b. Shah Jahan.
c. Aurangzeb.
d. Akbar.

_____ 46. Although most people in the Safavid Empire were Sunni
a. the rulers closed the mosques.
b. the first shah converted to Buddhism.
c. the Shia paid the most in taxes.
d. the first shah made Shiism the official religion.

_____ 47. During the 1500s, the Ming dynasty became increasingly
a. agricultural.
b. militaristic.
c. isolated.
d. mercantilist.

_____ 48. Which of the following Europeans gained influence in Ming China?
a. Sir Francis Drake
b. Henry the Navigator
c. Lord George Macartney
d. Matteo Ricci

_____ 49. The people that started the Qing dynasty were the
a. Ming.
b. Manchu.
c. Mughals.
d. Persians.

PRACTICING SOCIAL STUDIES SKILLS Study the visual below and answer the question that follows.

Return of the Hunters by Pieter Brueghel the Elder/© Bridgeman Art Linbrary, London SuperStock

_____ 50. This painting is an example of
- a. Italian Renaissance art.
- b. religious art of the Middle Ages.
- c. Leonardo da Vinci's work.
- d. Northern Renaissance art.

New Ideas, New Empires

Unit Test

Form B

SHORT ANSWER On a separate sheet of paper, answer each of the following questions in complete sentences. Remember to use specific examples to support your answers.

1. Explain the *encomienda* system.

2. How is Leonardo da Vinci a good example of the spirit of the Renaissance?

3. What events led to the ex-communication of Martin Luther?

4. What were major accomplishments of the Ming dynasty?

5. Describe feudalism in Japan.

6. Describe the trading network known as triangular trade.

PRACTICING SOCIAL STUDIES SKILLS Study the map below and, on a separate sheet of paper, answer the question that follows in complete sentences.

The Slave Trade

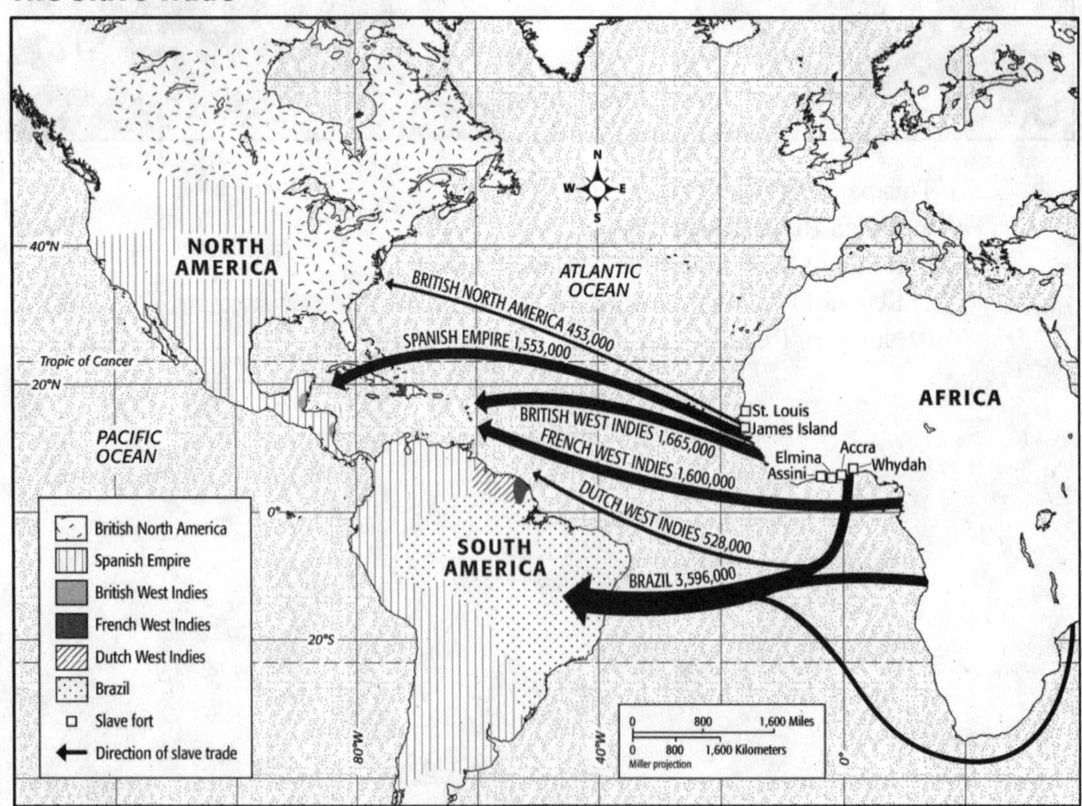

7. Why do you think the slave forts were located in a particular region of Africa?

Name ______________________ Class ______________ Date ______________

The Monarchs of Europe

Section Quiz

Section 1

MATCHING In the space provided, write the letter of the term, person, or place that matches each description. Some answers will not be used.

_____ 1. A ruler whose power was not limited by having to consult with nobles, common people, or their representatives

_____ 2. Concept that monarchs received their power from God

_____ 3. Became king of Spain in 1516

_____ 4. Treaty which gave each German prince the right to decide whether his state would be Catholic or Protestant

_____ 5. Author of *Don Quixote de la Mancha*

_____ 6. Spanish invasion fleet

_____ 7. The son of Charles V, he ruled the Netherlands, Spain, Sicily, and Spain's colonies in the Americas

_____ 8. Explorer supported by Charles V, who conquered the Aztec Empire

_____ 9. Period of artistic achievement in Spain from about 1550 to 1650

_____ 10. Source of Spain's wealth

a. divine right

b. Philip II

c. Peace of Augsburg

d. Spanish Armada

e. Ferdinand

f. Golden Century

g. El Greco

h. Diego Velázquez

i. absolute monarch

j. American colonies

k. Hernán Cortés

l. Charles I

m. Miguel de Cervantes

Name ______________________ Class ______________ Date ____________

The Monarchs of Europe

Section Quiz

Section 2

FILL IN THE BLANK For each of the following statements, fill in the blank with the appropriate word, phrase, or name.

1. By the 1560s, about one in ten French men and women was a Huguenot, or ______________________.

2. After the queen's assassins began killing French Huguenot nobles attending the wedding of Henry of Navarre, widespread fighting broke out. Between10,000 to 70,000 Huguenots were killed in the event known as ______________________.

3. Henry of Navarre was crowned king of ______________________.

4. King Henry IV earned acceptance by ______________________ to Catholicism in 1593.

5. The ______________________ granted some rights to French Huguenots, including limited freedom of worship.

6. After Henry IV was assassinated, the next king, ______________________ depended on his mother to serve as regent until he was old enough to rule.

7. A prominent Catholic churchman named ______________________ became Louis VIII's chief minister and most trusted advisor.

8. Known as the Sun King, ______________________ began a tradition of absolute monarchy in France.

9. The Sun King built an enormous palace at ______________________.

10. The most costly of the French wars was the ______________________, which began when the Spanish king died without an heir.

Name ______________________ Class ______________ Date ______________

The Monarchs of Europe

Section Quiz

Section 3

MATCHING In the space provided, write the letter of the term, person, or place that matches each description. Some answers will not be used.

_____ 1. Group that wanted to reform, or "purify" the Church of England

_____ 2. Became king after the death of Queen Elizabeth I

_____ 3. Stated the king could not levy taxes without the approval of Parliament

_____ 4. First European monarch to be executed by his own people

_____ 5. Bloodless transfer of power

_____ 6. War between Royalists and Roundheads

_____ 7. Leader of the Roundheads

_____ 8. A republican government based on the common good of all the people

_____ 9. Described humans as being naturally selfish and fearful

_____ 10. The return of the monarchy

a. James I

b. Petition of Right

c. the Glorious Revolution

d. commonwealth

e. Thomas Hobbes

f. Oliver Cromwell

g. Puritans

h. Charles I

i. Charles II

j. James II

k. William and Mary

l. the Restoration

m. the English Civil War

Name ______________________ Class ______________ Date ______________

The Monarchs of Europe

Section Quiz

Section 4

TRUE/FALSE Mark each statement **T** if it is true or **F** if it is false. If false explain why.

_____ 1. Ivan IV eventually became known as Ivan the Terrible for his strict policies and violent actions.

____

____

_____ 2. To learn more about western culture, Peter the Great traveled in disguise.

____

____

_____ 3. The new city of St. Petersburg featured traditional Russian-style architecture, similar to that found in Moscow.

____

____

_____ 4. Because serfs supported Pugachev, Catherine the Great realized she should begin to favor serfs over landowners and nobles.

____

____

_____ 5. Although the Thirty Years' War involved several European countries, most of the fighting took place in Germany.

____

____

Name ______________________ Class ______________ Date ______________

The Monarchs of Europe

Chapter Test

Form A

MULTIPLE CHOICE For each of the following, write the letter of the best choice in the space provided.

_____ 1. Absolute monarchs argued that their power must not be challenged because
a. the pope had crowned them.
b. they were the most intelligent men in their nations.
c. they were democratically elected.
d. they ruled by divine right.

_____ 2. Why did people in the Netherlands revolt against Spain?
a. because of corruption in the Spanish government
b. to protest Spain's treatment of slaves
c. because of religious differences
d. to stop the sea dogs

_____ 3. Why did King Philip decide to invade England?
a. because of English raids on ships and to return England to the Catholic Church
b. to regain the southern part of the Netherlands
c. to take control of England's gold and silver
d. to crush England's American colonies

_____ 4. One goal of Louis XIII was to
a. conquer England.
b. conquer Spain.
c. end the Saint Bartholomew's Day Massacre.
d. limit the power of nobles and Huguenots.

_____ 5. Which of the following monarchs is history's best example of an absolute monarch?
a. Louis XIV
b. Henry IV
c. Philip II
d. Charles II

_____ 6. Why were William and Mary crowned king and queen of England?
a. to prevent a Puritan monarch from occupying the throne
b. to prevent a Catholic monarch from occupying the throne
c. to restore the English monarchy
d. to end the English Civil War

_____ 7. Which of the following is a cause of the Thirty Years' War?
a. agitation by Pugachev
b. Catherine's refusal to marry or name a chancellor
c. Prussia's drive for empire
d. throwing the Holy Roman emperor's representatives out of a window

Name ______________________ Class ______________ Date ______________

The Monarchs of Europe

Chapter Test

Form A

PRACTICING SOCIAL STUDIES SKILLS Study the chart and passage below and answer the questions that follow.

Building Versailles

Costs	Benefits
• Cost five percent of the country's annual revenue • Created resentment among the people • Helped cause revolution years later	• Kept court safer from Paris crowds • Was clear symbol of king's power • Helped keep his nobles in check

_____ 8. Which cost or benefit on the chart was Louis XIV unlikely to have foreseen?
- a. Allowed the king to keep his nobles in check
- b. Created resentment among people
- c. Helped cause revolution years later
- d. Was clear symbol of king's power

> **"If anyone habitually living at Court absented himself he insisted on knowing the reason; those who came there only for flying visits had also to give a satisfactory explanation; any one who seldom or never appeared there was certain to incur his displeasure."**
>
> **—Duc de Saint-Simon**

_____ 9. In the quote above the author was referring to which of the following European monarchs?
- a. Peter the Great
- b. Louis XIV
- c. Charles I
- d. Czar Michael

FILL IN THE BLANK For each of the following statements, fill in the blank with the appropriate word, phrase, or name.

10. When Charles V abdicated in 1556, his son, ____________________, took over the Netherlands, Spain, Sicily, and Spain's colonies in the Americas.

11. In 1598, the compromise known as the ____________________ gave certain rights to Huguenots as a way to restore peace in France.

12. The ____________________ wanted to purify the Church of England.

Name ______________________ Class ______________ Date ______________

The Monarchs of Europe

Chapter Test
Form A

13. The War of the ______________________ was fought to prevent France and Spain from being ruled by members of the same family.

14. A republican government based on the common good of all the people is called a(n) ______________________.

15. Beginning with Ivan the Terrible, absolute monarchs in Russia were known as ______________________.

MATCHING In the space provided, write the letter of the term, person, or place that matches each description. Some answers will not be used.

_____ 16. Painter famous for his elongated human figures

_____ 17. Led the English government after the execution of Charles I

_____ 18. Fleet assembled by Philip's navy

_____ 19. French Protestant nobleman who became king after converting to Catholicism

_____ 20. Began the Stuart dynasty

_____ 21. Limited the power of monarchs

_____ 22. First European monarch to be formally tried and executed by his own people

_____ 23. Ended the Thirty Years' War

_____ 24. Czar who brought western culture to Russia

_____ 25. French Protestants

a. Charles I

b. Huguenots

c. Peace of Augsburg

d. Treaty of Westphalia

e. Petition of Right

f. Spanish Inquisition

g. Peter I

h. El Greco

i. Cardinal Richelieu

j. Oliver Cromwell

k. Spanish Armada

l. Henry of Navarre

m. James I

Name ________________________ Class ______________ Date ______________

The Monarchs of Europe

Chapter Test
Form B

SHORT ANSWER On a separate sheet of paper, answer each of the following questions in complete sentences. Remember to use specific examples to support your answers.

1. What problems did Charles V encounter in his attempt to keep Europe Roman Catholic?
2. What was the Court of Blood, and how did it contribute to the Dutch Revolt?
3. If you had lived in England in the mid-17th century, which side would you have supported in the English Civil War? Explain your answer.
4. Describe English society under Oliver Cromwell.
5. Compare and contrast the early years of Ivan IV's rule with his later years.
6. What did Peter the Great gain from the Great Northern War?

PRACTICING SOCIAL STUDIES SKILLS Study the chart below and, on a separate sheet of paper, answer the questions that follow in complete sentences.

Building Versailles

Costs	Benefits
• Cost five percent of the country's annual revenue • Created resentment among the people • Helped cause revolution years later	• Kept court safer from Paris crowds • Was clear symbol of king's power • Helped keep his nobles in check

7. What were the non-monetary costs of building the palace at Versailles?
8. Why did Louis XIV build a palace at Versailles? Use your knowledge of the chapter as well as information from the chart in your answer.

Name _______________ Class _______________ Date _______________

Enlightenment and Revolution

Section Quiz

Section 1

MATCHING In the space provided, write the letter of the term, person, or place that matches each description. Some answers will not be used.

_____ 1. The belief that the earth is the center of the universe

_____ 2. The new way of thinking that developed when scholars began to pose theories about the natural world and develop procedures to test those ideas

_____ 3. Described how blood and the circulatory system functioned

_____ 4. A Flemish doctor known for his work in anatomy

_____ 5. Copernicus created a model that supported this theory

_____ 6. Opposed the theories of Galileo

_____ 7. Built the first telescope used for astronomy

_____ 8. Developed a law of universal gravitation

_____ 9. Proved that matter could not be created or destroyed

_____ 10. Bacon and Descartes helped develop this five step approach to learning

a. scientific method

b. Sir Isaac Newton

c. Galileo Galilei

d. Robert Boyle

e. Antony van Leeuwenhoek

f. geocentric theory

g. the Church

h. William Harvey

i. Antoine-Laurent Lavoisier

j. heliocentric theory

k. calculus

l. Andreas Vesalius

m. Scientific Revolution

Name ______________________ Class ______________ Date ______________

Enlightenment and Revolution — Section Quiz

Section 2

FILL IN THE BLANK For each of the following statements, fill in the blank with the appropriate word, phrase, or name.

1. A new generation of philosophers believed that ____________________ could be used to solve all human problems.

2. The ____________________ was also called the Age of Reason.

3. The new philosophers in France were called the ____________________.

4. Ideas such as the separation of powers, and checks and balances were published in a book by ____________________.

5. The French thinker ____________________ believed that people were born good, but that society corrupted them.

6. Hobbes believed that people were not naturally ____________________.

7. Rousseau argued that government should protect the common good of ____________________ people.

8. Even though Enlightenment thinkers questioned established beliefs, they usually held traditional views about ____________________.

9. The English writer ____________________ argued that if men and women had equal education, they would hold equal places in society.

10. Frederick the Great, Catherine the Great, and Joseph II were known as ____________________ because of their interest in Enlightenment ideas and reform.

Name ______________________ Class ______________ Date ______________

Enlightenment and Revolution

Section Quiz

Section 3

TRUE/FALSE Mark each statement **T** if it is true or **F** if it is false. If false explain why.

_____ 1. The English class system continued in North America; few individuals could advance themselves through intelligence and hard work.

____

____

_____ 2. The Stamp Act required colonists to pay a tax for an official stamp on all newspapers, legal documents, and other papers.

____

____

_____ 3. The Articles of Confederation created a strong central government with broad powers to tax.

____

____

_____ 4. A pamphlet called *Common Sense,* by the writer Thomas Paine, helped the Patriots gain popular support for the cause of independence.

____

____

_____ 5. The United States Constitution and the Bill of Rights show the influence of Enlightenment thinkers such as Locke, Rousseau, Montesquieu, and Voltaire.

____

____

Name ______________________ Class ______________ Date ______________

Enlightenment and Revolution

Chapter Test
Form A

MULTIPLE CHOICE For each of the following, write the letter of the best choice in the space provided.

_____ 1. The new way of thinking that emerged in the mid-1500s is called the
a. geocentric theory.
b. Scientific Revolution.
c. Enlightenment.
d. American Revolution.

_____ 2. Until the Scientific Revolution, the traditional authorities were
a. Plato and Aristotle.
b. the Church and ancient scholars.
c. navigators and explorers.
d. Aquinas and his followers.

_____ 3. Which of the following posed theories that brought him into direct conflict with the Church?
a. Francis Bacon
b. Galileo
c. Aristotle
d. Ptolemy

_____ 4. Who argued that people had a right to overthrow a government that does not protect their natural rights?
a. Locke
b. Voltaire
c. Newton
d. Hobbes

_____ 5. Who wrote "Man is born free but everywhere is in chains"?
a. Locke
b. Montesquieu
c. Rousseau
d. Voltaire

_____ 6. How did Hobbes and Rousseau differ?
a. Rousseau believed in the idea of a social contract; Hobbes did not.
b. Rousseau believed an absolute monarchy was essential; Hobbes did not.
c. Rousseau believed people were naturally good; Hobbes did not.
d. Hobbes believed people needed protection from government; Rousseau did not.

_____ 7. American colonists objected to the Stamp Act because
a. they resented forced conscription in the British military to fight the Seven Years' War.
b. the Act restricted the colonists' trade.
c. contrary to British belief, Americans thought stamps were necessary.
d. they objected to taxes levied by the British Parliament without representation.

_____ 8. During the Boston Tea Party, the Sons of Liberty dumped tea into Boston Harbor to
a. protest the tax on tea.
b. raise money to fight the War for Independence.
c. get back at Boston merchants.
d. protest the Intolerable Acts.

Name ______________________ Class ______________ Date ______________

Enlightenment and Revolution

Chapter Test Form A

PRACTICING SOCIAL STUDIES SKILLS Study the visual and passage below and answer the questions that follow.

THE SCIENTIFIC METHOD
The Scientific Method is a set of techniques for acquiring new knowledge about the natural world based on observable, measurable evidence.
Step 1 Identify a problem
Step 2
Step 3 Perform experiments to test the hypothesis
Step 4 Record the results of the experiments
Step 5 Analyze the results and form a conclusion that either proves or disproves the hypothesis

_____ 9. Which of the following phrases belongs in Step 2 in the chart above?
a. Form a hypothesis that can be tested
b. Ask a question
c. Prove or disprove the hypothesis
d. Observe the natural world

"We hold these truths to be self-evident, that all men are created equal, that they are endowed by their Creator with certain unalienable Rights, that among these are Life, Liberty, and the pursuit of Happiness.—That to secure these rights, Governments are instituted among Men, deriving their just powers from the consent of the governed,—That whenever any Form of Government becomes destructive of these ends, it is the Right of the People to alter or to abolish it, and to institute new Government . . ."

_____ 10. The above quote is from the
a. United States Constitution.
b. Treaty of Paris.
c. Townshend Acts.
d. Declaration of Independence.

Name ______________ Class ______________ Date ______________

Enlightenment and Revolution

Chapter Test

Form A

FILL IN THE BLANK For each of the following statements, fill in the blank with the appropriate word, phrase, or name.

11. The ______________ theory held that the earth was the center of the universe and that the sun, moon, and planets revolved around it.

12. A new kind of mathematics called ______________ could be used to predict the effects of gravity.

13. English physician ______________ explained the workings of the human heart.

14. The purpose of the ______________ by Denis Diderot was to promote knowledge.

15. Parliament passed the ______________ in order for the colonists to pay for some of the costs of the French and Indian War

16. On July 4, 1776, the ______________ was adopted by the Continental Congress.

17. General ______________ led the American troops in the War for Independence.

TRUE/FALSE Indicate whether each statement below is true or false by writing **T** or **F** in the space provided.

_____ 18. Copernicus was the first scientist to create a complete model of the solar system combining physics, astronomy, and mathematics.

_____ 19. Brahe was the first astronomer to understand that the planets orbited the sun in an ellipse.

_____ 20. John Locke believed that the purpose of government was to protect people's natural rights.

_____ 21. In *The Spirit of the Laws*, Montesquieu argued that the best form of government included a separation of powers.

_____ 22. European monarchs who embraced Enlightenment ideals had no intention of giving up their own power.

_____ 23. Thomas Paine's pamphlet *Common Sense* argued that the American colonies deserved to be an independent nation.

_____ 24. The American victory at the Battle of Saratoga was a turning point in the War for Independence because it convinced the French to contribute to the American war effort.

_____ 25. Enlightenment ideals had little or no impact in the new nation known as the United States.

Name ______________________ Class ______________ Date ______________

Enlightenment and Revolution

Chapter Test

Form B

SHORT ANSWER On a separate sheet of paper, answer each of the following questions in complete sentences. Remember to use specific examples to support your answers.

1. What led scholars to begin to challenge traditional authorities in the mid-1500s?
2. Discuss three advances that occurred as a result of the Scientific Revolution.
3. How did the philosophers of the 1600s view reason?
4. How did enlightened despots both advance and undermine Enlightenment ideals?
5. What Enlightenment concepts did the Declaration of Independence express?

PRACTICING SOCIAL STUDIES SKILLS Study the chart below and, on a separate sheet of paper, answer the questions that follow in complete sentences.

THE SCIENTIFIC METHOD The Scientific Method is a set of techniques for acquiring new knowledge about the natural world based on observable, measurable evidence.
Step 1
Step 2 Form a hypothesis that can be tested
Step 3 Perform experiments to test the hypothesis
Step 4 Record the results of the experiments
Step 5

6. What completes Step 1 of the chart above?
7. What completes Step 5 of the chart above?

Name ______________________________ Class ________________ Date ________________

The French Revolution and Napoleon — Section Quiz

Section 1

MATCHING In the space provided, write the letter of the term, person, or place that matches each description. Some answers will not be used.

_____ 1. French social and political structure in which the king ruled over three distinct social groups

_____ 2. Law-making body formed by the Third Estate on June 17, 1789

_____ 3. Social group made up of Roman Catholic clergy, comprising about 1% of the population

_____ 4. Social group that comprised about 97% of the French population, including merchants, professionals, workers, and peasants

_____ 5. Traditional governing body made up of the three social groups

_____ 6. "Notebooks" in which grievances against the government were recorded

_____ 7. Ancient prison that became a symbol of the French Revolution

_____ 8. Wrote a declaration of rights for women

_____ 9. Abolished the monarchy, declared France a republic

_____ 10. Social group made up of the nobility who held important government and military positions but paid few taxes

a. Bastille

b. Versailles

c. First Estate

d. sans culottes

e. Estates General

f. cahiers

g. Old Order

h. Olympe de Gouges

i. National Convention

j. Second Estate

k. Third Estate

l. bourgeoisie

m. National Assembly

Name ______________________________ Class ________________ Date ________________

The French Revolution and Napoleon — Section Quiz

Section 2

TRUE/FALSE Mark each statement **T** if it is true or **F** if it is false. If false explain why.

_____ 1. The radical Montagnards were eager to execute the king as a way of protecting the Revolution and preventing a return to the monarchy.

____

____

_____ 2. Maximilien Robespierre led the peace-keeping efforts of the Committee of Public Safety.

____

____

_____ 3. The cult of the Supreme Being replaced Roman Catholicism and promoted enthusiasm for the Revolution as the object of worship.

____

____

_____ 4. The accusations, trials, and executions during the Revolution became known as the Reign of Terror.

____

____

_____ 5. When the Reign of Terror ended, a strong effective government called the Directory was formed.

____

____

Name ______________________ Class ______________ Date ______________

The French Revolution and Napoleon

Section Quiz

Section 3

TRUE/FALSE Mark each statement **T** if it is true or **F** if it is false. If false explain why.

_____ 1. In an 1804 plebiscite, the French voted to declare France an empire.

____

____

_____ 2. The Continental System was Napoleon's plan to weaken the economy of Great Britain by disrupting trade.

____

____

_____ 3. During the Napoleonic Wars, France became the dominant European power.

____

____

_____ 4. By 1812, Napoleon controlled all European nations except Great Britain, Sweden, Portugal, and the Ottoman Empire.

____

____

_____ 5. Napoleon abolished the tax system in France as a way to gain the trust and loyalty of the people.

____

____

The French Revolution and Napoleon

Section Quiz

Section 4

MULTIPLE CHOICE For each of the following, write the letter of the best choice in the space provided.

_____ 1. Which describes the greatest challenge faced by Napoleon's troops in Russia?
a. resistance by Russian peasants
b. harsh weather
c. reinforcements from Germany
d. desertion by French troops

_____ 2. The Hundred Days describes
a. the length of Napoleon's exile to Elba.
b. how long it took for Napoleon's army to return from Moscow to Paris.
c. the brief period between Napoleon's return from Elba and the Battle of Waterloo.
d. how long the Congress of Vienna met.

_____ 3. British troops at the Battle of Waterloo were led by
a. Horatio Nelson.
b. the Duke of Wellington.
c. Maurice de Talleyrand.
d. King Frederick William.

_____ 4. The Congress of Vienna was influenced by
a. Enlightenment thinkers.
b. the sans culottes.
c. Napoleon's supporters.
d. people with reactionary ideals.

_____ 5. Which of the following best describes the primary purpose of the Congress of Vienna?
a. to restore order and stability to Europe
b. to punish Germany for military aggression
c. to stimulate the sluggish European economy
d. to establish a common European currency

Name ______________________ Class ______________ Date ______________

The French Revolution and Napoleon

Chapter Test

Form A

MULTIPLE CHOICE For each of the following, write the letter of the best choice in the space provided.

_____ 1. Which of the following was one cause of the French Revolution?
a. new taxes on the Second Estate
b. the influence of Enlightenment ideas
c. strong leadership from Louis XVI
d. economic prosperity

_____ 2. Which of the following was one of the first acts of the National Convention?
a. a declaration of war against the Austrian Netherlands
b. convening of a Constitutional Convention
c. a declaration of war against England
d. the declaration that France was a republic

_____ 3. Which political faction was the most radical?
a. the Montagnards
b. the Girondins
c. the Louisites
d. the Plain

_____ 4. The Reign of Terror resulted in
a. increased foreign opposition to the French Revolution.
b. a strengthened National Assembly.
c. peace throughout France.
d. the election of Robespierre to the presidency.

_____ 5. Which legislative body was in place when Napoleon seized power?
a. the National Convention
b. the National Assembly
c. the Directory
d. the Legislative Assembly

_____ 6. The Continental System restricted
a. trade with Great Britain.
b. trade with French possessions in Asia.
c. freedom of speech and of the press.
d. the rights of women.

_____ 7. Which European campaign was a disaster for Napoleon?
a. the Russian Campaign
b. the Saint Domingue Expedition
c. the Peninsular War
d. the Continental System

_____ 8. The Congress of Vienna
a. rewarded Napoleon's supporters with large tracts of land.
b. made France a colony of Great Britain.
c. outlawed monarchies.
d. strengthened nations surrounding France.

The French Revolution and Napoleon

Chapter Test

Form A

PRACTICING SOCIAL STUDIES SKILLS Study the map below and answer the question that follows.

Napoleon's Empire, 1812

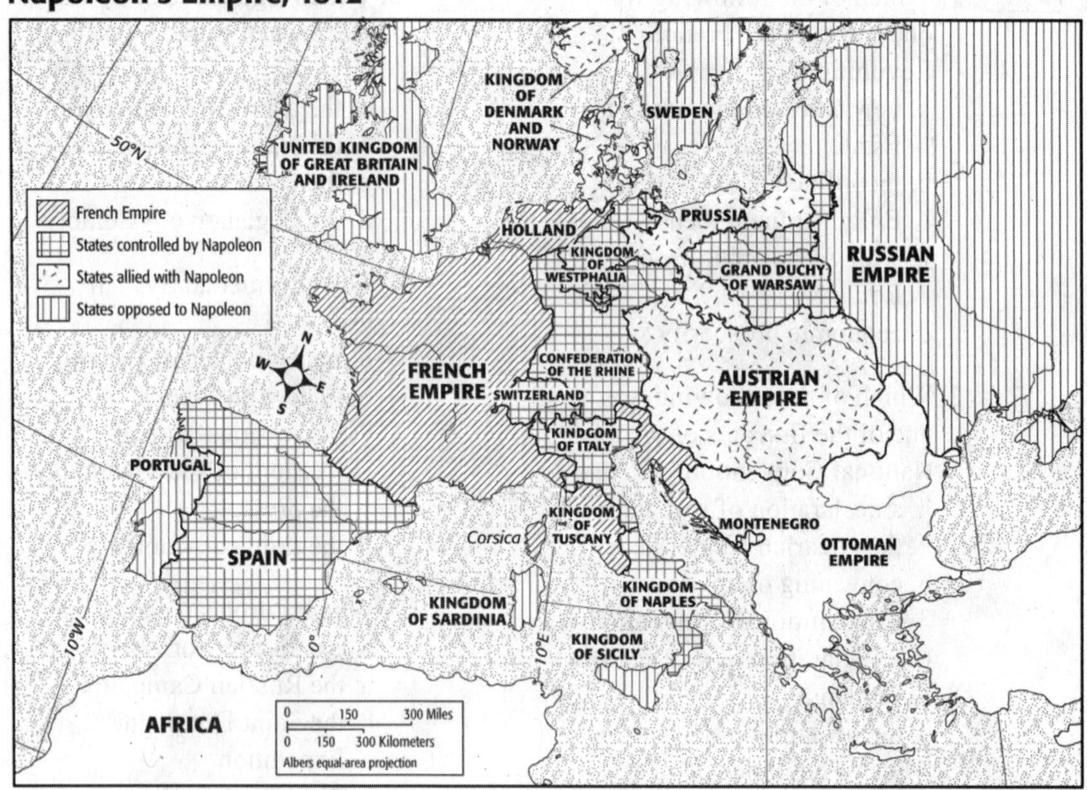

_____ 9. Which states were opposed to Napoleon in 1812?

a. All states were either controlled by or allied with Napoleon.

b. Grand Duchy of Warsaw, Confederation of the Rhine, Kingdoms of Denmark and Norway

c. Africa and the Ottoman Empire

d. Portugal, United Kingdom of Great Britain and Ireland, Kingdom of Sardinia, Kingdom of Sicily, Russian Empire, Montenegro, and Sweden

FILL IN THE BLANK For each of the following statements, fill in the blank with the appropriate word, phrase, or name.

10. The First Estate was made up of the ____________________.

11. The Third Estate called itself a legislature known as the ____________________.

12. The radical ____________________ Club adopted policies supported by the lower middle class and the poor.

13. A sense of patriotism and unity as a people is called ____________________.

The French Revolution and Napoleon

Chapter Test

Form A

14. The ______________________ eliminated many injustices in French law but also promoted order and authority over individual rights.

15. British and Prussian troops dealt a crushing defeat to Napoleon at the Battle of ______________________.

MATCHING In the space provided, write the letter of the term, person, or place that matches each description. Some answers will not be used.

_____ 16. Guaranteed freedom of speech, the press, and religion

_____ 17. A brief period when Napoleon regained control of France

_____ 18. A symbolic event of the Revolution

_____ 19. A forced transfer of power

_____ 20. Advocated violence to protect the Revolution

_____ 21. France's greatest enemy during the Napoleonic Wars

_____ 22. Used for executions

_____ 23. His views dominated the Congress of Vienna

_____ 24. The top of France's Old Order

_____ 25. People who wanted conditions to return to those of an earlier time

a. Great Britain

b. guillotine

c. King Louis XVI

d. Prince Klemens von Metternich

e. Civil Constitution of the Clergy

f. Hundred Days

g. the storming of the Bastille

h. coup d' état

i. Jean-Paul Marat

j. reactionaries

k. the Declaration of the Rights of Man and Citizen

l. plebiscite

m. Duke of Wellington

Name ______________________ Class ______________ Date ____________

The French Revolution and Napoleon — Chapter Test

Form B

SHORT ANSWER On a separate sheet of paper, answer each of the following questions in complete sentences. Remember to use specific examples to support your answers.

1. Name the three classes of French society before the Revolution and describe who made up each class.
2. Why did the National Convention attack the Catholic religion? How did they do so?
3. Why did the French people welcome Napoleon's seizure of power?
4. Describe the personality of Napoleon Bonaparte.
5. Why did the Congress of Vienna change many national borders in Europe?

PRACTICING SOCIAL STUDIES SKILLS Study the map below and, on a separate sheet of paper, answer the questions that follow in complete sentences.

Napoleon's Empire, 1812

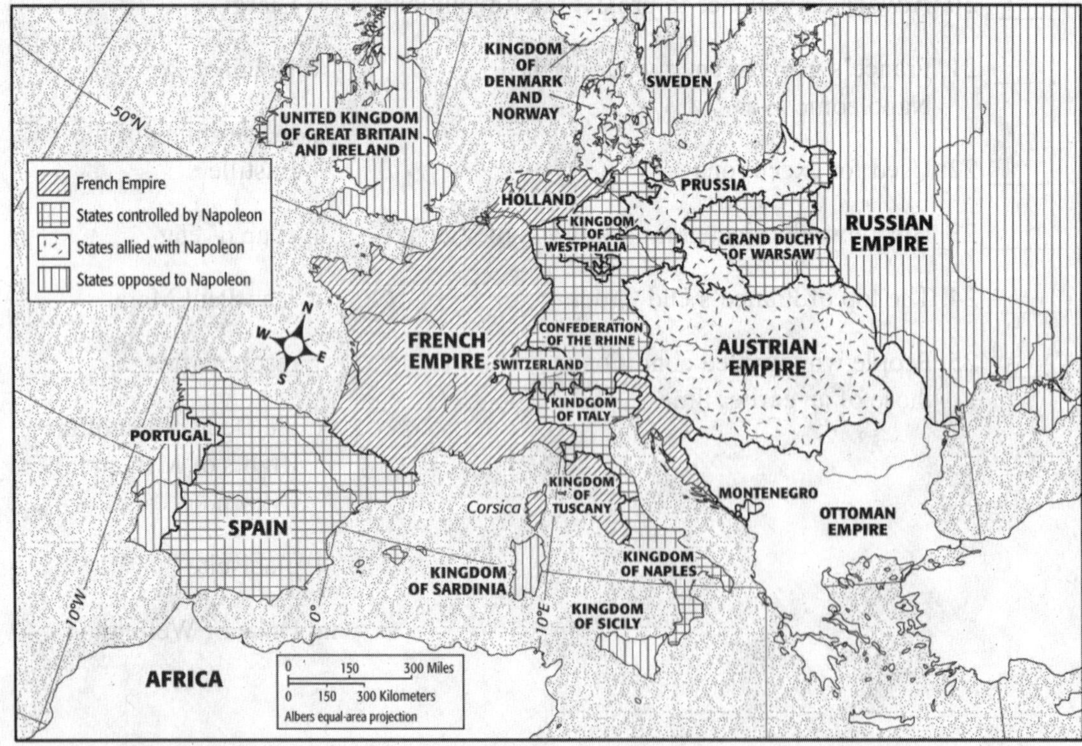

6. Identify two nations controlled by Napoleon in 1812.
7. Where might Napoleon have felt vulnerable to attack? Explain your answer.

Name ______________________ Class ______________ Date ______________

Changes in European Society

Unit Test

Form A

MATCHING In the space provided, write the letter of the term that matches each description. Some answers will not be used.

_____ 1. The concept that monarchs receive their power from God

_____ 2. A ruler whose power is not limited by having to consult with others

_____ 3. Agreement that gave each German prince the right to decide whether his state would be Catholic or Protestant

_____ 4. A famous fleet of about 130 ships and 20,000 soldiers and sailors

_____ 5. French Protestants

_____ 6. A religious group demanding further reform of the Church of England

_____ 7. The belief that the earth was the center of the universe

_____ 8. Workers of the Third Estate

_____ 9. A series of accusations, trials, and executions implemented to prevent a possible counterrevolution in France

_____ 10. A forced transfer of power

a. Peace of Augsburg
b. geocentric theory
c. heliocentric theory
d. coup d'état
e. divine right
f. sansculottes
g. absolute monarch
h. Reign of Terror
i. nationalism
j. Spanish Armada
k. Huguenots
l. plebiscite
m. Puritans

FILL IN THE BLANK For each of the following statements, fill in the blank with the appropriate word, phrase, or name.

11. The five-step method of investigation and discovery is called the ______________________.

12. ______________________ were European monarchs who developed a system of government in which they ruled according to Enlightenment ideas.

13. Inspired by Enlightenment thinkers, the ruler ______________________, intended to reform Russia, but had no intention of giving up power.

14. Another name for the Enlightenment is the Age of ______________________.

15. ______________________ was a philosopher who despised inequality in society and believed all people were equal.

16. The ______________________ Revolution was the first war in which old ideas about government were challenged by the ideas of the Enlightenment

17. After the king locked them out of the meeting place, the Third Estate swore the ______________________, stating they would not leave until they had written a constitution for France.

18. Under Napoleon's leadership, French scholars created the ______________________, which promoted order and authority over individual rights.

19. The ______________________ was Napoleon's plan to disrupt trade in Great Britain.

20. Led by Prince Metternich, the ______________________ restored monarchies in much of Europe.

TRUE/FALSE Indicate whether each statement below is true or false by writing **T** or **F** in the space provided.

_____ 21. Charles V was successful in his goal of establishing a Catholic Europe.

_____ 22. King Louis XIV ruled as an absolute monarch.

_____ 23. The War of the Spanish Succession united France and Spain under a single monarch.

_____ 24. The English Civil War resulted in a commonwealth led by Oliver Cromwell.

_____ 25. Thomas Hobbes called giving up some freedoms for peace, safety, and order the social contract.

_____ 26. John Locke believed that if a government failed to protect its citizens' natural rights, they had the right to overthrow it.

_____ 27. After the Battle of Saratoga, Benjamin Franklin was unable to convince the French to financially contribute to the American Revolution.

_____ 28. The most radical enlightened despot was Joseph II, the son of Maria Theresa of Austria.

Changes in European Society

Unit Test

Form A

_____ 29. On July 14, 1789, an angry mob stormed the Bastille after King Louis XVI brought troops into Paris.

_____ 30. The Continental System was Napoleon's plan for an improved legal code for the French Empire.

MULTIPLE CHOICE For each of the following, write the letter of the best choice in the space provided.

_____ 31. Henry IV became the king of France after he
a. arrested the Huguenots.
b. converted to Catholicism.
c. declared *un roi, une loi, une foi.*
d. issued the Edict of Nantes.

_____ 32. Louis XIV led France during a time of power and glory and was known as
a. the Sun King.
b. the Honored King.
c. Louis the Powerful.
d. Louis the Magnificent.

_____ 33. Russia's main goal in the Great Northern War was to
a. regain control of the capital.
b. westernize Russian society.
c. block Swedish trade routes.
d. secure a warm-water port.

_____ 34. The return to monarchy in Great Britain is known as the
a. Restoration.
b. Reformation.
c. Petition of Right.
d. Edict of Nantes.

_____ 35. To squash opposition, Ivan the Terrible created
a. the Bill of Opposition.
b. the Russian Redcoats.
c. a private police force.
d. a national assembly.

_____ 36. After Pugachev's rebellion, Catherine II decided to
a. free the Russian serfs.
b. strengthen her authority in rural areas.
c. grant independence to Poland.
d. tax the Catholic Church.

_____ 37. What did the Treaty of Westphalia accomplish?
a. It led to the Peace of Augsburg, which gave German princes the right to decide whether their states would be Catholic or Protestant.
b. It forced Philip to send the Spanish Armada to England.
c. It led to 100 years of peace between the Ottoman Empire and the Holy Roman Empire.
d. It ended the Thirty Years' War, extended religious toleration, and diminished the power of the Holy Roman Empire.

Changes in European Society

Unit Test

Form A

_____ 38. Which of the following scientists was the first to observe that the earth revolved around the sun?
a. Newton
b. Galileo
c. Ptolemy
d. Copernicus

_____ 39. Enlightenment philosophers were thinkers who
a. studied the solar system.
b. fought in the American Revolution.
c. focused their attention on government or chose to deal with social issues such as religious toleration, women's rights, and economic issues.
d. finally concluded that reason could be applied to issues of science, but had no religious application.

_____ 40. Which of the following men influenced the foundation of modern democracy with his belief in government by consent?
a. John Locke
b. Francis Bacon
c. Thomas Hobbes
d. Jean-Jacques Rousseau

_____ 41. In response to the Stamp Act, American colonists
a. began growing tobacco.
b. raised taxes on exports.
c. boycotted British goods.
d. dumped tea in the harbor.

_____ 42. Which of the following was a cause of the French Revolution?
a. heavy taxes on the nobility
b. inequalities in society
c. the constant threat of British aggression
d. strong leadership from Louis XVI

_____ 43. The Declaration of the Rights of Man and of the Citizen
a. abolished slavery in the French colonies.
b. was historic because it applied to women and men.
c. stated that all men are born equal and remain equal before the law.
d. was turned down by the National Assembly.

_____ 44. One of the first acts of the National Convention
a. was to free the king and his family from prison.
b. was to ask Napoleon to lead the country.
c. was to abolish the monarchy and declare France a republic.
d. was to give all French citizens, including women, the right to vote.

_____ 45. During a coup d'état, armed supporters of Napoleon seized power from
a. King Louis XVI.
b. the National Assembly.
c. the National Convention.
d. the Directory.

Changes in European Society

Unit Test

Form A

_____ 46. Throughout the Napoleonic Wars
a. Spain remained an ally of France.
b. Portugal protected French troops.
c. Great Britain remained France's greatest enemy.
d. Great Britain worked to keep Napoleon in power.

_____ 47. Which was a key factor in Napoleon's defeat in Russia?
a. the Russian winter
b. superior Russian troops
c. inferior French weapons
d. armed Russian serfs

_____ 48. The Battle of Waterloo was significant because
a. Napoleon died in the battle.
b. it was Napoleon's first defeat.
c. it ended the Napoleonic Wars.
d. it secured freedom for England.

_____ 49. The Congress of Vienna restored
a. liberal reforms.
b. European monarchies.
c. personal freedoms.
d. democratic republics.

Changes in European Society

Unit Test

Form A

PRACTICING SOCIAL STUDIES SKILLS Study the map below and answer the question that follows.

Napoleon's Empire, 1812

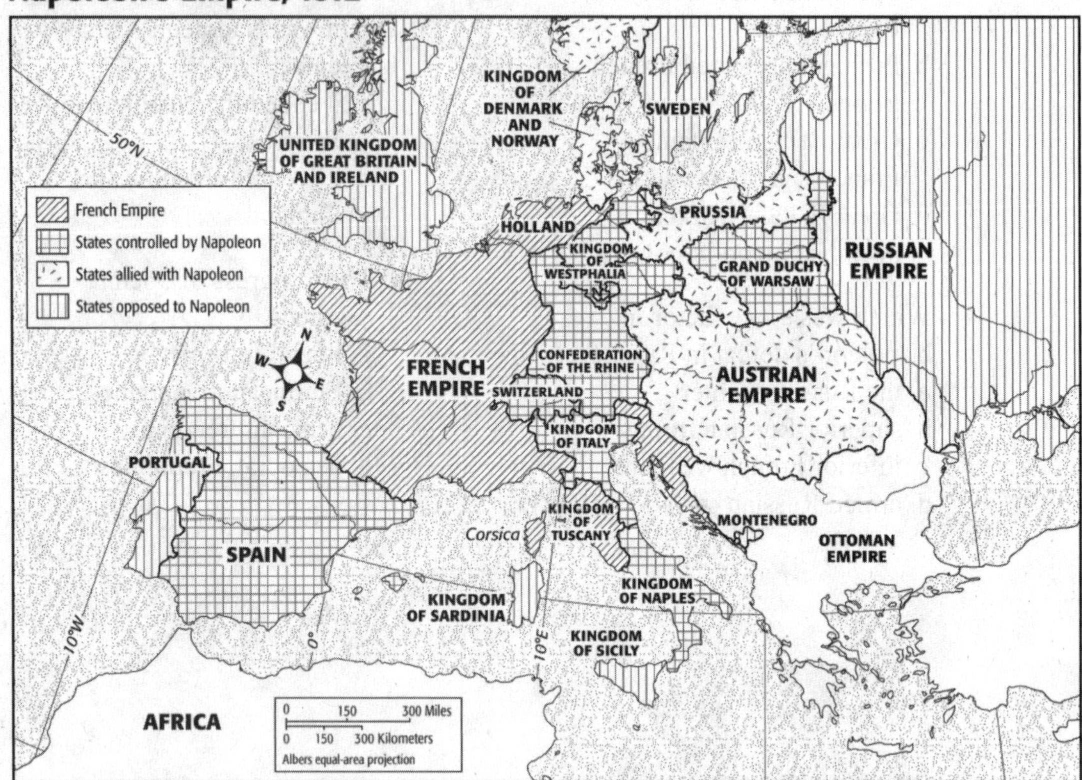

_____ 50. Which of the following statements is best supported by the map?

a. The states allied with Napoleon were Prussia, the Austrian Empire, and the Kingdom of Denmark and Norway.

b. The French Empire was surrounded by states opposed to Napoleon.

c. Over 2000 kilometers separated the French Empire from the United Kingdom of Great Britain and Ireland

d. Portugal and the Grand Duchy of Warsaw were both opposed to Napoleon.

Name ______________________ Class ______________ Date ______________

Changes in European Society

Unit Test

Form B

SHORT ANSWER On a separate sheet of paper, answer each of the following questions in complete sentences. Remember to use specific examples to support your answers.

1. What events led Charles V to abdicate his throne in 1556?
2. Describe Oliver Cromwell's rise to power and his leadership in England.
3. What were some of the results of the Scientific Revolution?
4. What were Thomas Hobbes' thoughts about people and government?
5. Summarize the causes of the French Revolution.

PRACTICING SOCIAL STUDIES SKILLS Study the map below and, on a separate sheet of paper, answer the question that follows in complete sentences.

Napoleon's Empire, 1812

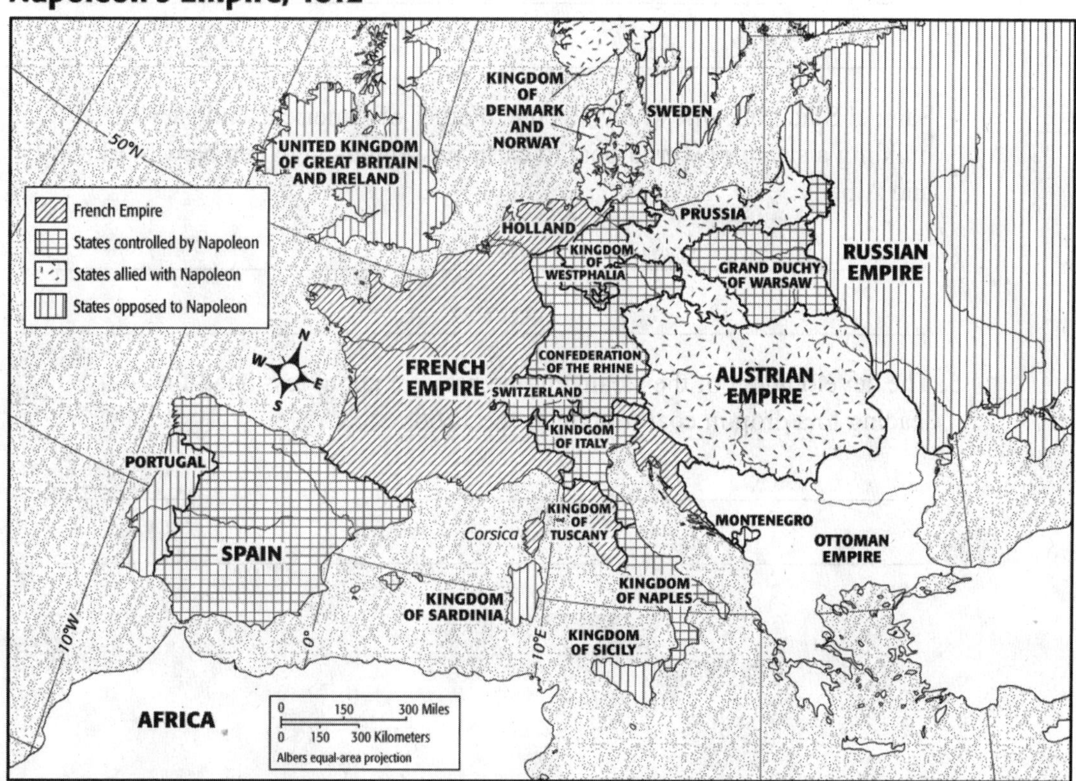

6. Napoleon placed his relatives as rulers in the following states: Spain, Kingdom of Italy, Kingdom of Tuscany, Kingdom of Naples, and the Kingdom of Westphalia. According to the map, what did those states have in common?

Name ______________________ Class ______________ Date ______________

The Industrial Revolution

Section Quiz

Section 1

TRUE/FALSE Mark each statement **T** if it is true or **F** if it is false. If false explain why.

_____ 1. The Industrial Revolution began in Great Britain around 1700.

____

____

_____ 2. The three basic factors of production needed for a nation's economic success are land, stable government, and a source of energy.

____

____

_____ 3. Eli Whitney, James Hargreaves, Richard Arkwright, and John Kay all made important contributions to the development of the textile industry.

____

____

_____ 4. Samuel Slater became known as the "Father of American Industry" after building a steam-powered boat to carry passengers between New York City and Albany.

____

____

_____ 5. The development of the steam engine brought about less need for coal, leading to a drop in coal mining in the 1700s.

____

____

Name ____________________ Class ______________ Date ______________

The Industrial Revolution

Section Quiz

Section 2

FILL IN THE BLANK For each of the following statements, fill in the blank with the appropriate word, phrase, or name.

1. Farming and weaving are examples of ____________________ industries, or occupations performed at home.

2. The British city of Manchester, with poor sanitation and polluted air and water, symbolized the problems of ____________________.

3. The ____________________ opposed machines that were "hurtful to the commonality." This group protested by burning buildings or smashing machinery but tried to leave people unharmed.

4. ____________________ are organizations designed to represent the interests of workers.

5. American industry became expert in ____________________, the system of manufacturing large numbers of identical items.

MULTIPLE CHOICE For each of the following, write the letter of the best choice in the space provided.

_____ 6. Labor unions pressured employers to improve conditions by
   a. employing Luddites.
   b. hiring families.
   c. organizing strikes.
   d. hiring only men.

_____ 7. The factory system caused the growth
   a. of the middle class.
   b. of more cottage industries.
   c. of mills near rivers.
   d. of improved air quality.

_____ 8. An increase in production led to
   a. custom parts.
   b. fewer employees.
   c. more skilled workers.
   d. lower prices.

_____ 9. The assembly line cut
   a. profits.
   b. production time.
   c. the need for managers.
   d. down on sick days.

_____ 10. Burning coal and iron-smelting
   a. powered cottage industries.
   b. closed factories.
   c. put soot and chemicals in the air.
   d. turned water wheels.

The Industrial Revolution

Section Quiz

Section 3

MATCHING In the space provided, write the letter of the term, person, or place that matches each description. Some answers will not be used.

_____ 1. Idea that governments should not interfere in business

_____ 2. Author of *The Wealth of Nations,* describing wealth and how it is created

_____ 3. Someone who starts a business

_____ 4. Demonstrated his ideas about socialism by founding a utopian community

_____ 5. Put forth a more radical view of socialism, declaring that more workers would sink into poverty with the growth of capitalism

_____ 6. American railroad industrialist

_____ 7. System in which the government controls the economy and most means of production

_____ 8. American oil industrialist

_____ 9. Level of material comfort

_____ 10. Believed that the population would always grow faster than food production

a. Great Exhibition of 1851

b. Karl Marx

c. entrepreneur

d. Robert Owen

e. Cornelius Vanderbilt

f. Adam Smith

g. John D. Rockefeller

h. communism

i. Thomas Malthus

j. leisure

k. standard of living

l. laissez-faire

m. means of production

Name _______________ Class _______________ Date _______________

The Industrial Revolution

Chapter Test
Form A

MULTIPLE CHOICE For each of the following, write the letter of the best choice in the space provided.

_____ 1. Britain's colonial empire fueled the development of industry in that country because
- a. the nation had access to vast amounts of raw materials.
- b. the war machine required quick and efficient production of goods.
- c. colonies provided slave labor for growing industries.
- d. workers in the colonies earned far less than workers in Britain.

_____ 2. Which of the following was a negative result of the growth of the textile industry in Great Britain?
- a. fewer cotton farms in Great Britain
- b. the huge population growth in the country
- c. the expansion of agriculture in India
- d. the spread of slavery in the United States

_____ 3. A region in northwestern England became known as the "black country" because
- a. laborers there smudged coal dust on their faces to keep the sun out of their eyes.
- b. iron-smelting factories polluted the air.
- c. industries located there were all immensely profitable.
- d. the sand on the beaches was dark gray.

_____ 4. The Luddite movement emerged in order to
- a. agitate for the ten-hour day.
- b. oppose industrial changes that were putting weavers out of work.
- c. direct strikes breaking out all over Great Britain.
- d. abolish child labor.

_____ 5. What led to the growth of the middle class?
- a. industry's need for managers and other mid-level employees
- b. the increasing profit earned from small, family-owned farms
- c. the increase in prices of manufactured goods
- d. the growth of universities

_____ 6. The mercantile system in Britain was replaced by
- a. entrepreneurship.
- b. socialism.
- c. department stores.
- d. laissez-faire economics.

_____ 7. According to Marx and Engels, establishing a society based on cooperation and equal distribution of wealth would require
- a. an energy crisis.
- b. development of a wealthy industrial class.
- c. universal public education.
- d. a revolution.

Name ______________ Class ______________ Date ______________

The Industrial Revolution Chapter Test

Form A

PRACTICING SOCIAL STUDIES SKILLS Study the map below and answer the question that follows.

Industrialized Europe, 1900

_____ 8. Including railroads and industrialized areas, which two countries were most heavily industrialized?

a. Spain and Italy
b. United Kingdom and Belgium
c. United Kingdom and Italy
d. Germany and Sweden

Name ______________________ Class ______________ Date ______________

The Industrial Revolution

Chapter Test

Form A

MATCHING In the space provided, write the letter of the term, person, or place that matches each description. Some answers will not be used.

_____ 9. System of manufacturing large numbers of identical items

_____ 10. The "Father of America's Industrial Revolution"

_____ 11. Level of material comfort for people in industrialized countries

_____ 12. Built to house machines

_____ 13. Theory that society as a whole should own property and control industry

_____ 14. Invented a machine that made planting grain more efficient

_____ 15. Work stoppage organized by laborers

_____ 16. Founded New Harmony

_____ 17. Invented a machine that pulled seeds from raw cotton

_____ 18. Invented the assembly line

a. Robert Owen
b. factories
c. mass production
d. Eli Whitney
e. socialism
f. Samuel Slater
g. standard of living
h. entrepreneur
i. Jethro Tull
j. strike
k. assembly line
l. James Watt
m. Henry Ford

TRUE/FALSE Indicate whether each statement below is true or false by writing **T** or **F** in the space provided.

_____ 19. The enclosure movement not only supported population growth, but also helped make all farmers wealthier.

_____ 20. As steam power began to be used commercially, factories began to be built near coal mines rather than near rivers and streams.

_____ 21. The industrialization of France was delayed by British secrecy, the French Revolution, and the Napoleonic Wars.

_____ 22. The change from the cottage industry system to the factory system was beneficial for all workers.

_____ 23. Labor unions, organizations of workers that represent workers' interests, emerged in the early 1800s in Great Britain.

_____ 24. In his classic work, *The Wealth of Nations,* Adam Smith defended the mercantile system, arguing that government regulations on restricting imports protected a nation's wealth.

_____ 25. Negative effects of industrialization included crowded, dirty cities and polluted air and water.

Name ______________________ Class ______________ Date ______________

The Industrial Revolution

Chapter Test
Form B

SHORT ANSWER On a separate sheet of paper, answer each of the following questions in complete sentences. Remember to use specific examples to support your answers.

1. What are the factors of production? Define each of them.
2. Inventor John Kay was attacked and had to flee the country after he patented the "flying shuttle." How does this incident illustrate the negative effects of industrial progress?
3. Describe the working conditions for children in early factories.
4. Why do you think Andrew Carnegie was generally admired?

PRACTICING SOCIAL STUDIES SKILLS Study the map below and, on a separate sheet of paper, answer the question that follows in complete sentences.

Industrialized Europe, 1900

5. According to this map, what was the relationship between industrialization and railroads?

Name ______________________ Class ______________ Date ______________

Life in the Industrial Age

Section Quiz

Section 1

MATCHING In the space provided, write the letter of the term, person, or place that matches each description. Some answers will not be used.

_____ 1. Developed a process for cheaper and more efficient production of steel

_____ 2. Invented the telegraph and a language for sending messages

_____ 3. Developed the first powered airplane that was able to sustain flight

_____ 4. Created the world's first central electric power plant

_____ 5. Put an internal combustion engine on a horse carriage and developed the carburetor

_____ 6. Used mass production methods to make a line of affordable cars

_____ 7. Generated electricity by moving a magnet through a coil of copper wire

_____ 8. Developed the wireless telegraph, or radio

_____ 9. Created a device to transmit the human voice electronically

_____ 10. Developed a primitive electric light bulb that produced a dim light

a. Michael Faraday

b. Joseph Swan

c. Thomas Edison

d. Henry Bessemer

e. switchboard operator

f. Gottlieb Daimler

g. Henry Ford

h. Wilbur and Orville Wright

i. Samuel Morse

j. William Kelly

k. Alexander Graham Bell

l. Thomas Watson

m. Guglielmo Marconi

Name ______________________ Class ______________ Date ______________

Life in the Industrial Age

Section Quiz

Section 2

MULTIPLE CHOICE For each of the following, write the letter of the best choice in the space provided.

_____ 1. Charles Darwin's observations led him to conclude that
a. there is little difference among the various types of finches.
b. because of their diet, birds are able to survive in cold climates.
c. the strongest creatures are those that live in cold climates.
d. creatures that are well adapted are those that survive to produce offspring.

_____ 2. In 1871, Dmitri Mendeleyev
a. succeeded in proving that atoms are real.
b. created a periodic table for elements.
c. discovered polonium.
d. developed the idea of natural selection.

_____ 3. Which of the following is true about Albert Einstein's theory of relativity?
a. It identified particles of matter that move faster than the speed of light.
b. It overturned what Newton and other scientists said about how the universe worked.
c. It stated that all living things are related to one another.
d. It identified the nucleus that lay within the center of an atom.

_____ 4. The development of ether helped medical patients by
a. reducing pain during surgery.
b. killing disease-causing germs.
c. eliminating the threat of anthrax.
d. reducing recovery time from surgery.

_____ 5. Which of the following individuals concluded that human behaviors are a series of connected conditioned reflexes?
a. Joseph Lister
b. Ivan Pavlov
c. Sigmund Freud
d. Louis Pasteur

Name ______________________ Class ______________ Date ______________

Life in the Industrial Age

Section Quiz

Section 3

TRUE/FALSE Mark each statement **T** if it is true or **F** if it is false. If false explain why.

_____ 1. In the Industrial Age, cities became less important as centers for manufacturing and distribution and, instead, began to play a greater role in political, military, religious, and trade functions.

____

____

_____ 2. In the late 1800s, the population of cities declined as many people moved to the countryside hoping to escape hunger, political oppression, and discrimination.

____

____

_____ 3. In the early 1800s, a movement called romanticism emerged as a reaction to Enlightenment rationalism and the early abuses of the Industrial Revolution.

____

____

_____ 4. In 1881, Booker T. Washington founded a private school in Alabama to train African American teachers.

____

____

_____ 5. As leisure time increased, cultural events, such as concerts and museum visits, became more popular.

____

____

Name ______________________ Class ______________ Date ______________

Life in the Industrial Age

Chapter Test
Form A

MULTIPLE CHOICE For each of the following, write the letter of the best choice in the space provided.

_____ 1. Which of the following was a significant factor in the expansion of the railroad system in the 1800s?
a. the invention of the Bessemer process
b. the discovery of electricity
c. production of the Model T
d. preparation for the Paris Exhibition of 1900

_____ 2. One effect of the expansion of the railroads was that
a. horse-drawn carriages were no longer used.
b. consumers had a greater choice of low-cost products.
c. the population of the East declined.
d. the price of steel rose.

_____ 3. In addition to personal communication the telegraph was used to
a. speak with loved ones who lived far away.
b. conduct business and transmit news from far away places quickly.
c. help hearing-impaired students learn to speak.
d. advance the study of aerodynamics.

_____ 4. The work of Joseph Lister with an antiseptic would have been impossible without the discoveries of
a. Marie Curie.
b. Isaac Newton.
c. Albert Einstein.
d. Louis Pasteur.

_____ 5. Charles Darwin's work contributed to the advancement of which of the following disciplines?
a. physical anthropology
b. cultural archaeology
c. psychology
d. medicine

_____ 6. What development was essential to the expansion of cities to the suburbs?
a. the growth of sports
b. the invention of the telegraph
c. the emergence of public transportation systems
d. the professionalization of nursing

_____ 7. Which art form or style does the phrase "the spontaneous overflow of powerful feelings from emotions recollected in tranquility" represent?
a. realism
b. rationalism
c. romanticism
d. Enlightenment thought

Name ______________________ Class ______________ Date ______________

Life in the Industrial Age

Chapter Test

Form A

PRACTICING SOCIAL STUDIES SKILLS Study the map and passage below and answer the questions that follow.

Expansion of Railroads

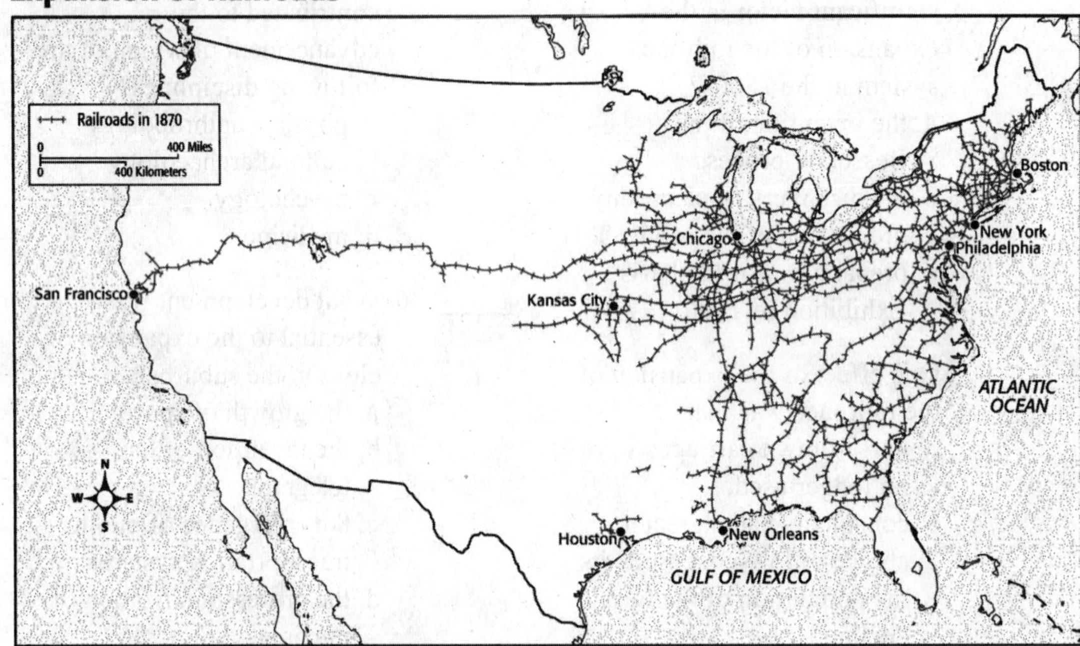

_____ 8. In what part of the country did people have the most access to railroads in the 1870s?
a. the Southeast
b. Kansas City
c. the frontier
d. the Northeast

> **"Bedrooms in tenements were dark closets, utterly without ventilation. There couldn't be any. The houses were built like huge square boxes, covering nearly the whole lot. Some light came in at the ends, but the middle was always black."**
>
> **—Jacob Riis, The Battle with the Slum, 1902**

_____ 9. What is Jacob Riis describing in this quote?
a. why governments should build parks in cities
b. the poor ventilation and lack of light in tenements
c. the homes immigrants had before arriving in the United States
d. the poor ventilation and lack of light in factories

Name ______________________ Class ______________ Date ______________

Life in the Industrial Age

Chapter Test

Form A

MATCHING In the space provided, write the letter of the term, person, or place that matches each description. Some answers will not be used.

_____ 10. Introduced the idea of the unconscious mind

_____ 11. Developed a new, fast way to send long-distance messages

_____ 12. Artistic style that portrayed details of everyday life

_____ 13. Developed vaccines for anthrax and rabies

_____ 14. Invented the first usable, practical light bulb

_____ 15. Energy released from certain elements as they break down

_____ 16. Artistic style concerned with capturing an impression of a scene

_____ 17. Arrangement that revealed previously unknown patterns among the elements

_____ 18. First to succeed in flying a powered airplane in sustained flight

_____ 19. Concluded that human behaviors are a series of connected conditioned reflexes

a. Albert Einstein
b. radio
c. radioactivity
d. Thomas Edison
e. realism
f. Hull House
g. Wilbur and Orville Wright
h. Sigmund Freud
i. impressionism
j. Ivan Pavlov
k. periodic table
l. Louis Pasteur
m. Samuel Morse

FILL IN THE BLANK For each of the following statements, fill in the blank with the appropriate word, phrase, or name.

20. When ______________________ used electricity to power a motor, it paved the way for the development of electrical generators.

21. In the early 1900s, Henry Ford built an affordable car known as the ______________________.

22. To destroy the bacteria that caused disease in milk, cheese, and juice, these products went through the process of ______________________.

23. Sigmund Freud developed a form of therapy during the early 1900s called ______________________.

24. Increased industrialization created a need for a more _______________ workforce, as factories need managers who could read and write.

25. Cities began printing _______________ with expanded coverage including current events and information about arts and science.

Name ______________________ Class ______________ Date ______________

Life in the Industrial Age

Chapter Test

Form B

SHORT ANSWER On a separate sheet of paper, answer each of the following questions in complete sentences. Remember to use specific examples to support your answers.

1. Explain two ways electricity impacted industry.
2. Summarize two of the medical breakthroughs of the Industrial Age.
3. Why was Charles Darwin's book, *On the Origin of Species,* controversial?
4. Describe two of the art forms or styles that developed during the Industrial Age.
5. What were some of the characteristics of an industrial city?

PRACTICING SOCIAL STUDIES SKILLS Study the map below and, on a separate sheet of paper, answer the questions that follow in complete sentences.

Expansion of Railroads

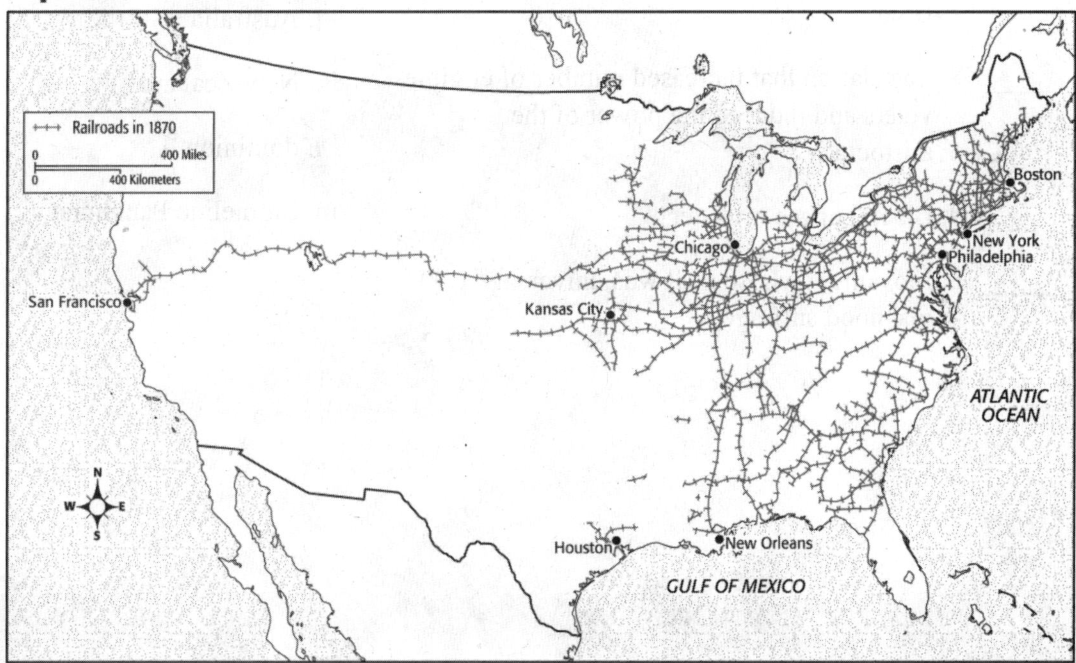

6. What areas may have seen population growth as a result of the expansion of the railroads? Explain.
7. Based on what you have learned from the chapter, what would this map look like if it illustrated railroad routes up to 1850?

Name ________________ Class ________________ Date ________________

MATCHING In the space provided, write the letter of the term, person, or place that matches each description. Some answers will not be used.

_____ 1. Conservative prime minister who argued for women's voting rights

_____ 2. The first country to grant women the right to vote

_____ 3. Wanted to preserve the best traditions of the past

_____ 4. The right to vote

_____ 5. A self-governing colony

_____ 6. Member of Parliament whose textile industry investigations led to the Factory Act of 1833

_____ 7. Founder of the Women's Social and Political Union

_____ 8. Legislation that increased number of eligible voters and reduced the power of the aristocracy

_____ 9. Liberal prime minister

_____ 10. Movement whose goal was universal manhood suffrage

a. Reform Act of 1832

b. Conservative party

c. Fawcett Act

d. Chartism

e. Michael Sadler

f. Benjamin Disraeli

g. William Gladstone

h. suffrage

i. Lord Durham

j. Australia

k. New Zealand

l. dominion

m. Emmeline Pankhurst

Reforms, Revolutions, and War

Section Quiz

Section 2

TRUE/FALSE Mark each statement **T** if it is true or **F** if it is false. If false explain why.

_____ 1. As a result of the Revolution of 1830 in France, Charles X gave up the throne and fled to England.

____

____

_____ 2. Louis Philippe, the "citizen king", limited the power of the government and allowed his opponents to criticize him.

____

____

_____ 3. As a result of the Revolution of 1848, the move for women's rights lost support in France.

____

____

_____ 4. After Napoleon III surrendered to the Prussians, the French Assembly deposed Napoleon and declared the Third Republic.

____

____

_____ 5. The Dreyfus affair and the letter of Émile Zola divided France into two groups—those who supported Dreyfus, and those who opposed him.

____

____

Name ______________________ Class ______________ Date ______________

Reforms, Revolutions, and War

Section Quiz

Section 3

MATCHING In the space provided, write the letter of the term, person, or place that matches each description. Some answers will not be used.

_____ 1. People of European descent who were born in the Spanish colonies of Latin America

_____ 2. Priest known as the Father of Mexican Independence

_____ 3. Translated the Declaration of the Rights of Man and of the Citizen into Spanish

_____ 4. Latin American colonists who were born in Spain

_____ 5. The Liberator's actions brought independence to Spain's colonies in South America

_____ 6. Caribbean French colony that declared independence

_____ 7. Declared Brazil independent

_____ 8. Took military and political action against French settlers in Hispaniola

_____ 9. Leader who won independence for Argentina and Chile

_____ 10. Leader who created a three-part proposal for the liberation of Mexico

a. Toussaint L'Ouverture

b. Haiti

c. Antonio Nariño

d. creoles

e. peninsulares

f. Miguel Hidalgo

g. José Maria Morelos

h. Agustín de Iturbide

i. Stephen Austin

j. Honduras

k. Simón Bolívar

l. Prince Pedro

m. José de San Martín

Name ______________________ Class ______________ Date ______________

Reforms, Revolutions, and War — Section Quiz

Section 4

TRUE/FALSE Mark each statement **T** if it is true or **F** if it is false. If false explain why.

_____ 1. The War of 1812 consisted of a series of battles between France and the United States.

____

____

_____ 2. After Mexico gained independence from Spain, strict laws imposed on American settlers led Texas to fight for its own independence.

____

____

_____ 3. Manifest destiny was the term used to describe the rush to find gold in California in the 1840s.

____

____

_____ 4. The Indian Removal Act of 1830 called for the relocation of five Indian nations to part of the Louisiana Territory in the Great Plains.

____

____

_____ 5. President Lincoln's Emancipation Proclamation helped the South in its fight against the Union.

____

____

Name ______________________ Class ______________ Date ______________

Reforms, Revolutions, and War — Chapter Test

Form A

MULTIPLE CHOICE For each of the following, write the letter of the best choice in the space provided.

_____ 1. What was the effect of the Reform Act of 1832?
- a. It gave industrial cities representation in Parliament for the first time.
- b. It gave women the right to vote for members of Parliament.
- c. It regulated working conditions and minimum wages in industry.
- d. It created the United Kingdom by joining England, Ireland, Scotland, and Wales.

_____ 2. Despite Queen Victoria's views,
- a. Pankhurst did not want women's suffrage.
- b. Disraeli voted against extending the vote to women.
- c. Gladstone insisted on independence for Ireland.
- d. Disraeli supported women's voting rights.

_____ 3. The Revolution of 1830 in France replaced Charles X with
- a. Klemens von Metternich.
- b. Émile Zola.
- c. Louis Phillipe.
- d. Emperor Napoleon III.

_____ 4. The Dreyfus affair had a lasting impact because it
- a. kept women from voting for another sixty years.
- b. led to the Revolution of 1848.
- c. barred Jews from holding military commissions for almost a century.
- d. inspired the Zionist movement.

_____ 5. How did Agustín de Iturbide become emperor of Mexico?
- a. by bringing together creoles, peninsulares, royalists, and revolutionaries
- b. by overthrowing the democratically-elected government in a bloodless coup d'etat
- c. by cultivating the favor of the Roman Catholic Church and receiving the title from the pope
- d. by marrying the daughter of the king of Spain

_____ 6. Brazilian colonists achieved their independence from Portugal when
- a. they threatened to fight to the death.
- b. they hired José de San Martín to lead their army.
- c. they attacked the capital city.
- d. Prince Pedro declared Brazil independent.

_____ 7. Americans went to war with Great Britain in 1812 in part because
a. they wanted independence from Britain.
b. Britain was seizing American sailors.
c. Britain blocked the purchase of the Louisiana Territory.
d. Americans wanted to admit Texas as a state.

_____ 8. The Kansas-Nebraska Act
a. set off a bitter debate between proslavery and antislavery Americans.
b. created the Confederate States of America.
c. forced Native Americans to Indian Territory.
d. finalized the Louisiana Purchase.

PRACTICING SOCIAL STUDIES SKILLS Study the graph and passage below and answer the questions that follow.

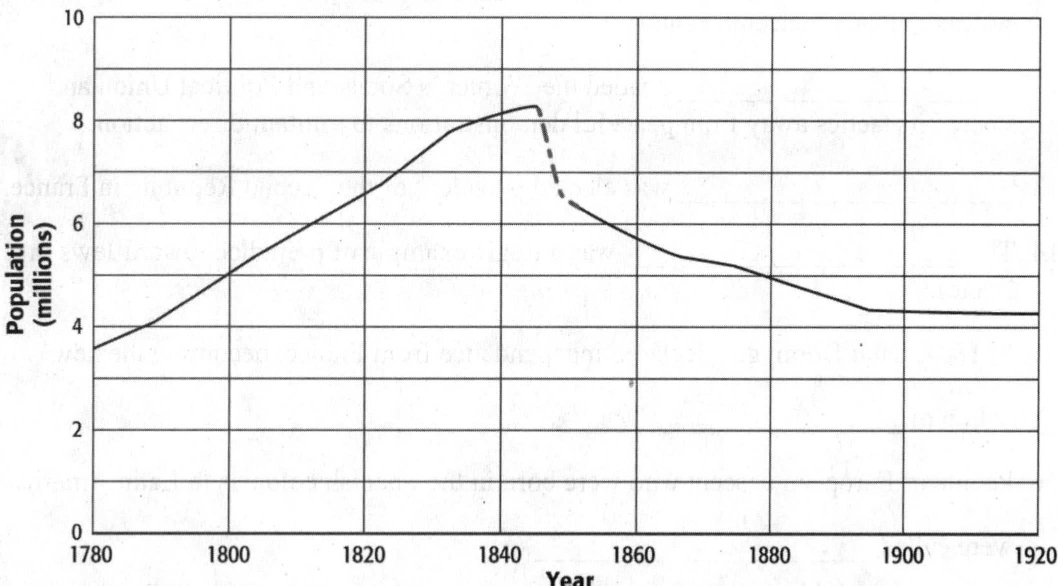

_____ 9. In approximately what year did the Irish population reach its height?
a. 1830
b. 1845
c. 1850
d. 1860

Name ______________ Class ______________ Date ______________

Reforms, Revolutions, and War

Chapter Test

Form A

> **"Other nations have tried to check... the fulfillment of our manifest destiny to overspread the continent allotted by Providence for the free development of our yearly multiplying millions."**
>
> **—John O'Sullivan, editorial, 1845**

_____ 10. This writer referred to the American belief that
- a. Texas was God's country.
- b. Native Americans had no right to any land on the North American continent.
- c. slavery was a just and humane institution.
- d. Americans had a right to settle land all the way to the Pacific Ocean.

FILL IN THE BLANK For each of the following statements, fill in the blank with the appropriate word, phrase, or name.

11. The group known as ______________________ worked for universal manhood suffrage in the nineteenth century.

12. ______________________ headed the Women's Social and Political Union and steered its tactics away from peaceful demonstrations to militant direct action.

13. ______________________ was elected president of the Second Republic in France.

14. The ______________________ was a tragic example of prejudice toward Jews in France.

15. In 1804, Saint Domingue declared independence from France, becoming the new nation of ______________________.

16. People of European descent who were born in the Spanish colonies in Latin America were called ______________________.

17. Spanish colonists in Latin America who were born in Spain were called ______________________.

18. In the ______________________, President James Monroe declared the Americas off limits to further European colonization.

19. After the Civil War, during ______________________, some important legislation and amendments were passed to protect the rights of formerly enslaved people.

Name ______________________________ Class ________________ Date ______________

Reforms, Revolutions, and War

Chapter Test

Form A

TRUE/FALSE Indicate whether each statement below is true or false by writing **T** or **F** in the space provided.

_____ 20. All women in Britain gained the right to vote in 1918.

_____ 21. Benjamin Disraeli argued for women's voting rights in a speech before the House of Commons.

_____ 22. The Revolution of 1848 in France had a far-reaching impact because it inspired similar revolutions across Europe.

_____ 23. The Third Republic began when the French Assembly deposed Napoleon III after he surrendered in the Franco-Prussian War.

_____ 24. José de San Martín wanted to form an independent Federation of the Andes.

_____ 25. The Emancipation Proclamation freed all enslaved people in the United States.

Name ______________________ Class ______________ Date ______________

Reforms, Revolutions, and War

Chapter Test

Form B

SHORT ANSWER On a separate sheet of paper, answer each of the following questions in complete sentences. Remember to use specific examples to support your answers.

1. The Reform Act of 1832 was passed to address what issues?
2. Why was Klemens von Metternich dismayed by events in Europe in the 1830s and 1840s?
3. Describe the compromise that allowed Mexico to win its independence from Spain in 1821.
4. Summarize how the Indian Removal Act of 1830 was one consequence of American belief in manifest destiny.

PRACTICING SOCIAL STUDIES SKILLS Study the graph below and, on a separate sheet of paper, answer the questions that follow in complete sentences.

Population of Ireland, 1780–1920

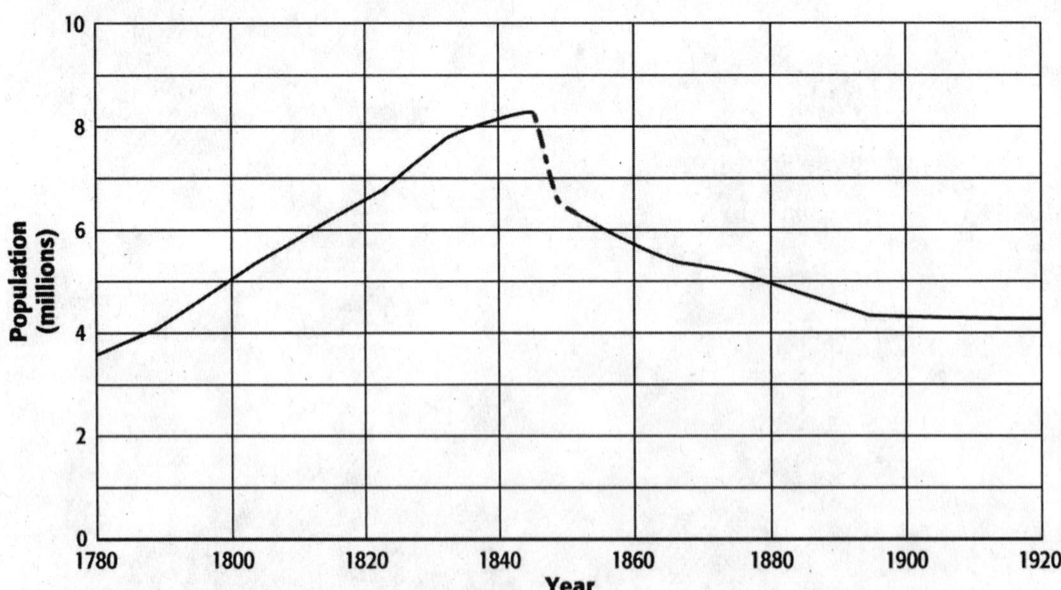

Source: Hearth Tax Returns, Irish Census

5. What accounted for the steep population decline in the 1840s?
6. What might have accounted for the population change that continued after the Great Famine?

Name ______________________ Class ______________ Date ____________

Nationalism in Europe

Section Quiz

Section 1

TRUE/FALSE Mark each statement **T** if it is true or **F** if it is false. If false explain why.

_____ 1. An Italian named Giuseppe Mazzini formed a nationalist group called Young Italy to fight for the unification of the separate Italian states.

____

____

_____ 2. Both Giuseppe Garibaldi and Camillo di Cavour wanted united Italy to be a republic.

____

____

_____ 3. Giuseppe Garibaldi and his followers, known as the Red Shirts, used guerrilla warfare tactics in the military campaign to unify Italy.

____

____

_____ 4. Once southern and northern Italy were united, Giuseppe Garibaldi became the king of Italy.

____

____

_____ 5. After unification, social and economic problems, as well as regional differences, led to a lack of unity among many Italians.

____

____

Name ______________________ Class ______________ Date ______________

Nationalism in Europe

Section Quiz

Section 2

MULTIPLE CHOICE For each of the following, write the letter of the best choice in the space provided.

_____ 1. The Zollverein
a. required Frederick Wilhelm IV to enact democratic reforms.
b. allowed the removal of taxes on products traded between the German states.
c. legislated that the people have the right to elect a king.
d. required composers to write music glorifying German culture.

_____ 2. Otto von Bismarck's political philosophy, later known as realpolitik, meant
a. he developed policies based on the interests of Prussia.
b. he weighed what was best for Europe.
c. he was unwilling to use military force.
d. he insisted that the borders of weaker nations should be protected.

_____ 3. After the Franco-Prussian War
a. Prussia surrendered to France.
b. a unified German empire was established.
c. Germany divided into two nations.
d. Napoleon III ruled the German Confederation.

_____ 4. Bismarck's efforts to limit the influence of the Catholic Church in Germany was called
a. realpolitik.
b. Kulturkampf.
c. reich.
d. Zollverein.

_____ 5. Bismarck sought to reduce the appeal of socialism by
a. vetoing all legislation that aided workers.
b. refusing to invest in industry.
c. assassinating the emperor.
d. enacting his own reforms.

Name ____________________ Class ______________ Date ______________

Nationalism in Europe

Section Quiz

Section 3

MATCHING In the space provided, write the letter of the term, person, or place that matches each description. Some answers will not be used.

_____ 1. The Austrian emperor in 1848

_____ 2. Laws that established censorship of newspapers and created a secret police

_____ 3. Russian troops helped Austria crush this Hungarian group's revolt

_____ 4. Two separate, equal states under one ruler

_____ 5. The possible collapse of the Ottoman Empire that worried European powers

_____ 6. Austrian prince who worked to maintain power of Austrian Empire

_____ 7. Britain, France, and the Ottoman Empire fighting against Russia

_____ 8. Group who fought against the absolute power of the ruler of the Ottoman Empire

_____ 9. Series of conflicts and wars in the Balkans

_____ 10. Event where leaders agreed to provide military intervention to support governments against internal revolution

a. Metternich

b. Magyars

c. "The Eastern Question"

d. Crimean War

e. Congress of Troppau

f. Dual Monarchy

g. Bosnia and Herzegovina

h. Franz Joseph I

i. Carlsbad Decrees

j. Frederick Wilhelm

k. Young Turks

l. Middle East and Africa

m. Balkan Wars

Name ______________________ Class ______________ Date ______________

Nationalism in Europe

Section Quiz

Section 4

FILL IN THE BLANK For each of the following statements, fill in the blank with the appropriate word, phrase, or name.

1. Russian monarchs called ______________________ ruled with absolute power.

2. ______________________ were agricultural peasants who were considered part of the land on which they worked.

3. A government led by one ruler with unlimited power is called a(n) ______________________.

4. ______________________ was convinced that reforms were necessary and freed the serfs.

5. ______________________, the leader of the Russian Marxists, called for the overthrow of the Russian monarch.

6. Russian Marxists wanted to create a ______________________, a government in which there would be no private property, and the state would collectively own and distribute goods.

7. Widespread violent attacks by Russians against Jews were called ______________________.

8. During Nicholas II's reign, Russia began building the ______________________, linking western Russia to Siberia.

9. Troops killed hundreds when an Orthodox priest and a group of protesters marched to the Winter Palace to bring a petition to the czar on a day that became known as ______________________.

10. Rebellions broke out, workers went on strike, university students protested, and peasants rebelled against landlords during the ______________________ of 1905.

Name ______________________ Class ______________ Date ______________

Nationalism in Europe

Chapter Test
Form A

MULTIPLE CHOICE For each of the following, write the letter of the best choice in the space provided.

_____ 1. What goal did Giuseppe Mazzini, Camillo di Cavour, and Giuseppe Garibaldi all have in common?
a. a democratic republic in Italy
b. the unification of Germany
c. the unification of Italy
d. the return of Italy to the glory of the Roman Empire

_____ 2. Giuseppe Garibaldi's actions show that he was most committed to
a. a republican government.
b. achieving political power.
c. the independence of the Catholic Church.
d. a unified Italy.

_____ 3. After Prussian king Frederick Wilhelm IV promised a constitution and reforms
a. he went back on many of his promises.
b. he worked hard to promote democracy.
c. he gave up his throne.
d. war ended his plans.

_____ 4. Which of the following leaders began a program of reforms in Russia?
a. Nicholas I
b. Karl Marx
c. Alexander II
d. Alexander III

_____ 5. What did Otto von Bismarck mean by the phrase "blood and iron"?
a. Germany needed railroads to unite the country.
b. Prussia would fight to obtain iron.
c. He would continue to fight until he was named emperor.
d. He would use the Prussian military as a force for German unification.

_____ 6. Nationalism remained a problem under the Dual Monarchy because
a. Marxists spread discontent.
b. ethnic minorities continued to seek self-government.
c. Franz Joseph I was not a strong leader.
d. Magyars felt they should have special privileges.

_____ 7. What were the Young Turks fighting against in 1908?
a. independence from the Ottoman Empire
b. the absolute power of the sultan
c. reforms and a representative government
d. religious freedom

Name ______________________ Class ______________ Date ______________

Nationalism in Europe

Chapter Test

Form A

PRACTICING SOCIAL STUDIES SKILLS Study the maps below and answer the questions that follow.

The Unification of Italy, 1858–1870

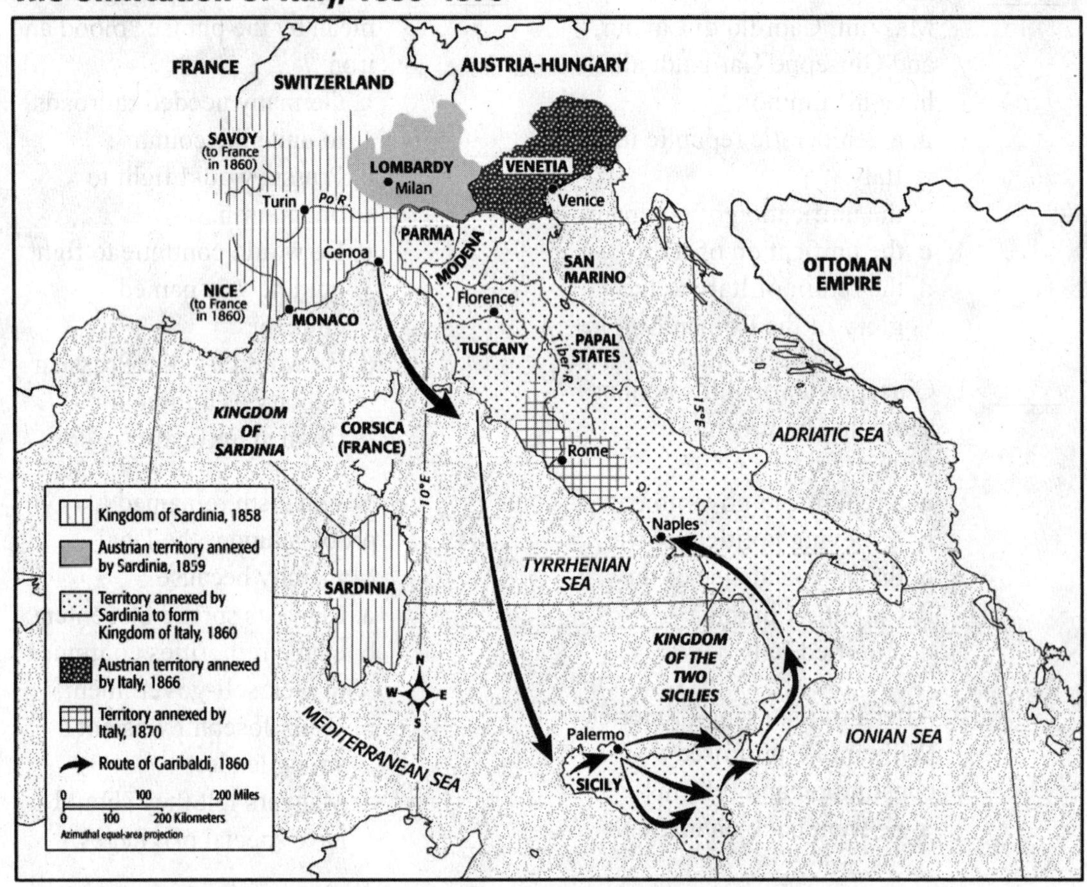

_____ 8. Which area was the last to be annexed by Italy?

a. Sicily
b. the territory surrounding Rome
c. Sardinia
d. the northern states of Savoy, Lombardy, and Venetia

Name ______________________________ Class ________________ Date ________________

Nationalism in Europe

Chapter Test

Form A

The Unification of Germany, 1865–1871

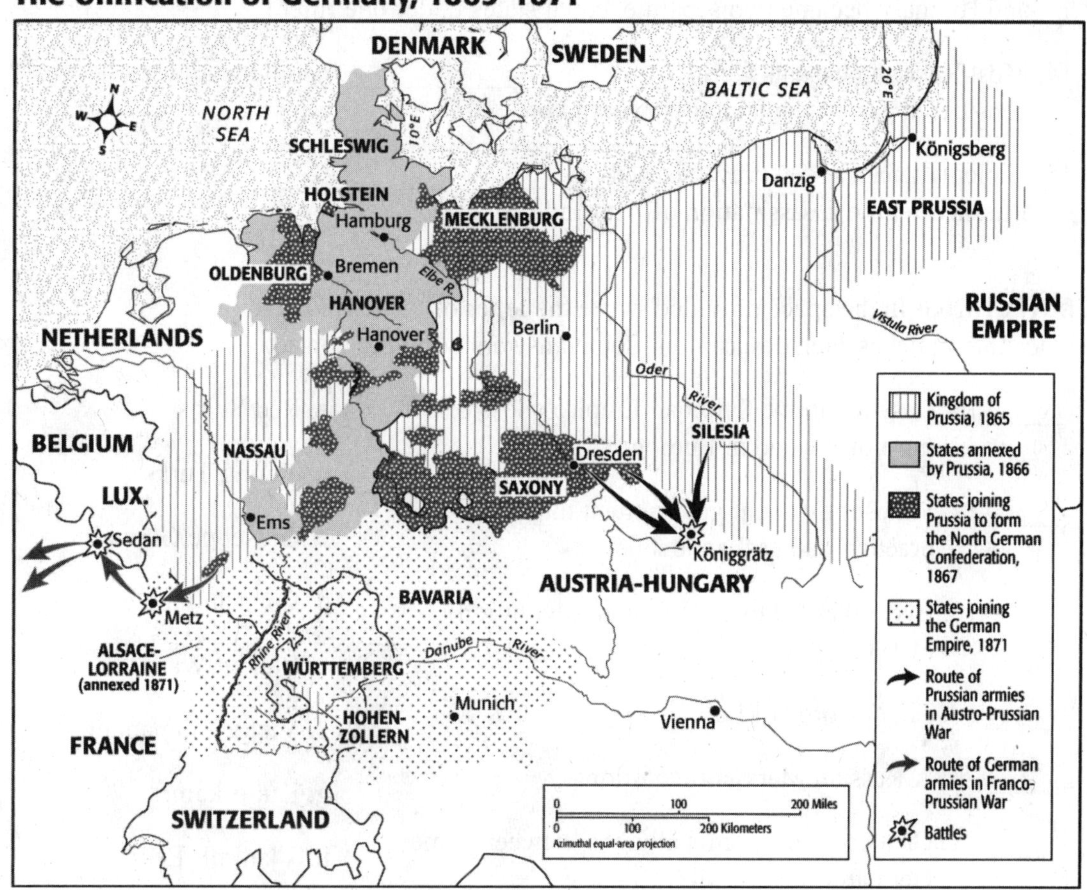

_____ 9. In which direction did the German armies advance during the Franco-Prussian War?

a. west
b. north
c. east
d. northeast

FILL IN THE BLANK For each of the following statements, fill in the blank with the appropriate word, phrase, or name.

10. Devotion to one's national group, or ______________________, was an important force in Europe during the nineteenth century.

11. The disagreement over Schleswig and Holstein gave ______________________ a way to start a war with Denmark.

12. The ______________________ were passed with Metternich's help. They prohibited any reforms that conflicted with absolute monarchy.

Nationalism in Europe

Chapter Test

Form A

13. The Compromise of 1867 created a(n) ______________________ in which Austria and Hungary became two separate, equal states under one ruler.

14. Most Russian peasants were ______________________, people who were considered part of the land they worked on.

15. Violent attacks against Jews, called ______________________, were widespread in Russia after the assassination of Alexander II.

MATCHING In the space provided, write the letter of the term, person, or place that matches each description. Some answers will not be used.

_____ 16. Resulted in the Ottoman Empire's loss of most of its land in Europe

_____ 17. Philosophy about government that was practical rather than idealistic

_____ 18. Event that led to the Russian Revolution of 1905

_____ 19. The "sword" of Italy

_____ 20. A Russian Marxist revolutionary

_____ 21. Created an economic alliance between some German states

_____ 22. Nationalist group in the Ottoman Empire

_____ 23. Struggle between the German government and the Catholic Church

_____ 24. Event where military group refused to declare allegiance to Nicholas I

_____ 25. Defeat in this war added to unrest in Russia

a. Red Shirts
b. Young Turks
c. Giuseppe Garibaldi
d. Constantinople
e. Balkan Wars
f. Victor Emmanuel
g. Kulturkampf
h. Vladimir Lenin
i. Russo-Japanese War
j. Decembrist Revolt
k. realpolitik
l. Zollverein
m. Bloody Sunday

Name ______________________ Class ______________ Date ______________

Nationalism in Europe

Chapter Test

Form B

SHORT ANSWER On a separate sheet of paper, answer each of the following questions in complete sentences. Remember to use specific examples to support your answers.

1. Describe Camillo di Cavour's contribution to the unification of Italy.
2. What challenges did Italy face in the years following unification?
3. How did Prince Metternich try to prevent liberal ideas and movements from endangering the Austrian Empire?
4. Describe the reforms instituted by Alexander II in Russia. Why do you think he enacted these reforms?
5. What was the October Manifesto?

PRACTICING SOCIAL STUDIES SKILLS Study the map below and, on a separate sheet of paper, answer the questions that follow in complete sentences.

The Unification of Germany, 1865–1871

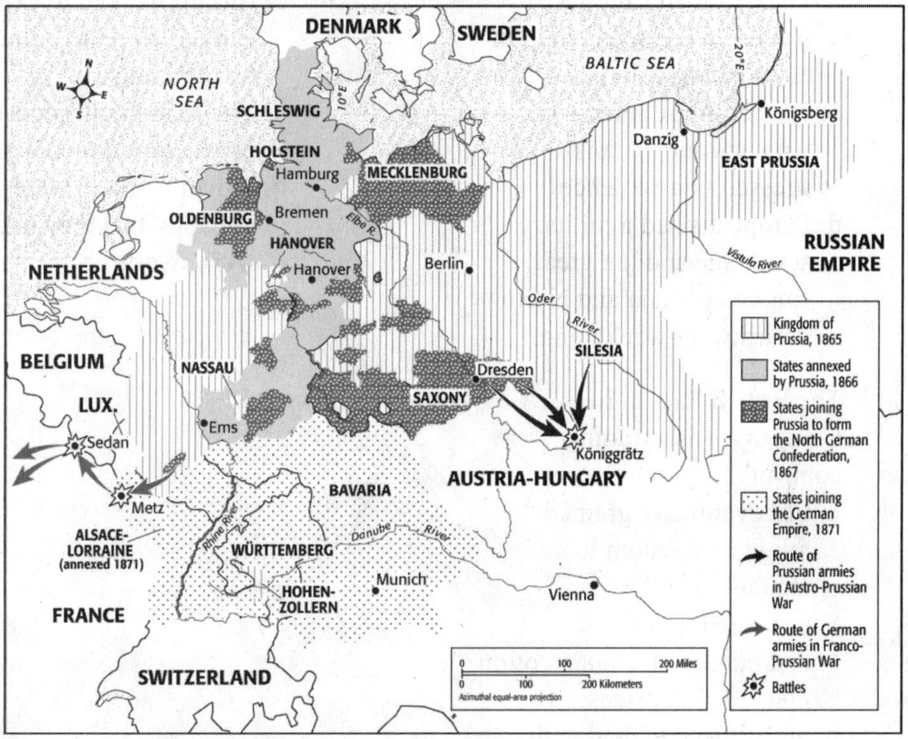

6. Describe how the borders of Prussia changed in 1867.
7. How did the borders of the German Empire in 1871 differ from the borders of Prussia in 1865?

Name ______________________ Class ______________ Date ______________

The Age of Imperialism

Section Quiz

Section 1

MULTIPLE CHOICE For each of the following, write the letter of the best choice in the space provided.

_____ 1. Which of the following phrases describes imperialism?
   a. the process of one people ruling or controlling another
   b. a situation in which one nation trades exclusively with another
   c. the deliberate effort to westernize a country
   d. a equal relationship between two nations

_____ 2. Why were Europeans able to expand their power in Africa and Asia?
   a. Ethnic groups in Africa and Asia invited European rule.
   b. The Ottoman Empire requested European help in establishing colonies.
   c. The religious beliefs of Africans and Asians stressed non-violence.
   d. Europeans had a military advantage and the great empires of Asia and North Africa were weakening.

_____ 3. The British East India Company was a trading company
   a. that eventually granted religious freedom to Hindus.
   b. that ruled India.
   c. that purchased Indian cotton goods at fair prices.
   d. that refused to deal with Indians.

_____ 4. The Sepoy Mutiny was significant because
   a. it led to direct British rule in India.
   b. it ended the relationship between India and Britain.
   c. it forced the British to release the sepoys from duty.
   d. it led to a direct democracy in Indian government.

_____ 5. How did British rule affect the Indian textile industry?
   a. The British closed Indian textile factories, which devastated the industry.
   b. Britain worked to expand and develop the Indian textile industry.
   c. The British introduced new products and techniques.
   d. Indian workers were unhappy that they had to work overtime.

Name ______________________________ Class ________________ Date ________________

The Age of Imperialism

Section Quiz

Section 2

FILL IN THE BLANK For each of the following statements, fill in the blank with the appropriate word, phrase, or name.

1. In the late 1700s, the Chinese restricted trade with Europeans to the city of ________________________.

2. The Treaty of Nanjing is an example of a(n) ________________________ because it benefited the British at the expense of the Chinese.

3. The ________________________ began in 1899 when rebels attacked missionaries and Chinese converts to Christianity.

4. After the Taiping Rebellion, reform-minded Qing officials tried to make changes because of strong resistance from ________________________ scholars and powerful officials.

5. In 1911, after 268 years of Qing rule, revolutionaries declared China a ________________________.

6. The Treaty of Kanagawa and other treaties, allowed American ships to stop at Japanese ports and established ________________________ for Westerners in Japan.

7. In Tokugawa Japan, the primary source of power lay in the hands of the supreme military ruler, or ________________________.

8. In Japan, the Meiji period began when the ________________________ returned to power.

9. The ________________________ took control of Vietnam and annexed Laos and Cambodia.

10. ________________________, the only Southeast Asian country to retain its independence in the 1800s, served as a buffer between British-controlled Burma and French Indochina.

The Age of Imperialism

Section Quiz

Section 3

TRUE/FALSE Mark each statement **T** if it is true or **F** if it is false. If false explain why.

_____ 1. The "Scramble for Africa" is a term describing a new type of imperialism in which European countries rushed to settle colonies on the African continent so that people from the home countries could move there.

____

____

_____ 2. Imperialism in Africa reflected struggles for power among European nations, such as the long-term rivalry between France and Britain.

____

____

_____ 3. The United States occupied Egypt in 1882 to protect its interests and maintain the security of the Suez Canal.

____

____

_____ 4. In the early 1800s, Zulu leader Shaka built a strong kingdom, which the British invaded and annexed as a colony.

____

____

_____ 5. Ethiopian forces led by Menelik II were defeated by the Italians at the Battle of Adowa.

____

____

Name ______________________ Class ______________ Date ______________

The Age of Imperialism

Section Quiz

Section 4

MATCHING In the space provided, write the letter of the term, person, or place that matches each description. Some answers will not be used.

_____ 1. Rebel leader in the Philippines who had cooperated with U.S. forces against the Spanish

_____ 2. The 1910 Mexican presidential candidate who called for a revolution against the Díaz government

_____ 3. U.S. vow to use military might to keep Europeans out of the Americas

_____ 4. Rebel leader who attacked the U.S. for supporting Carranza as president of Mexico

_____ 5. One of Spain's colonies in the Americas

_____ 6. Proclamation that the Americas were off-limits to new European imperialist efforts

_____ 7. Sensationalist style of reporting

_____ 8. Part of the constitution of Cuba

_____ 9. Exiled poet and journalist who founded the Cuban Revolutionary Party

_____ 10. Result of U.S. support of an uprising against Colombia

a. Roosevelt Corollary

b. yellow journalism

c. Emilio Aguinaldo

d. Panama Canal

e. Philippines

f. José Martí

g. Francisco Madero

h. Monroe Doctrine

i. Emilliano Zapata

j. Victoriano Huerta

k. Francisco "Pancho" Villa

l. Cuba

m. Platt Amendment

Name ______________________ Class ______________ Date ______________

The Age of Imperialism

Chapter Test
Form A

MULTIPLE CHOICE For each of the following, write the letter of the best choice in the space provided.

_____ 1. Which of the following was one factor that allowed European nations to extend their control over Asia and Africa after 1800?
a. military advantages such as superior weapons
b. the rise of great empires in Asia and North Africa
c. the superiority of European trading networks
d. European democratic traditions

_____ 2. What led the British government to take control of India from the British East India Company?
a. the Mughal Revolt
b. the spice trade
c. missionary impulses
d. the Sepoy Mutiny

_____ 3. Why did Britain begin exporting opium to China?
a. to prevent opium from going to British subjects
b. to change the balance of trade in favor of Britain
c. to make colonization of China easier
d. to improve the health of Chinese citizens

_____ 4. The Treaty of Kanagawa contributed to
a. the shogun's power.
b. a rise in nationalism.
c. the prestige of the Tokugawas.
d. Japanese wealth through high tariffs.

_____ 5. Why did the British occupy Egypt in 1882?
a. to rebuild the Suez Canal to accommodate larger ships
b. to set up trading posts along the coast
c. to maintain access to the Suez Canal
d. to secure the Congo River

_____ 6. How did the politics of General Antonio López de Santa Anna change during his years in power?
a. He first allied with liberal reformers but later became conservative.
b. He seized power in a conservative military coup, but became a liberal reformer.
c. He first courted the United States and then rebelled against it.
d. He used the Catholic Church to gain power but then limited the Church's power.

Name ______________ Class ______________ Date ______________

Form A

PRACTICING SOCIAL STUDIES SKILLS Study the print below and answer the question that follows.

The Art Archive/British Museum

_____ 7. This Japanese print depicts the arrival of Commodore Perry in Edo Bay in 1853. Which statement below does the print help to illustrate?

a. There was growing tension between young and old in Japanese society.

b. The military might of Japan forced Commodore Perry to surrender his warships.

c. The United States warships were meant to send the Japanese a message about American military strength.

d. Commodore Perry failed to establish contact with the Japanese people.

Name ______________________ Class ______________ Date ______________

The Age of Imperialism — Chapter Test

Form A

Imperialism in Africa

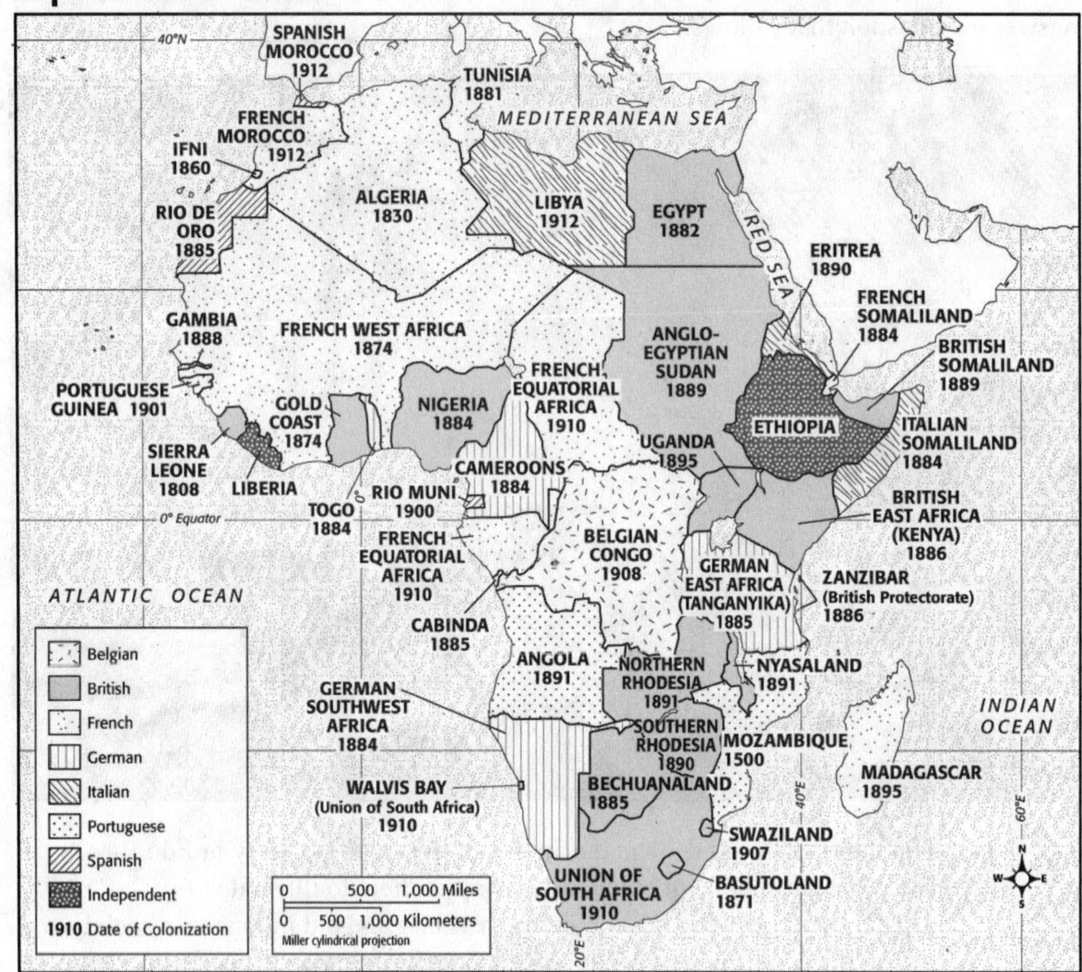

_____ 8. By what year had most of Africa been colonized?

a. 1850
b. 1880
c. 1910
d. 1940

FILL IN THE BLANK For each of the following statements, fill in the blank with the appropriate word, phrase, or name.

9. By 1800, the ______________________ Company ruled much of India.

10. The British ______________________ is the era of British rule in India.

11. The most prominent radical calling for revolutionary change in early 20th-century China was ______________________.

12. One motive for imperialism was economic. Europeans wanted

    ________________________ such as cotton and rubber to manufacture goods.

13. ________________________ is a philosophy that argues that certain nations or races are more fit than others, and that it is natural for the "fit" to rule the "less fit."

14. The ________________________ linked the Mediterranean with the Red Sea.

15. The United States sent ________________________ to several Latin American countries with the stated goal of restoring civil order.

16. The ________________________ declared the Americas off-limits to European imperialism except for colonies that already existed.

TRUE/FALSE Indicate whether each statement below is true or false by writing **T** or **F** in the space provided.

_____ 17. If the Mughal Empire had remained strong, British trade in India would have remained limited.

_____ 18. Indian elites and middle classes welcomed British rule because the British strengthened the market for goods manufactured in India.

_____ 19. The Treaty of Nanjing was the first of the unequal treaties between China and Western European countries.

_____ 20. In the late nineteenth century, Germany, Russia, Britain, and France all carved out spheres of influence in China.

_____ 21. Key reforms during the Meiji era helped Japan quickly become one of the world's great industrial powers.

_____ 22. The "Scramble for Africa" was prompted by economic interests, political competition between European powers, and cultural motives such as teaching European customs.

_____ 23. Political turmoil in Mexico ended when Mexico became a republic in 1823.

_____ 24. The Spanish-American War began when a U.S. battleship exploded in a Cuban harbor.

_____ 25. For their support in the Spanish-American War, the United States granted independence to the Philippines in 1900.

SHORT ANSWER On a separate sheet of paper, answer each of the following questions in complete sentences. Remember to use specific examples to support your answers.

1. What conditions in India led to the Sepoy Mutiny?
2. What was the Taiping Rebellion and what were its costs?
3. If you had lived in China in 1911, would you have supported or opposed the 1911 Revolution? Explain your answer.
4. How did the imperialism of the late 19th century differ from the imperialism of the 1500s and 1600s?
5. What was the purpose of the Roosevelt Corollary?

PRACTICING SOCIAL STUDIES SKILLS Study the image below and, on a separate sheet of paper, answer the question that follows in complete sentences.

The Art Archive/British Museum

6. The image above is a Japanese print of Commodore Perry's arrival in Edo Bay in 1853. Based on your knowledge of the chapter, what do you think the artist was trying to convey about this event?

Name ______________________ Class ______________ Date ______________

Industrialization and Nationalism

Unit Test

Form A

MATCHING In the space provided, write the letter of the person that matches each description. Some answers will not be used.

_____ 1. The Father of American Industry

_____ 2. Built an affordable line of cars

_____ 3. Concluded that human behaviors are a series of connected conditioned reflexes

_____ 4. Developed the first usable and practical light bulb

_____ 5. Founder of a women's suffrage group that adopted destructive tactics

_____ 6. Began a movement called Zionism

_____ 7. A leading force behind German unification in the late 1800s

_____ 8. the "sword" of Italy

_____ 9. Served as Mexico's president seven times

_____ 10. Filipino rebel who cooperated with U.S. forces against the Spanish

a. Theodor Herzl

b. Giuseppe Garibaldi

c. Thomas Edison

d. Emilio Aguinaldo

e. Otto von Bismark

f. Samuel Slater

g. Giuseppe Mazzini

h. Franz Joseph

i. Louis Kossuth

j. Henry Ford

k. Emmeline Pankhurst

l. Antonio López de Santa Anna

m. Ivan Pavlov

FILL IN THE BLANK For each of the following statements, fill in the blank with the appropriate word, phrase, or name.

11. The era when the use of power-driven machinery was developed is called the ______________________.

12. The ______________________ movement was started by people opposed to the machines that put them out of work.

13. In his book, *On the Origin of the Species*, ______________________ discussed his concept of natural selection.

14. In the 1890s, the study of the mind and human behavior emerged as a separate field known as ______________________.

15. Parliament passed the ______________________ Act of 1833 to limit the working hours of children in the textile industry.

16. In 1839, a group in Great Britain called the _________________ worked for voting rights for all men.

17. The ______________________ declared the Americas off limits to further European colonization.

18. The ______________________, led by Garibaldi, used guerrilla warfare tactics to unify Italy.

19. Nicholas II issued the ______________________, which promised a Russian constitution and guaranteed individual liberties to all Russians in 1905.

20. The Treaty of ____________________, and other treaties, humiliated the Japanese because they opened Japanese ports to Westerners.

TRUE/FALSE Indicate whether each statement below is true or false by writing **T** or **F** in the space provided.

_____ 21. The famine in Ireland that resulted from potato crop failures increased Irish resentment against the British.

_____ 22. The Meiji Restoration marked the emperor's return to power in Japan.

_____ 23. The enclosure movement resulted in an increased food supply.

_____ 24. The coal that was burned to run steam engines and warm homes created health problems for people in industrial cities.

_____ 25. Michael Faraday's discoveries led to the development of electrical generators.

_____ 26. The Theory of Relativity was Darwin's belief that species change and adapt over time.

_____ 27. New Zealand became the first country to give women the vote.

_____ 28. The period of Reconstruction following the Civil War was a period of rebuilding in the North.

_____ 29. The Compromise of 1867 created the Dual Monarchy of Austria-Hungary with two separate, equal states and two rulers.

_____ 30. Bloody Sunday is the day in Russian history when the czar's supporter rose up against the Russian ruler Vladimir Lenin.

Name ______________________ Class ______________ Date ______________

Industrialization and Nationalism

Unit Test

Form A

MULTIPLE CHOICE For each of the following, write the letter of the best choice in the space provided.

_____ 31. What factors of production led to Great Britain's economic success in the 1700s?
a. water, steam, and coal
b. land, labor, and capital
c. credit, risk, and exploration
d. politics, military, and farming

_____ 32. Factory employees hired women and children because women and children
a. were paid less.
b. were better educated.
c. could work longer hours.
d. could be easily trained.

_____ 33. Factory working conditions improved after the formation
a. of the Luddites.
b. of work teams.
c. of labor unions.
d. of craft guilds.

_____ 34. An increase in the availability of cheaper goods in America in the mid-1800s was a result
a. of mass production.
b. of increased imports.
c. of increased exports.
d. of economic recession.

_____ 35. Which was a result of the development of public transportation?
a. urbanization
b. industrialization
c. decreased auto production
d. development of suburbs

_____ 36. Adam Smith became the leading advocate of
a. mass production.
b. agriculture reform.
c. laissez-faire economics.
d. public education for all.

_____ 37. In 1840, the first women's rights convention was organized by Elizabeth Cady Stanton and
a. Florence Kelly.
b. Lucretia Mott.
c. Jane Addams.
d. Sojourner Truth.

_____ 38. The Reform Act of 1832 gave more British citizens the chance to
a. live in new cities.
b. start businesses.
c. work fewer hours a day.
d. take part in politics

_____ 39. Manifest Destiny contributed
a. to suburban spread.
b. to industrial centers.
c. to westward expansion.
d. to public transportation.

_____ 40. The secession of South Carolina led to the
a. Civil War.
b. War of 1812.
c. expansion of Texas.
d. Louisiana Purchase.

Name ______________ Class ______________ Date ______________

_____ 41. The Austro-Prussian War was the first step towards
a. Austrian dominance.
b. German unification.
c. a military dictatorship.
d. lasting peace in Europe.

_____ 42. As revolts spread in Europe, Metternich helped to pass the Carlsbad Decrees which
a. squashed the revolution brewing in Hungary.
b. prevented reforms that conflicted with absolute monarchy.
c. allowed Serbian representation in their government.
d. forced Austria, Russia, and Prussia to control nationalism.

_____ 43. The efforts of the Young Turks in the Ottoman Empire brought about
a. the return of the monarchy.
b. military domination.
c. civil war.
d. a more representative, liberal government.

_____ 44. Czar Alexander II took the historic step of
a. freeing the Russian serfs.
b. forming a socialist republic.
c. expanding the Russian borders.
d. restoring an absolute monarchy.

_____ 45. The Sepoy Mutiny was caused
a. by a decrease in textile exports.
b. by social segregation in India.
c. by the introduction of a new type of rifle.
d. by conflicts between Muslims and Hindus.

_____ 46. When Chinese officials ordered the destruction of British opium in Guangzhou, the British
a. responded by attacking China.
b. sold the opium to the Japanese.
c. agreed that smuggling opium was immoral.
d. used diplomatic means to negotiate the Opium Treaty with China.

_____ 47. The requests of the Indian National Congress to the British were
a. radical and caused British outrage.
b. modest and later became radical.
c. benefited Muslims.
d. led to a Bengal state.

_____ 48. Kipling's phrase " the white man's burden"

a. represents the view of Europeans who felt that imperialism was difficult to fund.

b. represents the view of Indians and Africans who felt British were an imperialist burden they had to bear.

c. became the slogan of the Berlin Conference.

d. represents the view of Europeans who believed they had a duty to educate those they saw as inferior.

Name ______________________ Class ______________ Date ______________

PRACTICING SOCIAL STUDIES SKILLS Study the map below and answer the questions that follow.

Expansion of Railroads

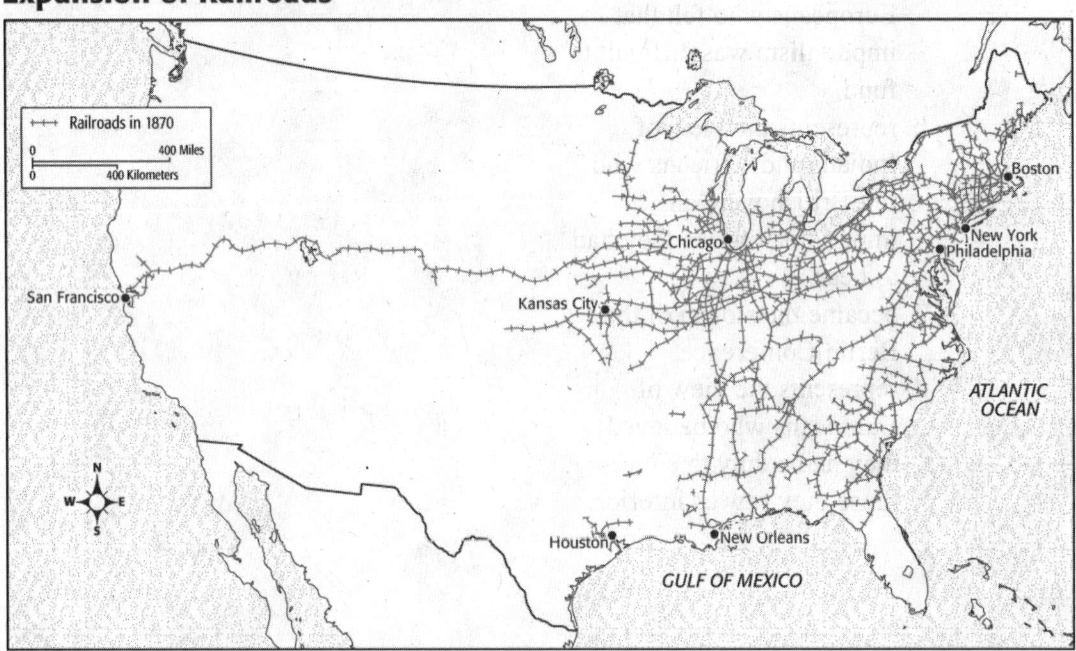

_____ 49. According to the map, in the late 1800s, manufactured goods became more available in the American West because

a. from Houston, goods were shipped by train to San Francisco.
b. industrialists funded a highway to San Francisco.
c. the Panama Canal was completed.
d. by 1870 there was a railroad line across the United States.

_____ 50. As shown on the map, railroad lines in 1870

a. all led to Houston.
b. were concentrated between Houston and New Orleans.
c. connected Mexico and Canada.
d. were concentrated in the northeast.

Industrialization and Nationalism

Unit Test

Form B

SHORT ANSWER On a separate sheet of paper, answer each of the following questions in complete sentences. Remember to use specific examples to support your answers.

1. What five factors made Great Britain the ideal location for the birth of the Industrial Revolution?
2. Describe the working conditions in British factories in the late 1700s and early 1800s.
3. Describe life in an American industrial city in the early 1900s.
4. Explain how the Reform Act of 1832 dealt with the inequalities of representation in the British government.
5. Describe the events that led to the Civil War.
6. How did British imperialism contribute to the Sepoy Mutiny?
7. What led to the Opium Wars?
8. What challenges did Italy face in the years after unification?
9. Explain Otto von Bismarck's political philosophy.
10. Explain how the Bessemer process contributed to transportation and trade.

Name ____________________ Class ____________ Date ____________

Industrialization and Nationalism

Unit Test

Form B

PRACTICING SOCIAL STUDIES SKILLS Study the map below and, on a separate sheet of paper, answer the question that follows in complete sentences.

Imperialism in Africa

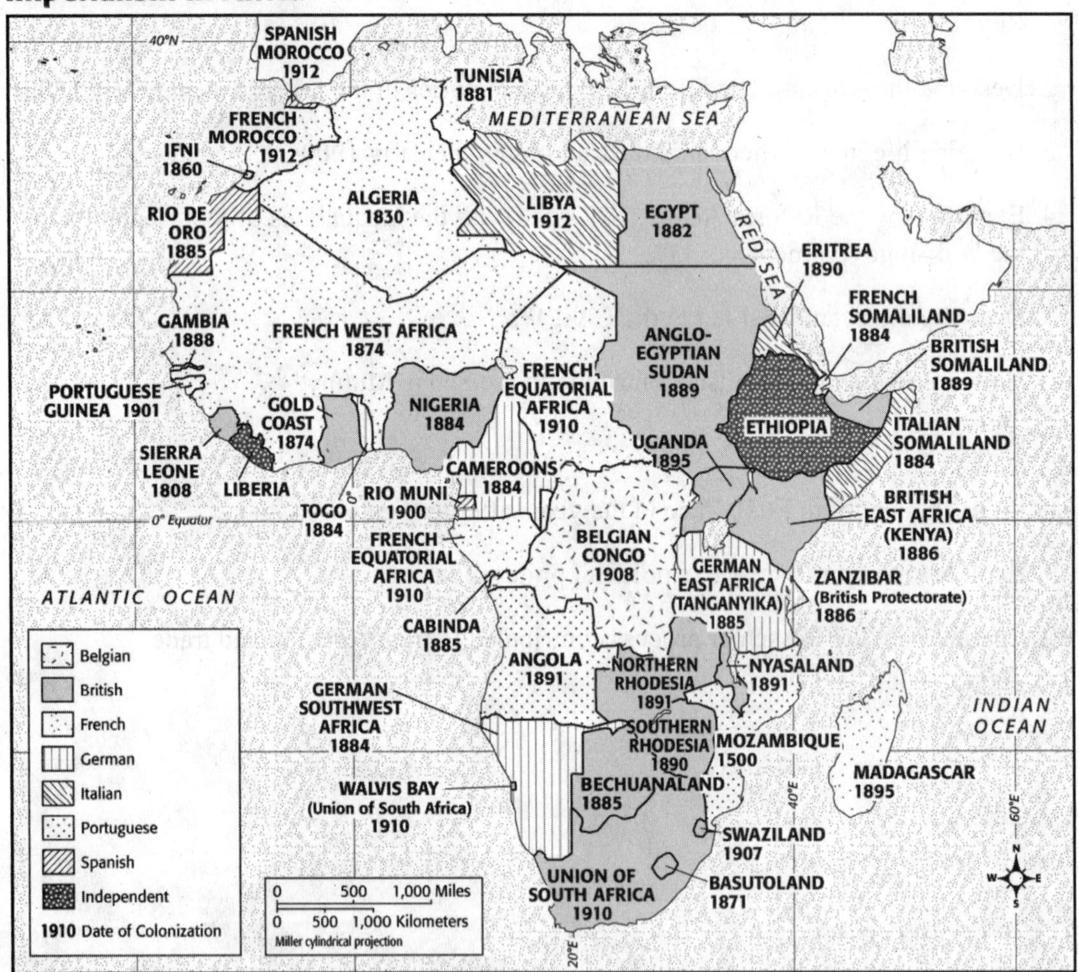

11. Use information from the map to summarize what you have learned about imperialism in Africa.

Name ______________________ Class ______________ Date ______________

World War I

Section Quiz

Section 1

MULTIPLE CHOICE For each of the following, write the letter of the best choice in the space provided.

_____ 1. In 1914, which factor created tensions in Europe?
a. militarism
b. alliances
c. imperialism
d. all of the above

_____ 2. Nationalism
a. was the sole cause of World War I.
b. is a partnership between allies.
c. was exclusive to Serbia.
d. is devotion to one's national group or culture.

_____ 3. The Triple Alliance united
a. Germany, France, and Italy.
b. Germany, Austria-Hungary, and Italy.
c. France, Russia, and Great Britain.
d. Germany, France, and Russia.

_____ 4. France, Russia, and Great Britain became known as the
a. Central Powers.
b. Triple Entente.
c. Ottoman Empire.
d. Triple Alliance.

_____ 5. Austria-Hungary declared war on Serbia because
a. a Serb assassinated the Austrian archduke.
b. Serbia was a military threat.
c. Serbia was a Central Power.
d. Serbia had vast resources.

_____ 6. The Allied Powers were made up of
a. Great Britain, France, Russia, and Serbia.
b. Germany and Austria-Hungary.
c. Belgium and Serbia.
d. Germany, France, Russia, and Serbia.

_____ 7. When the war began, Germany moved through Belgium towards
a. Serbia.
b. Russia.
c. France.
d. Austria.

_____ 8. German forces awaited the Allied attack along the Aisne River in
a. tents.
b. trees.
c. trenches.
d. tunnels.

_____ 9. Another name for World War I is the
a. Trench War.
b. Allied War.
c. Great War.
d. Western War.

_____ 10. By late 1914 it was clear
a. the Western Front had become deadlocked.
b. few soldiers would die.
c. Germany would win.
d. France would surrender.

Name ______________________ Class ______________ Date ______________

World War I

Section Quiz

Section 2

MATCHING In the space provided, write the letter of the term or place that matches each description. Some answers will not be used.

_____ 1. Fighting from deep ditches

_____ 2. One of the new weapons used in the war

_____ 3. Pioneered the use of tanks in World War I

_____ 4. When a society uses all its resources to fight a war

_____ 5. Information designed to influence people's opinions

_____ 6. Purpose of this battle was to "bleed France white"

_____ 7. British attack that took place in the Somme River area of France

_____ 8. A disastrous British offensive in Belgium

_____ 9. The fight over an important sea passage called the Dardanelles

_____ 10. The deliberate destruction of a racial, political, or cultural group

a. the British

b. propaganda

c. genocide

d. the Battle of Verdun

e. poison gas

f. the Battle of the Somme

g. the Ottoman Empire

h. the Gallipoli Campaign

i. trench warfare

j. the Third Battle of Ypres

k. the Turks

l. the Caucasus

m. total war

World War I

Section Quiz
Section 3

TRUE/FALSE Mark each statement **T** if it is true or **F** if it is false. If false explain why.

_____ 1. A small Marxist group called the Bolsheviks wanted to lead a revolution against Czar Nicholas' government.

____

____

_____ 2. Russia's military was strong due to efficient factories, a strong transportation system and high quality military leaders.

____

____

_____ 3. Czar Nicholas II took charge of the Russian forces because he had a strong military background.

____

____

_____ 4. Grigory Rasputin helped raise Russia's morale after doing poorly in the war.

____

____

_____ 5. After taking over leadership of Russia, Vladimir Lenin established a radical Communist program, making private ownership of land illegal.

____

____

Name ______________________ Class ______________ Date ______________

World War I

Section Quiz

Section 4

FILL IN THE BLANK For each of the following statements, fill in the blank with the appropriate word, phrase, or name.

1. The German submarine attack on the ____________________, as well as attacks on other ships carrying American passengers, influenced the United States to enter World War I.

2. In the early years of World War I, the United States was a ____________________ country because President Woodrow Wilson did not want to become involved in a huge conflict on the other side of the Atlantic Ocean.

3. Germany's attacks on civilian ships were part of a policy called ____________________.

4. German submarines were known as ____________________.

5. The secret message from a German diplomat to officials in Mexico encouraging Mexico to attack the United States is known as the ____________________.

6. In April 1917, the United States entered World War I on the side of the ____________________.

7. After Allied forces broke through the Hindenburg Line, German leaders approached the Allies seeking a(n) ____________________, or truce.

8. Woodrow Wilson's plan for world peace was called the ____________________.

9. The ____________________ forced Germany to pay money to war victims, return seized land, and to reduce its military.

10. The organization of world governments Woodrow Wilson had envisioned in his plan for world peace was called the ____________________.

World War I

Chapter Test

Form A

MULTIPLE CHOICE For each of the following, write the letter of the best choice in the space provided.

_____ 1. Austria-Hungary opposed the formation of a "greater Serbia" because
a. its leaders strongly supported the principle that all people should choose their own government.
b. the government's policy forbade negotiating with terrorists.
c. any Serbian expansion might encourage other ethnic groups to rebel.
d. the Serbs had pledged to join the Triple Entente once they achieved independence.

_____ 2. Which of the following best describes Germany's position for much of the war?
a. All of Germany's military efforts were focused on Serbia.
b. Germany faced war on two fronts.
c. Germany did not have a military strategy for this war.
d. Germany was a neutral country.

_____ 3. Why did both sides in World War I turn to new weapons?
a. because trench warfare had led to a stalemate
b. because there were not enough weapons to arm the millions of soldiers
c. because advances in radar technology made bombers almost useless
d. because both sides wanted to avoid the deaths of too many soldiers

_____ 4. Which of the following was a social change influenced by the war?
a. The government took permanent control of heavy industry.
b. Universal public education was implemented.
c. All men won the right to vote, regardless of race or class.
d. Public views of what women could do were transformed.

_____ 5. Many colonial people volunteered to fight for the Allied forces because they
a. hated Communism.
b. hoped their service would win their colony's independence.
c. believed in the German cause.
d. supported the terrorist acts used by the Serbians.

_____ 6. Czar Nicholas II welcomed World War I because he
a. hated the United States and wanted to defeat them.
b. believed that all ethnic groups should have the right to rule themselves.
c. hoped a surge of patriotism would overcome domestic problems and unite the country around his leadership.
d. was a brilliant military commander and led most effectively on the battlefield.

_____ 7. Bolshevik opponents came to be called
a. the Red Army.
b. Soviets.
c. Marxists.
d. the White Army.

_____ 8. What was the Zimmermann Note?
a. the German policy of attacking all ships entering or leaving Great Britain
b. Wilson's speech detailing reasons why the United States should remain neutral
c. a note left behind by a suicide bomber in Serbia
d. a proposal by a German official that Mexico attack the United States in return for territory

_____ 9. Which of the following battles signified a turning point in the Allied Powers' favor in the war?
a. the Second Battle of the Marne
b. the Battle of the Frontiers
c. the Battle of Verdun
d. The Battle of Caporetto

PRACTICING SOCIAL STUDIES SKILLS Study the passage and the photo below and answer the questions that follow. COMP: do photo credit per Holt style

> **"All private ownership of land is abolished immediately without compensation [payment to the owners]. All landowners' estates and all land belonging to the Crown, to monasteries, church lands and all their livestock and… property… are transferred to the disposition of [control of] the township Land Committees…"**

_____ 10. The policy described above was put in place by which of the following?
a. Bolsheviks
b. the Russian monarch
c. the Russian czar
d. Russian capitalists

World War I

Chapter Test

Form A

Hulton-Deutsch/CORBIS

_____ 11. What aspect of World War I is best illustrated by this photo?
a. total war
b. trench warfare
c. the effects of poison gas
d. the Russian Revolution

FILL IN THE BLANK For each of the following statements, fill in the blank with the appropriate word, phrase, or name.

12. The partnership formed between Germany, Austria-Hungary, and Italy in the late 1800s was called the ______________________.

13. During World War I, Serbia, Russia, France, and Great Britain were known as the ______________________.

14. ______________________ is information designed to influence people's opinions.

15. Ottoman leaders were accused of ______________________ when some 600,000 Armenians died in the process of being forcibly removed from the Caucasus.

16. Czarina Alexandra's reliance on ______________________ for advice weakened any remaining public support for the Russian monarchy.

17. The German attack on a passenger liner called the ______________________ helped propel the United States into World War I.

18. Treaties turned a portion of the Ottoman Empire into ______________________, or territories to be ruled by European powers.

TRUE/FALSE Indicate whether each statement below is true or false by writing **T** or **F** in the space provided.

_____ 19. The murder of Archduke Franz Ferdinand of Austria led to the outbreak of World War I.

_____ 20. After being forced to retreat in the Battle of the Marne, Germans were able to defend their position on the Western Front by digging heavily defended trenches.

_____ 21. The Battle of Verdun, the Battle of the Somme, and the Third Battle of Ypres dramatically changed the position of the frontlines.

_____ 22. The Allied Powers gained control of the Dardanelles in the Gallipoli Campaign.

_____ 23. Bolsheviks were able to take over Russia because the Russian people were opposed to the provisional government's continued involvement in World War I.

_____ 24. Lenin's introduction of limited capitalist activity led to improvements in the Russian economy.

_____ 25. The Fourteen Points included provisions for a worldwide reduction of weapons, an affirmation of the right of all people to choose their own governments, and plans to form an organization of the world's nations to protect one another.

Name ______________________ Class ______________ Date ______________

World War I

Chapter Test

Form B

SHORT ANSWER On a separate sheet of paper, answer each of the following questions in complete sentences. Remember to use specific examples to support your answers.

1. How did imperialism and militarism lead Europe to the brink of war in 1914?

2. How did the conflict between Serbia and Austria-Hungary widen into the Great War?

3. Describe the uses and effectiveness of two new weapons developed the war.

4. What conditions in Russia led to the February Revolution?

5. How was Germany punished by the Treaty of Versailles?

PRACTICING SOCIAL STUDIES SKILLS Study the photo below and, on a separate sheet of paper, answer the question that follows in complete sentences.

Hulton-Deutsch/CORBIS

6. Use the photo to describe trench warfare.

Name ______________________ Class ______________ Date ______________

The Interwar Years

Section Quiz

Section 1

MATCHING In the space provided, write the letter of thc term, person, or place that matches each description. Some answers will not be used.

_____ 1. Event that convinced many Indians that they must rid themselves of their British rulers

_____ 2. Nonviolence toward living things

_____ 3. Man who led 100,000 Communist supporters on a 6,000 mile trek

_____ 4. Nationalist party that joined with the Communists in opposing China's warlords

_____ 5. Ruler who wanted to make Iran a modern, independent nation

_____ 6. British proclamation of 1917 declaring support for a Jewish homeland in Palestine

_____ 7. Strikes and protests that swept China in 1919, demanding widespread change

_____ 8. Leader who came to be known as "Father of the Turks"

_____ 9. Indian lawyer who organized nonviolent protests against British policies

_____ 10. Man who led Arab nationalists in seeking the creation of an independent Arab state

a. May Fourth Movement

b. Guomindang

c. Jiang Jieshi

d. Mao Zedong

e. Amritsar Massacre

f. Rowlatt Acts

g. Mohandas Gandhi

h. ahimsa

i. Kemal Atatürk

j. Husayn bin Ali

k. Reza Shah Pahlavi

l. Balfour Declaration

m. Pan-African Congresses

Name ______________________ Class ______________ Date ______________

The Interwar Years Section Quiz

Section 2

TRUE/FALSE Mark each statement **T** if it is true or **F** if it is false. If false explain why.

_____ 1. In the United States during the 1920s, stock market prices were pushed higher as people borrowed money in order to buy the stocks.

____

____

_____ 2. President Hoover believed that the federal government should do more, not less, to regulate business affairs, as his policy decisions showed.

____

____

_____ 3. Under President Roosevelt's New Deal policies, the federal government's role in the lives of Americans greatly decreased.

____

____

_____ 4. British economist John Maynard Keynes believed that governments could limit or prevent economic downturns by spending money.

____

____

_____ 5. The Smoot-Hawley Tariff Act was designed to stimulate trade by encouraging Americans to buy imported goods.

____

____

Name ______________________ Class ______________ Date ______________

The Interwar Years

Section Quiz

Section 3

MULTIPLE CHOICE For each of the following, write the letter of the best choice in the space provided.

_____ 1. Which best describes Japanese industry in the years following World War I?
- a. Many industries experienced a slowdown.
- b. Japan's vast natural resources enabled the country to remain self-sufficient.
- c. The number of strikes and labor disputes decreased after the war.
- d. Japan's exports enabled the country to survive economically.

_____ 2. Which best describes the foreign policy of the Japanese civilian government after World War I?
- a. refusal to honor the requests of other nations
- b. tried to get other nations to turn against one another
- c. willing to cooperate with other nations
- d. only willing to compromise in dealing with other Asian nations

_____ 3. The nationalistic spirit in Japan after World War I can best be described as
- a. belief in a society devoted to the interests of the West.
- b. dedication to protecting the rights of individuals rather than the government.
- c. belief in a strong military and the glory of the nation.
- d. pride in the civilian government.

_____ 4. The Manchurian Incident occurred as a result of
- a. Japan's desire to gain natural resources and compete with large industrial nations.
- b. China's desire to get the United States involved in the conflict between China and Japan.
- c. Japan's desire to stop the Manchurian army from invading.
- d. Japan's attempt to solve the problem of widespread unemployment.

_____ 5. The Anti-Comintern Pact was an agreement between the nations of
- a. China and Japan.
- b. China and Germany.
- c. China and the United States.
- d. Japan and Germany.

Name ______________________ Class ______________ Date ______________

The Interwar Years

Section Quiz

Section 4

FILL IN THE BLANK For each of the following statements, fill in the blank with the appropriate word, phrase, or name.

1. In 1919, Benito Mussolini founded a political party based on ____________________, an authoritarian system that places the good of the nation above all else.

2. A government that practices ____________________ attempts to control all aspects of life.

3. Mussolini's forces successfully invaded ____________________ in 1935.

4. Joseph Stalin's plans to modernize the economy reflected the Soviet system of ____________________, in which the government makes major decisions about the production of goods.

5. In the 1930s, Stalin began a campaign known as the ____________________, designed to get rid people or things considered undesirable, such as opponents of his rule.

6. Many ____________________ starved to death after Stalin punished the republic for opposing collectivism.

7. Peasants who resisted Stalin's taking land from them were executed or sent to the ____________________ in Siberia.

8. In 1933 Hitler was appointed to the position of ____________________, the most powerful post in the German government.

9. In 1935, the ____________________ created a separate legal status for German Jews.

10. Anti-Jewish riots across Germany and Austria on the nights of November 9 and 10, 1938, came to be known as ____________________.

Name ______________________ Class ______________ Date ______________

The Interwar Years

Chapter Test

Form A

MULTIPLE CHOICE For each of the following, write the letter of the best choice in the space provided.

_____ 1. Which of the following helped convince many Indians to rid themselves of their British rulers?
   a. the Long March
   b. the Amritsar Massacre
   c. the Balfour Declaration
   d. the Pan-African Congress

_____ 2. What did Kemal Atatürk and Reza Shah Pahlavi have in common?
   a. Both fought against British colonial rule.
   b. Both honored the requests of the Allied Powers after World War I.
   c. Both wanted to make their nations modern and independent.
   d. Both sought to create religious nations.

_____ 3. How did President Franklin Delano Roosevelt propose to fight the Great Depression?
   a. with a government program known as the New Deal
   b. by increasing production of military weapons and equipment
   c. by buying up stocks at pre-October 1929 prices
   d. by heavily taxing exported goods

_____ 4. Which event caused many Japanese people to question their government's foreign policy with the West?
   a. The United States barred Japanese immigration.
   b. Japan lost territory as a result of the Treaty of Versailles.
   c. The Japanese military demanded final approval of all government decisions.
   d. China won several small skirmishes on the border with Korea.

_____ 5. The Nuremberg Laws differed from earlier anti-Semitism because they
   a. allowed Jewish people to reclaim their citizenship if they renounced their faith.
   b. deported all Jews from Germany for the first time.
   c. defined a person as Jewish based on ancestry of grandparents, not religious beliefs.
   d. aimed at excluding Jews from mainstream life in Germany.

Name ____________________ Class ______________ Date ______________

The Interwar Years

Chapter Test

Form A

PRACTICING SOCIAL STUDIES SKILLS Study the map below and answer the questions that follow.

Japanese Aggression, 1931–1937

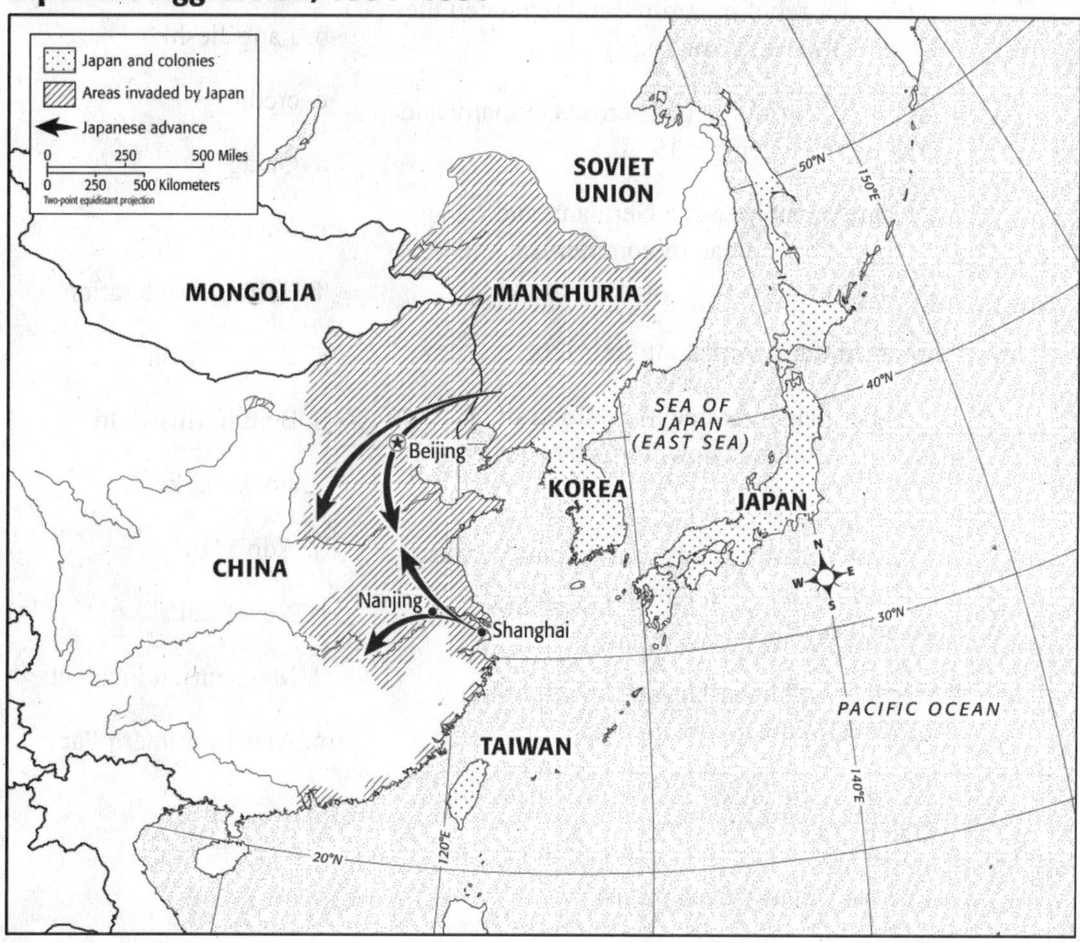

_____ 6. What boundary served as the northern limit of Japanese military aggression?

a. the Chinese boundary with Mongolia
b. the Manchurian boundary with the Soviet Union
c. the Taiwanese boundary with China
d. the Korean boundary with China

_____ 7. How does the map help to explain Japan's lack of success in China?

a. China was too far away for Japan to govern.
b. Countries to the east of Japan were easier to conquer.
c. China was too large for Japan to conquer.
d. Japan did not need the land or resources of China.

Name ____________________ Class ____________ Date __________

The Interwar Years — Chapter Test

Form A

MATCHING In the space provided, write the letter of the term, person, or place that matches each description. Some answers will not be used.

_____ 8. Gave jobs to the unemployed, provided money for relief programs, and regulated the stock market and banking system

_____ 9. Anti-Jewish riots staged across Germany and Austria in November 1938

_____ 10. An agreement between Germany and Japan to oppose the spread of communism and defend one another in case of attack

_____ 11. Boomed during much of the 1920s

_____ 12. Argued that governments could limit or prevent economic downturns by spending money

_____ 13. System of labor camps used to punish those opposed to the Soviet policy of taking land from peasants

_____ 14. Carried out by the Japanese military in defiance of the government

_____ 15. Led the nationalist Guomindang party in China

_____ 16. Led the Chinese Communists

_____ 17. Founded the National Fascist Party in Italy

a. John Maynard Keynes
b. Jiang Jieshi
c. credit
d. Gulag
e. Mao Zedong
f. Balfour Declaration
g. Kristallnacht
h. Benito Mussolini
i. stock market
j. Adolf Hitler
k. New Deal
l. Manchurian Incident
m. Anti-Comintern Pact

FILL IN THE BLANK For each of the following statements, fill in the blank with the appropriate word, phrase, or name.

18. ____________________ was known as "Father of the Turks" because he led in the creation of the Republic of Turkey.

19. Although many Africans fought for independence from European domination, only ____________________ won independence during the interwar years.

20. Gandhi believed in two important concepts—ahimsa, or non-violence, and ____________________.

The Interwar Years

21. On a day known as ______________________, investors in the U.S. stock market sold off 16 million shares.

22. The Japanese invaded and set up a new state in China called ______________________, in order to gain its rich natural resources.

23. Japanese troops killed as many as 300,000 Chinese men, women, and children in the ______________________.

24. An authoritarian form of government that places the good of the nation above all else is called ______________________.

25. A ______________________ government attempts to control all aspects of political, social, and economic life.

Name ______________________ Class ______________ Date ______________

The Interwar Years

Chapter Test

Form B

SHORT ANSWER On a separate sheet of paper, answer each of the following questions in complete sentences. Remember to use specific examples to support your answers.

1. Explain two important concepts that guided the protest movement led by Mohandas Gandhi.

2. Compare and contrast the attitudes of Herbert Hoover and Franklin Roosevelt regarding government response to the Great Depression.

3. Describe characteristics that the governments of Italy, the Soviet Union, and Germany had in common in the interwar years.

4. What factors contributed to Hitler's rise to the most powerful post in the German government?

PRACTICING SOCIAL STUDIES SKILLS Study the map below and, on a separate sheet of paper, answer the question that follows in complete sentences.

Japanese Aggression, 1931–1937

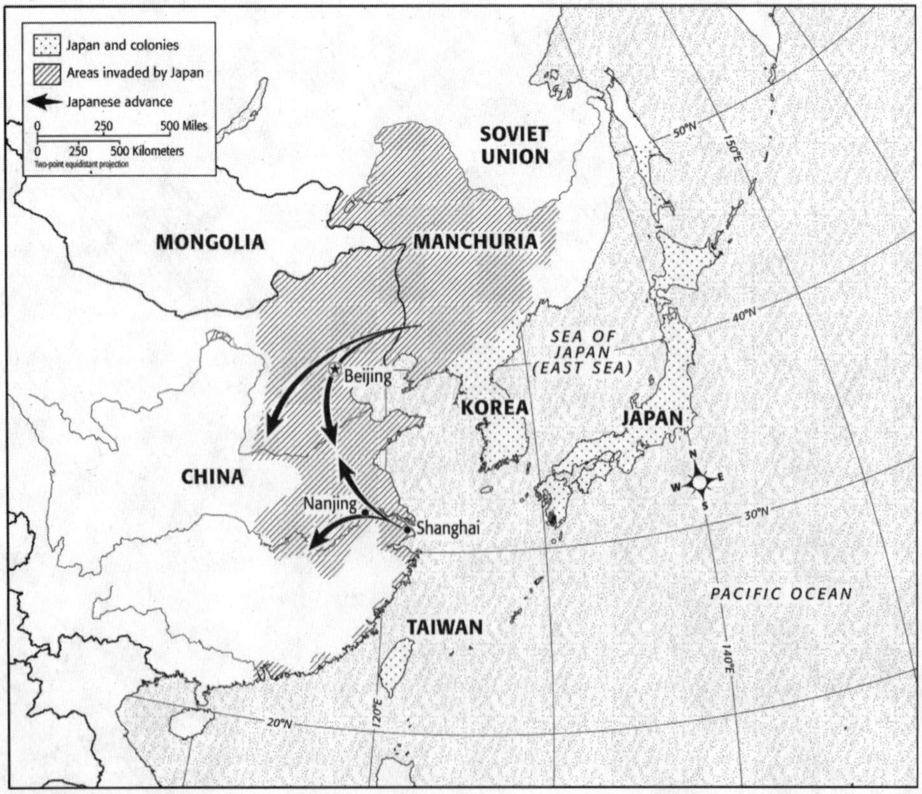

5. How did Japan compare in size to its colonies and the areas it invaded?

Name ______________________ Class ______________ Date ______________

World War II

Section Quiz

Section 1

MATCHING In the space provided, write the letter of the term, person, or place that matches each description. Some answers will not be used.

_____ 1. Formally joined to a country

_____ 2. To give into aggressive demands in order to maintain peace

_____ 3. Prime minister of Great Britain

_____ 4. The military alliance of Germany, Italy, and Japan

_____ 5. When countries agree not to attack each other

_____ 6. German for "lightning war"

_____ 7. Location of the attack that led the U.S. Congress to declare war on Japan

_____ 8. Conflict in which new technology called radar allowed the British to detect German air attacks

_____ 9. Japanese military leader

_____ 10. A desire to stay out of the affairs of other nations

a. allies

b. annexation

c. appeasement

d. Axis Powers

e. Battle of Britain

f. blitzkrieg

g. Francisco Franco

h. Hideki Tojo

i. isolationism

j. nonaggression pact

k. Pearl Harbor

l. sitzkrieg

m. Winston Churchill

Name ______________________ Class ______________ Date ____________

World War II | **Section Quiz**

Section 2

FILL IN THE BLANK For each of the following statements, fill in the blank with the appropriate word, phrase, or name.

1. Bringing military forces to readiness, or ____________________, was an enormous task.

2. British forces not only eliminated the Italian threat to Egypt, they drove into Libya and threatened to gain control of all of ____________________.

3. ____________________ was a German commander known as the Desert Fox.

4. American general ____________________ landed in French North Africa with strong Allied forces.

5. After the Battle of ____________________ in Egypt, Axis power in North Africa was severely weakened.

6. In 1941–1942, Hitler ordered a ____________________, or military blockade of the Russian city of Leningrad.

7. Although over a million Soviet soldiers died in defense of Stalingrad, the result was a ____________________ for Hitler.

8. Although the Americans had fewer ships and aircraft carriers than the Japanese, Americans won the ____________________ because they had broken the secret Japanese code.

9. Japanese pilots known as ____________________ deliberately crashed their planes into Allied ships.

10. The Allied strategy in the Pacific was known as ____________________.

Name ______________________ Class ______________ Date ______________

World War II **Section Quiz**

Section 3

TRUE/FALSE Mark each statement **T** if it is true or **F** if it is false. If false explain why.

_____ 1. Adolf Hitler blamed the German people for many of the country's problems.

____

____

_____ 2. The Final Solution was the deliberate, mass execution of Jewish prisoners.

____

____

_____ 3. Concentration camps were labor camps meant to hold the people Hitler called enemies of the state.

____

____

_____ 4. The Nazi campaign of genocide against the Jews is known today as the "Day of Mourning."

____

____

_____ 5. Although the Germans tried to cover up or destroy evidence of the death camps, Allied troops discovered the camps as they pushed back the Germans.

____

____

Name ______________________ Class ______________ Date ______________

World War II Section Quiz

Section 4

FILL IN THE BLANK For each of the following statements, fill in the blank with the appropriate word, phrase, or name.

1. On June 6, 1944, known as ____________________, nearly 150,000 Allied troops landed on the beaches of Normandy.

2. ____________________ or Victory in Europe Day ended the nearly six years of war in Europe.

3. After capturing the islands of Iwo Jima and ____________________, the next step for the Allies was Japan itself.

4. After Franklin Roosevelt died, ____________________ became president.

5. Truman decided to use the atomic bomb in hopes that ____________________ would surrender.

6. The Japanese emperor, ____________________, acknowledged defeat by surrendering on August 15, 1945.

7. In 1945, at the ____________________ held in Soviet territory, the Allies met to discuss what to do with Europe after the war.

8. The ____________________ was organized to encourage international cooperation and prevent war.

9. August 15, 1945 was the end of World War II and became known as ____________________.

10. At the ____________________ in July 1945, leaders met despite the ill will between the Soviet Union and other Allies.

Name ______________________ Class ____________ Date ____________

World War II

Chapter Test Form A

MULTIPLE CHOICE For each of the following, write the letter of the best choice in the space provided.

_____ 1. Which of the following military alliances became known as the Axis Powers?
a. England and France
b. Germany, Italy, and Japan
c. Czechoslovakia, Poland, and the Rhineland
d. Germany and the Soviet Union

_____ 2. When Hitler attacked the Soviet Union in June 1941, he
a. was breaking the Soviet-German nonaggression pact.
b. threatened the alliance between the Axis Powers.
c. felt invincible because of his victory in Great Britain.
d. hoped to draw the United States into war.

_____ 3. Which group was treated most harshly by the U.S. government during World War II?
a. German Americans
b. African Americans
c. Italian Americans
d. Japanese Americans

_____ 4. Before World War II, Hitler's Nazi government
a. sent *Einsatzgruppen* into the Soviet Union.
b. outlawed emigration.
c. passed restrictive laws severely limiting the rights of Jews.
d. did not limit the rights of any German citizens.

_____ 5. Hitler's Final Solution included
a. opening a second front in Western Europe.
b. less restrictive laws benefiting Germany's Jewish population.
c. concentration camps, death camps, and *Einsatzgruppen*.
d. deportation of European Jews.

_____ 6. How did Hitler respond to the successful invasion of France by the Allies?
a. He ordered a counterattack in Belgium.
b. He invaded the Soviet Union.
c. He reconquered the beaches of Normandy.
d. He personally surrendered to Soviet troops in Berlin.

_____ 7. Roosevelt and Churchill's joint declaration proclaiming what they viewed as the purpose of going to war is called the
a. Atlantic Charter.
b. Treaty of Versailles.
c. Declaration of the Three Powers.
d. Yalta Charter.

PRACTICING SOCIAL STUDIES SKILLS Study the passage and visual below and answer the question that follows.

> **"Here was the greatest misery that I have seen in my whole life. An endless wailing of wounded and dying men… most of them had received nothing to eat for days."**
>
> **—Alois Dorner, German Soldier, January 1943**

_____ 8. This German soldier was referring to
- a. the Battle of Stalingrad.
- b. the Bataan Death March.
- c. the Battle of Midway.
- d. the Battle of Britain.

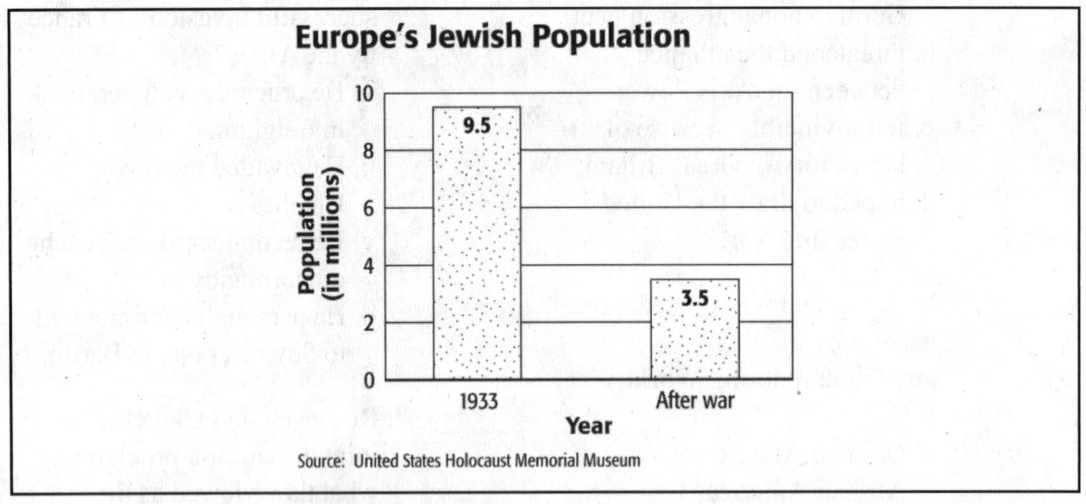

_____ 9. This graph illustrates the
- a. migration of European Jews to Israel after World War II.
- b. deportation of thousands of German Jews by Nazi Germany.
- c. deaths of 6 million Jews worldwide during World War II.
- d. decrease in Europe's Jewish population between 1933 and the conclusion of the war.

World War II

Chapter Test

Form A

MATCHING In the space provided, write the letter of the term, person, or place that matches each description. Some answers will not be used.

_____ 10. A huge death camp

_____ 11. Spoke out against Britain's policy of appeasement

_____ 12. Resulted in the deaths of as many as one million Russian civilians

_____ 13. Celebrated Germany's surrender

_____ 14. War tactic combining air and ground attacks and emphasizing speed

_____ 15. Formed to encourage international cooperation and prevent war

_____ 16. Desire to stay out of the affairs of other nations

_____ 17. The deliberate, mass execution of Jews by the Nazis

_____ 18. Severely weakened the Axis Powers in North Africa

_____ 19. Diminished the Japanese advantage on the seas

a. Battle of Midway

b. isolationism

c. United Nations

d. Battle of El Alamein

e. Auschwitz

f. V-J Day

g. Winston Churchill

h. kamikaze

i. blitzkrieg

j. V-E Day

k. Siege of Leningrad

l. Neville Chamberlain

m. Final Solution

TRUE/FALSE Indicate whether each statement below is true or false by writing **T** or **F** in the space provided.

_____ 20. The militarization of the Rhineland violated the Treaty of Versailles.

_____ 21. The annexation of Austria began World War II.

_____ 22. The United States provided military aid to Great Britain before entering the war.

_____ 23. Many German Jews could not flee Nazi Germany because the United States and many European nations would not allow them to enter.

_____ 24. Only Jews were targeted by the Nazi campaign to kill "inferior" people.

_____ 25. Allied leaders had difficulty reaching agreement at the Potsdam Conference.

World War II

Chapter Test
Form B

SHORT ANSWER On a separate sheet of paper, answer each of the following questions in complete sentences. Remember to use specific examples to support your answers.

1. What two actions that Hitler took convinced him that his European rivals would not stop his aggression against Czechoslovakia?
2. What was the result of the Battle of Midway? Why was it significant?
3. Evaluate the response of the U.S. government to evidence of the widespread killing of Jews in Europe.
4. What was D-Day, and how did it help defeat Germany in Europe?
5. Explain the rationale behind the U.S. government's decision to use the atomic bomb.

PRACTICING SOCIAL STUDIES SKILLS Study the image below and, on a separate sheet of paper, answer the questions that follow in complete sentences.

© Swim Ink 2, LLC/Corbis

6. Explain the purpose of this U.S. propaganda poster.
7. How do you think Americans would have responded to this poster?

Name ____________________ Class ______________ Date ______________

The World at War

Unit Test

Form A

MULTIPLE CHOICE For each of the following, write the letter of the best choice in the space provided.

_____ 1. In 1914, Great Britain declared war on Germany because
a. Germany attacked Belgium.
b. Germany attacked France.
c. Russia supported Serbia.
d. Austria threatened Russia.

_____ 2. What resulted from trench warfare in World War I?
a. Fewer soldiers died in battle.
b. The Allies captured Serbia.
c. The German troops retreated.
d. The Western Front was deadlocked.

_____ 3. How did World War I affect the home front in many nations?
a. Governments eased travel restrictions.
b. Militaries controlled all activity in cities.
c. Civilians conserved food and other goods for military use.
d. Fewer women worked outside the home.

_____ 4. The peace agreement between the nations after World War I is called the
a. New Economic Policy.
b. Treaty of Versailles.
c. Fourteen Points.
d. League of Nations.

_____ 5. The Guomindang of China was the party of the
a. warlords.
b. nationalists.
c. Communists.
d. Chinese separatists.

_____ 6. Which is a result of nationalism in Africa in the post-World War I years?
a. Most African nations became independent.
b. Pan-African Congresses began.
c. Africans participated in the Versailles talks.
d. War broke out between Germany and Egypt.

_____ 7. Several factors contributed to the stock market crash of 1929 including
a. the threat of war.
b. fewer consumer goods were available.
c. increasing consumer reliance on credit.
d. the Smoot-Hawley Tariff Act.

_____ 8. Stalin's Five-Year Plan reflected the Soviet system of
a. central planning.
b. military rule.
c. capitalism.
d. nonviolent change.

_____ 9. The Manchurian Incident showed
   a. the strength of the Japanese military and the weakness of the Japanese government.
   b. the strength of the League of Nations and the weakness of the Japanese military.
   c. the strength of the Chinese military and the weakness of the Japanese military.
   d. the strength of the Japanese government and the weakness of the Japanese military.

_____ 10. The Nuremberg Laws were established to
   a. stop the immigration of Jews to Germany.
   b. include Jews in mainstream German life.
   c. exclude Jews from mainstream German life.
   d. increase government representation for Jews.

_____ 11. What prompted Japan's attack on Pearl Harbor?
   a. Japan wanted to stop the shipment of goods to Europe.
   b. Japan knew the United States had atomic bombs.
   c. The United States threatened Japan with war.
   d. The United States banned the sale of oil to Japan.

_____ 12. The Battle of Midway was significant because it
   a. was the halfway mark of the war.
   b. was the Allies' first major sea battle.
   c. changed the balance of power in the Pacific.
   d. drew the United States into the war.

_____ 13. Hitler's Final Solution called for the
   a. end to World War II.
   b. relocation of prison camps.
   c. the establishment of a separate Jewish state.
   d. deliberate, mass execution of Jewish prisoners.

_____ 14. One result of the Yalta Conference was
   a. establishing a world economy.
   b. that Stalin agreed to join the United Nations.
   c. that Stalin refused to join the fight against Japan.
   d. the Allies had no trouble agreeing on plans for peace.

Name ______________________ Class ______________ Date ______________

The World at War

Unit Test
Form A

PRACTICING SOCIAL STUDIES SKILLS Study the graphs below and answer the question that follows.

Unemployment, 1929–1933

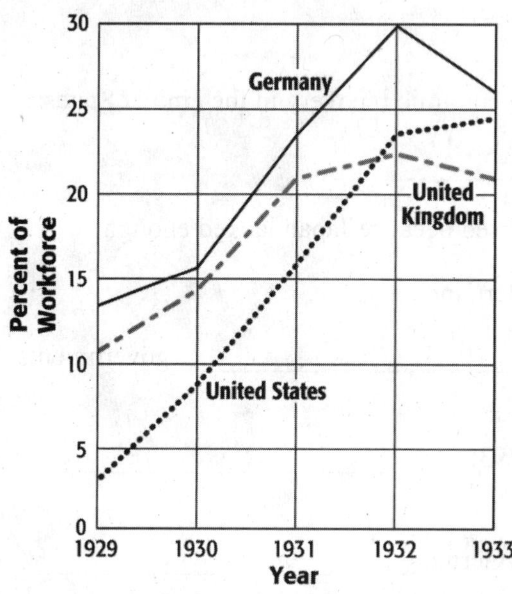

Source: Historical Statistics of the United States; European Historical Statistics

Decline of World Trade, 1929–1933

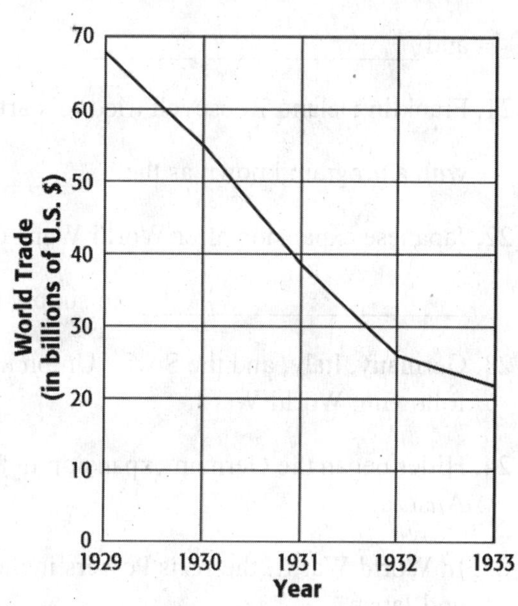

Source: Economic Discrimination and Political Exchange

_____ 15. Which of the following statements best explains the relationship between the information in the charts?
a. Only the United States was affected by the decline in world trade.
b. More people were unemployed in 1929 despite the fact that world trade had not yet declined.
c. More people became unemployed as world trade continued to decline.
d. all of the above

FILL IN THE BLANK For each of the following statements, fill in the blank with the appropriate word, phrase or name.

16. The causes of World War I include militarism, alliances, imperialism, and

______________________.

17. The main players in what came to be called World War I were the Allied Powers and

the ______________________.

18. The Russian monarchy came to an end when ______________________ stepped down.

Name ______________________ Class ______________ Date ______________

The World at War

Unit Test

Form A

19. Mao Zedong led 100,000 Communists on the ____________________ through China, searching for a region safe from the Guomindang.

20. Mohandas Gandhi believed in change through two important concepts, nonviolence and ____________________.

21. Franklin Delano Roosevelt tried to start an economic recovery in the United States with a program known as the ____________________.

22. Japanese expansion after World War I occurred because Japan lacked enough ____________________ to supply modern industry.

23. Germany, Italy, and the Soviet Union had ____________________ governments following World War I.

24. Hitler began the German expansion in the 1930s by ____________________ Austria.

25. In World War II, the Axis Powers included Germany, ____________________ and Japan.

26. Japan's attack on Pearl Harbor resulted in the end of ____________________ in the United States.

27. The Allies gained power in Northern Africa by taking advantage of the Afrika Korps's ____________________ problems.

28. The German army was without food, ammunition, and medicine when the Soviet army surrounded them at the ____________________, a turning point in World War II.

29. In response to reports of widespread killing of Jews in Europe, the United States established the ____________________.

30. Germany's defeat in the ____________________ marked the end of major German resistance at the close of World War II.

Name ______________________ Class ______________ Date ______________

The World at War

Unit Test

Form A

MATCHING In the space provided, write the letter of the term or place that matches each description. Some answers will not be used.

_____ 31. Desert Fox who led the Afrika Korps

_____ 32. Early Bolshevik leader

_____ 33. Leader who wrote the Fourteen Points

_____ 34. Guomindang leader who turned against his Communist allies

_____ 35. "Father of the Turks"

_____ 36. British economist who believed governments could limit economic downturns by spending

_____ 37. Founder of the National Fascist Party

_____ 38. Started collectivization in the Soviet Union

_____ 39. General who led Japan in World War II

_____ 40. Prime minister of Great Britain who supported policy of appeasement

a. John Maynard Keynes
b. Jiang Jieshi
c. Hideki Tojo
d. Benito Mussolini
e. Adolf Hitler
f. Winston Churchill
g. Neville Chamberlain
h. Vladimir Lenin
i. Woodrow Wilson
j. Joseph Stalin
k. Erwin Rommel
l. Kemal Atatürk

TRUE/FALSE Indicate whether each statement below is true of false by writing **T** or **F** in the space provided.

_____ 41. In World War I, after three years of battles, the battle positions at the Western Front were virtually unchanged.

_____ 42. Grigory Rasputin was an exceptional military advisor to Czar Nicholas II.

_____ 43. Russian factories were unable to produce military supplies quickly enough to meet the army's needs in World War I.

_____ 44. The White Army fought Lenin's Red Army and ultimately defeated the Bolsheviks in 1920.

_____ 45. Negotiations were difficult after World War I because the leaders of the four major Allies had very different ideas about a peace treaty.

_____ 46. After World War I, the Turks defeated the Greeks and announced the establishment of the Republic of Turkey.

_____ 47. Before entering World War II, the United States had been helping the Allies by shipping supplies across the Atlantic Ocean.

_____ 48. American leaders considered using the atomic bomb to spare huge Allied casualties that might result from invading Japan.

_____ 49. The world organization called the League of Nations replaced the earlier organization, the United Nations.

_____ 50. Propaganda was only used by Axis nations during World War II.

Name ____________________ Class ____________ Date ____________

The World at War

Unit Test

Form B

SHORT ANSWER On a separate sheet of paper, answer each of the following questions in complete sentences. Remember to use specific examples to support your answers.

1. Explain the four factors that put Europe on the brink of war in 1914.
2. Why did the United States enter World War I?
3. What factors contributed to the 1929 stock market crash in the United States?
4. What are the common features of totalitarian governments?
5. Explain two ways the terms of the Treaty of Versailles impacted the interwar years.

PRACTICING SOCIAL STUDIES SKILLS Study the visuals below and, on a separate sheet of paper, answer the question that follows in complete sentences.

Unemployment, 1929–1933

Germany
United Kingdom
United States
Percent of Workforce
0 5 10 15 20 25 30
1929 1930 1931 1932 1933
Year

Source: Historical Statistics of the United States; European Historical Statistics

Decline of World Trade, 1929–1933

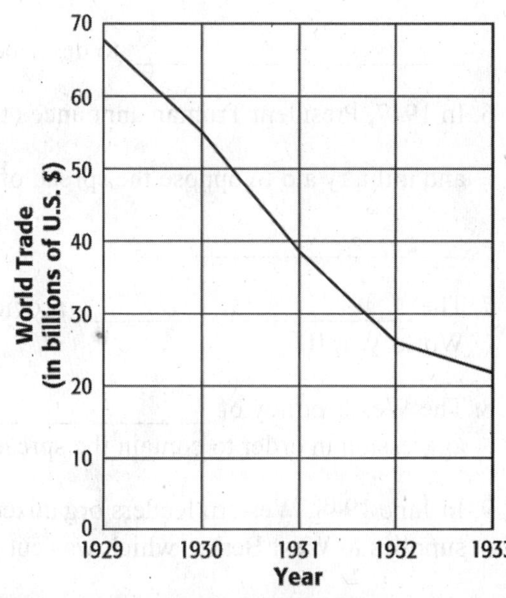

Source: Economic Discrimination and Political Exchange

6. Use the information in both graphs to describe some key economic events and figures of the interwar years.

Name ______________________ Class ______________ Date ______________

Europe and North America

Section Quiz

Section 1

FILL IN THE BLANK For each of the following statements, fill in the blank with the appropriate word, phrase, or name.

1. After World War II, the Allies temporarily divided Germany into four zones of occupation, with about one-third of the country controlled by ______________________.
2. Former Nazi and military leaders were brought to justice at the ______________________ for crimes committed during the war.
3. At the ______________________ in the summer of 1945, the major Allied powers argued over what to do with Eastern Europe.
4. Soon after World War II, the United States and the Soviet Union entered an era of hostility and tension, which became known as the ______________________.
5. In a speech in the United States, Winston Churchill used the image of an ______________________ to describe the division of Europe due to Soviet actions.
6. In 1947, President Truman announced that the United States would provide economic and military aid to oppose the spread of communism. This pledge was known as the ______________________.
7. The ______________________ provided $13 billion for rebuilding Europe after World War II.
8. The West's policy of ______________________ involved resisting Soviet aggression in order to contain the spread of communism.
9. In June 1948, Western leaders organized the ______________________ to provide supplies to West Berlin, which was cut off by the Soviets.
10. Communist Chinese troops fought on the side of ______________________ in the Korean War.

Name ______________________ Class ______________ Date ______________

Europe and North America

Section Quiz

Section 2

MATCHING In the space provided, write the letter of the term or place that matches each description. Some answers will not be used.

_____ 1. Destructive weapon powered by fusion

_____ 2. Struggle between nations to gain an advantage in weapons

_____ 3. History's first artificial satellite

_____ 4. Barrier built to stop East Germans from fleeing to the West

_____ 5. Failed event in which U.S. officials trained Cuban forces to invade Cuba and start an uprising against Castro

_____ 6. Confrontation between the United States and the Soviet Union over the installation of Soviet nuclear missiles near Florida

_____ 7. Countries who refused to support either side during the Cold War

_____ 8. Reduced tension between the superpowers

_____ 9. U.S. proposal that would allow the United States and the Soviet Union to fly over each other's territory and gather information about its weapons

_____ 10. Agreement between the United States and the Soviet Union calling for the elimination of certain types of missiles

a. hydrogen bomb

b. *Sputnik*

c. arms race

d. deterrence

e. nonaligned nations

f. Bay of Pigs invasion

g. Intermediate-Range Nuclear Forces Treaty

h. open skies treaty

i. détente

j. Red Scare

k. Test Ban Treaty

l. Cuban missile crisis

m. Berlin Wall

Name ______________________ Class ______________ Date ______________

Europe and North America

Section Quiz

Section 3

MULTIPLE CHOICE For each of the following, write the letter of the best choice in the space provided.

_____ 1. The postwar period in the United States was a time of
a. depression.
b. declining birthrates.
c. prosperity.
d. conflict.

_____ 2. In the 70s and 80s, the nation's heavy industry
a. posted record profits.
b. outpaced technology and banking services.
c. focused on defense.
d. had to compete with foreign companies.

_____ 3. The G.I. Bill of Rights helped millions of returning soldiers
a. return to duty.
b. attend college.
c. get medical care.
d. get jobs.

_____ 4. Racial segregation in U.S. military forces was ended by
a. the G.I. Bill of Rights.
b. President Truman in 1948.
c. the Supreme Court in 1954.
d. the Civil Rights Act of 1964.

_____ 5. *Brown* v. *Board of Education* was a ruling against racial segregation in
a. professional sports.
b. restaurants and hotels.
c. public schools.
d. the armed forces.

_____ 6. Which was responsible for the baby boom?
a. returning veterans
b. prosperity
c. consumer confidence
d. all of the above

_____ 7. *Glasnost* and *perestroika* were proposed by
a. Ronald Reagan.
b. Joseph Stalin.
c. Nikita Khrushchev.
d. Mikhail Gorbachev.

_____ 8. In which country did the Solidarity movement take place?
a. Hungary
b. Czechoslovakia
c. Poland
d. Soviet Union

_____ 9. The Berlin Wall represented
a. U.S. control of Germany.
b. Soviet repression.
c. détente.
d. the arms race.

_____ 10. The role of the United States in the Cold War was to prevent the spread of
a. capitalism.
b. prosperity in the Soviet Union.
c. European culture.
d. communism.

Name ____________________ Class ______________ Date ______________

Europe and North America

Section Quiz

Section 4

TRUE/FALSE Mark each statement **T** if it is true or **F** if it is false. If false explain why.

_____ 1. Boris Yeltsin was a hard-line Communist Party leader who sought to end Mikhail Gorbachev's reforms.

____

____

_____ 2. In the 1990s, the Soviet Union broke into several republics and introduced market reforms.

____

____

_____ 3. The European Union was established to build an economic and political union among the nations of Europe.

____

____

_____ 4. Much of the economic success of the United States in the 1990s came from developments in computer technology.

____

____

_____ 5. The leader of al Qaeda was Saddam Hussein.

____

____

Name ______________ Class ______________ Date ______________

Europe and North America

Chapter Test

Form A

MULTIPLE CHOICE For each of the following, write the letter of the best choice in the space provided.

_____ 1. The Soviet Union wanted to control Eastern Europe after World War II because
a. it wanted a buffer zone of friendly governments to protect against attack.
b. it needed the rich natural resources of the region.
c. otherwise it might be controlled by Germany.
d. Eastern European people had elected Communist governments.

_____ 2. Which of the following did Winston Churchill use as an image to describe the division of Europe?
a. a closed door
b. a steel fist
c. an iron curtain
d. the Grand Canyon

_____ 3. What was the goal of the United States when it went to war in Korea?
a. to end communism in Korea and China
b. to contain Communist expansion
c. to build up the United Nations
d. to eliminate Soviet nuclear missile sites in North Korea

_____ 4. Why did President Kennedy favor the Test Ban Treaty?
a. to force the Soviets to remove nuclear missiles from Cuba
b. to ensure that each side remained vulnerable to the other's weapons
c. to encourage the sharing of information between the superpowers
d. to slow the development of new, more deadly weapons

_____ 5. What helped drive the tremendous growth of the U.S. economy after World War II?
a. new oil supplies
b. consumer spending
c. an agricultural revolution
d. rising interest rates

_____ 6. One reason Western Europe made a rapid recovery from World War II was because
a. the war had caused only minor damage to property.
b. the United States provided massive economic aid.
c. strong Communist movements emerged in those countries.
d. sweeping social programs eliminated poverty.

_____ 7. What caused the breakup of Yugoslavia in the 1990s?
a. military occupation by NATO
b. democratic elections
c. the collapse of the Soviet Union
d. ethnic tensions coupled with a weakening government

_____ 8. One reason revolution spread across Eastern Europe in 1989
a. was that Gorbachev loosened Soviet control.
b. was that Soviet leaders wanted a smaller union.
c. was that Gorbachev increased Soviet control.
d. was that Boris Yeltsin demanded it.

PRACTICING SOCIAL STUDIES SKILLS Study the political cartoon below and answer the question that follows.

Dick Adair/Honolulu Advertiser/Rothco Cartoons

_____ 9. Which statement best describes the subject of the cartoon?
a. Cuba requests Soviet help during the Cuban missile crisis.
b. Western Europe is on the brink of chaos after World War II.
c. The United States faces a counterculture movement in the 1960s.
d. Economic problems and reforms weaken the Soviet Union.

Name ______________________ Class ______________ Date ______________

Europe and North America

Chapter Test
Form A

FILL IN THE BLANK For each of the following statements, fill in the blank with the appropriate word, phrase, or name.

10. In the ______________________, Allied military courts tried several dozen Nazi and military officials, sentencing many to death.

11. The Soviet Union and the Communist nations of Eastern Europe formed the ______________________ in response to the formation of NATO.

12. A(n) ______________________ is a struggle between nations to gain an advantage in weapons.

13. Fidel Castro alarmed the U.S. government when he installed a ______________________ government in Cuba.

14. ______________________ used techniques of nonviolence and civil disobedience to expose racial injustice in the United States.

15. In the 1960s, young people in the ______________________ adopted new styles of clothing and behavior and questioned U.S. actions in the Vietnam War.

16. Under communism, the Soviet Union had a(n) ______________________ economy, a system in which the government makes all economic decisions.

17. Mikhail Gorbachev's policy of ______________________ sought to restructure the Soviet economic and political system.

18. Osama bin Laden led an Islamist terrorist organization called ______________________.

TRUE/FALSE Indicate whether each statement below is true or false by writing **T** or **F** in the space provided.

_____ 19. The United States used the Truman Doctrine and the Marshall Plan as part of a policy of containment.

_____ 20. The success of the Berlin airlift was followed by the formation of the Federal Republic of Germany.

_____ 21. At the close of the 1950s, Americans thought they had a technological edge over the Soviets.

_____ 22. The United States supported Salvador Allende's government in Chile because it had been democratically elected.

_____ 23. All American women in the 1960s and 1970s wanted to change traditional ideas of women's roles.

_____ 24. The people of Eastern Europe all benefited immediately from the end of communism and the introduction of market reforms.

_____ 25. The Persian Gulf War was fought to free Kuwait and to protect oil supplies.

Name ______________________ Class ______________ Date ______________

Europe and North America

Chapter Test

Form B

SHORT ANSWER On a separate sheet of paper, answer each of the following questions in complete sentences. Remember to use specific examples to support your answers.

1. What was the policy of containment, and how was it carried out by the United States?
2. How did the superpowers' military strategies during the Cold War demonstrate the principle of deterrence?
3. What radical changes did Mikhail Gorbachev propose when he came to power in the Soviet Union?
4. How did the emergence of the Internet affect the U.S. economy in the 1990s?
5. How did fears associated with the Cold War affect the lives of ordinary Americans?

PRACTICING SOCIAL STUDIES SKILLS Study the political cartoon below. On a separate sheet of paper, answer the question that follows, using complete sentences.

Dick Adair/Honolulu Advertiser/Rothco Cartoons

6. Use elements within the political cartoon to describe the collapse of the Soviet Union.

Name ______________________ Class ______________ Date ______________

Asia **Section Quiz**

Section 1

TRUE/FALSE Mark each statement **T** if it is true or **F** if it is false. If false explain why.

_____ 1. The "Quit India" campaign was a non-violent protest designed to drive the British from India.

____

____

_____ 2. In 1947, Mohandas Gandhi became India's first prime minister.

____

____

_____ 3. The Muslim League wanted a united India and was opposed to partition.

____

____

_____ 4. In 1971, East Pakistan declared independence from Pakistan and changed its name to Bangladesh.

____

____

_____ 5. Today, both India and Pakistan are among the nations that have tested nuclear weapons.

____

____

Name ______________________ Class ______________ Date ____________

Asia

Section Quiz

Section 2

MULTIPLE CHOICE For each of the following, write the letter of the best choice in the space provided.

_____ 1. Before World War II, the Philippines was under the control of
a. Great Britain.
b. China.
c. the United States.
d. Japan.

_____ 2. The Gulf of Tonkin Resolution
a. ended the conflict between North Vietnam and South Vietnam.
b. allowed President Johnson to expand U.S. involvement in Vietnam without a declaration of war.
c. outlined the proper treatment for captured U.S. soldiers.
d. expanded the authority of the government of South Vietnam.

_____ 3. U.S efforts did not destroy the North Vietnamese supply network known as the
a. Tet Offensive.
b. Pathet Lao.
c. Myanmar Passage.
d. Ho Chi Minh Trail.

_____ 4. The Vietcong was a group opposed to the leadership of
a. Ngo Dinh Diem.
b. Ho Chi Minh.
c. Pol Pot.
d. Sukarno.

_____ 5. Cambodia's Khmer Rouge believed
a. all influences of urban life should be destroyed.
b. modernization was the key to prosperity in Democratic Kampuchea.
c. international cooperation would bring peace and prosperity after a successful revolution.
d. Democratic Kampuchea should form a strong partnership with Vietnam.

Name ______________________ Class ______________ Date ______________

Asia

Section Quiz

Section 3

MATCHING In the space provided, write the letter of the term, person, or place that matches each description. Some answers will not be used.

_____ 1. Group that wielded much of the power in China during the last years of Mao's life and was later imprisoned

_____ 2. Island to which China's Communists drove the previous government's forces in 1949

_____ 3. Nationalist leader whose corrupt government policies led many Chinese peasants to support the Communists

_____ 4. Failed plan to increase China's industrial and agricultural output

_____ 5. Where hundreds of thousands of protesters gathered, demanding more political freedoms

_____ 6. Put into place an economic reform plan called the Four Modernizations

_____ 7. Political party that was ousted when the Communists came to power

_____ 8. Movement that sought to rid China of its old ways and create a society in which peasants and physical labor were the ideal

_____ 9. Nation whose formation was announced on October 1, 1949

_____ 10. Militant high school and college students who murdered political opponents

a. Deng Xiaoping

b. Jiang Jieshi

c. Guomindang

d. Gang of Four

e. Mao Zedong

f. Taiwan

g. People's Republic of China

h. Soviet Union

i. Great Leap Forward

j. Cultural Revolution

k. Red Guards

l. Gang of Four

m. Tiananmen Square

FILL IN THE BLANK For each of the following statements, fill in the blank with the appropriate word, phrase, or name.

1. The ______________________ refers to the nations that border the Pacific Ocean.
2. After World War II, U.S. troops occupied ______________________, and General Douglas MacArthur took control of the Allied efforts to rebuild the nation.
3. After ______________________ was elected president of the Philippines in 1986, the Philippines began a struggle to return to democracy.
4. In ______________________, Communist dictator Kim Il Sung formed a government based partly on the Soviet model.
5. Despite economic problems under Kim Jong Il's rule, North Korea continued to fund military programs and said it possessed ______________________ weapons.
6. South Korea, Hong Kong, Taiwan, and Singapore, the nations known as the ______________________, made great economic gains.
7. Today, China views Taiwan as part of China and insists that China and Taiwan will eventually be ______________________.
8. Japan and other successful Pacific Rim countries focused on growth though exports of ______________________, primarily to the United States.
9. These countries built skilled workforces by providing ample ______________________ and training.
10. A symbol of the success and optimism of Asian economies has been the construction of spectacular ______________________.

Name ______________________ Class ______________ Date ______________

Asia

Chapter Test

Form A

MULTIPLE CHOICE For each of the following, write the letter of the best choice in the space provided.

_____ 1. In 1947, India became the world's largest
a. democracy.
b. monarchy.
c. authoritarian state.
d. economy.

_____ 2. What helped to rebuild Japan's economy after World War II?
a. Emperor Hirohito's strong leadership
b. massive defense spending
c. U.S. economic aid and being a supply source during the Korean War
d. abolishing light industries

_____ 3. General Suharto's corrupt, authoritarian reign lasted until 1998 in
a. Indonesia.
b. East Timor.
c. Cambodia.
d. Myanmar.

_____ 4. The peace talks on dividing Vietnam into northern and southern halves reflected
a. lessons learned from World War II.
b. Cold War tensions.
c. hopes for a permanent division of Vietnam.
d. the impact of events in the Gulf of Tonkin.

_____ 5. Aung San Suu Kyi won the Nobel Peace Prize for working to promote democracy in
a. Nepal.
b. Pakistan.
c. India.
d. Myanmar.

PRACTICING SOCIAL STUDIES SKILLS Study the passage and graph below and answer the questions that follow.

> **"You have a row of dominoes set up, you knock over the first one, and what will happen to the last one is the certainty that it will go over very quickly. So you could have the beginning of a disintegration that would have the most profound influences. . ."**
>
> **—Dwight Eisenhower, April 7, 1954**

_____ 6. The passage above illustrates the belief that led to which of the following?
a. independence for the Philippines
b. the Vietnam War
c. a UN role in Korea
d. U.S. withdrawal from Indochina

Asia

Chapter Test

Form A

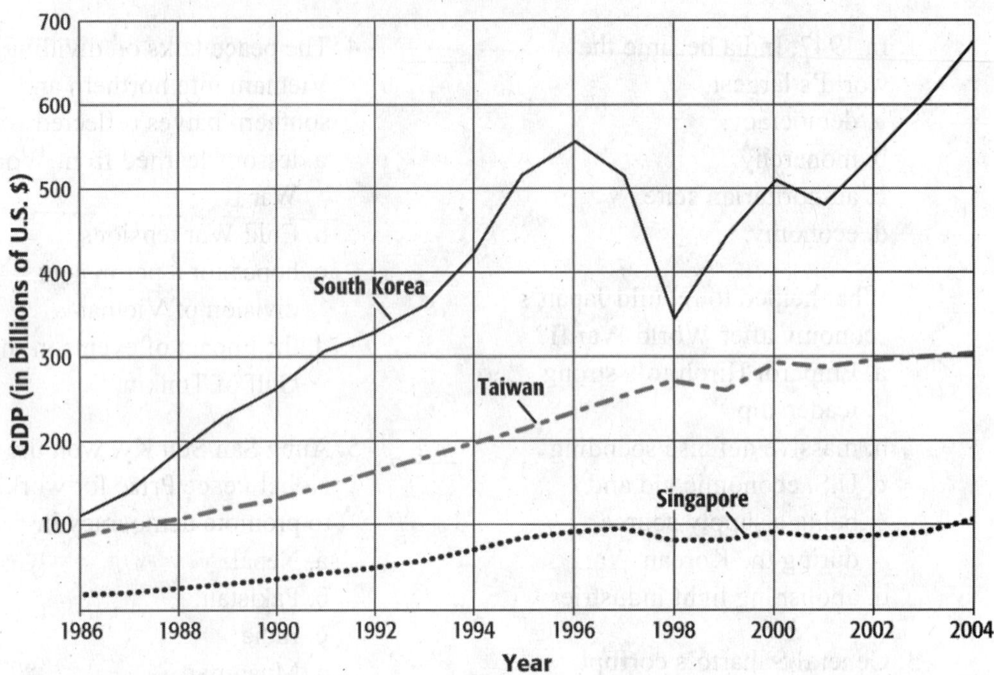

Sources: The World Bank; Asia Pacific Economic Cooperation; Singapore Department of Statistics; The Bank of Korea

_____ 7. According to this chart, the economies of South Korea, Taiwan, and Singapore
- a. remained flat.
- b. never recovered from the lows.
- c. consistently declined.
- d. all showed growth.

FILL IN THE BLANK For each of the following statements, fill in the blank with the appropriate word, phrase, or name.

8. ______________________ led the Muslim League, which favored a partition of India.

9. When East Pakistan became independent, it took the name ______________________.

10. ______________________ was the Communist leader of the Viet Minh.

11. The ______________________ were militant students who traveled through China's cities and villages, looking for those they believed to be corrupt.

Asia

Chapter Test
Form A

12. In Cambodia, the ______________ established a Communist government and renamed the country Democratic Kampuchea.

13. Mao Zedong's plan to increase China's industrial and agricultural output was called the ______________.

14. The rule of the Philippines' dictatorial President ______________ came to an end in 1986.

15. In 1989, the ______________, an event in which many supporters of democracy were killed, showed that true freedom had not arrived in China.

16. After Mao Zedong's death, ______________ eventually became China's leader and began economic reforms.

TRUE/FALSE Indicate whether each statement below is true or false by writing **T** or **F** in the space provided.

_____ 17. The British began the "Quit India" campaign because they wanted to help India make a gradual and peaceful transition to democratic self-rule.

_____ 18. Tension continues today between India and Pakistan over Kashmir.

_____ 19. The United States formally recognized the united Vietnam in 1995.

_____ 20. The Tet Offensive was a decisive victory for the American cause in Vietnam.

_____ 21. The United States and China improved their relations during the 1970s.

_____ 22. The Soviet Union and China ceased to be close allies during the 1950s.

_____ 23. The Cultural Revolution in China led to a golden age of art, architecture, and literature in the 1960s.

_____ 24. A strong Japanese work ethic contributed to Japan's stunning economic recovery after World War II.

_____ 25. Some predicted that the 2000s would see Europe and North America surpassing Asia as the dominant economic region in the world.

Asia

Chapter Test
Form B

SHORT ANSWER On a separate sheet of paper, answer each of the following questions in complete sentences. Remember to use specific examples to support your answers.

1. Explain how religious tensions in India led to partition.
2. What factors complicated the relationship between India and Pakistan after partition?
3. What was the domino theory? How did it lead to the Vietnam War?
4. Summarize Mao Zedong's attempts to transform the Chinese economy in the 1950s.
5. What were the three basic steps of the rebuilding process in postwar Japan?

PRACTICING SOCIAL STUDIES SKILLS Study the graph below and, on a separate sheet of paper, answer the question that follows in complete sentences.

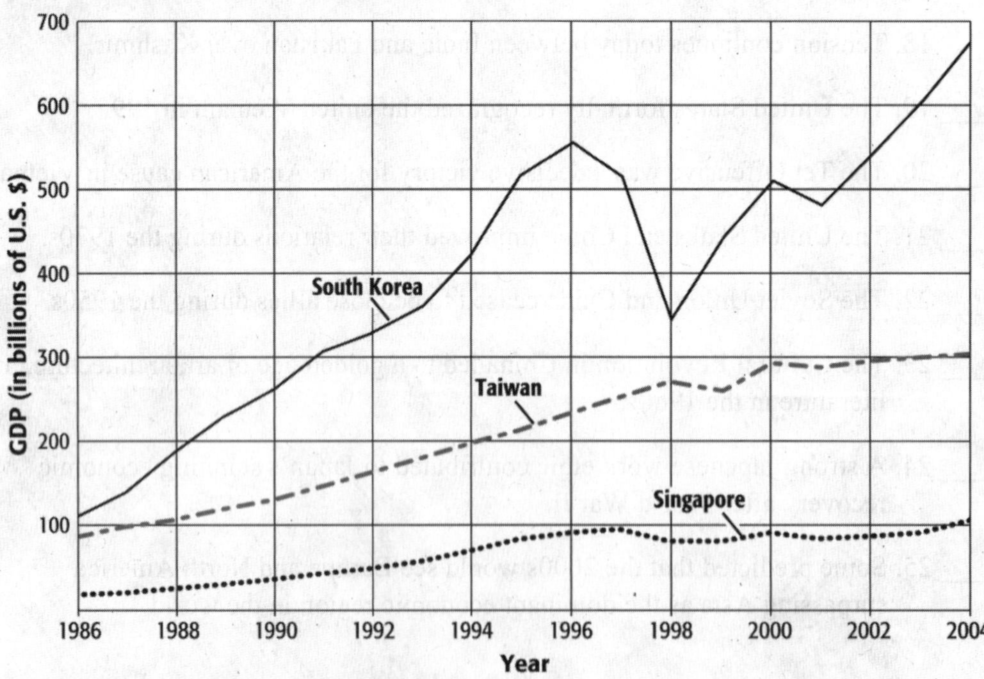

6. Use information from the chart and your knowledge of the chapter to describe how the Asian Tigers' economies grew.

Name ______________________ Class ______________ Date ______________

Africa and the Middle East

Section Quiz

Section 1

MULTIPLE CHOICE For each of the following, write the letter of the best choice in the space provided.

_____ 1. As leader of the Gold Coast nationalists, Kwame Nkrumah
- a. pressed for independence from France.
- b. hoped to keep the Gold Coast out of World War II.
- c. eventually became prime minister of the new nation of Ghana.
- d. led the Belgian Congo to independence.

_____ 2. Mau Mau was the name given to the violent movement formed by Kikuyu farmers in
- a. Ghana.
- b. South Africa.
- c. Egypt.
- d. Kenya.

_____ 3. Charles de Gaulle gave African leaders the choice of
- a. accepting French rule or having to fight for independence.
- b. remaining tied to France through an organization called the French Community or becoming independent.
- c. being absorbed into France or remaining a colony.
- d. becoming part of an organization called the Economic Community or holding democratic elections.

_____ 4. What was the result of Portugal's decision to hold onto its colonies?
- a. The leaders of the African colonies respected Portugal's decision.
- b. Nationalist movements in the colonies continued to press for independence using nonviolent means.
- c. There were long years of warfare between the Portuguese and Africans until it became impossible for Portugal to support its colonies.
- d. The African colonies placed sanctions on Portugal until the Portuguese economy was crippled.

_____ 5. Although South Africa was granted independence in 1910, under apartheid,
- a. blacks placed restrictions on white businesses.
- b. blacks were denied citizenship.
- c. blacks and whites both ran for political office.
- d. the larger black population had the best farmland.

Name ______________________ Class ______________ Date ______________

Africa and the Middle East

TRUE/FALSE Mark each statement **T** if it is true or **F** if it is false. If false explain why.

_____ 1. The Sharpeville Massacre was significant because it led the African National Congress to adopt a policy of peaceful resistance to apartheid.

_____ 2. Nelson Mandela became the first president of a democratic South Africa.

_____ 3. By the end of the 1960s, almost all independent African countries had adopted multi-party systems.

_____ 4. After independence, most African nations had fragile economies that depended on one or two products for export.

_____ 5. As part of the revival of African culture after independence, both Kenya and Tanzania adopted French as their national language.

Name ______________________ Class ______________ Date ______________

Africa and the Middle East

Section Quiz

Section 3

MATCHING In the space provided, write the letter of the term, person, or place that matches each description. Some answers will not be used.

_____ 1. U.S.-led alliance against communism in the Middle East

_____ 2. European leader who signed an agreement granting Algeria independence

_____ 3. Mandate controlled by Britain in the Middle East

_____ 4. Iranian prime minister whose nationalist policies led to conflict with Western powers

_____ 5. Pro-British Egyptian monarch

_____ 6. First prime minister of Israel

_____ 7. Shah of Iran in 1941

_____ 8. Leader of young nationalist army officers who staged a military coup in Egypt in 1952

_____ 9. Algerian nationalist movement

_____ 10. Jewish nationalist movement

a. National Liberation Front

b. Suez

c. Baghdad Pact

d. Charles de Gaulle

e. Mohammad Reza Pahlavi

f. Palestine

g. Zionism

h. Aswan

i. King David

j. David Ben-Gurion

k. Gamal Abdel Nasser

l. Mohammad Mosadeq

m. King Farouk I

Name ______________________ Class ______________ Date ______________

Africa and the Middle East

Section Quiz

Section 4

FILL IN THE BLANK For each of the following statements, fill in the blank with the appropriate word, phrase, or name.

1. The regional issues that have led to conflict in the Middle East are the presence of huge ______________________ reserves, the growth of Islamism, and the conflict between Israel and its neighbors.

2. Islamism is a movement to reorder government and society according to ______________________ laws.

3. Several Middle Eastern countries belong to ______________________, which seeks to maximize revenues from oil exports.

4. In the ______________________ of 1967, Israel gained control of land with a large Palestinian population.

5. In 1977 Egyptian president Anwar Sadat declared that Egypt wanted ______________________ with Israel.

6. In 1964, the ______________________ was formed, pledging to destroy Israel and replace it with a Palestinian state.

7. As Iran changed from a rural society to a(n) ______________________ society, many Iranians felt threatened and betrayed by the government.

8. In 1980 Iraq attacked its neighbor ______________________, setting off a bitter war.

9. In an effort to end the Iraqi occupation of Kuwait, the UN passed economic ______________________ against Iraq.

10. A growing ______________________, or armed rebellion, in Iraq targeted coalition forces, their Iraqi allies, and innocent civilians.

Name ______________ Class ______________ Date ______________

Africa and the Middle East

Chapter Test Form A

MULTIPLE CHOICE For each of the following, write the letter of the best choice in the space provided.

_____ 1. The Kenyan struggle for independence was especially difficult because
a. the Kikuyu people were also fighting for independence in two other countries.
b. the French refused to give up control of any of their African colonies.
c. Nelson Mandela had to lead the independence movement from prison.
d. white settlers feared they would lose valuable cash crops.

_____ 2. Portugal's African colonies gained independence
a. through free elections.
b. immediately after World War II.
c. after long years of warfare.
d. because of action by the United Nations.

_____ 3. Which of the following organizations was influential in ending apartheid in South Africa?
a. Convention People's Party
b. African National Congress
c. Mau Mau
d. National Liberation Front

_____ 4. After the Cold War ended in 1989, democratic governments began to emerge in Africa because
a. the United States and Soviet Union no longer supported dictators friendly to their sides.
b. the United States promised massive economic aid.
c. colonial rule had just ended.
d. industrialists invested large amounts of money there.

_____ 5. Britain, France, and Israel attacked Egypt in October 1956 because Nasser
a. nationalized all personal property.
b. nationalized the Suez Canal.
c. was threatening to expel all Jews from Egypt.
d. had created the Palestine Liberation Organization.

_____ 6. France granted independence to Tunisia and Morocco in 1956 because
a. fighting nationalists in Algeria required France's full attention.
b. the country believed all people should have the right to self-determination.
c. the French liberated all their former colonies at that time.
d. economic sanctions forced them to.

_____ 7. How did Iran change under Ayatollah Ruhollah Khomeini's leadership?

a. It became less hostile to Israel.
b. It modernized and became more closely allied with the West.
c. It enforced strict religious and social values.
d. Orthodox Christianity replaced Islam as the state religion.

_____ 8. U.S.-led forces attacked Iraq in 2003 after Iraq

a. went to war against Israel.
b. invaded Iran.
c. invaded Kuwait.
d. resisted full cooperation with UN weapons inspectors.

PRACTICING SOCIAL STUDIES SKILLS Study the graph below and answer the question that follows

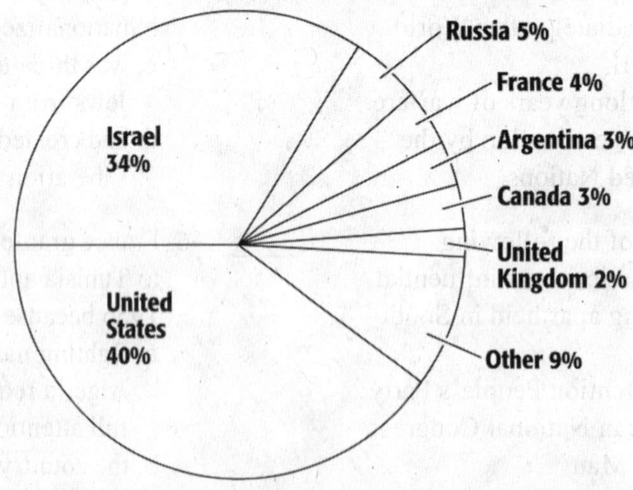

_____ 9. Which country has the highest percentage of the total Jewish population?

a. Israel
b. Germany
c. the United States
d. the United Kingdom

Name ______________________ Class ______________ Date ______________

Africa and the Middle East

Chapter Test

Form A

MATCHING In the space provided, write the letter of the term, person, or place that matches each description. Some answers will not be used.

_____ 10. Iraqi leader ousted in 2003

_____ 11. Dominant political system in newly independent African countries by 1960

_____ 12. United Nations proposal to divide Palestine

_____ 13. Led the radical Convention People's Party in the Gold Coast

_____ 14. Rebellion in the West Bank and Gaza in 1987

_____ 15. Type of literature that rejected European culture and focused on African culture and identity

_____ 16. Group that attempts to regulate the production of oil exports

_____ 17. Conflict that resulted in territorial gains for Israel

_____ 18. Leader of the African National Congress who became the first black president of South Africa

_____ 19. President of South Africa who held the country's first democratic election

a. Nelson Mandela

b. Yom Kippur War

c. OPEC

d. Kwame Nkrumah

e. Baghdad Pact

f. one-party system

g. Saddam Hussein

h. intifada

i. F.W. de Klerk

j. partition

k. Six-Day War

l. negritude movement

m. Soweto Uprising

FILL IN THE BLANK For each of the following statements, fill in the blank with the appropriate word, phrase, or name.

20. ______________________ led Kenya's nationalist movement and served as prime minister after independence was achieved.

21. Two serious diseases that take many lives in Africa are ______________________ and ______________________.

22. The revival of African culture includes ______________________ arts as well as new means of expressing African identity.

Name ______________________ Class ______________ Date ______________

Africa and the Middle East

Chapter Test
Form A

23. The 1978 peace agreement between Israel and Egypt is known as the

    ______________________ Accords.

24. In 1969, ______________________ became the leader of the Palestine Liberation Organization.

25. ______________________ are Muslims who seek to reorder government and society according to Islamic laws.

Name ______________________ Class ______________ Date ______________

Africa and the Middle East

Chapter Test

Form B

SHORT ANSWER On a separate sheet of paper, answer each of the following questions in complete sentences. Remember to use specific examples to support your answers.

1. How did the policy of apartheid limit the freedom of nonwhite South Africans?
2. Describe two ways in which Africans have experienced a cultural revival since independence.
3. What were the causes and effects of Gamal Abdel Nasser's rise to power in Egypt?
4. How has oil impacted life in the Middle East?

PRACTICING SOCIAL STUDIES SKILLS Study the graph below and, on a separate sheet of paper, answer the question that follows in complete sentences.

World Jewish Population by Country, 2005

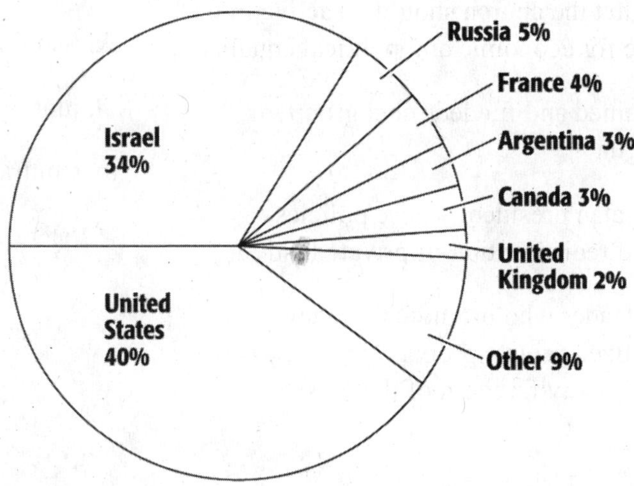

Source: Jewish Virtual Library

5. How do you think this graph would look different if it portrayed the world Jewish population in 1940?

Latin America

Section Quiz

Section 1

MATCHING In the space provided, write the letter of the term, person, or place that matches each description. Some answers will not be used.

_____ 1. Leader whose nation was described as "a rich country with too many poor people"

_____ 2. Revolutionary group that took over the Nicaraguan capital in 1979

_____ 3. Salvadoran archbishop whose murder sparked civil war between Communist-supported guerillas and the nation's army

_____ 4. Nation that was one of the richest countries in Latin America in the 1950s

_____ 5. Family forced to flee after ruling Nicaragua for four decades

_____ 6. A group of leaders who rule jointly

_____ 7. Belief that the church should be active in the struggle for economic and political equality

_____ 8. U.S.-trained and funded rebel group in Nicaragua

_____ 9. Guatemalan president whose policies included redistribution of private land

_____ 10. Cuban leader who promoted literacy, nationalized private property and businesses, and took away freedom of the press

a. Liberation Theology

b. Fulgencio Batista

c. Cuba

d. Fidel Castro

e. Che Guevara

f. Bay of Pigs

g. Jacobo Arbenz

h. Oscar Romero

i. Nicaragua

j. Somoza

k. Sandinistas

l. junta

m. Contras

Latin America Section Quiz

Section 2

TRUE/FALSE Mark each statement **T** if it is true or **F** if it is false. If false explain why.

_____ 1. Argentina's Juan Perón placed cattle and wheat industries under government control and turned the nation into a one-party state, suppressing opposition and freedom of speech.

____

____

_____ 2. During the "Brazilian miracle" of 1968-1973, wages grew more quickly than at any other time in the nation's history.

____

____

_____ 3. In Chile, Salvador Allende's leftist policies did not alarm the United States government.

____

____

_____ 4. In Haiti, the political and social reforms of the Duvaliers stimulated economic growth and enabled the economy to flourish.

____

____

_____ 5. In Peru, congressional complaints about abuse of power led Alberto Fujimori to disband the congress and suspend the constitution.

____

____

Latin America

Section Quiz

Section 3

FILL IN THE BLANK For each of the following statements, fill in the blank with the appropriate word, phrase, or name.

1. Pressure for reform came from lenders such as the International Monetary Fund and the ______________________ Bank.
2. When Latin Americans had a chance to vote, they often voted out the repressive ______________________ governments and voted in new civilian governments.
3. Because it enjoyed more economic success than most others in the region, the Pinochet regime in ______________________ was one of the last Latin American dictatorships to fall.
4. For more than 70 years, the Institutional Revolutionary Party governed ______________________ with almost no opposition.
5. The North American Free Trade Agreement was designed to eliminate tariffs on trade between Mexico, the United States, and ______________________.
6. In Latin America, nearly one-third of the population lives on less than ______________________ dollars a day.
7. ______________________ of Mexico was the first president in 71 years who was not a member of the PRI.
8. After winning election in 2006, Evo Morales nationalized the natural gas industry and supported the coca-growing industry in the country of ______________________.
9. Starting in the late 1990s, elections brought populist, left-leaning leaders such as ______________________ of Venezuela to power.
10. Under pressure from Western banks, deeply indebted Latin American countries began a series of reform measures, also called ______________________ reforms.

Name _______________ Class _______________ Date _______________

Latin America

Chapter Test

Form A

MULTIPLE CHOICE For each of the following, write the letter of the best choice in the space provided.

_____ 1. Why did many Latin American countries adopt a policy of import-substitution led industrialization?
a. to eliminate high tariffs that limited imports
b. to reduce the poor population's dependence on farming
c. to develop local industries to replace the need to import manufactured goods
d. to increase the amount of manufactured goods imported from foreign countries

_____ 2. What were Fidel Castro's goals in Cuba?
a. to impose moderate democratic reforms
b. to end U.S. dominance, redistribute wealth, and reform society
c. to establish a Marxist regime
d. to industrialize the country in order to pump money into the economy

_____ 3. What caused the hyperinflation in Brazil in the early 1990s?
a. growing national debt and rising oil prices
b. freezing wages
c. the loss of population to government death squads
d. the bloody military coup

_____ 4. What was true about U.S. foreign policy in Guatemala, El Salvador, and Nicaragua?
a. The United States supported the work of social reformers in each country.
b. The United States maintained a "hands-off" policy.
c. The United States worked to make democratically elected governments stable in all three.
d. The United States supported anticommunist, corrupt governments.

_____ 5. The military dictatorships of Chile, Brazil, and Argentina all
a. were put into power by the Soviet Union.
b. presided over economies undergoing rapid growth.
c. used torture and murder to silence opposition.
d. were populist.

_____ 6. Salvador Allende in Chile
a. oversaw several periods of rapid economic growth.
b. gradually transformed his government into a Marxist dictatorship.
c. was extremely popular for his social reforms and re-elected several times.
d. worried the U.S. government with his leftist policies.

Latin America

Chapter Test

Form A

_____ 7. Luiz Inácio Lula da Silva of Brazil was a leftist leader who
a. closed down the unions.
b. led a communist but not a totalitarian government.
c. balanced the interest of social reformers and businesses.
d. advanced the interests of large capitalists over poor people.

_____ 8. The election of Vicente Fox as president of Mexico was significant because
a. it ended 71 years of one-party rule.
b. his election was characterized by fraud.
c. he was Mexico's first socialist president.
d. he never took office.

_____ 9. While the North American Free Trade Agreement was intended to remove barriers to trade, many Mexicans worried that
a. their population would decrease as a result of free immigration.
b. their political system would suffer if a second party were allowed to run opposition candidates.
c. tourism would suffer from decreased competition.
d. increased competition from foreign imports would hurt their economy.

PRACTICING SOCIAL STUDIES SKILLS Study the graph below and answer the question that follows.

GDP Per Capita in Latin America

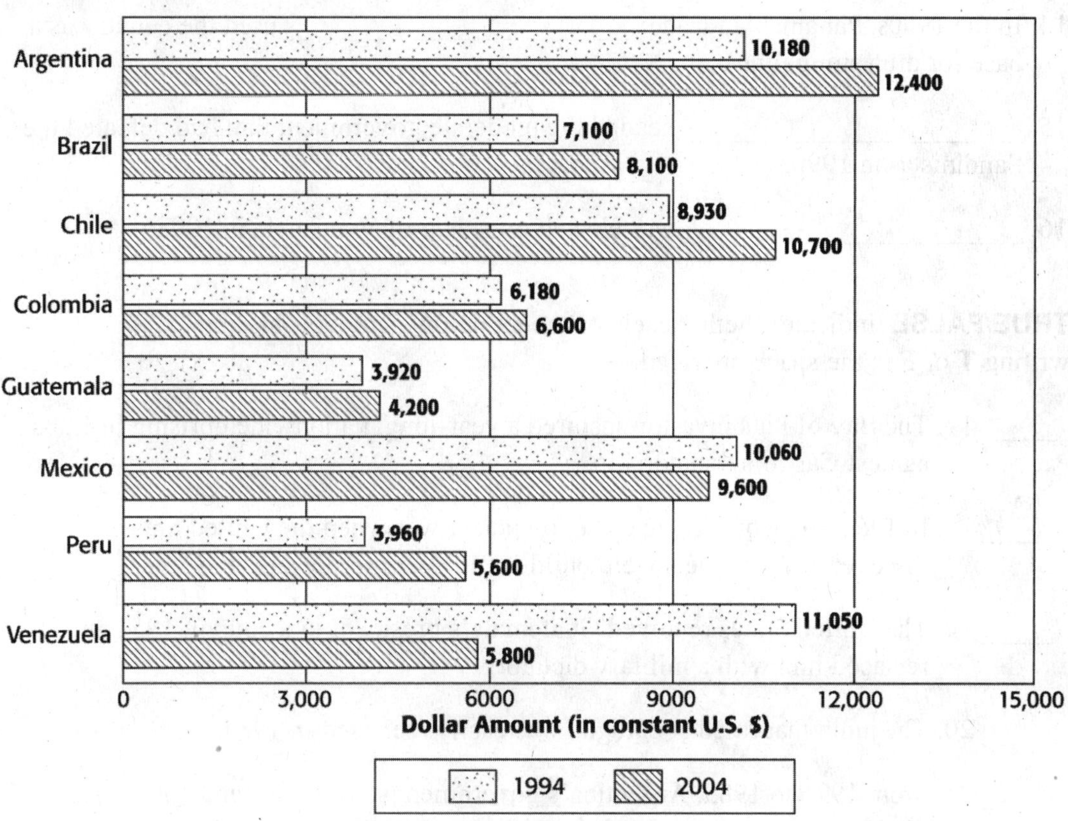

Sources: The World Almanac and Book of Facts, 1997; The World Almanac and Book of Facts, 2006

_____ 10. Which of the following statements is best supported by the information in the graph?
- a. All Latin American economies suffered setbacks between 1994 and 2004.
- b. The populations of Latin American countries are growing.
- c. More people in Latin American countries lived below the poverty line in 2004 than in 1994.
- d. In general, the economies of most Latin American countries grew.

FILL IN THE BLANK For each of the following statements, fill in the blank with the appropriate word, phrase, or name.

11. Catholics who support ______________________ Theology urge the Church to be active in the struggle for economic and political equality in Latin America.

12. The revolutionary group, the ______________________, established some collective farms and passed laws to protect workers' rights in Nicaragua.

13. A leader who supports the rights of the common people as opposed to the privileged elite is a ____________________.

14. In the 1980s, Panamanian leader ____________________ used the country as a base for drug smuggling.

15. ____________________ headed the moderate government that had defeated the Sandinistas in 1990.

16. ____________________ was elected president of Venezuela in 1998.

TRUE/FALSE Indicate whether each statement below is true or false by writing **T** or **F** in the space provided.

_____ 17. The Bay of Pigs invasion inspired a year-long, nationwide uprising in Cuba against Castro's dictatorship.

_____ 18. In 1962, the world came close to nuclear war when the United States discovered the Soviets were building nuclear missile sites in Cuba.

_____ 19. The United States removed Guatemala's president in a coup in 1952 and replaced him with a military dictator.

_____ 20. The junta that ruled Nicaragua was easily reelected in 1984.

_____ 21. From 1976 to 1983, Argentina's government seized thousands of suspected dissidents who were never heard from again.

_____ 22. In Chile, leftist leader Augusto Pinochet made sweeping changes intended to improve the lives of the working class and stimulate the slow economy.

_____ 23. In 1990, Peru faced the dual challenges of a poor economy and the terrorist activities of a group called the Shining Path.

_____ 24. Mexico's economy remained strong in the 1980s when world oil prices fell.

_____ 25. Many Latin American countries have instituted free-market reforms to stabilize economies, reduce inflation, and pay their debts.

Name ______________________ Class ______________________ Date ______________

Latin America

Chapter Test
Form B

SHORT ANSWER On a separate sheet of paper, answer each of the following questions in complete sentences. Remember to use specific examples to support your answers.

1. Describe the conditions in Cuba in the 1950s that made the island susceptible to a revolution.
2. What have been some positive effects of the Cuban Revolution?
3. Describe two ways the United States has influenced change in Latin America.
4. Why did Latin American military governments fall in the 1980s and 1990s?
5. Name three market reforms undertaken by Latin American governments in the 1990s.

PRACTICING SOCIAL STUDIES SKILLS Study the graph below and, on a separate sheet of paper, answer the question that follows in complete sentences.

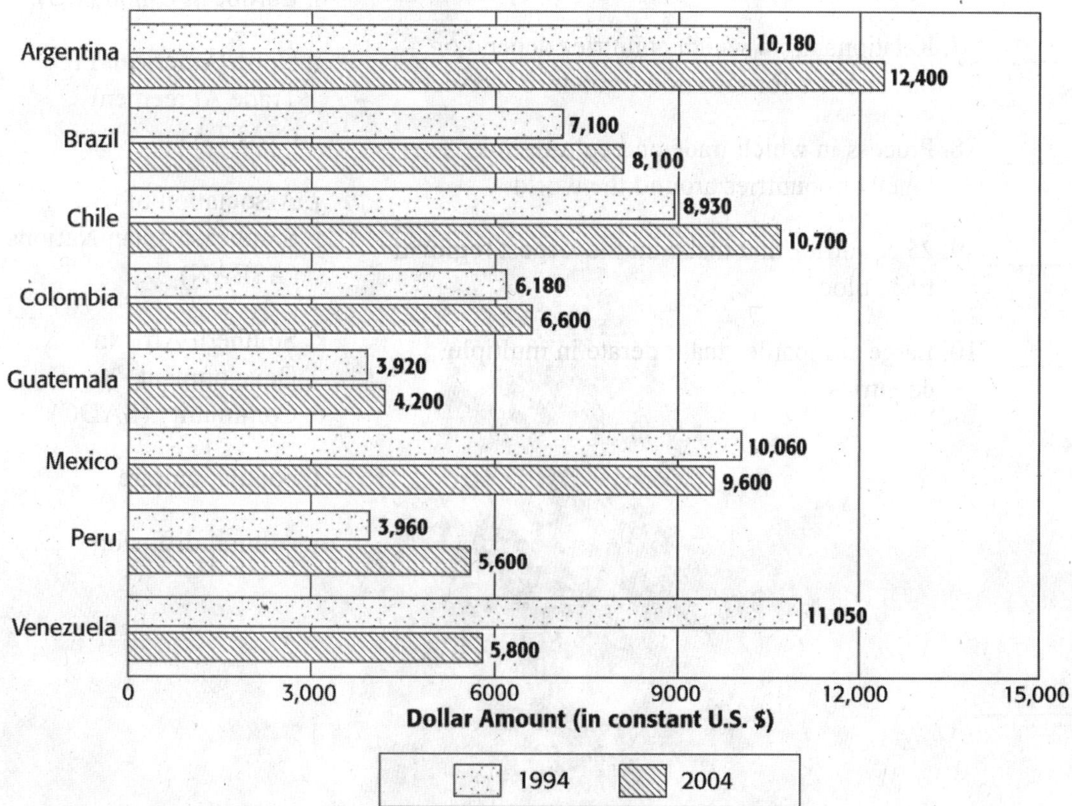

Sources: The World Almanac and Book of Facts, 1997; The World Almanac and Book of Facts, 2006

6. How does the graph illustrate some recent trends in Latin America?

Name ______________________ Class ______________ Date ______________

Today's World

Section Quiz

Section 1

MATCHING In the space provided, write the letter of the term or place that matches each description. Some answers will not be used.

_____ 1. Culture traits that are common within a group of people

_____ 2. First major international agreement on free trade, established in 1948

_____ 3. Group of approximately 150 countries that monitor national trade policies and help resolve trade disputes

_____ 4. Exchange of goods among nations without trade barriers

_____ 5. Practice of having work done elsewhere to cut costs or increase production

_____ 6. Spread of culture traits from one region to another

_____ 7. Relationship in which countries depend on one another for resources, goods, or services

_____ 8. Process in which trade and culture link together countries around the world

_____ 9. 25 countries that make up the largest regional trade bloc

_____ 10. Large companies that operate in multiple countries

a. globalization

b. interdependence

c. multinational corporations

d. outsourcing

e. General Agreement on Tariffs and Trade (GATT)

f. World Trade Organization (WTO)

g. free trade

h. European Union (EU)

i. North American Free Trade Agreement (NAFTA)

j. Association of Southeast Asian Nations (ASEAN)

k. Southern African Development Community (SADC)

l. popular culture

m. cultural diffusion

Name ______________________ Class ______________ Date ______________

Today's World

Section Quiz

Section 2

TRUE/FALSE Mark each statement **T** if it is true or **F** if it is false. If false explain why.

_____ 1. Countries that signed the Helsinki Accords in 1975 agreed to establish and regulate fair trade practices among developed nations.

____

____

_____ 2. An NGO is a government-sponsored agency dedicated to promoting human rights.

____

____

_____ 3. Factors that cause people to leave their homes and migrate are sometimes described as "push" and "pull" factors.

____

____

_____ 4. More than 20 percent of the world's people live on less than a $1 per day and do not have access to basic services such as education and health care.

____

____

_____ 5. The increase in the percentage of people who live in cities is called ruralization.

____

____

Name ______________________ Class ______________ Date ______________

Today's World

Section Quiz

Section 3

FILL IN THE BLANK For each of the following statements, fill in the blank with the appropriate word, phrase, or name.

1. The ______________________ used terrorist acts on British targets in an effort to end British control of Northern Ireland.

2. Due to the Arab-Israeli conflict and the region's history of Western colonial domination the ______________________ has become a focus of efforts against international terrorist groups.

3. In 2001, a U.S.-led military campaign invaded ______________________, where the Taliban government supported the terrorist group al Qaeda.

4. Weapons of mass destruction may include chemical weapons such as those used by Saddam Hussein against the Kurds in ______________________.

5. During the Cold War, the Soviet Union was among the nations that signed the ______________________ Non-proliferation Treaty designed to stop the spread of nuclear weapons.

6. It is difficult to control nuclear weapons because nuclear technology can be used for ______________________ purposes.

7. Tragically, tension between ______________________ groups, such as between the Tutsi and Hutu of Rwanda, can result in mass killings and other abuses.

8. In the early 2000s, a peacekeeping force sent by the African Union attempted to stop the loss of life and physical destruction caused by government-sponsored Arab militias in ______________________.

9. One way a country tries to force a change in policy on another country is through economic or political ______________________.

10. The International Atomic Energy Agency routinely monitors countries suspected of developing ______________________ weapons.

Name ______________________ Class ______________ Date ______________

Today's World

Section Quiz

Section 4

MULTIPLE CHOICE For each of the following, write the letter of the best choice in the space provided.

_____ 1. Deforestation in the Amazon region of Brazil
a. increased rainfall in the region.
b. resulted in the extinction of some species of plants and animals.
c. caused a loss of jobs in the mining industry.
d. prevented cattle ranching from being profitable.

_____ 2. Desertification is caused by drought and
a. too many trees in a particular region.
b. excessive rainfall in the same year.
c. human activity such as overgrazing livestock.
d. extreme temperatures.

_____ 3. Sustainable development can best be described as
a. economic development that relies on human activity to sustain a profit.
b. long-term jobs that permanently employ a nation's workforce.
c. natural resources that can be cultivated for profit.
d. economic development that does not permanently damage resources.

_____ 4. Genetic engineering can be described as
a. altering the genetic makeup of a plant or animal.
b. a rise in the surface temperature of the earth.
c. information technology.
d. sharing cultural ideas about agricultural technology.

_____ 5. The green revolution is
a. dedication to avoiding meat products in one's diet.
b. farming without pesticides.
c. a movement to grow food without relying on technology.
d. the attempt by agricultural scientists to increase food production by developing new food crops.

Today's World

Chapter Test

Form A

MULTIPLE CHOICE For each of the following, write the letter of the best choice in the space provided.

_____ 1. Some people argue against multinational corporations because they believe that
a. outsourcing causes a loss of jobs in a home country.
b. they improve the standard of living in developing countries.
c. developing countries are doing all right on their own.
d. developing countries will become wealthier than developed countries.

_____ 2. Opponents of free trade
a. believe that it does not provide new markets for goods.
b. support the work of the World Trade Organization.
c. believe that it encourages practices that exploit workers and damage the environment in developing countries.
d. do not support social responsibility in corporations.

_____ 3. Which system of government tends to best protect the human rights of its citizens?
a. military rule
b. dictatorship
c. autocracy
d. democracy

_____ 4. When a disease becomes an epidemic it means that
a. it is not contagious.
b. only people without access to medical care will be affected.
c. it is spreading quickly and affecting many people.
d. a vaccine has been developed.

_____ 5. In 1994, about 1 million people were massacred due to ethnic tension in
a. Rwanda.
b. Darfur.
c. Germany.
d. Iraq.

_____ 6. Some scientists believe that global warming
a. was caused by the meltdown of the nuclear plant in Chernobyl.
b. is due to cloning.
c. is the result of the green revolution.
d. is caused by air pollution from human activity.

_____ 7. Deforestation is a problem because
a. it causes the land to become useless.
b. plants and animals may become extinct.
c. it creates a protected area for threatened species.
d. it can lead to millions of illnesses and deaths each year.

______ 8. Genetically engineered plants
a. were modified to reduce food production.
b. may reduce pesticide use.
c. have well documented effects on humans and the environment.
d. have bankrupted small farmers.

PRACTICING SOCIAL STUDIES SKILLS Study the visuals below and answer the questions that follow.

Motor Vehicle Production, 1950–2000

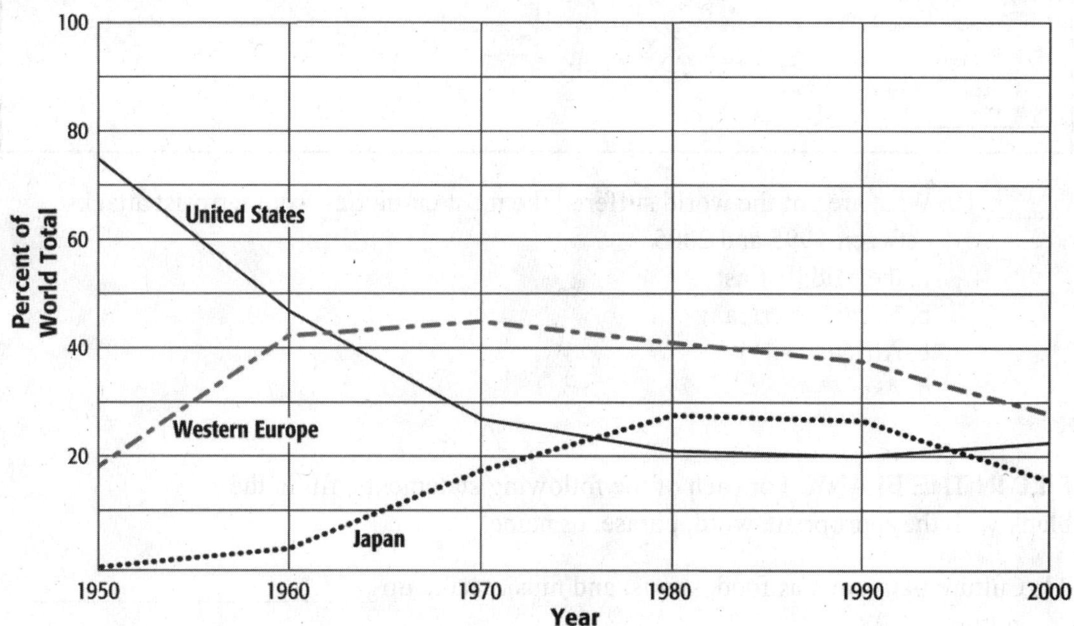

Source: The World Almanac and Book of Facts, 2006

______ 9. In the year 2000, the United States, Japan, and Western Europe combined produced about what percent of the world's motor vehicles?
a. 33%
b. 50%
c. 65%
d. 95%

Name ______________________ Class ______________ Date ______________

Today's World

Chapter Test

Form A

Worldwide Terrorism Incidents

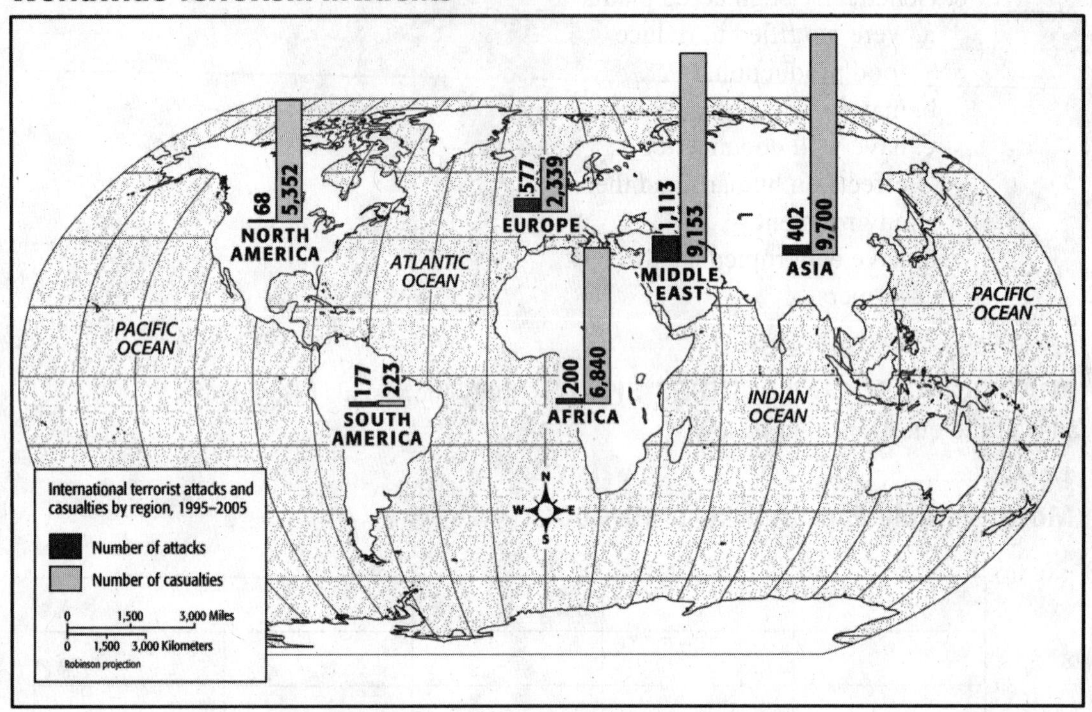

_____ 10. What area of the world suffered the most casualties from terrorist attacks between 1995 and 2005

a. the Middle East
b. North America
c. Africa
d. Asia

FILL IN THE BLANK For each of the following statements, fill in the blank with the appropriate word, phrase, or name.

11. Culture traits such as food, sports, and music make up ______________________ culture.

12. An extreme shortage of food, or ______________________, is one result of poverty.

13. The tsunami that devastated large areas of Southeast Asia in 2004 is an example of a(n) ______________________.

14. ______________________ are people who leave their home country to seek safety in another nation.

15. The Irish Republican Army, Tamil Tigers, and Hezbollah are examples of groups that have used ______________________.

16. ______________________ may help balance the need for economic development with protection of the environment.

17. The exchange of information has become such an important part of modern life that some people say we are living in a(n) ______________________.

MATCHING In the space provided, write the letter of the term or place that matches each description. Some answers will not be used.

_____ 18. Can include economic penalties imposed by one country on another

_____ 19. The use of biological research in industry

_____ 20. The process by which countries are linked to each other through trade and culture

_____ 21. The process of creating an identical organism from a cell of an original organism

_____ 22. Takes place when people from rural areas move to cities

_____ 23. A likely cause of global warming

_____ 24. The spread of culture traits from one region to another

_____ 25. Groups that have played key roles in the fight against slavery, violence against women, and apartheid

a. genetics

b. cultural diffusion

c. sanctions

d. air pollution

e. NGOs

f. urbanization

g. cloning

h. globalization

i. free trade

j. biotechnology

Name ______________________ Class ______________ Date ______________

Today's World

Chapter Test

Form B

SHORT ANSWER On a separate sheet of paper, answer each of the following questions in complete sentences. Remember to use specific examples to support your answers.

1. How do developing countries differ from developed countries?
2. Describe two ways in which cultural diffusion takes place.
3. Explain how migration is influenced by "push" and "pull" factors.
4. Describe two kinds of weapons of mass destruction.
5. Imagine you were growing up before the Information Age. How would your life be different than it is now?

PRACTICING SOCIAL STUDIES SKILLS Study the map below and, on a separate sheet of paper, answer the question that follows in complete sentences.

Worldwide Terrorism Incidents

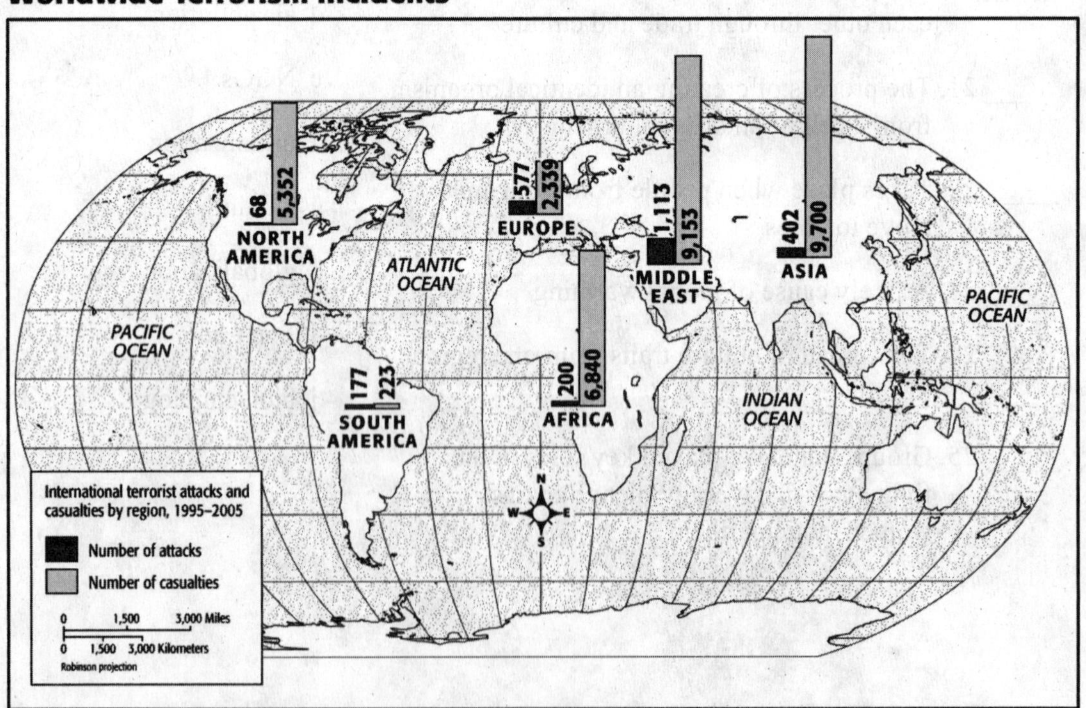

6. What area of the world saw the most terrorist attacks between 1995 and 2005? Based on your knowledge of the chapter why do you think this was so?

Name ______________________ Class ______________ Date ______________

The Contemporary World

Unit Test

Form A

MATCHING In the space provided, write the letter of the term that matches each description. Some answers will not be used.

_____ 1. Built to stop migration from East to West Germany

_____ 2. Economic or political penalties imposed by one country on another to try to force a change in policy

_____ 3. Belief that communism in Vietnam would spread to other Southeast Asian countries

_____ 4. Mao's plan to increase China's industrial and agricultural output

_____ 5. A violent movement to free Kenya of white farmers

_____ 6. U.S.-led alliance against communism in the Middle East during the 1950s

_____ 7. A period of growth in industrial exports, farming, and mining in a certain Latin American country

_____ 8. The belief that the church should be active in the struggle for economic and social equality

_____ 9. The process in which countries are linked together through trade and culture

_____ 10. Economic development that does not permanently damage resources

a. domino theory

b. Brazilian Miracle

c. global warming

d. globalization

e. Berlin Wall

f. green revolution

g. Mau Mau

h. sustainable development

i. sanctions

j. Warsaw Pact

k. Liberation Theology

l. Baghdad Pact

m. Great Leap Forward

FILL IN THE BLANK For each of the following statements, fill in the blank with the appropriate word, phrase, or name.

11. The purpose of the ______________________ was to help Western Europe make a rapid recovery from war and preserve political stability.

12. American officials believed that the 1961 U.S.-led invasion at the Bay of Pigs would start a massive uprising against ______________________.

13. After the death of ______________________ in 1976, Chinese leaders retreated from many of his policies.

The Contemporary World

Unit Test

Form A

14. The purpose of the ______________________ campaign was to drive the British from India.

15. South Africa's requirement that black students must be taught Afrikaans resulted in a protest movement called the ______________________.

16. F.W. de Klerk opened the way to a new constitution that ended the policy of ______________________ in South Africa.

17. Juan Perón was an example of a ______________________ leader—one who supports the rights of the common people, as opposed to the privileged elite.

18. In 1992 Mexico, the United States, and Canada signed an agreement known by the initials ______________________, eliminating tariffs on trade among the three countries.

19. The process of ______________________ leads to a scarcity of fertile farmland and threatens parts of North Africa with cycles of drought and famine.

20. Nuclear, ______________________, and chemical weapons are known as weapons of mass destruction.

TRUE/FALSE Indicate whether each statement below is true or false by writing **T** or **F** in the space provided.

_____ 21. The Cold War was a conflict between communism and capitalist democracy.

_____ 22. The arms race was a competition between the United States and the Soviet Union to gain new colonies.

_____ 23. Market reforms were made in many Latin American countries despite the opposition of the IMF and World Bank.

_____ 24. The Tet Offensive proved that U.S. forces were close to victory in Vietnam.

_____ 25. Tension between the Hutu and Tutsis that led to violence and genocide is an example of ethnic conflict.

_____ 26. Arab members of OPEC applied an oil embargo to nations supporting Israel.

_____ 27. The assassination of Archbishop Oscar Romero set off a civil war in El Salvador.

_____ 28. Juan Perón put an end to Argentina's one-party system.

_____ 29. Economic interdependence occurs because countries are quite similar in the types of goods and services they need and can provide.

_____ 30. One cause of poverty is rapid population growth.

MULTIPLE CHOICE For each of the following, write the letter of the best choice in the space provided.

_____ 31. The Cuban missile crisis occurred when
a. Cuban exiles invaded at the Bay of Pigs.
b. Fidel Castro installed a Communist government.
c. a Cuban missile landed in the Gulf of Mexico.
d. the United States spotted Soviet nuclear arms in Cuba.

_____ 32. Al Qaeda's forces in the Middle East were supported and protected by
a. the Muslim League.
b. the Taliban.
c. Corazon Aquino.
d. Suharto.

_____ 33. The Vietnam War resulted in
a. France regaining control.
b. victory for North Vietnam.
c. victory for South Vietnam.
d. U. S. colonization of Vietnam.

_____ 34. The two superpowers in the nuclear arms race were the United States and
a. China.
b. Germany.
c. the Soviet Union.
d. Great Britain.

_____ 35. The goal of the Anti-Ballistic Missile or ABM Treaty was to
a. end the arms race.
b. stop development of weapons that could shoot down missiles.
c. make the superpowers invulnerable to attack.
d. freeze all weapons development.

_____ 36. India's partition resulted in
a. tight British control.
b. creation of the Indian National Congress.
c. violent religious conflicts.
d. equal distribution of wealth.

_____ 37. What outside factor boosted Japan's economy in the 1950s?
a. the Korean War
b. the Vietnam War
c. China's Cultural Revolution
d. the nuclear arms race

_____ 38. China's student protests of 1989 ended with the
a. arrest of the Gang of Four.
b. creation of the Red Guards.
c. Cultural Revolution.
d. Tiananmen Square Massacre.

_____ 39. The first step toward the creation of a separate Jewish state was
a. the Suez Crisis.
b. the Yom Kippur War.
c. when Britain gave the UN control of Palestine.
d. the first Arab-Israeli war.

_____ 40. What event led to the Persian Gulf War?
a. an Iranian call for revolution among Iraq's Shiite population
b. Iraq's invasion of Kuwait
c. the attacks of September 11, 2001
d. Israeli air strikes in Gaza

_____ 41. The growth of Islamism has contributed to
a. globalization.
b. the success of OPEC.
c. peace agreements with Israel.
d. conflict in the Middle East.

_____ 42. The Cuban Revolution in the 1950s was sparked by Castro's distrust of
a. Liberation Theology.
b. Communist propaganda.
c. U.S. dominance in Cuba.
d. the financial support of the Soviet Union.

_____ 43. Following World War II, many countries in Latin America experienced
a. massive migration to rural areas.
b. a rise in dictatorships.
c. the withdrawal of religious leaders.
d. increased civilian participation in government.

_____ 44. Latin American leaders lost power in the 1980s and 1990s because of
a. election fraud.
b. massive emigration of skilled workers.
c. failure to make social and economic progress.
d. a renewal of European imperialism.

_____ 45. North Korea's goal in the Korean War was to
a. protect its northern borders.
b. end South Korean aggression.
c. draw the United States into a war.
d. unite Korea under Communist rule.

_____ 46. The Korean War resulted in
a. a stalemate.
b. a North Korean victory.
c. a South Korean victory.
d. China's gaining control of Korea.

_____ 47. Which is a characteristic of a developing nation?
a. widespread technology
b. inadequate education
c. broad health care systems
d. an economy based on manufacturing

_____ 48. The green revolution is an attempt to increase
a. Internet access.
b. food production.
c. recycling of consumer goods.
d. land in rainforests.

PRACTICING SOCIAL STUDIES SKILLS Study the visual below and answer the questions that follow.

The Korean War, 1950–1951

June 1950

① In a surprise attack, North Korean troops invade the South.

Sept. 1950

② UN forces land at Inchon attacking behind North Korean lines.

Sept.–Oct. 1950

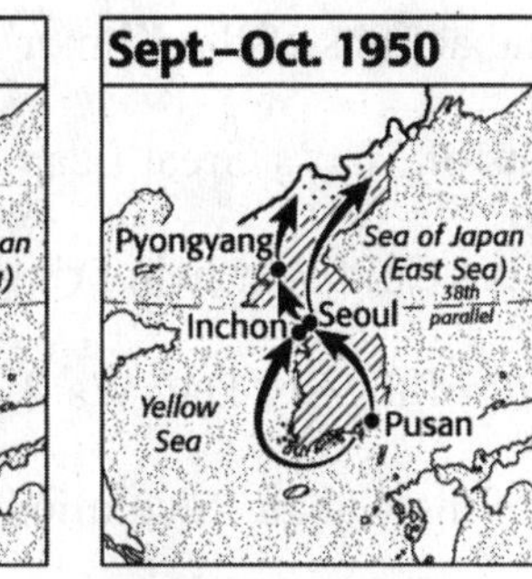

③ UN forces quickly push north from Pusan and Inchon.

Nov. 1950–Jan. 1951

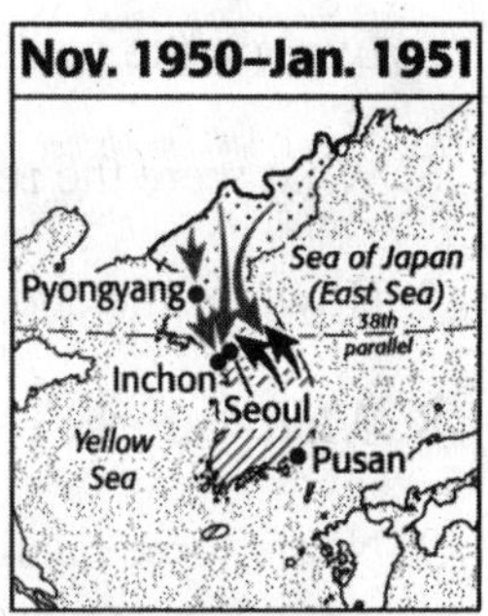

④ China enters the war on the side of North Korea.

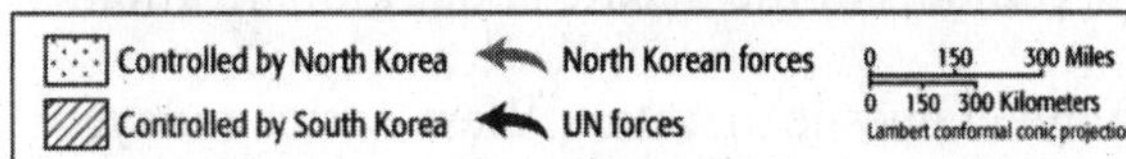

_____ 49. Which of the following cities is north of the 38th parallel?
a. Pyongyang
b. Seoul
c. Inchon
d. Pusan

_____ 50. During which period did South Korea control the largest amount of territory?
a. June 1950
b. September 1950
c. Sept.-Oct. 1950
d. Nov. 1950-Jan. 1951

Name ______________________ Class ______________ Date ______________

The Contemporary World

Unit Test

Form B

SHORT ANSWER On a separate sheet of paper, answer each of the following questions in complete sentences. Remember to use specific examples to support your answers.

1. Explain how the Truman Doctrine and the Marshall Plan are products of the Cold War.
2. What were the causes and effects of the Soviet blockade in Berlin?
3. What caused worsening relations between the United States and Britain, on one side, and the Soviet Union, on the other, after World War II?
4. Describe one cause and one effect of partition in India.
5. Explain the goals and actions of the Khmer Rouge in Cambodia.
6. What were the results of Mao's Great Leap Forward?
7. How did the end of the Cold War help bring democracy to many African nations?
8. What were the results of the Six-Day War?
9. Name three results of the Cuban Revolution.
10. How did economic reforms in Latin America in the 1990s affect poverty?
11. Explain opposing arguments in the debate about globalization.
12. Describe an environmental issue affecting West Africa today.

Name ______________________ Class ______________ Date ______________

The Contemporary World Unit Test

Form B

PRACTICING SOCIAL STUDIES SKILLS Study the maps below and, on a separate sheet of paper, answer the question that follows.

The Korean War, 1950–1951

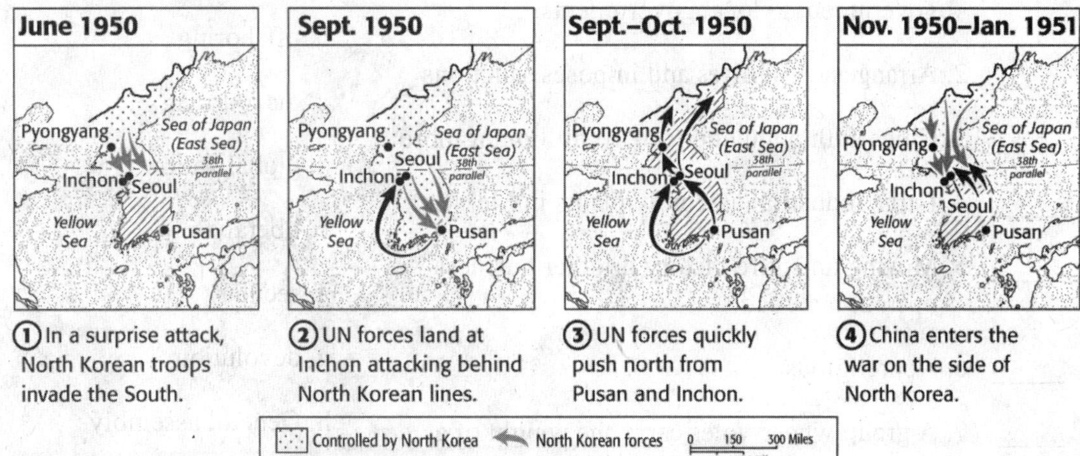

13. Based on the maps, describe how the control of territory changed at different stages of the Korean War.

Name ______________________ Class ______________ Date ______________

Issues in the Contemporary World — Unit Test

Form A

MATCHING In the space provided, write the letter of the term that matches each description. Some answers will not be used.

_____ 1. The redistribution of power from a central government to local governments

_____ 2. Arranges cease-fires and imposes sanctions

_____ 3. Cities with populations of 10 million or more

_____ 4. Large industrial assembly plants in Mexico

_____ 5. Moving an entire factory or other business operation abroad

_____ 6. Nonreligious

_____ 7. A group whose votes carry the weight of a statement of world opinion

_____ 8. To open up, such as an economy

_____ 9. Private ownership of industries

_____ 10. One of the world's strongest markers for disadvantage

a. megacities
b. offshoring
c. outsourcing
d. globalization
e. liberalize
f. secular
g. devolution
h. General assembly
i. privatization
j. gender
k. socialist market
l. maquiladoras
m. Security Council

FILL IN THE BLANK For each of the following statements, fill in the blank with the appropriate word, phrase, or name.

11. Since it was elected in 1997, Britain's ______________________ government has sought to reform the country's democratic institutions.

12. In South Africa, the ______________________ has seen its majorities rise in each of the three national elections since the end of apartheid.

13. ______________________ has the second largest economy in Latin America.

14. Mexico's location next to the ______________________ has made it possible to expand trade under the North American Free Trade Agreement (NAFTA).

15. China's economic liberalization was initially confined to the creation of a few ______________________ such as the city of Shenzen, which served as a testing ground for China's limited capitalism.

Issues in the Contemporary World

Unit Test

Form A

16. At first, foreign companies operated in India as ______________________, or business partnerships with Indian companies.

17. The ______________________ was created to settle disputes among nations and solve global problems.

18. In the 1990s, India embraced capitalism and began to move toward a ______________________ economy.

19. The ______________________ includes all member nations of the United Nations.

20. Permanent members of the Security Council have ______________________ power, which guarantees the interests of powerful nations.

TRUE/FALSE **Indicate whether each statement below is true or false by writing T or F in the space provided.**

_____ 21. Public participation in a democracy is limited to voting in public elections.

_____ 22. In a recent survey, two thirds of South Africans said they believe their country was governed by the will of the people.

_____ 23. In Rio de Janeiro, Brazil, the shantytowns called *favelas* are so dangerous that the police will not go there.

_____ 24. Mexico's assembly plants produce finished goods for export to the United States.

_____ 25. China's entry into the WTO blocked China from foreign investment and offshoring.

_____ 26. Low import tariffs have helped India's economy grow.

_____ 27. An economic boom in Ireland produced a need for workers, leading to increased employment for women.

_____ 28. Women's rights in Turkey were written into laws regarding property ownership, inheritance, and suffrage.

_____ 29. In Ireland, overall participation of women in public office is low.

_____ 30. The Secretariat carries out peacekeeping missions for the United Nations.

Issues in the Contemporary World

Unit Test

Form A

MULTIPLE CHOICE For each of the following, write the letter of the best choice in the space provided.

_____ 31. Both Great Britain and South Africa experienced a
a. rise in voter participation.
b. drop in voter participation.
c. recent change to democracy.
d. change in voter eligibility.

_____ 32. The lack of land in Mexico continues to draw peasants to the megacity of
a. Rio de Janeiro.
b. São Paulo.
c. Mexico City.
d. Shenzen.

_____ 33. What event caused a temporary rise in voter turnout in South Africa?
a. independence
b. the founding of the ANC
c. government reward for participation
d. the uncovering of government corruption

_____ 34. In the "Voice of the People" survey, the majority of respondents said that
a. they were generally satisfied with democracy.
b. they were generally unsatisfied with democracy.
c. their countries were ruled by the will of the people.
d. their countries were ruled by capable leaders.

_____ 35. Both Brazil and Mexico are trying to broaden their economic base by
a. increasing imports.
b. increasing urbanization.
c. establishing themselves as true democracies.
d. expanding their trade sources and foreign investment.

_____ 36. As Brazil's exports surged in the mid-1990s,
a. the economy weakened.
b. poverty rates decreased.
c. the economy grew.
d. school enrollment decreased.

_____ 37. To ease population pressures, Brazil
a. built new megacities.
b. designed multistoried homes.
c. encouraged emigration.
d. opened the interior region for resettlement.

_____ 38. International outcry has spurred Brazil to
a. gain control over the continent's trade.
b. build a partnership with the European Union.
c. limit rural overdevelopment.
d. become a political superpower in South America.

_____ 39. With the rise to power of Deng Xiaoping in 1978, China's government started to
a. decrease free-market incentives.
b. return many industries to state control.
c. take land away from peasants.
d. encourage foreign investment.

_____ 40. The lack of free-market incentives in 1960s China resulted in
a. low productivity.
b. foreign investments.
c. an increased standard of living.
d. strict curbs on population growth.

_____ 41. The great majority of India's population works
a. in large industries.
b. in government offices.
c. for foreign computer companies.
d. on farms and in small traditional businesses.

_____ 42. Already home to one-sixth of the world's people, the most populous nation in the world within the next 50 years is expected to be
a. the United States.
b. Japan.
c. China.
d. India.

_____ 43. Ireland's constitution was modified in 1972 to remove the clause that gave
a. equal rights to women.
b. the Catholic Church a "special position."
c. women equal pay as men in the same job.
d. Catholic women the vote.

_____ 44. As a member of the European Union, Ireland
a. has not attempted to conform to EU standards.
b. is not required to conform to EU standards.
c. has conformed to EU standards on the treatment of women.
d. no longer allows married women to work outside the home.

_____ 45. In 1923, Turkey was founded as a nation government and religion are
a. one and the same.
b. separated by law.
c. are part of every law passed.
d. essential to the continuation of the state.

_____ 46. One of the four major goals stated in the United Nations' charter is to
a. advance democracy worldwide.
b. promote respect for human rights.
c. spread power equally among all nations.
d. provide a voice for developing nations.

Name ______________ Class ______________ Date ______________

_____ 47. One recent criticism of the UN has been
- a. it reacts too quickly to world issues.
- b. it no longer attempts to maintain peace.
- c. it is not effective at combating terrorism.
- d. it does not guarantee the best interests of permanent members.

_____ 48. The five permanent members of the Security Council are France, Russia, the United Kingdom, the United States, and
- a. Japan.
- b. China.
- c. India.
- d. Israel.

_____ 49. The International Court of Justice is held at The Hague, in the Netherlands, but the rest of the UN's operations are based at its global headquarters in
- a. Geneva.
- b. New York.
- c. Paris.
- d. Rome.

PRACTICING SOCIAL STUDIES SKILLS Study the visual below and answer the question that follows.

Millennium Development Goals
1. Eradicate extreme poverty and hunger. 2. Achieve universal primary education. 3. Promote gender equality and empower women. 4. Reduce child mortality. 5. Improve maternal health. 6. Combat HIV/Aids, malaria, and other diseases. 7. Ensure environmental sustainability. 8. Develop a global partnership for development.

_____ 50. The Millennium Development Goals reflect the United Nation's emphasis on
- a. solving global problems.
- b. expanding the economies of developed nations.
- c. space exploration.
- d. peacekeeping programs.

Name ______________________ Class ______________ Date ______________

Issues in the Contemporary World

Unit Test

Form B

SHORT ANSWER On a separate sheet of paper, answer each of the following questions in complete sentences. Remember to use specific examples to support your answers.

1. What is civic participation?

2. Why and how has Britain's Labor government sought to reform the country's democratic institutions?

3. Describe some of the changes in the economies of China and India.

4. Explain how religious beliefs have influenced the roles of women in Turkey and Ireland.

5. What are the four main goals included in the United Nations charter?

PRACTICING SOCIAL STUDIES SKILLS Study the table below and, on a separate sheet of paper, answer the question that follows in complete sentences.

Megacities

City/Metropolitan areas (rank)	Population* (2000)	Percentage of population (2000)	Projected population growth (2000 – 2015)
Tokyo, Japan (1)	34,450	27.1%	5.1%
Mexico City, Mexico (2)	18,066	18.3%	14.3%
New York City (3)	17,846	6.3%	10.5%
Sao Paolo, Brazil (4)	17,099	10.0%	16.7%
Mumbai, India (5)	16,086	1.6%	40.8%
Rio de Janeiro, Brazil (14)	10,803	6.3%	14.4%

Source: *The World Almanac and Book of Facts*, 2006

* All population figures in thousands

6. What percentage of Brazil's total population lives in São Paulo and Rio de Janeiro? Use information from the unit to describe what life is like in the two cities.

Name ______________________ Class ______________ Date ______________

End-of-Year Test

MULTIPLE CHOICE For each of the following, write the letter of the best choice in the space provided.

_____ 1. Early humans living during the Stone Age most likely
a. lived in small groups and moved to new areas as food became scarce.
b. settled in permanent villages for common defense.
c. were uninterested in art or music.
d. worshipped one god.

_____ 2. What was an important development for early people of the Stone Age?
a. the use of tools
b. calendars
c. writing
d. cave art

_____ 3. The Neolithic Revolution marked the
a. end of Homo habilis.
b. creation of man-made fire.
c. beginning of agricultural societies.
d. introduction of stone tools.

_____ 4. Hammurabi's Code was an
a. early method of communication.
b. early written code of law.
c. effort to tax the Babylonians.
d. ethical code for waging war.

_____ 5 The world's first civilization arose
a. in China.
b. along the Nile River.
c. in Mesopotamia.
d. in the Indus Valley.

_____ 6. Many scholars believe that Judaism
a. developed under Julius Caesar.
b. died out in 1000 BC.
c. was founded by David, Israel's greatest king.
d. was the world's first monotheistic religion.

_____ 7. During the Old Kingdom, Egyptians built pyramids because of their belief in
a. archaeology.
b. reincarnation.
c. the afterlife.
d. medical studies.

_____ 8. The experience of Hyksos rule led pharaohs in the New Kingdom to
a. create Egypt's first permanent army.
b. pass laws forbidding weapons in Egypt.
c. organize teams of archers to protect the pyramids.
d. rely on geographical barriers for protection.

_____ 9. The Rosetta Stone helped historians to
a. understand the purpose of the pyramids.
b. understand Egyptian writing.
c. decipher Linear A.
d. find the source of the Nile.

_____ 10. The early Indus settlements of Harappa and Mohenjo Daro can best be described as
a. disorganized units.
b. small villages.
c. well planned and carefully laid out.
d. lacking clean water and sanitary conditions.

_____ 11. The *Vedas*, *Upanishads*, and *Mahabharata* are some of the sacred texts of
a. Islam.
b. Dualism.
c. Hinduism.
d. Buddhism.

_____ 12. What Zhou idea was used to explain the dynastic cycle?
a. Yin and Yang
b. Enlightenment
c. the Middle Road
d. Mandate of Heaven

_____ 13. The Mycenaean states formed
a. an early Greek civilization.
b. the first industrial empire.
c. an early African trading kingdom.
d. the first matriarchal society.

_____ 14. The world's first democracy existed in
a. Athens.
b. Sparta.
c. Knossos.
d. Carthage.

_____ 15. Which of the following Greeks is known for a method of learning through questions?
a. Plato
b. Socrates
c. Aristotle
d. Sophocles

_____ 16. Which of the following phrases describes the government of the Roman Republic?
a. unrestricted use of military rule
b. network of local governments
c. use of clergy to write and enforce laws
d. system of checks and balances

_____ 17. Law and order, a stable government, and widespread trade were characteristics of
a. the Pax Romana.
b. the Early Republic.
c. the Late Republic.
d. the Age of Constantine.

_____ 18. Caesar, Pompey, and Crassus are known as the
a. Good Emperors.
b. Julio-Claudians.
c. First Triumvirate.
d. Second Triumvirate.

_____ 19. The Hohokum people of North America adapted to desert farming by
a. using terraces.
b. planting crops in riverbeds.
c. using slash-and-burn techniques.
d. digging irrigation canals.

_____ 20. Mesoamerica is the region that includes
- a. South America and Central America.
- b. North America and Central America.
- c. southern Mexico and northern Central America.
- d. northern Mexico and the Mid-West.

_____ 21. The Olmec culture is called the "mother culture" of Mesoamerica
- a. because all Mesoamericans descend from one Olmec female.
- b. because the Olmec gave rise to all later civilizations in the area.
- c. because the Olmec were worshipped.
- d. and the Maya culture is called the "father culture."

_____ 22. During the Qin dynasty, strict laws and harsh penalties were the result of a political philosophy called
- a. Daoism.
- b. Legalism.
- c. Imperialism.
- d. Confucianism.

_____ 23. The Mauryan Empire was the first empire to
- a. unite much of India.
- b. allow elected officials.
- c. encourage private businesses.
- d. expand through peaceful means.

_____ 24. A characteristic of the Gupta golden age was
- a. great works of art and architecture.
- b. equal distribution of wealth.
- c. the introduction of democracy.
- d. the end of the caste system.

_____ 25. Sharia, the Muslim legal system,
- a. regulated trade.
- b. is made up of opinions and writings over several centuries.
- c. was written by Muhammad.
- d. only applies to Muslim men.

_____ 26. The conflict over the successor to Muhammad
- a. was negotiated peacefully.
- b. was confined to Mecca.
- c. never divided the followers of Islam.
- d. led to the Sunni-Shia division.

_____ 27. The actions of the Umayyad dynasty conflicted with the Muslim belief in equality when
- a. they used military power to grow.
- b. they converted to Sufism.
- c. Arab Muslims became a ruling class.
- d. they split into Shia and Sunni groups.

_____ 28. The African kingdom of Aksum thrived
a. due to a monopoly on salt.
b. because of its location along the Mediterranean.
c. due to advanced iron technology.
d. because its location on the Red Sea was ideal for controlling trade.

_____ 29. Ghana became a wealthy kingdom
a. by conducting silent auctions.
b. by taxing ships in Ghana's ports.
c. through sales of camels to Bedouins.
d. by controlling the gold and salt trade.

_____ 30. Islam was introduced to West Africa
a. by Muhammad.
b. by Muslim traders.
c. by Sunni Ali.
d. after the Jesuits arrived in Timbuktu.

_____ 31. In China, under Song rule, the civil service exam system tested a person's
a. ability to add and subtract large sums.
b. skills as a diplomat.
c. knowledge of Confucianism.
d. knowledge of Chinese history.

_____ 32. One result of Mongol rule in China was
a. foreign trade increased.
b. increased violence.
c. that the Mongol culture died out over time.
d. that the country was closed to all foreigners.

_____ 33. What factor allowed Japan to limit contact with other cultures?
a. climate
b. religion
c. language
d. geography

_____ 34. The Eastern Roman Empire
a. fell to Germanic tribes called Vandals.
b. became known as the Byzantine Empire.
c. relocated to Damascus.
d. rejected all forms of Christianity.

_____ 35. Who were the Rus?
a. three brothers from Rome who set up a trading post in Moscow
b. northern Europeans, perhaps Vikings, who united the Slavs and formed a state called Kievan Rus
c. three sisters who liberated the Slavs to form a state called Kievan Rus
d. monks who migrated from Constantinople to Moscow

_____ 36. Charlemagne, who created an empire in Western Europe in the late 700s, is also known for
a. allowing the Muslims to build the city of Tours.
b. his opposition to Christianity and missionaries.
c. his interest in education and religion.
d. his interest in exploration of the New World.

_____ 37. The Vikings were successful raiders because
a. they lived in dense forests across Europe.
b. they were skilled riders with fast horses.
c. their nomadic lifestyle made them difficult to find and capture.
d. they built fast moving ships that allowed for surprise attacks.

_____ 38. In the Middle Ages, the feudal system was the political and social system, while the manorial system was the
a. legal system.
b. educational system.
c. religious system.
d. economic system.

_____ 39. The document known as the Magna Carta
a. limited the king's power.
b. favored the monarchy.
c. abolished the monarchy.
d. gave commoners the vote.

_____ 40. The goal of the Crusades was
a. to reclaim the Holy Land.
b. to show allegiance to the patriarch.
c. to convert Muslims to Christianity.
d. to preserve the Byzantine Empire.

_____ 41. In the High Middle Ages, new farming technology required fewer people to produce food and enabled more people to
a. move to towns.
b. buy their own farms.
c. become knights.
d. live on manors.

_____ 42. Scholasticism is the
a. belief in public education.
b. translation of Greek texts into Arabic.
c. use of intellect and logic to bring together opposing ideas.
d. systematic approach to cultural diffusion.

_____ 43. Which of the following statements describes humanism?
a. The purpose of all human work is to glorify God.
b. The potential of the human mind is almost limitless.
c. A spiritual focus leads to personal fulfillment.
d. A person's potential is reached through meeting the needs of others.

_____ 44. One of the causes of the Renaissance was
a. limited trade following the Crusades.
b. increased interest in spiritual matters.
c. the growth of large, wealthy city-states in Italy.
d. decreased interest in scientific and technical knowledge.

_____ 45. The concern that the church was moving from its spiritual roots led to the
a. Edict of Worms.
b. Protestant Reformation.
c. Age of Reason.
d. start of the church court.

_____ 46. How did the compass and the astrolabe aid the Age of Exploration?
a. Explorers went in search of new technology.
b. Explorers hoped to trade these items to the Chinese.
c. Marco Polo took these items to Kublai Khan.
d. They enabled sailors to plot courses and sail long distances.

_____ 47. The primary cause for the drastic drop in the Native American population of the Americas in the 1500s was
a. massive migration.
b. harsh climatic events.
c. the introduction of guns.
d. the introduction of diseases.

_____ 48. Mercantile nations established colonies in order to
a. trade with other colonies.
b. control sources of raw materials and provide markets for manufactured goods.
c. increase imports of manufactured goods to the home country.
d. more easily trade with other mercantile nations.

_____ 49. One section of the Atlantic Slave Trade network was called the
a. Middle Passage.
b. Columbian Exchange.
c. Encomienda System.
d. Mississippi Waterway.

_____ 50. The Mughal Empire was the
a. first civilization in India.
b. first Muslim empire in India.
c. only governing republic in India.
d. only civilization without religion.

_____ 51. The purpose of the Great Wall of China was
a. as an observatory for Asian astronomers.
b. to protect China from invasions from the north.
c. to limit trade with India.
d. as a memorial to Chinese emperors.

Name ______________________ Class ______________ Date ______________

End-of-Year Test

_____ 52. Ming emperors isolated China because
a. they thought European weapons might cause the peasants to rebel.
b. they were disappointed with the tribute gained from Zheng He's voyages.
c. they did not want to divert attention from building the Great Wall.
d. they disliked European influence and sought to preserve China's traditions.

_____ 53. The Spanish Armada revealed
a. England's growing military power.
b. Spain's invincible naval forces.
c. Spain's opposition to the Catholic Church.
d. Charles V's goal of a Catholic Europe.

_____ 54. Restoration was the name given to the
a. the growing gold trade in the Netherlands.
b. return to a monarchy in England.
c. establishment of Puritanism.
d. reign of Oliver Cromwell in England.

_____ 55. For what is Peter the Great best known?
a. as the cause of the Time of Troubles
b. for abdicating the throne
c. for the westernization of Russia
d. for the death of Ivan the Terrible

_____ 56. The Enlightenment was the
a. idea that all physical objects exert force.
b. belief that the earth is the center of the universe.
c. emphasis on using reason to understand truth.
d. five basic steps used to form and test a hypothesis.

_____ 57. Enlightenment thought had a profound influence on
a. Louis XIV.
b. the Carlsbad Decrees.
c. Otto von Bismarck.
d. the U.S. Constitution.

_____ 58. What was a major cause of the French Revolution?
a. strong leadership
b. ambitious generals
c. inequalities in society
d. foreign intervention

_____ 59. The chaos following the Reign of Terror
a. allowed Napoleon to rise to power.
b. forced the United States to intervene.
c. positioned the Catholic Church to take over.
d. allowed Horatio Nelson to rule France.

_____ 60. The purpose of the Napoleonic Wars was to
a. unite the French people.
b. defend France's borders.
c. establish Napoleon as king.
d. expand the French Empire.

_____ 61. The Industrial Revolution was
a. the formation of cottage industry guilds.
b. the conflict between cottage and factory workers.
c. a race between Great Britain and the United States for higher production rates.
d. a shift to power driven machinery and factory production.

_____ 62. Factory working conditions in Britain improved as a result of
a. labor strikes.
b. American unions.
c. the Luddite Movement.
d. new education laws.

_____ 63. A characteristic of socialism is
a. corporate empires.
b. increased mercantilism.
c. privately owned property.
d. that society controls industry.

_____ 64. Industry was transformed in the late 1800s due to the availability of
a. coal.
b. electric power.
c. steam power.
d. water power.

_____ 65. The construction of vast railroad systems was made possible
a. because of electric engines.
b. by the Bessemer process.
c. through the use of assembly lines.
d. through improved communication.

_____ 66. Which aspect of city life made migration to the suburbs possible?
a. city green spaces
b. skilled factory jobs
c. public transportation
d. multistoried buildings

_____ 67. In Great Britain, the goal of Chartism was
a. voting rights for all men.
b. voting rights for all women.
c. protection for child workers.
d. standardized factory wages and hours.

_____ 68. In 1804, Haiti became
a. the final resting place of Napoleon.
b. the first Latin American colony in the Caribbean.
c. the first Latin American territory to break its ties with Europe.
d. the first Latin American colony to obtain independence through peaceful means.

_____ 69. The U.S. Civil War was about
a. voting rights for African Americans.
b. Reconstruction.
c. taxation without representation.
d. states' rights and the issue of slavery.

_____ 70. Key figures in the unification of Italy were
a. Napoleon, Victor Emmanuel, and the Medici.
b. the Medici, Garibaldi, and Cavour.
c. Garibaldi, Mazzini, and Cavour.
d. the Medici, Mazzini, and Metternich.

_____ 71. Bismarck hoped realpolitik would help him achieve his goal of
a. ruling Germany.
b. unifying Germany.
c. spreading idealism.
d. overthrowing the king.

_____ 72. In the early 1900s, unrest in Russia
a. caused Lenin to call for the overthrow of the czar.
b. ultimately increased the power of the czar.
c. triggered World War II.
d. improved the status of Russian Jews.

_____ 73. The Sepoy Mutiny in India resulted in
a. India gaining self-rule.
b. India becoming two nations.
c. the East India Company taking control of India.
d. the British government taking direct control of India.

_____ 74. The British took control of Egypt in 1882 to
a. slow the spread of Islam.
b. control the diamond mines.
c. ensure the security of the Suez Canal.
d. remove the French imperialists.

_____ 75. The Spanish-American War
a. gained more colonies for Spain.
b. resulted in the Philippines becoming an American colony.
c. forced Cuba to become a monarchy.
d. was a victory for Spain.

_____ 76. The four factors that led to World War I were militarism, imperialism, nationalism, and
a. socialism.
b. isolationism.
c. nuclear power.
d. alliances.

_____ 77. Russia entered World War I because Czar Nicholas
a. wanted to expand the empire.
b. took advice from Grigory Rasputin.
c. hoped the cause would unite his country.
d. feared an attack from Great Britain.

_____ 78. One reason the United States entered World War I was
a. Germany's policy of unrestricted submarine warfare.
b. the hope it would stabilize the United States economy.
c. the belief it would bring a quick end to the war.
d. to get backing for the League of Nations.

_____ 79. The peace agreement ending World War I was called the
a. Call to Power.
b. Zimmerman Note.
c. Treaty of Versailles.
d. New Economic Policy.

_____ 80. The Stock Market Crash of 1929 signaled the beginning of
a. the New Deal.
b. World War II.
c. the Great Depression.
d. an economic rebound.

_____ 81. Mussolini, Stalin, and Hitler
a. were benevolent dictators.
b. ran totalitarian governments.
c. headed democratic nations.
d. led anarchist movements.

_____ 82. The goal of the Nuremberg Laws was to
a. guarantee Hitler's absolute power in Germany.
b. exclude Jews from mainstream German life.
c. end the reign of violence spreading through Germany.
d. form an alliance between Germany, Italy, and Japan.

_____ 83. Control of the Atlantic was critical in World War II because
a. Axis powers dominated on land.
b. Japan controlled all shipping routes on the Pacific.
c. it protected the United States from direct attack.
d. it was the supply route to Britain and the Soviet Union.

_____ 84. The Nazi campaign to systematically kill Jews, Poles, Slavs, Gypsies, homosexuals, and disabled people is known today as the
a. Sitzkreig.
b. Holocaust.
c. Blitzkreig.
d. Higher Order.

_____ 85. In World War II, fighting with Japan ended
a. with an Allied victory in Iwo Jima.
b. after the Battle of Midway.
c. with MacArthur's victory in the Battle of the Bulge.
d. after the United States dropped atomic bombs on Japan.

_____ 86. The purpose of the Marshall Plan was to
a. provide support for the Warsaw Pact.
b. maintain political stability in Europe.
c. gain control over Eastern Europe.
d. rebuild European military power.

_____ 87. The goal of the North Koreans in 1950 was to
a. unite their divided nation under a communist government.
b. participate in the space race.
c. make Asia a communist continent.
d. isolate Korea from communist influence.

_____ 88. The Cold War ended when the
a. Solidarity Movement failed.
b. Soviet Union collapsed.
c. United States won the arms race.
d. Soviet Union held a democratic election.

_____ 89. The Berlin Wall was built to
a. end the spread of communism.
b. block supplies to the west.
c. prevent an invasion from Great Britain.
d. stop migration from East to West Germany.

_____ 90. The "Quit India" campaign became violent when
a. Indira Gandhi was elected prime minister.
b. the British informed India it was not required to fight for the Allies in World War II.
c. the British imprisoned Gandhi and thousands of others.
d. Pakistan was created.

_____ 91. The United States supported South Vietnam because of U.S. concerns about
a. another war.
b. the spread of communism.
c. Vietnam's economy.
d. French imperialism.

_____ 92. The Tet Offensive in 1968 resulted in
a. the end of the Vietnam War.
b. the surrender of North Vietnam.
c. the destruction of the Ho Chi Minh Trail.
d. increased American opposition to the war.

_____ 93. President Nixon's visit to China ended
a. the Cultural Revolution.
b. communism in China.
c. China's isolation from the world.
d. the Tiananmen Square Massacre.

_____ 94. Democracy spread through African nations in the 1990s in part because
a. public education grew.
b. the Cold War ended.
c. the United Nations forced out the dictatorships.
d. missionaries introduced ideas of democracy.

_____ 95. An independent Jewish state was achieved through
a. the Peel Commission.
b. Arab-Israeli negotiations.
c. a United Nations proposal.
d. the Haganah military power.

_____ 96. The United States led a multinational force in the Persian Gulf War in 1990 to
a. free Kuwait.
b. find the Taliban.
c. block trade routes.
d. empower the Kurds.

_____ 97. Castro's goals for Cuba included
a. restoring the free press.
b. redistribution of wealth.
c. establishing a Marxist regime.
d. friendly relations with the United States.

_____ 98. For more than seventy years, Mexico's government was not a true democracy because
a. it was run by dictatorships.
b. the church ruled Mexico.
c. it was a one-party system.
d. the militia was in control.

_____ 99. Economic interdependence occurs when
a. transportation creates a demand for new goods.
b. cultural diffusion is a goal of developing nations.
c. developed nations control all aspects of life in developing nations.
d. countries can't provide all of the raw materials and finished goods they need.

_____ 100. The purpose of the green revolution is to
a. stop pesticide use on plants.
b. decrease water pollution.
c. help build developing economies.
d. increase the world's food supply.

Diagnostic Test

1. a
2. a
3. c
4. b
5. c
6. d
7. c
8. a
9. b
10. c
11. c
12. d
13. a
14. a
15. b
16. d
17. a
18. c
19. d
20. c
21. b
22. b
23. a
24. a
25. b
26. d
27. c
28. d
29. d
30. b
31. c
32. a
33. d
34. b
35. b
36. c
37. d
38. d
39. a
40. a
41. a
42. c
43. b
44. c
45. b
46. d
47. d
48. b
49. a
50. b
51. b
52. d
53. a
54. b
55. c
56. c
57. d
58. c
59. a
60. d
61. d
62. a
63. d
64. b
65. b
66. c
67. a
68. c
69. d
70. c
71. b
72. a
73. d
74. c
75. b
76. d
77. c
78. a
79. c
80. c
81. b
82. b
83. d
84. b
85. d
86. b
87. a
88. b
89. d
90. c
91. b
92. d
93. c
94. b
95. c
96. a
97. b
98. c
99. d
100. d

Chapter 1: The Beginnings of Civilization

Section Quiz

SECTION 1

1. d
2. h
3. l
4. k
5. g
6. f
7. e
8. a
9. c
10. b

SECTION 2

1. d
2. c
3. b
4. c
5. a
6. b
7. e
8. d
9. c
10. a

SECTION 3

1. traditional
2. civilization
3. labor
4. artisans
5. abstract
6. F; The earliest civilizations grew up in fertile river valleys.
7. T
8. T
9. F; Priests were powerful figures, interpreting the will of the gods.
10. T

Chapter Test, Form A

1. b
2. a
3. d
4. b
5. a
6. c
7. c
8. c
9. c
10. c
14. f
15. j
16. c
17. i
18. d
19. h
20. e
21. artifacts
22. Neanderthals
23. tools

11. l
12. m
13. a
24. surplus
25. trade

Chapter Test, Form B

Possible responses:

1. Scholars rely on material remains to learn about prehistory. Students should mention two of the following specialists: Archaeologists dig into ancient settlements to find objects used by early people called artifacts. Anthropologists study fossils, items or their imprints preserved in rock. Some anthropologists study human culture, the set of beliefs, knowledge, and patterns of living that a group of people develop.
2. In hunter-gatherer societies, most hunters were men who hunted in groups. Women took responsibility for collecting plants and fruits. They probably stayed near camps and took care of children.
3. Because farming allowed people to adopt settled lifestyles, communities grew. Simple governments were formed. As trade and wealth increased, social ranking became more defined, and people owned more private property.
4. Village populations consisted of a few families or clans; city populations were larger and more diverse, including migrants. Cities had large public buildings, well-defined centers, and boundaries. Cities and surrounding rural communities were interdependent; cities relied on farmlands for food, while they also acted as religious, economic, and cultural centers.
5. Cultural diffusion is the spreading of cultural traits from one society to another through trade (for example, merchants learned other languages to conduct trade with other groups), migration (for example, immigrants brought their languages, customs, and traditions with them to their new homeland), and invasion (civilizations often imposed their cultures on conquered peoples). As a result, societies changed. Cultural diffusion often brought new languages, writing, improved technology and farming techniques, as well as influencing artists and craftspeople.
6. Humans may have been able to make the journey from Asia to the Americas by crossing land that was exposed during an ice age. Because of the cold climate they would have needed tools to create warm clothes, the ability to make fire, and tools for hunting and gathering food.

Chapter 2: The Ancient Near East

Section Quiz

SECTION 1

1. m
2. k
3. e
4. g
5. h
6. l
7. d
8. b
9. j
10. c

SECTION 2

1. T
2. F; They used Sumerian cuneiform and developed a code of law similar to the Code of Hammurabi.
3. F; Assyrian power relied on military strength.
4. T
5. T

SECTION 3

1. Judaism
2. Torah
3. Exodus
4. Ten Commandments
5. covenant
6. Canaan
7. Saul
8. Judah
9. monotheism
10. Talmud

SECTION 4

1. T

2. F; Cyrus the Great led a revolt against the Medes and united the kingdoms.
3. T
4. T
5. F; During the reign of Darius, Persian culture reached a high point.

Chapter Test, Form A

1. c	6. b
2. d	7. a
3. d	8. b
4. b	9. c
5. a	10. c

11. Mesopotamia
12. Sargon I
13. Assyrian
14. sailors
15. Exodus
16. monotheism
17. Ten Thousand Immortals
18. Satraps

19. T	23. T
20. T	24. F
21. T	25. F
22. F	

Chapter Test, Form B

Possible responses:

1. Large cities began to appear in Sumer by 4000 BC. Over time, each city in Sumer and the land around it formed a city-state, a political unit with its own government. Priests held high status and initially they governed the city-states. As the city-states battled for dominance, however, war chiefs began to rule as kings. In time, many of the city-states' kings formed dynasties. Dynasties are a series of rulers from one family.
2. Men held political power and made laws while women took care of the home and children. Some upper-class women also served as priestesses in the temples.
3. First, the Hittites were among the first people to master ironworking techniques. Iron produced stronger weapons than the bronze weapons used by the Hittites' enemies. Second the Hittites' war chariot was light and quick. The chariot seated three soldiers rather than two; the extra soldier held shields, enabling the Hittites to move their chariots close to enemy forces while remaining protected.
4. The Jewish belief in monotheism is a key feature of western culture. In addition, the values regarding human life, self-control, and justice contained in the Ten Commandments influenced the laws and values of Western civilization.
5. Student answers should include several of the following points: Darius reorganized and strengthened the empire in many ways, including creating a permanent, paid, well-trained army; surrounding the kingship with ceremony and ritual to demonstrate his power to everyone; changing the structure of the empire by appointing governors called satraps to govern regions in the emperor's name, yet ensuring that they remained loyal; strengthening the economy and building roads throughout the empire. This was the high point of Persian culture because the emperors who followed never achieved the level of power and prestige that Darius enjoyed.
6. The region was valuable because it contained fertile land, good rainfall, and lay along major trade routes.
7. Geographic factors may have prevented the Assyrians from expanding. It would be difficult to live and grow food in the desert. The Mediterranean and Black seas may have prevented expansion. There may have been strong tribes in the north.

Chapter 3: Nile Civilizations

Section Quiz

SECTION 1

1. T
2. F; The kingdom was unified, not divided, at that time.
3. F; The pyramids were built as tombs for Egypt's rulers.

4. T
5. T

SECTION 2

1. d
2. e
3. g
4. a
5. i
6. b
7. f
8. j
9. h
10. l

SECTION 3

1. c
2. a
3. a
4. b
5. d

Chapter Test, Form A

1. b
2. b
3. a
4. d
5. b
6. d
7. a
8. c
9. g
10. m
11. l
12. k
13. i
14. h
15. c
16. e
17. f
18. j
19. desert
20. Pyramids
21. scribe
22. hieroglyphics
23. peasant farmers
24. archers
25. Meroë

Chapter Test, Form B

Possible responses:

1. Hatshepsut was officially ruling in the name of her young son after her husband died, a fact that indicates that Egypt didn't normally have female rulers. However, Hatshepsut declared herself Egypt's pharaoh. She wanted to be accepted as pharaoh even though she was a woman. One of the ways she tried to do this was to dress like a man. She even referred to herself as the son of the sun god and had statues made in which she appeared as a man.
2. The primary duty of an Egyptian woman was to take care of the home and children. However, they had more rights than women in most other ancient civilizations: they could own and inherit property, create wills, and be granted divorce. They also could work as singers, hairdressers, and wigmakers.
3. Egyptian paintings tend to be both detailed and colorful. In addition, in Egyptian portraits, human torsos are seen straight on, but their heads, arms, and legs are seen from the side. Also, major figures such as gods and pharaohs were drawn larger than other people. These characteristics give Egyptian art a unique style.
4. The Egyptian economy depended on farming the fertile river valley around the Nile. The Nubian economy, on the other hand, depended on exporting its great mineral resources of gold, granite, and other precious stones. Nubia's location also made it a central trading post.
5. One possible response is that gold could be shipped down the Nile from Thebes to Memphis. Another possible response is that gold could be shipped from Punt to Thebes via the Red Sea and then on to Memphis down the Nile.
6. The areas into which the New Kingdom of Egypt expanded were all along water routes. For example, as the New Kingdom expanded southward it followed the Nile River. Expansion into East Asia followed the coastline of the Mediterranean Sea. The desert prevented the kingdom from expanding very far from sources of water.

Chapter 4: Ancient India and China

Section Quiz

SECTION 1

1. T
2. T
3. F; Evidence of planning and uniformity suggests a central authority held power over the civilization.
4. T
5. T

SECTION 2

1. d
2. a
3. a
4. c
5. d

SECTION 3

1. c
2. h
3. i
4. a
5. j
6. e
7. k
8. b
9. l
10. d

SECTION 4

1. Huang He
2. loess
3. Himalayas
4. Gobi
5. Shang
6. oracle
7. Mandate of Heaven
8. Confucius
9. *Analects*
10. Laozi

Chapter Test, Form A

1. c
2. a
3. d
4. c
5. b
6. b
7. b
8. a
9. h
10. d
11. a
12. f
13. c
14. b
15. l
16. g
17. e
18. i
19. *Vedas*
20. reincarnation/*samsara*
21. yoga
22. Eightfold Path
23. trade
24. Mandate of Heaven
25. Daoism

Chapter Test, Form B

Possible responses:

1. Some scholars believe that the Indus civilization was a single society, not a collection of independent city–states. They base this on the similarity of the cities and towns. The people shared common tool designs and a standard set of weights and measures. These factors suggest a single authority was in control.
2. A group of Hindus broke away from Hinduism and founded Jainism. They thought there was too much emphasis on rituals in Hinduism. Although most Hindus practice *ahimsa*, Jains take it further and carefully avoid harming any living creature, from people to insects.
3. After the Buddha's death, differing opinions arose concerning the correct teachings and practices of Buddhism. Eventually three main traditions formed—Theravada, Mahayana, and Tibetan. After his death Buddha's followers spread his teachings. Buddhism spread beyond India into East and Southeast Asia. As Buddhism encountered other religions it continued to change and develop. Today it is a very diverse religion.
4. Any three of the following are acceptable: The Shang developed the earliest Chinese writing; they made great advances in working with bronze, creating highly decorative bronze vessels and objects; they were able to build huge, stable structures such as tombs quickly and efficiently; Shang astronomers created a precise calendar based on the cycles of the moon; and the Shang may have created one of the world's first systems of money.
5. The Zhou introduced the idea of the Mandate of Heaven to gain acceptance for their rule after conquering the Shang. The principle stated that the gods would support a just ruler, but they would not allow anyone corrupt to hold power.
6. Mahayana Buddhism is practiced in both China and Japan. From Bodh Gaya the Mahayana form spread to Central Asia and Southeast Asia. From those two regions it spread to China. It spread to Japan from both Korea and China.

Unit 1: The Dawn of Civilization

Unit Test, Form A

1. e	6. k
2. i	7. b
3. l	8. h
4. a	9. c
5. g	10. f

11. fossils
12. Neolithic
13. Sumerians
14. Phoenicians
15. monotheism/one God
16. the Persian Empire/Persia
17. the Nile River
18. afterlife
19. Indus
20. *Vedas*

21. T	36. a
22. F	37. c
23. F	38. a
24. T	39. d
25. F	40. d
26. T	41. a
27. F	42. a
28. T	43. c
29. T	44. d
30. F	45. d
31. a	46. b
32. c	47. a
33. b	48. d
34. c	49. d
35. b	50. b

Unit Test, Form B

Possible responses:

1. The first civilizations grew from settled farming communities. River valleys provided water for drinking and growing crops. Flooding deposited fertile soil necessary for growing crops. Some communities had to organize to control annual flooding or build large irrigation projects.
2. Without written history, scientists rely on human material remains to learn about prehistory. They study fossils and artifacts including: clothing, artwork, tools, weapons, homes, temples, and tombs.
3. The Phoenicians developed extensive sea trade routes which spread their products to other areas. They developed glass blowing and a valuable purple dye. They also developed an alphabet that served as a basis for the Greek alphabet and our alphabet today.
4. Originally pyramids were built as tombs for Egyptian pharaohs. Inside each pyramid, tunnels led to a hollow central chamber that held the pharaoh's body. The pyramids were built by craftsmen and peasants who were paid for their work. Limestone blocks were floated down the river and then dragged to the building site. The pyramids took so long to build that kings often started the project as soon as they took the throne. The pyramids contained all the items the pharaoh's ka would need in the afterlife.
5. Students will summarize one of the following: Judaism, Hinduism, or Buddhism. Judaism was developed by the ancient Hebrews. They believe God made a covenant with Abraham. Their belief in one God made them unique among ancient peoples. Judaism stresses justice, ethics, and obedience to the law. Their sacred texts include the Torah and Talmud. Hinduism has no founder and evolved over hundreds of years. Hindus believe that an eternal being (Brahman) created and preserves the world. Everything in the world is an aspect of Brahman. Hindus believe in a pattern of birth, death, and rebirth. Hindu teachings and practices are based on many sacred texts including the *Vedas* and *Upanishads*. Buddhism is based on the teachings of Siddhartha Gautama, or Buddha. Like Hindus, Buddhists believe in reincarnation. Buddhists teach that following the Eightfold path will lead to enlightenment and salvation.
6. The Shang may be China's first dynasty. Much of what historians know has come

from studying tombs. The Shang believed in an afterlife. They consulted their ancestors using oracle bones. Shang writing appears on the bones. Wealthy Shang hunted for sport and collected expensive objects made of bronze or jade.

7. New Kingdom Egyptians were surrounded by desert. Where possible they used waterways such as the Nile, Euphrates or sea to transport trade goods. They used overland routes where the Nile was obstructed by cataracts.

Chapter 5: Classical Greece

Section Quiz

SECTION 1

1. F; The Mycenaean civilization developed after the Minoan civilization.
2. T
3. F; A polis was built around a high area called an acropolis.
4. T
5. T

SECTION 2

1. Athens
2. people
3. Draco
4. Solon
5. tyrant
6. Persians
7. Peloponnesian
8. Pericles
9. sea
10. Macedonia

SECTION 3

1. b
2. e
3. m
4. c
5. a
6. g
7. k
8. d
9. f
10. i

SECTION 4

1. T
2. F; Kingdoms replaced city-states.
3. T
4. F; There were tremendous advances in science and technology.
5. T

Chapter Test, Form A

1. b
2. a
3. a
4. d
5. c
6. b
7. c
8. e
9. h
10. c
11. k
12. a
13. m
14. i
15. d
16. g
17. j
18. Mycenaeans
19. agora
20. direct democracy
21. Peloponnesian War
22. Plato
23. Euripides
24. Phillip II
25. Hellenistic

Chapter Test, Form B

Possible responses:

1. The Mycenaean and Minoan civilizations were two distinct civilizations that developed in early Greece. The Minoan civilization was based on the island of Crete. The later Mycenaean civilization had cities on the Greek mainland. Mycenaeans copied Minoan writing to develop their own writing system. Both the Mycenaeans and the Minoans were great traders. However, Mycenaean society was dominated by competition, war, and powerful kings. Eventually, the Mycenaeans conquered the Minoans. Historians consider the Mycenaeans the first Greeks.
2. Athens became the leading city-state after the Greek victory in the Persian Wars. It was the head of the Delian League, and controlled the league's ships and money. Athens would not allow league members to quit. Over time the league turned into an Athenian empire. Athens used the league's treasury to rebuild the city with grand public buildings. In addition, Pericles, who led the city-state for many years, was a great patron of the arts.

During this time, trade turned Athens into a very cosmopolitan city.

3. Free men in Athens over the age of 20 who had completed military training were allowed to vote. Women, children, immigrants, and slaves could not participate in government. Those who could vote were required to vote in all elections, serve in office, on juries, and in the military. There were three main bodies of government, the assembly of all eligible voters, the Council of 500, and a series of courts.
4. The *Iliad* and the *Odyssey* were known throughout the Greek world. They became a basis for Greek education. Young men were encouraged to emulate the deeds of heroes. Homer's works inspired later Greek writers. Greek murals often included scenes from the *Iliad* and the *Odyssey*.
5. Alexander married two Persian princesses and encouraged his soldiers to marry Persian women as well. He appointed officials from various cultures to help rule the empire. He built dozens of new cities, most of them named Alexandria, in the lands he conquered, and encouraged Greek settlers to move into them. Cities in Egypt, Persia, and Central Asia became trading centers where goods and ideas were exchanged.
6. Sparta was part of the Peloponnesian League. Athens was part of the Delian League. The map shows the areas of both leagues. The map illustrates why Athens, with ships, was able to dominate the sea in the early years of the war. The map helps explain why the victor in the Peloponnesian War (Sparta) needed both an army and ships.

Chapter 6: Rome and Early Christianity

Section Quiz

SECTION 1

1. b
2. m
3. j
4. a
5. g
6. d
7. i
8. c
9. k
10. e

SECTION 2

1. T
2. F; The murder of Julius Caesar was an attempt on the part of some senators to save the republic.
3. T
4. T
5. T

SECTION 3

1. b
2. a
3. c
4. c
5. b

SECTION 4

1. T
2. F; Zealots were particularly vocal about overthrowing Roman rule.
3. T
4. T
5. F; Christianity was made legal in the Roman Empire with the Edict of Milan.

SECTION 5

1. T
2. F; Money decreased in value as new coins were minted with copper and lead.
3. T
4. T
5. T

Chapter Test, Form A

1. c
2. a
3. d
4. b

14. paterfamilias
15. Latin
16. Judaism
17. bishops

5. d
6. b
7. a
8. c
9. a
10. b
11. tribunes
12. Gracchi
13. Pax Romana
18. Alaric
19. Odoacer
20. F
21. T
22. T
23. T
24. T
25. T

Chapter Test, Form B

Possible responses:

1. The Italian peninsula is well situated to be the center of a mighty Mediterranean empire, because it juts into the Mediterranean nearly halfway to Africa and lies about halfway between the eastern and western boundaries of the Mediterranean world. In addition, the peninsula is protected by the Alps in the north, and to the south, east, and west, the sea provided protection as well as a means of rapid transportation. The climate and rich soil also could feed a large population.
2. In the Republic, citizens elected their leaders, and leaders served for designated terms. Although not a pure democracy, it was more democratic than the Roman Empire. In the Empire, the emperor was the most powerful individual. Although during the Empire many of the forms of the Republic still existed, Rome did not function as a republic. For example the emperor came to power through force or family connections and remained in power until death.
3. The poet was referring to the horrible living conditions in which the poor people of Rome lived. The government distributed free food and held free public entertainments to keep poor people from rebelling against the awful conditions, a policy that was in large part successful – leading to the statement that the poor only cared about bread (free food) and circuses (free entertainment).
4. The Christian message of love and eternal life after death, regardless of social position or wealth, appealed to the poor, the oppressed, and the enslaved. Many people were also attracted by the sense of community that Christianity offered.
5. Diocletian changed the empire into an absolute monarchy and placed himself above his subjects, with no accountability to anyone. He divided the empire in two. He also transformed Roman society into a bureaucratic and rigid order in which almost every aspect of life was regulated by the imperial administration.
6. The Senate checked the power of the magistrates by controlling the budget; they could refuse to give magistrates money.
7. Assemblies and tribunes could check the power of the Senate by refusing to approve laws passed by the Senate.

Chapter 7: The Americas

Section Quiz

SECTION 1

1. b
2. a
3. d
4. a
5. c

SECTION 2

1. T
2. F; The Olmec were the first group to build large towns in Mesoamerica.
3. T
4. T
5. F; Aztec society was highly organized and strictly divided into different social classes.

SECTION 3

1. i
2. j
3. a
4. m
5. e
6. b
7. f
8. h
9. k
10. c

Chapter Test, Form A

1. b
2. d
3. a
4. c
5. d
6. d
7. c
8. a
9. b
10. c
11. T
12. T
13. T
14. F
15. F
16. T
17. F
18. b
19. cliff dwellings
20. Mississippians
21. glyphs
22. Tenochtitlán
23. desert floor
24. quipu
25. elite

Chapter Test, Form B

Possible responses:

1. Mesoamerica is a region that includes present-day southern Mexico and northern Central America. Because warm temperatures, plentiful rainfall, and rich volcanic soils made the area ideal for growing crops, it was the site of the first farming settlements in the Americas.
2. Tenochtitlán, an Aztec city, covered five square miles and had a population of 200,000. At the center of the city was a huge walled compound that contained a pyramid with two temples on top. The rest of the city center had other temples, government buildings, palaces, and a ball court. The city was built on a swampy island in the middle of a lake.
3. The Maya worshipped many gods and believed the gods influenced daily life. They performed private and public rituals for the gods to prevent disasters and keep the gods happy. The Maya performed human sacrifice only on special occasions. The Aztecs also performed religious ceremonies to keep the gods happy, but they performed human sacrifice often: as many as 20,000 victims were sacrificed each year.
4. The government strictly controlled the Incan economy. Common people "paid" a labor tax called the mita. They fulfilled the mita by working on government projects such as farms, in mines, or building roads. Government officials, in return, distributed goods around the empire instead of having them sold in the marketplace. There were no merchants or markets in the Inca Empire.
5. Students will write about one of the regions shown on the map. The Arctic and Subarctic groups lived in an area that included permanent snow and ice; all the peoples living there relied on fishing and hunting sea mammals for food; all peoples built houses out of ice. The Far West groups lived in an area that included rivers, forests, and a long coastline; fishing was a main method of getting food; all groups used wood from the forests to build houses and canoes. Groups in the Desert West lived in a dry, rocky environment; they learned irrigation techniques to farm maize, beans, and squash; they all built houses out of adobe or into the sides of cliffs. Groups in the Great Plains lived on treeless, grassy plains with fertile soil; they hunted buffalo for food; they made teepees made from buffalo skins. Groups in the Eastern Woodlands lived in warm and temperate forests; they relied on hunting and gathering as well as farming some native crops; they built log cabins out of forest materials.
6. The Artic and Subarctic region was the least populated because the permanent snow and ice made conditions there very harsh. The Eastern Woodlands region was most heavily populated, because the weather conditions were mild, and abundant food was available through agriculture and hunting.

Chapter 8: Empires of China and India

Section Quiz

SECTION 1

1. e
2. i
3. j.
4. a
5. l
6. d
7. k
8. c
9. g
10. m

SECTION 2

1. F; Women had fewer privileges and less status than men.
2. T
3. F; The rich grew richer and the poor grew poorer despite efforts at governmental control.
4. T
5. T

SECTION 3

1. F; The Indian force was defeated by the army of Alexander the Great.
2. T
3. F; Ashoka was India's greatest ruler and improved the lives of his people.
4. T
5. T

SECTION 4

1. caste
2. temples
3. Laws of Manu
4. Hinduism
5. carvings
6. Sanskrit
7. Kalidasa
8. Silk Roads
9. zero
10. Earth

Chapter Test, Form A

1. b
2. c
3. d
4. c
5. d
6. b
7. c
8. b
9. Qin
10. Xiongnu
11. silk
12. Sima Qian
13. Chandra Gupta II
14. Trade
15. Sanskrit
16. Faxian
17. F
18. T
19. F
20. T
21. F
22. T
23. T
24. F
25. T

Chapter Test, Form B

Possible responses:

1. Shi Huangdi took his title "first emperor" after conquering local states in China. He used harsh measures to unify and strengthen China. He most likely thought that these measures would ensure that the dynasty would last for a long time. However, when he died, his dynasty quickly fell apart because the harsh policies fueled anger and resentment among both peasants and nobles. In the end, the Qin dynasty lasted only one generation.
2. Possible response for a female student: Because I am a young woman, my marriage would be arranged and I would join my husband's household. Once married, I would be expected to obey my husband and my mother-in-law. As I grew older, I would achieve some power in the family because of the Confucian value of respect for elders and parents. Possible response for a male student: Because I am a young man, I would be expected to care for my parents as they age. My marriage would be arranged and my wife would come to live in my household. I would have complete authority over my wife and children.
3. Ashoka had wells dug and roads built to improve travel and provide water. He had shade trees planted and rest houses built for weary travelers along roads. He worked to spread Buddhist teachings, such as the importance of right conduct, being tolerant of other religions and ideas, and practicing nonviolence.
4. During the Gupta period increased trade led to a stable economy. Because of extensive trade routes the people of the empire were exposed to many new goods and ideas. A culture stressing luxury and

pleasure developed. During this period there were many cultural and scientific achievements including: literature, art, architecture, metallurgy, mathematics, medical science, and astronomy.

5. One route would follow the Silk Roads from Chang'an to Antioch. A much more circuitous route would go by boat, following the coastlines of Southeast Asia, India, and Persia, switching to the Silk Roads to cross Arabia to Antioch.
6. The Silk Roads were a network of routes that stretched from China 4,000 miles across the heart of Asia to the Mediterranean Sea. They became famous because they were extensive and linked China to the Mediterranean. Many new ideas, technologies, and even religions were diffused via the Silk Roads.

Unit 2: The Growth of Civilizations

Unit Test, Form A

1. b	26. T
2. h	27. F
3. c	28. T
4. j	29. T
5. k	30. F
6. e	31. a
7. f	32. b
8. g	33. a
9. d	34. c
10. a	35. d
11. Mycenaeans	36. b
12. Olympian	37. c
13. Athens	38. d
14. Senate	39. a
15. Augustus	40. d
16. Iroquois	41. c
17. South America	42. b
18. Legalism	43. a
19. Silk Roads	44. d
20. Hinduism	45. a
21. F	46. a
22. T	47. d
23. T	48. c
24. T	49. a
25. F	50. b

Unit Test, Form B

Possible responses:

1. As a democracy, Athens was ruled by the people. However, only about 10 percent of the total population was able to take part in government. Only free males over the age of 20 who had completed military training could vote. Women, children, immigrants, and slaves had no role in government. Individuals who could participate in government were expected to do so fully. They were expected to vote in all elections, serve office if elected, serve on juries, and in the military during war. At its height, the Athenian democracy included three main governing bodies: the assembly, the Council of 500, and a system of courts. In the assembly, all eligible voters voted directly on issues and laws.
2. Life during the Pax Romana was characterized by stable government, law that applied to all citizens, and widespread trade and transportation that helped build the empire and maintain peace. In the agricultural areas tenant farmers began replacing slaves. Manufacturing increased and there were many opportunities for trade. The Roman government was the strongest unifying force in the empire. Cities all over the Mediterranean were governed in imitation of Rome. Architecture was also modeled on buildings in Rome.
3. Both the Maya and Aztec civilizations were made up primarily of farmers. Maya farmers practiced slash-and-burn agriculture. Maya cities functioned as city-states, each with its own ruler and government. Trade, not government, linked the city-states. Kings, priests, and warriors were members of the upper class. Below them were merchants and skilled craftspeople. The lower class was made up of farmers and slaves. Maya achievements include advances in astronomy, writing,

and math. They were among the first people to use the concept of zero. Their writing consisted of glyphs. Written records were kept in bark-paper books. A lack of prime agricultural land forced Aztec farmers to seek new ways of raising crops. They created floating gardens and used canals to ship their crops. Poor farmers made up most of Aztec society. However, in Aztec civilization, farmers could move up in class by becoming warriors or studying at special schools. Priests and warriors were members of the Aztec. The Aztec Empire was based on trade and tribute. Like the Maya, the Aztec used glyphs and developed accurate calendars.

4. Ashoka of the Maurya Empire converted to Buddhism after a bloody military campaign. After converting, Ashoka sought to improve the lives of his people. He had wells dug and roads built. He worked to spread Buddhist teachings, encouraging his people to adopt right conduct, nonviolence, and tolerance. Hinduism flourished under the Guptas. They created beautiful temples, literature and art. As taught by the Brahmins, Hinduism maintained caste and gender roles in Indian society.
5. The map illustrates how the Silk Roads and other trade routes connected India, China, Southeast Asia, Africa and Europe. Traders carried goods, but also ideas. For example. Buddhism and Hinduism were carried from India by traders. Hindu-Arabic numerals may have also been diffused via the Silk Roads or other trade routes.

Chapter 9: Muslim Civilization

Section Quiz

SECTION 1

1. T
2. T
3. F; Some Meccans were angered by his criticism of their traditional beliefs.
4. T
5. F; The record of Muhammad's behavior and teachings is known as the Sunna.

SECTION 2

1. d
2. d
3. a
4. c
5. b
6. d
7. b
8. c
9. a
10. d

SECTION 3

1. c
2. f
3. h
4. m
5. i
6. a
7. g
8. l
9. d
10. j

Chapter Test, Form A

1. b
2. b
3. d
4. b
5. d
6. c
7. a
8. c
9. b
10. f
11. i
12. e
13. b
14. c
15. j
16. g
17. d
18. Qur'an
19. Muslims
20. Sunna
21. Shia
22. Abbasids
23. calligraphy
24. minarets
25. Omar Khayyam

Chapter Test, Form B

Possible responses:

1. Many Meccans were angered by Muhammad's criticism of their traditional beliefs in many gods. He told them their worship of idols was sinful. Meccans involved in the pilgrimage trade were worried that Muhammad's preaching would disrupt their business. For a time Muhammad was protected by his uncle Abu Talib, but when his uncle died he realized that he and his followers were not safe in Mecca.

2. The Five Pillars of Islam are basic acts of worship that are central to Islam and that Muhammad himself fulfilled. Muslims are required to fulfill the Five Pillars of Islam. The first pillar is the profession of faith. The second pillar is the performance of five daily prayers. Worshippers always face Mecca to pray. The third pillar is the giving of charity for the poor and needy. The fourth pillar is fasting from dawn to dusk during the month of Ramadan. The fifth pillar is undertaking a journey to Mecca, or the hajj.
3. In general, Muslims allowed considerable religious freedom. Christians and Jews were allowed to practice their religion. However non-Muslims had to pay taxes and had some restrictions on their lives.
4. A man was the head of the family. Men could marry several wives, but were supposed to treat them all equally. Islamic law protected the rights of women and children. According to the Qur'an women are equal to men before Allah. In early Muslim communities women played key roles. Under the Abbasid dynasty women lost status.
5. Learning and scholarship in Muslim civilization were highly valued. Muslim scholars translated many ancient texts into Arabic. Scholars studied astronomy and improved the astrolabe. Muslim thinkers developed algebra and trigonometry. Medicine was highly developed in the Muslim world. Doctors had to pass rigorous tests. Because of the importance of Mecca, geographers wrote travel guides describing the journey to Mecca. Other contributions include history, music, logic, and philosophy.
6. Between 662 and 750 Islam spread west across northern Africa and into Spain, and east into parts of India and Asia, including the cities of Kabul and Samarqand.
7. Islamic lands touch the continents of Africa, Europe, and Asia.

Chapter 10: African Kingdoms

Section Quiz

SECTION 1

1. three
2. Sahara
3. Sahel
4. savanna
5. parasites
6. pastoralism
7. age-sets
8. griots
9. Iron
10. Bantu

SECTION 2

1. i
2. a
3. m
4. b
5. k
6. d
7. g
8. f
9. h
10. j

SECTION 3

1. T
2. T
3. T
4. F; By the 1460s the rulers of Songhai had become strong and rich enough to take control of the former empire of Mali.
5. F; Askia Muhammad was a strong leader who is credited with being the first Muslim ruler of Songhai.

Chapter Test, Form A

1. b
2. b
3. d
4. c
5. a
6. b
7. d
8. C
9. Sahara
10. savanna
11. age-sets
12. Nok
13. Ge'ez
14. Solomonid
15. camels
16. Sundiata
17. Askia Muhammad
18. T
19. F
20. F
21. F
22. T
23. T
24. F
25. T

Chapter Test, Form B

Possible responses:

1. Tropical rain forests lie near the equator and on Madagascar, an island off the

southeast coast. The hot and humid climate supports a broad range of plant and animal life. This region receives year-round rainfall.
2. All village members worked together. Men hunted and farmed. Women cared for children, farmed, collected firewood, ground grain, and carried water.
3. Aksum's stelae were inscribed with records of important events. They provide examples of Ge'ez, Aksum's written and spoken language. Ge'ez was one of the first written languages developed in Africa and is the basis of the written language used in Ethiopia today.
4. I would wait to leave until between May and September, when the monsoon winds blow toward India and the Persian Gulf. There I would exchange my goods for rice and bananas. I would have to wait to return until between November and March, when the monsoon winds change directions and blow toward Africa.
5. Musa returned to Mali with artists and architects who designed beautiful mosques. He built schools and libraries where people could study Islamic writings. Musa's pilgrimage also brought Mali to the attention of people in Europe, and Mali began to appear on European maps for the first time.
6. Desert traders brought goods like cloth, salt, and gold across the Sahara to Ghana.
7. These empires probably arose in similar places because desert trade routes had been established in the area; because the area had many rivers; and because there was gold in the area.

Chapter 11: Cultures of East Asia

Section Quiz

SECTION 1

1. Grand Canal
2. Tang dynasty
3. Wu Zhao
4. Neo-Confucianism
5. movable type
6. population
7. poets
8. merchants
9. Sea
10. peasants

SECTION 2

1. T
2. T
3. F; Kublai Khan defeated the Chinese and established the Yuan dynasty.
4. T
5. F; Kublai Khan was not successful in his attempts to invade Japan.

SECTION 3

1. g
2. a
3. b
4. d
5. l
6. c
7. f
8. e
9. m
10. j

SECTION 4

1. d
2. a
3. a
4. b
5. c

Chapter Test, Form A

1. c
2. b
3. a
4. b
5. d
6. a
7. b
8. Wu Zhao
9. Age of Buddhism
10. Genghis Khan
11. Marco Polo
12. kami
13. Yamato
14. Confucian
15. Angkor
16. Anawrahta
17. d
18. T
19. T
20. F
21. F
22. T
23. T
24. T
25. T

Chapter Test, Form B

Possible responses:

1. As trade increased during the Tang period, merchants became more important members of society. Passing the civil

service exams was a way to gain wealth and status. As the power of aristocratic families declined, a new class, the gentry, arose. It was made up of scholar-officials (those who had passed the civil service exams) and leading landowners. During the Song period the status of women declined as upper-class women were encouraged to stay in the home. Most people in China, however, remained peasants. They farmed the land and paid most of the taxes.

2. Any two of the following are acceptable. The Tang perfected the magnetic compass, which contributed to an increase in world exploration. The Tang also developed woodblock printing. Gunpowder was used in fireworks and later in weapons. The Song government adopted paper money which took the place of bulky metal disks. The Song experimented with movable type, which made printing easier.
3. First, a Mongol fleet of some nine hundred ships was sent to Japan. After the Mongols won a brief battle, the entire fleet was destroyed in a storm, killing 10,000 people. Later, the Mongols sent an even larger fleet to try to conquer Japan. Another storm wiped out the entire fleet. The Mongols never attempted to invade Japan again.
4. The early Japanese turned to the sea for food and transportation. The sea has also served as a protective barrier against foreign invasion. Separated from the mainland the early Japanese were able to develop their culture in isolation.
5. During the Heian period the Fujiwara family controlled Japan. Many Fujiwaras served as regents, and the family married their daughters to heirs to the throne. When the Japanese emperor moved the capital to Heian, an elegant and stylish court society developed. Court life was so removed from the life of the common people that the nobles referred to themselves as "dwellers among the clouds." Rules of etiquette governed all aspects of court behavior and dress. Rules governed how to wear elaborate clothing, how to write notes, and poetry. Women of the court enjoyed reading and writing. They produced some of the best works of early Japanese literature.
6. The mainland kingdoms are Pagan, Khmer, and Dai Viet.
7. The Srivijaya Empire differs from the others because it is based on the island of Sumatra and extends to a portion of the Malay Peninsula and the island of Borneo.

Unit 3: Cultures in Contact

Unit Test, Form A

1. g	26. T
2. j	27. T
3. b	28. T
4. l	29. T
5. c	30. F
6. a	31. a
7. h	32. b
8. d	33. b
9. k	34. c
10. i	35. d
11. hegira	36. d
12. Allah	37. a
13. Shia	38. c
14. Christianity	39. d
15. monsoon	40. b
16. age-sets	41. d
17. trade	42. a
18. Grand Canal	43. a
19. archipelago	44. c
20. Buddhism	45. a
21. T	46. c
22. F	47. d
23. T	48. b
24. T	49. c
25. F	50. b

Unit Test, Form B

Possible responses:

1. The Five Pillars of Islam are central acts of worship. The pillars include the profession of faith, the performance of

five daily prayers, and the giving of alms. Additionally, Muslims are required to fast from dawn to dusk during Ramadan. Finally, Muslims who are physically and financially able must make a trip to Mecca at some time in their lives.

2. The Abbasid moved the capital to Baghdad and adopted a Persian style of government. Under the Abbasids, the nature of Islam changed. By inviting all peoples of the community to join in, they made Islam a universal religion. Abbasid scholars translated the works of ancient Greek scholars into Arabic at the House of Wisdom in Baghdad.
3. Many African societies developed village-based cultures. At the heart was the extended family, including parents, children, and close relatives. Each member contributed to the household. The men hunted, farmed, and raised animals. The women cared for the children, ground the grain, and carried the water. The elders in the household taught family traditions to the children. The children worked beside the adults as soon as they were able to do so. In some areas people took part in another group called age-sets. Men or women born within the same two or three-year period had a duty to help each other.
4. The Bantu migrations began in the first centuries AD. Bantu-speaking people began to migrate east and south. The reason for their migration is not known. As they traveled they carried knowledge of agriculture and iron working. They developed complex societies where cattle was an important resource.
5. In 1279 Kublai Khan defeated the Song and created the Yuan dynasty in China. The Chinese resented the Mongols and considered them rude and uncivilized. Instead of forcing the Chinese to adopt Mongol ways, the Mongols adopted some Chinese customs. However Mongols lived apart from the Chinese. Friendships were discouraged and Mongols were forbidden to marry Chinese. The Mongols had different laws and taxes for the Chinese.
6. Japan is a chain of islands close to mainland Asia. Most of Japan is mountains. The land best-suited for farming is near the coasts.

Chapter 12: Kingdoms and Christianity

Section Quiz

SECTION 1

1. i
2. j
3. a
4. f
5. c
6. h
7. b
8. g
9. m
10. l

SECTION 2

1. T
2. T
3. T
4. T
5. F; Alexander Nevsky was a brilliant military leader.

SECTION 3

1. Britain/England
2. Danes
3. adults
4. medieval
5. Gregory the Great
6. Augustine of Hippo
7. Benedictine
8. monasteries
9. abbots
10. missionaries

Chapter Test, Form A

1. b
2. d
3. b
4. b
5. c
6. c
7. d
8. b
9. d
14. Alfred the Great
15. Hagia Sophia
16. Augustine
17. iconoclasts
18. T
19. T
20. T
21. F
22. F

10. Justinian's Code
11. Belisarius
12. mosaics
13. Methodius
23. T
24. F
25. T

Chapter Test, Form B

Possible responses:

1. Constantinople was a large wealthy city. Its location on the Bosporus allowed it to control trade between Asia and Europe. The location also helped guard it from attacks. The sea protected it on two sides, and heavily fortified walls protected the landward side. These factors allowed the empire centered in Constantinople to thrive for centuries.
2. Most Byzantine art and architecture was based on religious themes. Many of the human subjects of Byzantine art were saints or figures from the Bible. Byzantine churches were built by placing a round dome over a square foundation. This style of architecture influenced building styles across Europe and Asia.
3. The Slavs of Russia practiced a native religion. In 863 a churchman in Constantinople sent two Greek monks, Cyril and Methodius, to Moravia to convert the Slavs to Christianity. The monks spoke the Slavonic language and celebrated the mass in that language. They also developed an alphabet to translate religious texts into the Slavonic language. This alphabet is called Cyrillic. The alphabet and Slavonic mass helped to spread the Byzantine version of Christianity in Russia. Then in 988, Vladimir of Kiev made Christianity the state religion of Kievan Russia.
4. Alexander encouraged the Russians not to rebel against the Mongols. As a result, the Mongols did not destroy as much as they had in other lands they had conquered and complete disaster was avoided.
5. Alfred was king of Wessex. The Anglo-Saxons united under him. Together they expelled the Danes from England. Alfred was recognized as king of all England. He reorganized the army, issued his own code of laws, reformed the justice system, and established a system of schools that educated adults as well as children. Clovis was king of the Franks. He converted to Christianity after winning a difficult battle. Under Clovis and his successors, the Franks became a major power in western Europe.
6. Monks ran schools, copied ancient manuscripts, advised rulers, created beautiful manuscripts, and spread Christianity.
7. Byzantine art was often done in mosaic, the subjects were often religious figures, and the art often contained symbols. This piece is a mosaic of Jesus. The circular design behind his head, the book, and the way he gestures with his right hand may be interpreted as symbols.

Chapter 13: The Early Middle Ages

Section Quiz

SECTION 1

1. k
2. m
3. h
4. f
5. e
6. d
7. b
8. c
9. i
10. a

SECTION 2

1. F; Even before Charlemagne died invaders began attacking his empire.
2. T
3. T
4. F; The Magyars were the ancestors of the present-day Hungarians and raided northern and western Europe from the east.
5. F; Muslims from Spain and North Africa destroyed many of Rome's ancient churches, including Saint Peter's Basilica.

SECTION 3

1. c
2. a

3. d
4. c
5. knights
6. feudalism or feudal system
7. oath of fealty or loyalty
8. manorial
9. protection
10. self-sufficient

SECTION 4

1. d	6. c
2. m	7. h
3. f	8. b
4. j	9. g
5. a	10. i

SECTION 5

1. Christian
2. Piety
3. Leo IX
4. Orthodox
5. pontificate
6. Gregory VII
7. clergy/religious officials
8. excommunication
9. Cluny
10. pope

Chapter Test, Form A

1. b	11. l
2. b	12. h
3. d	13. a
4. a	14. b
5. b	15. k
6. c	16. d
7. a	17. m
8. d	18. j
9. b	19. g
10. f	

20. counts
21. navigation/sailing/shipbuilding
22. Leif Eriksson
23. serfs
24. Parliament
25. pontificate

Chapter Test, Form B

Possible responses:

1. Answers will vary, and may be politics, education, religion, or law, as long as the answer is well supported. Sample answer: Charlemagne's religious reforms had the greatest impact. He wanted to spread Christian teachings, and did so by ordering the people he conquered to convert to Christianity and then sending missionaries to live among them to help Christianity take root. Unlike some of his other reforms, this reform lasted; medieval Europe became almost uniformly Christian, which had an immeasurable impact on the history of Europe.
2. The Vikings launched their raids on towns and cities they could reach by ship. A favorite target was monasteries. Viking raids were lightening fast. Armed with swords, axes, spears, and shields, warriors leapt from their ships to attack, grab any precious items they could find, and return to their ships to sail off. The Muslims, on the other hand, attacked cities and towns across southern Europe by land. They also attacked European ships sailing the Mediterranean.
3. The primary duty of a knight was to provide military service to his lord. A knight was expected to remain loyal and faithful. On special occasions or in the event of ransom a knight was required to provide money. The lord gave land to his knights. The lord had to treat his knights fairly, protect his knights if attacked, and settle disputes between knights.
4. The Magna Carta was significant because it restricted the king's power, suggesting that even monarchs were not above the law. It is an important historical document in the development of modern democracy.
5. Cistercian monasteries were very strict and built far from cities, to ensure isolation. This order may have been the most popular of the new orders because, first, people across Europe were becoming

more pious; and second, Cistercian monasteries provided a life free from worldliness at a time when many religious people were frustrated by the politics of the church and corruption among bishops and the papacy.

6. Primarily the Vikings raided areas of northern France. The Magyars invaded France by land from the east. If I lived in northern France in AD 900, I would be most afraid of the Vikings. The Vikings frequently raided the coastline and even Paris was not safe. Because it was impossible to know when the Vikings were coming, and because of their viciousness, I would fear them most.

Chapter 14: The High Middle Ages

Section Quiz

SECTION 1

1. F; He set out to free Jerusalem.
2. T
3. T
4. F; Trade increased because the Crusaders brought back goods that Europeans had not seen before and now wanted.
5. T

SECTION 2

1. f
2. b
3. i
4. m
5. k
6. c
7. e
8. l
9. j
10. d

SECTION 3

1. d
2. c
3. a
4. a
5. b

SECTION 4

1. heresy/heretical
2. pope
3. Friars
4. France
5. Joan of Arc
6. French
7. Wars of the Roses
8. Black Death
9. About 25
10. manor

Chapter Test, Form A

1. c
2. d
3. a
4. c
5. b
6. d
7. b
8. b
9. d
10. First
11. Venice
12. credit
13. illumination
14. chivalry
15. Black Death
16. j
17. e
18. l
19. d
20. m
21. h
22. k
23. f
24. b
25. i

Chapter Test, Form B

Possible responses:

1. Relations between religious groups changed as a result of the Crusades. Although some people came to respect other cultures as a result of the Crusades, many other Europeans became more intolerant. Most Jews and Muslims saw the Crusaders as vicious invaders. Other changes include an increase in trade. Monarchs became more powerful because absent lords could not defend their own lands and kings seized the lands.
2. As a group, a guild could set standards and prices for everyone's product. They could provide training in the craft, making sure that not too many people began working in it, flooding the market and driving prices down.
3. Cities were small and crowded, and tall buildings blocked the sunlight. There was no public sanitation, so cities were dirty and smelly. Fire was a danger. Rats and insects lived in open waste, spreading diseases. Violence was common. Cities offered many things village life did not. There were many public places to meet and socialize, such as churches, eating halls, and markets.
4. The plague may have been spread by the increased trade that resulted from the Crusades. Mongol armies may have been one source. Plague resulted in many

deaths. So many people died that labor became valuable, ultimately ending the manor system.

5. The image shows the high roofs, the light airy feel, the use of windows. All of this was made possible by the architectural innovation called the flying buttress that enabled buildings to be built much taller than before.

Unit 4: Medieval Europe

Unit Test, Form A

1. e	6. a
2. l	7. k
3. g	8. h
4. d	9. c
5. m	10. j

11. medieval
12. Byzantine
13. trade
14. Magyars
15. monasteries
16. guilds
17. Richard the Lion-Hearted
18. Hanseatic League
19. trade fair
20. Scholasticism

21. F	36. a
22. T	37. c
23. T	38. d
24. T	39. d
25. T	40. a
26. T	41. a
27. F	42. a
28. T	43. d
29. T	44. c
30. T	45. d
31. b	46. b
32. c	47. c
33. d	48. d
34. c	49. a
35. b	50. b

Unit Test, Form B

Possible responses:

1. Several issues divided the eastern and western churches and eventually resulted in a schism in 1054. The Church in the east used Greek, the church in the west used Latin. In the east the emperor oversaw church law. In the west the pope was the supreme patriarch. The Byzantines did not accept that the pope had supreme religious authority, they placed authority in church councils.
2. Brothers Cyril and Methodius were Greek monks who were sent as missionaries to Moravia. Their goal was to convert the Slavs to Christianity. They achieved this goal by celebrating Mass in the Slavonic language and developing a written alphabet for the Slavonic language called Cyrillic, which was based on Greek characters. The alphabet enabled them to translate religious texts for a larger group of readers. Use of the Cyrillic alphabet and the Slavonic mass became popular in what is now Serbia and Bulgaria, and beyond. The Byzantine version of Christianity was the one that spread to Russia, thanks in part to the monks.
3. Many historians consider Charlemagne one of the most important leaders in European history. Each year, he assembled an army, which he then led into battle against one of his foes. He incorporated the defeated peoples into his sphere of influence and formed alliances with their leaders. In the process, he increased the size and power of the Carolingian kingdom. He twice answered Pope Leo III's call for help, first in 774 when the Lombards attacked the Papal States, then in 799 when angry supporters of the previous pope attacked Leo and ran him out of town. Leo named Charlemagne Emperor of the Roman People, which showed that Leo credited him with restoring glory to the Roman Empire in Europe and that Charlemagne had the full backing of the church and God. He was the first Frankish king to establish a permanent capital at Aachen, and he established a system of counts and inspectors to rule parts of the empire and

make sure that the empire was well-run by loyal subjects, respectively. Charlemagne ordered churches and monasteries to start schools where educated priests and monks were teachers, and he had monks copy ancient texts to send to other monasteries, where still more copies where made. Without these efforts, many ancient texts may have disappeared completely in the Middle Ages. Charlemagne also worked closely with the church to create a unified Christian empire. He had many tribal laws recorded and allowed tribal legal codes to maintain their separate existence, and also created new laws to enforce Christian teaching. Western European reached great heights during his reign.

4. The purpose of feudalism was to protect Europe against invaders. Feudalism came about in part as a result of invasions of Magyars, Vikings, and Muslims in Europe. To defend their castles, nobles needed trained soldiers because they were no longer able to depend on kings' armies. Knights on horseback with heavy armor and weapons offered their services to lords, not for money, but in exchange for land, called a fief. In accepting the fief, a knight became a vassal of the lord by pledging loyalty, called fealty. The lord was obligated to protect his knights and treat them fairly. Knights were allowed to give parts of their land to other knights in exchange for loyalty. Everyone in a country was supposed to be loyal to the king, but some nobles grew to be just as strong as the kings they served. As a result, the king's power declined. Loyalties grew more complex, as did feudal obligations, which varied according to time and place.
5. Life on a manor was often difficult for peasants and serfs. They had to provide the lord with labor and other services in exchange for protection and a plot of land to cultivate for their own use. Serfs were tied to the land; they could not leave or marry without permission. Most serfs and peasants worked in farming although manors attempted to be self-sufficient, with some work being done by mill workers and blacksmiths. The lord and family lived in a castle, which could be quite uncomfortable. It was built to protect them, their soldiers and servants. There was little privacy. However peasants lived in smoky, one-room huts shared with animals. Rising before dawn, the men, boys, and sometimes women worked in the fields. Women and girls grew vegetables, cared for animals, cooked, and sewed, unless it was harvest time, when everyone worked in the fields.
6. The primary cause of the Crusades was the desire for Christians to control Jerusalem and the area around it, called the Holy Land. Many Christians felt it was vital to control the land that held the Holy Temple of the Jews, and where Jesus was crucified, buried, and would return. Stories of Muslim persecution of Christians visiting the Holy Land also spread throughout Europe. Fearful that the Turks would destroy Constantinople the Byzantine emperor turned to Pope Urban II for help. Believing the Turkish Muslims were persecuting Christians and might turn on the Byzantine Empire, the pope called on Christian warriors to unite and fight the Muslims. The Crusades impacted life in Europe. Trade increased with the awareness of products from around the world. The land that once belonged to knights and nobles killed in the Crusades was returned by other nobles, increasing their power. The Crusades brought knowledge of Muslim culture to Europe but relations between Christians, Jews, and Muslims remained strained for a long time after the Crusades. The most desired effect of the Crusades—Christian control of the Holy Land—did not happen.
7. The Crusaders states were far from Europe. They may have been difficult to keep supplied. The Europeans were very isolated. In the event of battle the only

place to retreat was the sea. Compared to areas under Muslim control the area of the Crusader states was small, suggesting it could be easily overthrown.

Chapter 15: Renaissance and Reformation

Section Quiz

SECTION 1

1. e
2. h
3. d
4. a
5. c
6. i
7. j
8. m
9. f
10. b

SECTION 2

1. Hanseatic League
2. Albrecht Dürer
3. Johannes Gutenberg
4. books/printed material
5. Desiderius Erasmus
6. Sir Thomas More
7. William Shakespeare
8. Christine de Pisan
9. Jan van Eyck
10. everyday peasant life

SECTION 3

1. T
2. F; He believed selling indulgences was sinful and flatly denied that indulgences had any power to remit sin.
3. T
4. F; He asked for an annulment because he believed Catherine would produce no male heir; he wanted to be able to marry again.
5. T

SECTION 4

1. k
2. m
3. a
4. f
5. l
6. d
7. c
8. b
9. j
10. e

Chapter Test, Form A

1. a
2. c
3. a
4. d
5. b
6. b
7. b
8. d
9. Leonardo da Vinci
10. humanists/humanism
11. Martin Luther
12. predestination
13. Counter-Reformation
14. Roman Inquisition
15. b
16. g
17. k
18. b
19. i
20. e
21. j
22. l
23. m
24. f
25. c

Chapter Test, Form B

Possible responses:

1. The city-states were bustling centers of commerce, dominated by the Church, nobles, merchants, and artisans. As nobles and merchants sought to display their new wealth, knowledge of arts such as painting, sculpture, and architecture increased. All of these areas saw achievements in the Renaissance.
2. Humanism had at its root a strong belief in individual accomplishment. Humanists believed that the human mind was almost limitless. They rediscovered ancient texts and made advances in medicine and astronomy. Philosophers and writers produced works that influenced Europe for centuries. Scientists began to challenge the church's teachings about the world. Humanists argued that individual achievement and education could be fully expressed only if people used their talents and abilities in the service of their cities.
3. Trade between northern Europe and Italy spread ideas. In addition, some Italian Renaissance artists fled to northern Europe to escape war and political unrest, taking their ideas with them; some northern scholars traveled to Italy for an education,

where they learned humanist ideas. The explosion of printed materials also helped ideas spread to new places.

4. The Council of Trent met off and on from 1545 to 1563. During this time delegates clarified Catholic teaching on important points. The council rejected some Protestant teachings, but did correct church abuses, address corruption in the clergy, and abolish the sale of indulgences. The bold pronouncements of the council gave Catholics renewed energy and confidence. An example of this is the work of the Jesuits around the world.
5. Both Savonarola and Ignatius of Loyola worked to reform the Catholic Church. However, they did this in different ways. Savonarola called for the churches to melt down their gold and silver to buy bread for the hungry and poor members of the church. Later, a pope excommunicated him for spreading dangerous ideas. Ignatius of Loyola founded the Jesuits, a religious order that emphasized obedience to the church above all. Jesuits concentrated on education as a means of combating the Protestant Reformation. They established missions, schools, and universities.
6. The painter of this scene likely came from northern Europe, because the subject matter is a scene of daily life and the scene is painted in detail. Italian painters, on the other hand, usually painted mythological scenes.

Chapter 16: Exploration and Expansion

Section Quiz

SECTION 1

1. b
2. d
3. d
4. d
5. a
6. b
7. b
8. b
9. a
10. c

SECTION 2

1. diseases
2. Hernán Cortés
3. Aztec
4. Peru
5. conquistadors
6. *encomienda*
7. Treaty of Tordesillas
8. New Netherland
9. priest
10. Jamestown

SECTION 3

1. F; The Columbian Exchange was the exchange of plants, animals, and disease between the Americas and the rest of the world. It began with large-scale contact between Europe and the Americas following the voyages of Columbus.
2. T
3. T
4. F; Capitalism is an economic system in which private individuals or organizations carry on most economic activities in order to seek a profit.
5. T

SECTION 4

1. c
2. c
3. a
4. a
5. d

Chapter Test, Form A

1. b
2. c
3. d
4. c
5. b
6. b
7. a
8. b
9. caravel
10. Prince Henry
11. Pedro Cabral
12. indentured servants
13. Jamestown
14. plantations
15. mercantilism
16. f
17. m
18. h
21. b
22. c
23. e

19. i
20. a
24. d
25. g

Chapter Test, Form B

Possible responses:

1. Europeans were searching for luxury goods and wealth. They wanted to spread Christianity. They desired fame and glory. They were driven by curiosity.
2. Sample answer: I have been forced to work for the Spanish landowner. I work long hours and am treated very badly. Many of my friends and family have died of disease and overwork. The landowner tells me I must believe in the Christian God.
3. Although the French did not find gold, silver, or riches in North America, they did find plentiful fish and furs. They began a profitable trade in these items.
4. Plants and animals used for food were exchanged between Europe and the Americas. Crops native to the Americas, such as corn and potatoes, provided substantial nutrition and helped people in Europe and in other parts of the world live much longer lives. Native Americans gained access to new foods and new beasts of burden.
5. Captive Africans resisted enslavement in many ways. Some slowed down their work or destroyed equipment. Some revolted, attacking slaveholders and their families. Some escaped and established communities of runaways. Enslaved people found ways to preserve their African traditions. And some turned to religion for strength and hope.
6. Most enslaved Africans came from an area of West Africa where there were many slave forts, including St. Louis, James Island, Elmina, Assini, Accra and Whydah.

Chapter 17: New Asian Empires

Section Quiz

SECTION 1

1. T
2. F; Mehmed II led the siege that resulted in the fall of Constantinople.
3. T
4. F; Though the Savavid and Ottomans did have Islam in common, they were from different sects. Conflict, not alliance, occurred between the groups.
5. T

SECTION 2

1. c
2. a
3. d
4. a
5. d

SECTION 3

1. Kublai Khan
2. Hongwu
3. 300
4. Beijing
5. Zheng He
6. isolate
7. Matteo Ricci
8. Qing
9. tea
10. porcelain

SECTION 4

1. f
2. i
3. a
4. g
5. h
6. e
7. b
8. l
9. c
10. j

Chapter Test, Form A

1. b
2. c
3. d
4. a
5. b
6. d
7. c
8. b
9. c
10. j
14. f
15. b
16. d
17. h
18. c
19. m
20. sultans
21. Suleyman I
22. Babur
23. Taj Mahal

11. e
12. g
13. l
24. Yonglo
25. shogun

Chapter Test, Form B

Possible responses:

1. The Ottoman Empire reached its height under Suleyman. During his reign, from 1520 to 1566, Ottoman forces pushed through Hungary up to Vienna. Meanwhile, the navy gained control of the eastern Mediterranean and the North African coast. Suleyman's domestic achievements included reforming the tax system, and the bureaucracy. He improved the court system and legal code, and issued new laws to address corruption. During his reign, architects built magnificent mosques and palaces, many of which showed a Byzantine influence. There were two classes in Ottoman society; a privileged ruling class, and a second class that consisted of everyone else. This group included people of diverse cultures and religions.
2. The Safavid culture blended Shia religion and Persian tradition. This gave the state a unique identity and laid the foundation for the national culture of present-day Iran. The greatest Safavid leader, 'Abbas, brought in Chinese potters to improve the quality of glazed tiles and ceramic. Public spaces had graceful arches and lush gardens. Colorful tiles and domes appeared on mosques. During the 1600s, the capital Esfahan was one of the world's most magnificent cities. Handwoven Persian carpets became an important industry. Trade goods brought wealth to the Safavid Empire and helped establish it as a major Muslim civilization.
3. Shah Jahan forced the people of India to pay high taxes to cover the enormous expense of the monuments he built. Many faced hardship and famine as a result. Shah Jahan was also intolerant toward Christians and Hindus. His son Aurangzeb declared himself emperor after killing his brother, ending a power struggle between them. After expanding the empire's borders, Aurangzeb issued and enforced strict decrees about morality and personal behavior. He persecuted Sikhs and Hindus, and had soldiers on elephants crush those who protested. These policies led many peasants to rebel. Invaders and rival claims to the throne led to disorder after Aurangzeb's death. The Mughals held on to power for another 150 years. Then India became a colony of Britain.
4. Under the Ming, improved methods of irrigation increased farm production. Peasants produced huge crops of rice in the southern river valleys. New crops from the Americas, such as corn and sweet potatoes, further increased farm output. The increased food supply led to population growth. As the population grew, so did the cities. These new cities produced silk and porcelain goods that were traded to Europeans.
5. In the Japanese feudal system, noble landowners received the allegiance and military service of samurai. In exchange the nobles gave land or rice. Only the most powerful samurai received land. Samurai were highly skilled warriors and very respected. They followed a code of ethics called Bushido. Most samurai were men, but women could also be samurai. However women did not often go into battle.
6. The vase is from the Ming period. Ming porcelain was blue and white. Its beauty made it a valuable trade item. Porcelain was one of the items that was part of Chinese trade to Europeans.

Unit 5: New Ideas, New Empires

Unit Test, Form A

1. d
2. i
3. j
4. c
6. b
7. h
8. e
9. k

5. a
10. l
11. detail
12. Humanists
13. Council of Trent
14. *encomienda*
15. Jamestown
16. Columbian Exchange
17. joint-stock
18. triangular trade
19. Bushido
20. Mughal

21. T	36. a
22. T	37. d
23. F	38. a
24. T	39. c
25. F	40. b
26. T	41. b
27. F	42. a
28. F	43. d
29. T	44. a
30. F	45. c
31. c	46. d
32. c	47. c
33. a	48. d
34. d	49. b
35. a	50. d

Unit Test, Form B

Possible responses:

1. The *encomienda* system was one in which a colonist was given a certain amount of land. The colonist was also given a number of Native Americans to work the land. In exchange, the colonist was required to teach the native workers about Christianity. Overwork and mistreatment took a heavy toll on the native population. Even worse were the effects of diseases spread by Europeans. Millions died, as they had no natural resistance to diseases such as smallpox, tuberculosis, and measles.
2. The Renaissance was a time of renewed interest and remarkable developments in art, literature, science, and learning. Leonardo da Vinci succeeded in many areas including: painting, writing, inventing, engineering, music, mathematics, philosophy, and architecture.
3. Events leading to Luther's excommunication began with his public complaints about the church. Intended for church leaders, Luther's theses denied that indulgences had any power to remit sin. He also criticized the power of the pope and the wealth of the church. Soon, university intellectuals were discussing Luther's ideas, and later, his theses were published. The desire for reform grew among those who felt Luther's theses made sense. After publication, Luther continued to study and debate. He contradicted basic Catholic beliefs when he insisted God's grace could be earned through faith alone, not also through good works. He also declared that only Jesus, not the pope, was the head of the church. Luther insisted that individuals interpret the Bible for themselves and that Christian practices should come only from the Bible. Finally, he translated the Bible into German so that many more people could read it without the aid of the clergy. Luther was summoned before the emperor where Luther refused to change his opinions and was excommunicated.
4. The Ming dynasty brought stability and prosperity to China. A more powerful emperor, improved agriculture and trade, set the stage for accomplishments such the new capital of Beijing, and rebuilding the Great Wall. The Ming dynasty sponsored seven voyages around the Indian Ocean as far as Africa. This extended China's influence and demonstrated its growing sea power. Ming artisans produced blue and white porcelain that became a valuable trade item. Rising literacy rates contributed to the growth of popular fiction.
5. In feudal Japan, noble landowners gave property or payment to samurai warriors in exchange for allegiance and military service. Unlike feudal knights in Europe, only the most powerful samurai received

land; most were paid in food, generally rice. The samurai who did receive land did not live or work on it, but rather received money or food from the peasants who worked it. Samurai were expected to be ready to fight at all times. They followed a strict code of ethics known as Bushido, and in time rose to such high a status that they had the right to kill anyone who showed disrespect. Likewise, samurai were expected to serve and obey their lords without hesitation. Should they fail to do this, they were expected to commit suicide rather than live with their shame.

6. Triangular trade was the trading network between Europe, Africa, and North America. During the first leg of the triangle ships carried European goods to Africa to be exchanged for captured Africans. The Africans were shipped to the Americas. This leg of the triangle was known as the Middle Passage. Travel conditions were brutal and many of the Africans did not survive the journey. On the third leg ships carried American products such as sugar, rum, rice, and tobacco to Europe.
7. The slave forts were located on the west coast of Africa. From there the British and Spanish had relatively short routes to their colonies in North America. Other slave forts were located further south along the coast, which enabled the ships bound for Dutch and Brazilian colonies to have a shorter route.

Chapter 18: The Monarchs of Europe

Section Quiz

SECTION 1

1. i
2. a
3. l
4. c
5. m
6. d
7. b
8. k
9. f
10. j

SECTION 2

1. French Calvinist Protestant
2. Saint Bartholomew's Day Massacre
3. France
4. converting
5. Edict of Nantes
6. Louis XIII
7. Cardinal Richelieu
8. Louis XIV
9. Versailles
10. War of the Spanish Succession

SECTION 3

1. g
2. a
3. b
4. h
5. c
6. m
7. f
8. d
9. e
10. l

SECTION 4

1. T
2. T
3. F; St. Petersburg featured Western architecture.
4. F; She realized she needed to strengthen her authority in rural areas.
5. T

Chapter Test, Form A

1. d
2. c
3. a
4. d
5. a
6. b
7. d
8. c
9. b
10. Phillip II
11. Edict of Nantes
12. Puritans
13. Spanish Succession
14. commonwealth
15. czars
16. h
17. j
18. k
19. l
20. m
21. e
22. a
23. d
24. g
25. b

Chapter Test, Form B

Possible responses:

1. Charles V encountered several problems. During his reign, a growing Protestant

movement threatened his influence. Charles confronted Martin Luther and declared him an outlaw. However, rebellions against Catholic rulers spread. After years of war, Charles had to sign the Peace of Augsburg in 1555. This gave each German prince the right to decide whether his state would be Lutheran or Catholic.

2. Calvinist Protestantism was spreading through the Low Countries. A revolt began when the Dutch refused to declare allegiance to Philip. To punish them he sent an army under the command of the Duke of Alba. Alba set up a court (Court of Blood) that tortured and executed thousands of people suspected of being rebels. After years of revolt a truce was reached in 1609. The southern provinces remained under Spanish rule. The northern provinces formed the independent nation of the Netherlands.
3. Sample answer: I would support Parliament, along with those who decided to rise up against Charles I because he intended to take back power from Parliament. Or: I would support Charles I, because I would oppose changes likely to be put in place by a Puritan government, including laws restricting entertainment.
4. Oliver Cromwell, a Puritan, was given the title Lord Protector of England, Scotland and Ireland. He demanded complete obedience. He also closed theaters and limited other forms of entertainment. Eventually he dissolved Parliament and ruled alone until his death.
5. During Ivan's early years, he made many reforms. He created a general council that included merchants and lower-level nobles. He promoted military officers on merit, drew up a new legal code, and reduced the power of the boyars. During the 1560s, Ivan changed dramatically, and he became known as "Ivan the Terrible." He became suspicious, and created a royal police force to investigate and punish any opposition. He ordered the killing of thousands of people in the city of Novgorod. He even killed his own son, leaving no heir to the throne.
6. Peter gained a port that would not freeze and would be open to western trade all year long.
7. Non-monetary costs of building the palace at Versailles include creating resentment among French people and helping to cause a revolution years later.
8. It helped him reduce the power of the nobles. They were required to attend him at Versailles where he could keep an eye on them. In addition the palace was a symbol of the Sun King's power as an absolute monarch.

Chapter 19: Enlightenment and Revolution

Section Quiz

SECTION 1

1. f	6. g
2. m	7. c
3. h	8. b
4. l	9. i
5. j	10. a

SECTION 2

1. reason
2. Enlightenment
3. philosophes
4. Baron de Montesquieu
5. Jean-Jacque Rousseau
6. good
7. all
8. women
9. Mary Wollstonecraft
10. enlightened despots

SECTION 3

1. F: The class system was not in place. Individuals could advance themselves through intelligence and hard work.
2. T
3. F: The Articles of Confederation created a weak government with no power to tax.

4. T
5. T

Chapter Test, Form A

1. b
2. b
3. b
4. a
5. c
6. c
7. d
8. a
9. a
10. d
11. geocentric
12. calculus
13. William Harvey
14. Encyclopedia
15. Stamp Act
16. Declaration of Independence
17. George Washington
18. T
19. F
20. T
21. T
22. T
23. T
24. T
25. F

Chapter Test, Form B

Possible responses:

1. The age of exploration showed scholars that there were new lands that the ancient scholars knew nothing about—perhaps there were other things to be discovered that the ancients had not known. In addition, the age of exploration led scientists to study the natural world more closely; for example, they needed more accurate instruments and geographic knowledge for world travel.
2. Student answers will discuss three of the following: The geocentric theory, which held that the sun was the center of the solar system, Newton's ideas about gravity and the invention of calculus, discoveries in biology such as drawings of human anatomy, explanations for the working of the human heart and the circulatory system, technical advances such as the telescope and microscope, new information about matter and elements.
3. Philosophers began to view reason as a concept that was unique to human beings. They credited reason as why humans instead of other creatures were making advances in science, art, and philosophy. They believed reason was a tool that could be used to solve problems such as poverty, war, and ignorance.
4. Enlightened despots were attracted to Enlightenment ideals and were willing to make some reforms. But they were not willing to make reforms at the expense of their own power. Most were attracted to ideas and reforms that built their country's strength and made their own rule more powerful.
5. The Declaration of Independence drew on the Enlightenment ideas that citizens had important civil rights (including the right to trial, the right to elect members of Parliament, and the right to an independent judicial system); and that people had the right to overthrow a government that did not protect those rights.
6. Step 1 of the Scientific Method is: Identify a Problem.
7. Step 5 of the Scientific Method is: Draw a conclusion that either proves or disproves the hypothesis.

Chapter 20: The French Revolution and Napoleon

Section Quiz

SECTION 1

1. g
2. m
3. c
4. k
5. e
6. f
7. a
8. h
9. i
10. j

SECTION 2

1. T
2. F; Robespierre led the Committee during the Reign of Terror.
3. T
4. T
5. F; The Directory was a weak and ineffective government.

SECTION 3

1. T
2. T
3. T
4. T
5. F; Napoleon established an efficient tax system to strengthen the government.

SECTION 4

1. b
2. c
3. b
4. d
5. a

Chapter Test, Form A

1. b
2. d
3. a
4. a
5. c
6. a
7. a
8. d
9. d

10. Roman Catholic clergy
11. National Assembly
12. Jacobin
13. nationalism
14. Napoleonic Code
15. Waterloo

16. k
17. f
18. g
19. h
20. i
21. a
22. b
23. d
24. c
25. j

Chapter Test, Form B

Possible responses:

1. The First Estate was made up of the Roman Catholic clergy. The Second Estate was made up of the nobility. The Third Estate, most of the population, was made up of the bourgeoisie—city-dwelling merchants, factory owners, and professionals; the artisans and workers of the cities; and the peasants.
2. The Catholic religion provided a connection to old ways of life that the National Convention wanted to erase. Clergy who refused to abide by the Civil Constitution of the Clergy lost their positions; in Paris, churches were closed; and Robespierre created another religion, the cult of the Supreme Being, where enthusiasm for the revolution became the object of worship.
3. The French welcomed Napoleon because they were tired of the constant warfare and chaos of the Revolution, and Napoleon promised order. He also pledged to uphold some key revolutionary reforms.
4. Student answers will vary. Students should mention that Napoleon was a brilliant military leader, was very courageous and ambitious, and he did not hesitate to use dishonest means to seize power.
5. The Congress changed many national borders in order to strengthen the nations surrounding France. In this way, they hoped to lessen the chance that France would invade its neighbors again.
6. In 1812, in addition to land in the French Empire, Napoleon controlled Spain, the Kingdoms of Naples and Italy, Switzerland, the Confederation of the Rhine, Holland, Kingdom of Westphalia, Tuscany, and the Grand Duchy of Warsaw.
7. Napoleon would have felt vulnerable to attack from states opposed to him that bordered the empire and had strong militaries. These nations would include Great Britain and the Russian Empire.

Unit 6: Changes in European Society

Unit Test, Form A

1. e
2. g
3. a
4. j
5. k
6. m
7. b
8. f
9. h
10. d

11. scientific method
12. Enlightened despots
13. Catherine II
14. Reason
15. Jean-Jacques Rousseau
16. American
17. Tennis Court Oath
18. Napoleonic Code
19. Continental System

20. Congress of Vienna
21. F
22. T
23. F
24. T
25. T
26. T
27. F
28. T
29. T
30. F
31. b
32. a
33. d
34. a
35. c
36. b
37. d
38. d
39. c
40. a
41. c
42. b
43. c
44. c
45. d
46. c
47. a
48. c
49. b
50. a

Unit Test, Form B

Possible responses:

1. Charles V's hoped to establish a Catholic Europe. After the Protestant Reformation took hold in Germany, rebellions against Catholic leaders spread. In 1555, Charles was forced to sign the Peace of Augsburg. This gave each German prince the right to decide if his state would be Catholic or Lutheran. This made his vision of a Catholic Europe impossible.
2. Cromwell was a Puritan army general who rose in power until he became commander-in-chief of Parliament's army. Once the king surrendered and Cromwell was in charge of Parliament, he dismissed all members who disagreed with him. He took the title, Lord Protector of England, Scotland, and Ireland. Under Cromwell's leadership England's government changed completely. It became a commonwealth. Eventually Cromwell dismissed Parliament and ruled alone. He clamped down on social life and forms of entertainment. Many people were unhappy under Cromwell's reign.
3. Instead of looking to traditional authorities for answers to questions about the natural world, scholars in the 1500s began to think in new ways. They developed the scientific method, a five-step process to aid investigation and discovery. They began to emphasize reason. Scientists made important discoveries about the solar system and human anatomy. They developed new tools such as the telescope and the microscope to aid investigation. Newton developed calculus to explain the effects of gravity. Ultimately the Scientific Revolution paved the way for the Enlightenment.
4. Hobbes believed that monarchy was the best form of government because it limited the freedoms of the individual. Hobbes believed people were not naturally good, so a strong government was needed to prevent chaos. He described the exchange of personal freedom for peace, safety, and order as the social contract.
5. Some of the causes of the French Revolution were: inequalities in French society, the influence of the ideas of Enlightenment thinkers, a financial crisis in France, widespread hunger and cold, and poor leadership from the king.
6. All the states were controlled by Napoleon.

Chapter 21: The Industrial Revolution

Section Quiz

SECTION 1

1. T
2. F; The factors are land, labor, and capital.
3. T
4. F; He built Slater's Mill on the Blackstone River in Pawtucket, Rhode Island.
5. F; It led to an increased need to use coal as fuel.

SECTION 2

1. cottage
2. industrialization
3. Luddites or Luddite Movement
4. Labor unions
5. mass production
6. c
7. a

8. d
9. b
10. c

SECTION 3

1. l	6. e
2. f	7. h
3. c	8. g
4. d	9. k
5. b	10. i

Chapter Test, Form A

1. a	14. i
2. d	15. j
3. b	16. a
4. b	17. d
5. a	18. m
6. d	19. F
7. d	20. T
8. b	21. T
9. c	22. F
10. f	23. T
11. g	24. F
12. b	25. T
13. e	

Chapter Test, Form B

Possible responses:

1. The factors of production are the essential elements that a nation needs to achieve economic success. The three factors are land, labor, and capital. Land means all of the natural resources in a place. Labor means the people available to go to work in industry. Capital refers to funds for investment in business.
2. The flying shuttle doubled the speed at which a single weaver could weave yarn into fabric. Once it was patented, many workers lost their jobs as a result. This event illustrates the negative effects of industrial progress: as machines made tasks traditionally done by hand faster and more efficient, many skilled workers were put out of work.
3. Factory work held dangers for all workers, but children faced special hazards. They often lost fingers or other body parts in the machines because there were no safety protections. The work day was long, and the factories were noisy and poorly-ventilated with inadequate food and poor sanitation. In addition the children's wages were even lower than the poor wages of adult workers.
4. Andrew Carnegie was admired because he was a common man who made it—a real rags-to-riches story. He epitomized the American dream. He was born in Scotland. His father was a weaver who was driven out of work by the textile mills. Carnegie started working in the mills at age 13, after his family immigrated to the United States. Only with his own hard work, creativity, and tough business practices, did he become a vastly wealthy entrepreneur.
5. More railroads are found in heavily industrialized areas and countries, like Great Britain. Several railroad lines tended to come together in an industrialized area. In non-industrialized areas, there are far fewer railroad lines.

Chapter 22: Life in the Industrial Age

Section Quiz

SECTION 1

1. d	6. g
2. i	7. a
3. h	8. m
4. c	9. k
5. f	10. b

SECTION 2

1. d	4. a
2. b	5. b
3. b	

SECTION 3

1. F; The industrial city served to gather raw materials, produce manufactured goods, and distribute those goods. Before the Industrial Age, most cities existed to serve

political, military, religious, or trade functions.

2. F; In the 1800s, people moved to cities to find factory jobs and to escape hunger, political oppression, or discrimination. The population of cities grew.
3. T
4. T
5. T

Chapter Test, Form A

1. a	14. d
2. b	15. c
3. b	16. i
4. d	17. k
5. a	18. g
6. c	19. j
7. c	20. Michael Faraday
8. d	21. Model T
9. b	22. pasteurization
10. h	23. psychoanalysis
11. m	24. educated
12. e	25. newspapers
13. l	

Chapter Test, Form B

Possible responses:

1. Students will discuss two of the following: First, by using electric power, factories no longer relied on large steam engines to power machines. Second, factories did not have to depend on water sources to power the steam engines. Third, factory production increased because with electric lighting in factories, workers could work well after dark.
2. Students will discuss two of the following: pasteurization, vaccines, anesthetic, and antiseptic.
3. *On the Origin of Species* described Darwin's theory that species change, or evolve, over time. His theory was controversial because it indicated that human beings were descended from other animals, which some people thought was ridiculous. In addition, his theory offended some because it opposed the creation story in the Bible.
4. Students will describe two of the following: Romanticism developed as a reaction to Enlightenment rationalism and early abuses of the Industrial Revolution. Romanticism was literature, paintings, poetry, or music filled with a love of nature, deep emotion, the value of the individual, affection for the past, and the importance of imagination. As a reaction to the exuberance of romanticism, a style called realism developed. Artists portrayed the rugged and disturbing details of everyday life. Subjects included war, pollution, and exploitation. Impressionism developed as an art form that looked to capture an impression of a scene, not an exact record.
5. Industrial cities had to have a large workforce, a reliable transportation network, factories, warehouses, stores, and offices. They were often crowded and dirty. On the other hand they provided entertainment not available in rural areas. They were lively and fastpaced places to live. Cities also attracted many immigrants looking for work.
6. Generally, areas near manufacturing cities and transportation areas would see population growth.
7. There would be fewer railroad lines and there would not be a railroad line across the United States.

Chapter 23: Reforms, Revolutions, and War

Section Quiz

SECTION 1

1. f	6. e
2. k	7. m
3. b	8. a
4. h	9. g
5. l	10. d

SECTION 2

1. T

2. F; Louis Philippe increased the power of the government and silenced those who opposed him.
3. F; The Revolution of 1848 fueled a new women's rights movement.
4. T
5. T

SECTION 3

1. d	6. b
2. f	7. l
3. c	8. a
4. e	9. m
5. k	10. h

SECTION 4

1. F; The War of 1812 was a war involving Great Britain and the United States.
2. T
3. F; Manifest destiny was the term used to describe the belief that Americans had a God-given right to settle the land all the way to the Pacific Ocean.
4. T
5. F; Lincoln's Emancipation Proclamation helped the North in its fight against the Confederacy.

Chapter Test, Form A

1. a	6. d
2. d	7. b
3. c	8. a
4. d	9. b
5. a	10. d

11. Chartists
12. Emmeline Pankhurst
13. Louis Napoleon
14. Dreyfus affair
15. Haiti
16. creoles
17. peninsulares
18. Monroe Doctrine
19. Reconstruction

20. F	23. T
21. T	24. F
22. T	25. F

Chapter Test, Form B

Possible responses:

1. The Reform Act of 1832 was passed after ordinary people demanded greater political participation. Before the Act, landowning aristocrats made up most of Parliament. Industrial cities had no representatives. The Act gave the vote to middle-class men, giving industrial cities the representation they wanted. However, women and many working-class men were still excluded from voting.
2. Metternich had worked hard at the Congress of Vienna to restore monarchies and prevent revolution. Now revolutions and revolutionary ideas were spreading once again. He felt his life's work was destroyed.
3. Agustín de Iturbide was asked by Spanish authorities to lead a final battle against the revolutionaries. Instead, Iturbide proposed to the revolutionary leader that Mexico would gain its independence but be ruled by a monarch; that creoles and peninsulares would have equal rights, and that the Roman Catholic Church would be the official church. This compromise satisfied both revolutionaries and royalists, allowing them to join together to win independence from Spain.
4. Manifest destiny was the term for the belief that Americans had a right to settle all the land up to the Pacific Ocean. By moving west, American settlers were moving onto land occupied by Native Americans. In order to access the land, they had to forcibly remove the Native Americans who lived in those territories,
5. The steep population decline beginning in 1845 was due to the Great Famine, which lasted from 1845-1851. The potato crop failed in those years, and about a million Irish died from starvation. In addition about 1.5 million people emigrated.
6. Many people lost everything during the famine, including their homes and loved ones. Many may have decided to emigrate

after the famine when they realized things were not going to get better. The political, economic, and social situation had not improved.

Chapter 24: Nationalism in Europe

Section Quiz

SECTION 1

1. T
2. F; Camillo di Cavour wanted Italy to be a monarchy.
3. T
4. F; Victor Emmanuel became king of Italy.
5. T

SECTION 2

1. b
2. a
3. b
4. b
5. d

SECTION 3

1. h
2. i
3. b
4. f
5. c
6. a
7. d
8. k
9. m
10. e

SECTION 4

1. czars
2. Serfs
3. autocracy
4. Alexander II
5. Vladimir Lenin
6. socialist republic
7. pogroms
8. Trans-Siberian Railroad
9. Bloody Sunday
10. Russian Revolution

Chapter Test, Form A

1. c
2. d
3. a
4. c
5. d
6. b
7. b
8. b
9. a
10. nationalism
11. Bismarck/Prussia
12. Carlsbad Decrees
13. Dual Monarchy
14. serfs
15. pogroms
16. e
17. k
18. m
19. c
20. h
21. l
22. b
23. g
24. j
25. i

Chapter Test, Form B

Possible responses:

1. Camillo di Cavour founded a nationalist newspaper. As prime minister of Sardinia, he worked to build the economy. He felt that a thriving economy would be helpful to a unified Italy. He also cultivated France as an ally. France agreed to support Sardinia in a war against Austria for lands in northern Italy. Cavour asked Garibaldi to lead part of the army. Some call Cavour the "brain" of Italian unification.
2. Italy faced a number of social and economic problems. Regional differences kept the new nation from truly being unified. In addition, the Catholic Church did not recognize Italy as a legitimate nation and prohibited Catholics from voting. Widespread poverty led to rioting and violence. Large numbers of Italians left the country.
3. Metternich clamped down on universities. He accused them of creating revolutionaries. He helped pass the Carlsbad Decrees, which prohibited reforms that conflicted with absolute monarchy. Newspapers were censored and a secret police force was created to spy on students suspected of liberal or nationalist activities. Metternich formed alliances with other European powers. They agreed to provide military intervention to support governments against internal revolution.
4. The Crimean War had shown how far behind Russia was from the rest of Europe. Alexander II freed the Russian serfs. He believed a peasant rebellion was likely if terrible conditions continued. He also hoped a market economy might develop if peasants owned land. He tried

to modernize Russia by setting up a judicial system and allowing some local self-government. He also reorganized the army and navy.

5. The October Manifesto was an official promise for reform and a more democratic government. It was issued by Czar Nicholas II in response to the rebellions and strikes in Russia in 1905. It guaranteed freedom of speech and assembly. Many Russians gained the right to vote. The manifesto stated that voters would elect representatives to the Duma, and that the czar would not pass laws without the approval of the Duma.
6. With the addition of the states that formed the North German Confederation, Prussia was united from east to west.
7. The German Empire was much larger than the Kingdom of Prussia, perhaps twice the size.

Chapter 25: The Age of Imperialism

Section Quiz

SECTION 1

1. a
2. d
3. b
4. a
5. a

SECTION 2

1. Guangzhou
2. unequal treaty
3. Boxer Rebellion
4. Confucian
5. republic
6. extraterritoriality
7. shogun
8. emperor
9. French
10. Siam

SECTION 3

1. F; The "Scramble for Africa" was the rapid division of Africa by the European powers, not to settle colonies, but to directly govern large areas occupied by non-European peoples.
2. T
3. F; The British occupied Egypt in 1882 to protect its interests and maintain the security of the Suez Canal.
4. T
5. F; It was the Ethiopians who defeated the Italians at the Battle of Adowa.

SECTION 4

1. c
2. g
3. a
4. k
5. l
6. h
7. b
8. m
9. f
10. d

Chapter Test, Form A

1. a
2. d
3. b
4. b
5. c
6. a
7. c
8. c
9. British East India
10. Raj
11. Sun Yixian
12. materials/resources
13. Social Darwinism
14. Suez Canal
15. troops
16. Monroe Doctrine
17. T
18. F
19. T
20. T
21. T
22. T
23. F
24. T
25. F

Chapter Test, Form B

Possible responses:

1. Under the British, changes were made to Indian society. The banning of some customs, the appearance of Christian missionaries, a new education system, and use of the English language strained relations between Indians and the British. Some Indians suspected that the British wanted to eliminate Indian customs and Hinduism completely. The Sepoy Mutiny was sparked when the British required Indian soldiers to use rifle cartridges greased with animal fat. Before using the cartridge, the soldier had to bite off the tip. Offended on religious grounds, some sepoys refused to use the rifles. They were punished. In response, sepoys all

over India rose up against their British officers.

2. The failure of the Qing dynasty to resist Western powers led some Chinese to conclude that the dynasty had lost the mandate of heaven. This led to a series of rebellions. The Taiping Rebellion was led by Hong Xiuquan, who wanted to reform society. He wanted to create a "Heavenly Kingdom of Great Peace" where no one would be poor. He set out to capture large territories in southeastern China. By 1853, Hong controlled the city of Nanjing and territories in southeastern China. With the help of French and British soldiers, the Qing put down the rebellion in 1864. Over 20 million Chinese died as a result of the rebellion.
3. Sample answers: I would have supported the revolution, because one of the principles of Sun Yixian's revolutionary philosophy was "people's livelihood." This meant equality in land ownership, which I would have wanted. Or, I would have opposed the revolution, because the Qing dynasty was beginning to make reforms such as provincial assemblies and schools. I would have been concerned that the revolution would erase Chinese culture and tradition.
4. The new imperialism sought to directly govern large areas occupied by non-European peoples. This differed from earlier colonialism. In the 1500s and 1600s Europeans intended to settle in the colonies.
5. The Roosevelt Corollary was added to the Monroe Doctrine. Although the doctrine proclaimed that the Americas were off-limits to European imperialism, some Europeans felt it was an idle threat. Latin American nations were deep in debt to foreign creditors. Some creditors threatened to use military force to collect their debt. Roosevelt wanted to protect U.S. interests in Latin America and keep the region stable. The Roosevelt Corollary stated that the United States would use military force to keep Europeans out of the Americas.
6. The Japanese boats in front look small and harmless compared to the warship. Although the ship is in the background, the dark color and absence of people convey a sense of foreboding. The ship looks threatening. The print illustrates that the Japanese felt forced to give in to Western demands.

Unit 7: Industrialization and Nationalism

Unit Test, Form A

1. f
2. j
3. m
4. c
5. k
6. a
7. e
8. b
9. l
10. d
11. Industrial Age
12. Luddite
13. Charles Darwin
14. psychology
15. Factory
16. Chartists
17. Monroe Doctrine
18. Red Shirts
19. October Manifesto
20. Kanagawa
21. T
22. T
23. T
24. T
25. T
26. F
27. T
28. F
29. T
30. F
31. b
32. a
33. c
34. a
35. d
36. c
37. b
38. d
39. c
40. a
41. b
42. b
43. d
44. a
45. c
46. a
47. b
48. d
49. d
50. d

Unit Test, Form B

Possible responses:

1. One factor that made Great Britain ideal for the birth of the Industrial Revolution was exploration and colonialism. The colonies gave Great Britain a vast supply of raw materials such as cotton fiber.

Seapower was a second factor. Great Britain had the largest and most powerful navy and merchant fleets in the world. Another factor was political stability. Although Great Britain fought in North America there was peace at home. A fourth factor was government support. The British government passed laws that favored businesses. A final factor was private investment. Private businessmen funded experiments (research) for creating better products.

2. Typical textile factories employed workers as young as six years old. Factories were noisy and lacked ventilation. Children often had to reach into running machines to catch broken threads, and without safety measures, severe injuries were common. Workers toiled more than twelve hours a day. They worked without adequate food and under poor sanitary conditions.
3. Industrial cities had factories, a large workforce, reliable transportation, warehouses, stores, and offices. The streets were crowded with people and streetcars. People hurried off to work on subways or streetcars, and came home at night to multi-storied buildings and skyscrapers. Streets and homes were lit with electric lights. Modern water and waste systems improved health and living conditions. Following the European example, the cities maintained green spaces—parks and recreational areas.
4. Landowning aristocrats made up most of Parliament. Some industrial cities had no representation in Parliament. Only wealthy male property owners could vote. The working and middle classes demanded political reform. The reform act did gave representation to some industrial cities for the first time. It also increased the number of eligible voters by allowing middle class men with property and an education to vote. These reforms reduced the power of the aristocrats. Yet many working class men and all women could not vote.
5. There were several events that led to the Civil War. The Kansas-Nebraska Act allowed residents of new territories to choose whether to allow slavery. This started a bitter debate. Tensions grew so great that after Lincoln was elected president, South Carolina decided to secede from the United States. Several other states followed. They formed the Confederate States of America. Lincoln did not believe that the constitution gave states the right to secede. He sent supplies to an American fort in South Carolina, Fort Sumter. There, the first shots of the Civil War were fired.
6. The British East India Company forced cultural changes on India such as a new educational system and the English language. They outlawed certain customs and brought Christian missionaries into India. Some Indians felt the British were trying to eliminate their customs and Hinduism completely. Then the British introduced a rifle that used cartridges greased in animal fat, which was offensive to both Hindus and Muslims. Sepoys in the town of Meerut refused to use the rifles. When they were punished, sepoys all over northern India rose up against their British officers. Brutalities were committed by both the sepoys and the British.
7. Great Britain imported tea from China. The Chinese were not interested in European exports. To try to fix the trade imbalance, Britain began smuggling opium in China. This addictive drug had been banned into China but it was still in demand. In 1838, Chinese officials ordered the destruction of British opium. In response the British attacked China and captured Shanghai.
8. Italy faced many changes after unification. Regional differences led to a lack of unity among the people, some of whom resented being governed by Rome, the new capital of Italy. The Catholic Church did not recognize Italy as a nation and forbid

Catholics from voting. Widespread poverty led to massive emigration of skilled workers from Italy. Voting reform was a major priority.

9. Otto von Bismarck's political philosophy became known as realpolitik. His philosophy was practical rather than idealistic. He developed his policies based on the interests of Prussia. For example, when Prussia's liberal government would not approve funds to expand the military, Bismarck dismissed them and collected the taxes anyway.
10. The Bessemer process allowed manufacturers to make cheaper, stronger steel more efficiently. By 1860, a network of tracks linked the major American cities, bringing goods to many areas. The stronger steel was used in the production of railroad bridges that allowed trains to cross any type of terrain. The expansion of railroads increased trade. Trains could move huge loads efficiently. As transportation costs declined, goods became more available and more affordable.
11. The map shows the effects of the "Scramble for Africa." Seven different European nations controlled all of Africa, except Liberia and Ethiopia. Most of the dates on the map show that Africa was carved up after the Berlin Conference of 1884.

Chapter 26: World War I

Section Quiz

SECTION 1

1. d
2. d
3. b
4. b
5. a
6. a
7. c
8. c
9. c
10. a

SECTION 2

1. i
2. e
3. a
4. m
5. b
6. d
7. f
8. j
9. h
10. c

SECTION 3

1. T
2. F; Factories were not able to supply the army, transportation was weak and military leaders were chosen through connections, not ability.
3. F; Nicholas knew very little about military matters.
4. F; Rasputin was viewed by most Russians as corrupt and immoral.
5. T

SECTION 4

1. *Lusitania*
2. neutral
3. unrestricted submarine warfare
4. U-boats
5. Zimmermann Note
6. Allied Powers
7. armistice
8. Fourteen Points
9. Treaty of Versailles
10. League of Nations

Chapter Test, Form A

1. c
2. b
3. a
4. d
5. b
6. c
7. d
8. d
9. a
10. a
11. b
12. Triple Alliance
13. Allied Powers
14. Propaganda
15. genocide
16. Grigory Rasputin
17. *Lusitania*
18. mandates
19. T
20. T
21. F
22. F
23. T
24. T
25. T

Chapter Test, Form B

Possible responses:

1. The drive to build empires in the late 1800s and early 1900s had created much rivalry and ill will among the nations of Europe. Germany, France, Russia, and

Great Britain each saw themselves as great imperial nations and believed they could not afford to stand by while a rival empire gained power. Their imperialism was accompanied by a massive military buildup caused by each nation's desire to protect overseas colonies from other nations. The growing power of Europe's armed forces left all sides anxious and ready to act at the first sign of trouble.

2. When Austria-Hungary identified the assassin of Franz Ferdinand as a Serb, Austria decided to punish Serbia. Russia had promised to support the Serbs, and so prepared for war. Germany saw Russia's actions as a threat, and so declared war on Russia, and then on France, Russia's ally. When Germany struck Belgium, a neutral country, Great Britain declared war on Germany.
3. Any two of the following are acceptable: Poison gas could blind, choke, or burn victims, but its effectiveness was limited because a change in wind direction could blow it back into the troops who had launched it; rapid-firing machine guns and high-explosive artillery were very effective and killed many soldiers; tanks could be used to cross rough battlefield terrain, but were not reliable or used widely until late in the war; aircraft with machine guns or bombs proved increasingly useful in attacking battlefield positions, factories, and cities.
4. Food and fuel supplies were growing low, Russians were unhappy with the government, especially with the corrupt influence of Grigory Rasputin, and also very unhappy about the terrible results of the war.
5. Germany was forced to pay an enormous amount of money to the war's victims (called reparations), to limit the size of its military, to return conquered lands to France and to Russia, to give up their colonies around the world, and to give up other German lands to form the newly independent nation of Poland.
6. Trenches were deep ditches dug by soldiers for protection. Because of the deadlock on the Western Front, soldiers remained in trenches for a long time. Trenches were dirty, unsanitary, and filled with rats and lice. At times, soldiers were ordered over the top only to be cut down by enemy fire. The photo shows a tank. This was one of the technologies created to break the deadlock. Poison gas was used, and aircraft too. Unfortunately none of these new technologies brought a quick end to trench warfare.

Chapter 27: The Interwar Years

Section Quiz

SECTION 1

1. e
2. h
3. d
4. b
5. k
6. l
7. a
8. i
9. g
10. j

SECTION 2

1. T
2. F; President Hoover believed the federal government should play a limited role in business affairs. He eventually took some actions to fight the Depression, but many felt he did too little.
3. F; The New Deal established public works programs that gave jobs to the unemployed, provided money for welfare and other relief programs, and created new regulations to reform and protect the stock market.
4. T
5. F; The Smoot-Hawley Tariff Act placed heavy taxes on imported goods to encourage Americans to buy goods and products made in the United States.

SECTION 3

1. a
2. c
3. c
4. a
5. d

SECTION 4

1. fascism
2. totalitarianism
3. Ethiopia
4. central planning
5. Great Purge/Great Terror
6. Ukrainians
7. Gulag/system of labor camps
8. chancellor
9. Nuremberg Laws
10. Kristallnacht

Chapter Test, Form A

1. b	14. l
2. c	15. b
3. a	16. e
4. a	17. h
5. c	18. Kemal Atatürk
6. b	19. Egypt
7. c	20. civil disobedience
8. k	21. Black Tuesday
9. g	22. Manchukuo
10. m	23. Nanjing Massacre
11. i	24. fascism
12. a	25. totalitarianism
13. d	

Chapter Test, Form B

Possible responses:

1. Gandhi believed in two important concepts. One was nonviolence toward living things, or ahimsa. The other was civil disobedience, or a refusal to obey unjust laws.
2. Herbert Hoover believed that the federal government should have a limited role in business affairs, and so he favored a minimal governmental response to the Great Depression. In time he took some action, but many Americans felt that he did too little. Franklin Roosevelt, however, believed the government should fight the Depression using government spending to help start an economic recovery. His New Deal created jobs, provided government money for relief programs, and created new regulations to reform and protect the stock market and the banking system.
3. Italy, Germany, and the Soviet Union all were totalitarian governments. In all three cases, the government viewed the state as more important than individuals; the government was controlled by a single political party; and a powerful dictator united the people and symbolized the government.
4. Hitler came to power during a time of conflict and political instability. While the Weimar Republic was in power after World War I, many Germans blamed its leaders for the humiliating Versailles Treaty and economic problems such as inflation, the German mark becoming virtually worthless, and many Germans losing their savings. The German people were desperate for a strong leader who could improve their lives. Hitler's talent for public speaking and leadership, along with his claims about German greatness won the Nazi Party many new supporters who wanted to believe him.
5. Japan itself was approximately the same geographic size as its two colonies, Korea and Taiwan. The area of China that Japan invaded was 3-4 times the area of Japan itself.

Chapter 28: World War II

Section Quiz

SECTION 1

1. b	6. f
2. c	7. k
3. m	8. e
4. d	9. h
5. j	10. i

SECTION 2

1. mobilizing or mobilization
2. North Africa
3. Erwin Rommel
4. Dwight D. Eisenhower
5. El Alamein
6. siege
7. defeat
8. Battle of Midway

9. kamikaze
10. island hopping

SECTION 3

1. F; Hitler blamed the Jews.
2. T
3. T
4. F; The genocidal campaign is known as the Holocaust.
5. T

SECTION 4

1. D-Day
2. V-E Day
3. Okinawa
4. Truman
5. Japan
6. Hirohito
7. Yalta Conference
8. United Nations
9. V-J Day
10. Potsdam Conference

Chapter Test, Form A

1. b	14. i
2. a	15. c
3. d	16. b
4. c	17. m
5. c	18. d
6. a	19. a
7. a	20. T
8. a	21. F
9. d	22. T
10. e	23. T
11. g	24. F
12. k	25. T
13. j	

Chapter Test, Form B

Possible responses:

1. First, Hitler violated the Treaty of Versailles by militarizing the Rhineland in March 1936. Second, Hitler annexed Austria in March 1938. In neither case did France or Europe take direct action to stop him, convincing him that he could invade Czechoslovakia unopposed.
2. Japanese and American carriers fought on the high seas in the Battle of Midway in June 1942. Because Americans had broken a secret Japanese code, they knew the details of the planned attack. As a result, they won the battle decisively, destroying four Japanese carriers. The battle changed the balance of power in the Pacific, and the Allies could finally go on the offensive.
3. When reports were investigated and confirmed, the United States established the War Refugee Board to aid the rescue of Jews in Europe. This helped save about 200,000 Jews. However, the U.S. government did not do all that it could to save Jews in Europe. The government did not establish the board until 1944, and leaders were unwilling to take actions that might interfere with the larger war effort.
4. D-Day opened a second, Western front in Europe, putting the Axis Powers on the defensive. On June 6, 1944, Allied forces invaded France. Nearly 150,000 troops landed on the beaches of Normandy and forced through strong German defenses. Nearly a million soldiers had come ashore by July. The Allies reconquered most of France in July, and Germans surrendered in Paris.
5. In early 1945, battles for two islands close to Japan, Iwo Jima and Okinawa, convinced American leaders that the Japanese defenders' willingness to fight to the death would be incredibly costly in American lives. They believed that using the atomic bomb would help bring the war to a quick end and save American lives.
6. Student answers will vary. A sample answer is that this poster was meant to show that the efforts of ordinary Americans to recycle metal through scrap metal drives was directly helping the war effort.
7. Student answers will vary. A sample answer is that this poster would make Americans who participated in scrap metal drives feel proud and patriotic, and

encourage more Americans to get involved in the war effort.

Unit 8: The World at War

Unit Test, Form A

1. a
2. d
3. c
4. b
5. b
6. b
7. c
8. a
9. a
10. c
11. d
12. c
13. d
14. b
15. c
16. nationalism
17. Central Powers
18. Czar Nicholas II
19. Long March
20. civil disobedience
21. New Deal
22. natural resources
23. totalitarian
24. annexing
25. Italy
26. isolationism
27. supply
28. Battle of Stalingrad
29. War Refugee Board
30. Battle of the Bulge
31. k
32. h
33. i
34. b
35. l
36. a
37. d
38. j
39. c
40. g
41. T
42. F
43. T
44. F
45. T
46. T
47. T
48. T
49. F
50. F

Unit Test, Form B

Possible responses:

1. The four factors that put Europe on the brink of war were militarism, alliances, imperialism, and nationalism. Throughout the late 1800s and early 1900s, European countries underwent a massive build up of military force. This left all sides worrying about aggression. To protect themselves some nations formed alliances with other nations. Germany, France, Russia, and Great Britain were imperial nations and did not want another empire to have more power. Nationalism was spreading across Europe and leading to the formation of new countries and a struggle for power.
2. Two major factors prompted the United States to enter World War I. Germans attacked the *Lusitania* and other ships carrying American passengers. The United States complained to German leaders, who agreed to stop attacking passenger ships. The Germans resumed unrestricted submarine warfare, ignoring their promise. Additionally, the United States learned via the Zimmermann Note that Germany proposed that Mexico attack the U.S. This action stirred the American public out of isolationism.
3. Several factors contributed to the stock market crash of 1929. The booming economy of the early 1920s had produced an unequal distribution of wealth. More people began investing in the stock market and stock prices reached unrealistic levels. Businesses began giving credit to consumers. When people reached their credit limits, they stopped purchasing products. The decline in consumer spending caused many businesses to suffer or fail. This led to concerns over the stock market and a huge sell-off of stock.
4. Common features of totalitarian governments include political, social, and economic factors. In totalitarian governments, the state is more important than the individual. The government is controlled by a single party and a dictator. The government controls all aspects of a citizen's life with the use of terror and violence. The government directs the national economy and controls businesses. Labor and businesses are used to serve the state.
5. The terms of the Treaty of Versailles were very damaging to Germany. The economy

was crippled due to demands for reparations. The punitive terms of the treaty made Hitler's ideas more appealing to the German people. Africans were upset because they were left out of negotiations and Europeans simply transferred control of Germany's African colonies to other countries. In this way the treaty increased unrest and stirred feelings of nationalism in Africans. China was hoping that the treaty would restore lands taken by the Japanese. Chinese disappointment with the West opened the door to communism.

6. Key events include the stock market crash or Black Tuesday, and the Great Depression. Disappointment with President Hoover's response led to the election of Roosevelt. He initiated New Deal programs such as public works programs, and new regulations to reform the banking system. The British economist John Maynard Keynes advocated government spending to control economic downturns. The worldwide nature of the depression created a desire for strong leaders, which resulted in Fascism and totalitarianism. In Germany, Hitler blamed the Jews for the economic problems of the country.

Chapter 29: Europe and North America

Section Quiz

SECTION 1

1. the Soviet Union
2. Nuremberg trials
3. Potsdam Conference
4. Cold War
5. iron curtain
6. Truman Doctrine
7. Marshall Plan
8. containment
9. Berlin airlift
10. North Korea

SECTION 2

1. a
2. c
3. b
4. m
5. f
6. l
7. e
8. i
9. h
10. g

SECTION 3

1. c
2. d
3. b
4. b
5. c
6. d
7. d
8. c
9. b
10. d

SECTION 4

1. F; Boris Yeltsin did not want to see hard-liners take over the Soviet Union.
2. T
3. T
4. T
5. F; al Qaeda was led by Osama bin Laden.

Chapter Test, Form A

1. a
2. c
3. b
4. d
5. b
6. b
7. d
8. a
9. d
10. Nuremberg trials
11. Warsaw Pact
12. arms race
13. Communist
14. Martin Luther King Jr.
15. counterculture
16. command
17. *perestroika*
18. al Qaeda
19. T
20. T
21. F
22. F
23. F
24. F
25. T

Chapter Test, Form B

Possible responses:

1. The policy of containment involved resisting Soviet aggression in order to contain the spread of communism. The

Truman Doctrine was a pledge to provide economic and military aid to countries in danger of becoming Communist. The Marshall Plan was a massive program of economic aid to Europe to prevent Europeans from turning to communism in desperation.

2. Deterrence is the development of, or maintenance of, military power in order to prevent an attack by a rival nation. This strategy fueled the arms race, in which the Soviet Union and the United States each struggled to gain an advantage in weapons. The goal was to have enough nuclear weapons to strike back against any attacker and cause terrible destruction, thus making it too dangerous for the other side to start a war.
3. Gorbachev proposed two radical concepts: *glasnost*, or "openness," meaning a willingness to discuss openly the problems of the Soviet Union, and *perestroika*, or "restructuring," referring to the reform of the Soviet economic and political system. His actions included introduction of free-market mechanisms, pursuit of arms control agreements, and reduction of Soviet troop strength in Eastern Europe.
4. The development of the Internet seemed to create tremendous opportunities for commerce. Entrepreneurs started hundreds of Internet-related companies known as "dot-coms." Although investors bought billions of dollars worth of stock, many of these companies never turned a profit. The collapse of the dot-com boom by the end of the decade contributed to a slowdown of the U.S. economy.
5. One possible answer: The Cold War made many Americans fearful of the prospect of nuclear war. Air-raid drills in schools made this danger seem quite real. Some people built bomb shelters for protection. Also, the Red Scare raised fears of Communist subversion in American life. During this period, unfounded accusations of Communist ties sometimes harmed innocent people.
6. The cartoon depicts Communist leaders facing an angry protest. Demonstrators are protesting problems in Soviet life that Gorbachev tried to solve with his policies of *glasnost* and *perestroika*. The "Free Lithuania" sign refers to efforts of the Baltic republics, other Soviet republics, and Eastern European nations to break free of Soviet rule. Their success brought the breakup of the Soviet Union.

Chapter 30: Asia

Section Quiz

SECTION 1

1. T
2. F; In 1947, Jawaharlal Nehru became India's first prime minister.
3. F; The Muslim League formally called for a partition, or division, of India and the creation of separate Muslim and Hindu countries.
4. T
5. T

SECTION 2

1. c
2. b
3. d
4. a
5. a

SECTION 3

1. l
2. f
3. b
4. i
5. m
6. a
7. c
8. j
9. g
10. k

SECTION 4

1. Pacific Rim
2. Japan
3. Corazon Aquino
4. North Korea
5. nuclear
6. Asian Tigers
7. reunited
8. consumer goods
9. education
10. skyscrapers

Chapter Test, Form A

1. a
2. c
3. a
5. d
6. b
7. d

4. b
8. Muhammad Ali Jinnah
9. Bangladesh
10. Ho Chi Minh
11. Red Guards
12. Khmer Rouge
13. Great Leap Forward
14. Ferdinand Marcos
15. Tiananmen Square Massacre
16. Deng Xiaoping

17. F
18. T
19. T
20. F
21. T
22. T
23. F
24. T
25. F

Chapter Test, Form B

Possible responses:

1. India was home to 255 million Hindus and 92 million Muslims. As hope for Indian independence grew, so did religious tensions. Some Muslims feared that Hindus would dominate an independent India. Arguing that Indian Muslims should have a separate nation in order to protect their rights, the Muslim League in 1940 called for partition. Violence between Hindus and Muslims increased. Finally, British leaders decided that partition was the best way to ensure a safe and stable region.
2. A wave of violence followed partition and independence, as millions of people on each side of the border tried to flee. Muslims in India headed for Pakistan, and Hindus in Pakistan headed for India. Nearly a million people died. Since independence, border disputes and other problems have caused continuing hostility. A key issue has been the conflicting claims of India and Pakistan to the region of Kashmir. The role of India in the independence of East Pakistan and the tensions caused by testing nuclear weapons in India and Pakistan have also complicated relations between the two countries.
3. The domino theory was the belief that if all of Vietnam fell to communism, other Southeast Asian countries would quickly follow. With North Vietnam already under Communist rule, the United States began sending military assistance to the non-Communist government in South Vietnam, which faced a guerrilla war led by Vietcong guerrillas. The United States sent thousands of military advisors to help South Vietnamese forces fight the Vietcong and the North Vietnamese. The American presence in Vietnam expanded greatly after the Gulf of Tonkin Resolution of 1962.
4. Mao Zedong seized the property of rural landowners and redistributed it among the peasants, then adopted Soviet-style five-year plans for industrial development. The first five-year plan doubled China's small industrial output and helped to raise living standards. But in 1958, Mao broke with Soviet-style policies and announced a program called the Great Leap Forward, creating thousands of communes with the goal of increasing industrial and agricultural output. The program had disastrous results. Droughts, floods and farmers' neglect led to sharp drops in agricultural production. Millions died in the famine that followed.
5. The three steps for rebuilding Japan were: demilitarizing Japan, creating a democratic government, and establishing an economy that could support a peaceful and democratic Japan.
6. The Asian Tigers achieved impressive economic growth by following a pattern similar to the one used by postwar Japan. They provided education and training to produce a skilled workforce, they received large amounts of economic aid from the United States, and they focused on growth through exports of consumer goods. Despite a severe economic crisis in Asia in 1997, the Asian Tigers worked together to stabilize their economies and keep growing.

Chapter 31: Africa and the Middle East

Section Quiz

SECTION 1

1. c
2. d
3. b
4. c
5. b

SECTION 2

1. F; The Sharpeville Massacre led some ANC leaders to resist apartheid by meeting violence with violence.
2. T
3. F; By the end of the 1960s, almost all the independent African countries had adopted one-party systems.
4. T
5. F; After independence, both Kenya and Tanzania adopted Swahili as their national language.

SECTION 3

1. c
2. d
3. f
4. l
5. m
6. j
7. e
8. k
9. a
10. g

SECTION 4

1. oil
2. Islamic
3. the Organization of Petroleum Exporting Countries (OPEC)
4. Six-Day War
5. peace
6. Palestine Liberation Organization (PLO)
7. urban
8. Iran
9. sanctions
10. insurgency

Chapter Test, Form A

1. d
2. c
3. b
4. a
5. b
6. a
7. c
8. d
9. c
10. g
11. f
12. j
13. d
14. h
15. l
16. c
17. k
18. a
19. i
20. Jomo Kenyatta
21. malaria; AIDS
22. traditional
23. Camp David
24. Yasser Arafat
25. Islamists

Chapter Test, Form B

Possible responses:

1. Apartheid kept nonwhites apart from whites and barred them from voting. It divided nonwhites into three separate racial categories: Black, Colored, and Asian. Apartheid laws banned interracial marriages, restricted nonwhite ownership of land and businesses, and required blacks to carry identity documents that limited where they could live or travel. Under apartheid, millions of blacks were deprived of South African citizenship and required to live in designated "homelands."
2. Any two of the following are acceptable: East Africans have emphasized the use of the Swahili language in maintaining a strong tradition of poetry, plays, and novels. Some African writers developed a new type of literature known as the negritude movement. They rejected European culture and focused on African identity. Other writers such as Wole Soyinka have focused on African culture and identity while daring to challenge repressive governments. Artists have revived traditional African arts such as sculpture (ceremonial masks), music (often blending African and Western styles), and ceremonial dance.
3. The Arab-Israeli war of 1948 discredited Middle Eastern leaders because they had been unable to prevent the creation and expansion of Israel. Egypt's Gamal Abdel Nasser was one of a number of young nationalist leaders who came to power in the war's aftermath. Blaming Egypt's failures on weak leadership and

corruption, Nasser and his associates seized power, abolished Egypt's monarchy, banned existing political parties, and created a strong one-party state. Nasser became the most important figure in the Arab world after his confrontation with Britain, France, and Israel over the Suez Canal. Nasser's policy of Pan-Arabism served to rally Arabs against Israel and the Western powers. Other Middle Eastern countries experienced similar nationalist ferment.

4. About two-thirds of the world's known oil reserves are located in the Middle East. These reserves have been a vast source of wealth for some countries. Oil revenues allowed governments to sponsor modernization efforts, bolster industrialization, improve health care, provide education, and increase national prosperity. At the same time, oil has been a source of conflict in the region. OPEC nations wield a tremendous influence over the world's economy.
5. Answers will vary, but should indicate that Israel was not a nation until 1948. Prior to World War II Germany might have been one of the countries represented on the chart. In addition there may have been a smaller percentage of Jews living in the Untied States.

Chapter 32: Latin America

Section Quiz

SECTION 1

1. b
2. k
3. h
4. c
5. j
6. l
7. a
8. m
9. g
10. d

SECTION 2

1. T
2. F; During this time, Brazil's economy grew faster than any other in the world. At the same time, wages were frozen.
3. F; Salvador Allende's leftist policies worried the United States government.
4. F; Under the Duvaliers, Haiti's economy became worse.
5. T

SECTION 3

1. World
2. military
3. Chile
4. Mexico
5. Canada
6. two
7. Vicente Fox
8. Bolivia
9. Hugo Chávez
10. free-market

Chapter Test, Form A

1. c
2. b
3. a
4. d
5. c
6. d
7. c
8. a
9. d
10. d
11. Liberation
12. Sandinistas
13. populist
14. Manuel Noriega
15. Violeta Chamorro
16. Hugo Chávez
17. F
18. T
19. T
20. T
21. T
22. F
23. T
24. F
25. T

Chapter Test, Form B

Possible responses:

1. U.S. businesses, wealthy Americans, and Cuba's elite earned a large part of Cuba's wealth. Most Cubans were poor. The United States supported a string of corrupt dictators, which stirred discontent and nationalism.
2. Some positive results of the Cuban revolution include free, nationwide medical care and free education.
3. Students will discuss two of the following: In order to prevent communist or socialist governments the United States has intervened in the politics of several Latin American countries. At times the U.S worked to keep a government in power. Other times it funded rebel groups who opposed the government in power. In

addition the U.S. has worked to protect its economic interests.

4. Latin America's military governments fell because they had not brought about needed economic and social changes, nor did they bring stability and security to their countries.
5. Any three of the following are acceptable: they drastically cut government spending; they ended some government subsidies for businesses; they turned over some government services to private enterprise; they returned some inefficient, government owned businesses to private ownership; they strengthened and made new regional trade agreements.
6. The graph illustrates the effects of economic reforms and increased stability in Latin American countries. It also shows that not all countries have benefited.

Chapter 33: Today's World

Section Quiz

SECTION 1

1. l
2. e
3. f
4. g
5. d
6. m
7. b
8. a
9. h
10. c

SECTION 2

1. F; Countries that signed the Helsinki Accords agreed to respect human rights.
2. F; An NGO is a non-governmental organization formed to provide services or promote certain public policies.
3. T
4. T
5. F; The increase in the percentage of people who live in cities is called urbanization.

SECTION 3

1. Irish Republican Army/IRA
2. Middle East
3. Afghanistan
4. Iraq
5. Nuclear
6. legitimate
7. ethnic
8. Darfur/Darfur region of Sudan
9. sanctions
10. nuclear

SECTION 4

1. b
2. c
3. d
4. a
5. d

Chapter Test, Form A

1. a
2. c
3. d
4. c
5. a
6. d
7. b
8. b
9. c
10. d
11. popular
12. famine
13. natural disaster
14. Refugees
15. terrorism/terrorist tactics
16. Sustainable development
17. Information Age
18. c
19. j
20. h
21. g
22. f
23. d
24. b
25. e

Chapter Test, Form B

Possible responses:

1. Developed countries are industrialized nations with strong economies and a high standard of living. People in developed countries generally have access to good health care, education, and technology. About 20% of the world's nations are considered developed. Developing countries have less productive economies and a lower standard of living. People often lack adequate education and health care. The poorest or least developed countries suffer from extreme poverty, a lack of political and social stability, and may have ongoing conflict.

2. Any two of the following are acceptable. Global trade and multinational corporations make it possible for people in one country to buy products produced in another country; rapid transportation systems allow many people to travel to or even move to different countries, bringing with them elements of their own culture; mass media makes it possible for people around the world to watch news, television, and movies, or hear music from other nations around the world, and the Internet is a major source for the exchange of images and ideas.
3. Push factors displace people. They include war, persecution, or poverty. Pull factors are things that people are drawn to, that provide opportunities. They include job opportunities or a better life.
4. Any two of the following are acceptable. Weapons of mass destruction include biological, chemical, and nuclear weapons. Biological weapons are organisms or toxins found in nature, including diseases or poisons such as anthrax, plague, or smallpox. Chemical weapons are chemicals that can be used against groups of people and can cause a great deal of damage; for example, the nerve gas sarin was released by a religious group in a Tokyo subway in 1995. Nuclear weapons are extremely destructive weapons that harness nuclear energy; eight countries are known to possess them today.
5. Sample answer: If I were growing up before the Information Age, I would not have access to the Internet, so I would have to go to a library to do research for homework, drive to stores to shop, and maintain friendships in person or through the mail; I would not have a personal computer, so would have to type my papers on a typewriter; and I would not have a cell phone, so my friends and parents could not call me wherever I was.
6. The Middle East saw the most terrorist attacks in the period from 1995 to 2005. Reasons for this include ongoing Arab-Israeli conflict, as well as Arab resentment of the West. There are some radical Muslim organizations that claim Islam justifies terrorist attacks. Some groups want to destroy Israel and create an independent Palestinian state. Other groups want to end Western influence.

Unit 9: The Contemporary World

Unit Test, Form A

1. e
2. i
3. a
4. m
5. g
6. l
7. b
8. k
9. d
10. h
11. Marshall Plan
12. Fidel Castro
13. Mao Zedong
14. Quit India
15. Soweto Uprising
16. apartheid
17. populist
18. NAFTA
19. desertification
20. biological
21. T
22. F
23. F
24. F
25. T
26. T
27. T
28. F
29. F
30. T
31. d
32. b
33. b
34. c
35. b
36. c
37. a
38. d
39. c
40. b
41. d
42. c
43. b
44. c
45. d
46. a
47. b
48. b
49. a
50. c

Unit Test, Form B

Possible responses:

1. Both the Truman Doctrine and the Marshall Plan reflected the United States' policy of containment, or desire to keep communism from spreading. The Truman Doctrine provided economic and military aid in the hope that it could help free peoples to resist takeover by "armed

minorities or outside pressures." The Truman Doctrine resulted in millions of dollars in aid going to Turkey and Greece. U.S. leaders feared that if conditions did not improve throughout Europe, more countries might turn to communism. The Marshall Plan provided billions of dollars in economic aid to keep that from happening. The aid was intended to help Western European countries recover quickly from World War II. The United States believed this would keep Europe politically stable.

2. A chief cause of the Berlin blockade was that Western leaders were about to form a new independent democratic German nation from the three Western zones. They also wanted to establish a democratic government in West Berlin, even though it was located deep within the Soviet zone. The Soviets opposed this plan and tried to block all food, coal, and other vital supplies from reaching Berlin. They hoped this would force the West to leave Berlin. An effect of the blockade was that the Western nations organized the Berlin airlift and successfully supplied West Berlin. The Soviets called off the blockade in May 1949. A second effect was that West Germany and East Germany then came into being. Other effects: The United States, Canada, and most Western European nations formed a military alliance called NATO to counter Soviet power in Europe. And the Soviet Union then formed the Warsaw Pact linking it to the Communist countries of Eastern Europe.
3. Tensions began to grow once the war ended. The Soviet Union wanted to create a buffer zone of friendly governments in Eastern Europe. The Western nations saw this as a threat and objected to Soviet actions that imposed Communist governments on Eastern Europe. Soon the United States and the Soviet Union entered an era of tension and hostility that became known as the Cold War.
4. A chief cause of partition was the fear among some Muslims that an independent India would be dominated by Hindus. Such fears led the Muslim League to call for separate Muslim and Hindu countries. One effect of partition was to create Muslim East and West Pakistan and Hindu India. Another effect was waves of violence as millions of people fled their homes to seek safety with other members of their own religious groups.
5. The Khmer Rouge established a Communist government in Cambodia and renamed the country Democratic Kampuchea. They wanted to create a society in which almost everyone was a simple peasant. To achieve this goal, they believed they had to destroy every influence of urban life and modern civilization. They were ruthless in this objective, killing anyone who seemed to be educated or who seemed to oppose their goal.
6. Mao's Great Leap Forward had disastrous results. The plan included the creation of thousands of communes of about 20,000 people each. Each commune was to produce its food and have its own small-scale industry. Small commune factories failed to produce the needed goods. Poor weather and farmer neglect led to sharp decreases in agricultural production. Famine was widespread in rural China. Tens of millions of Chinese starved to death between 1959 and 1961.
7. The end of the Cold War led to the collapse of dictatorships in many African nations. During the Cold War both the United States and the Soviet Union gave financial support to dictators who were friendly to their side. When the Cold War ended in 1989, most of that money dried up. Without such funding, many dictators had trouble maintaining control. Many Africans saw this as an opportunity to create democratic governments. Although more than 30 African countries abandoned one-party systems and held elections,

some dictators stayed in power due to election fraud, intimidation, or simply a lack of desirable alternatives.

8. As a result of the Six-Day War, Israel took control of the Golan Heights, Sinai Peninsula, Gaza Strip, West Bank, and East Jerusalem. This meant Israel had gained control of land in the West Bank and Gaza with a large Palestinian population. A delayed result was that Egypt and Syria went to war six years later to get their land back.
9. Results of the Cuban Revolution include a lack of political freedoms; free education and health care; a scarcity of food and goods; long-term hostility between Cuba and the United States; and Cuban reliance on Soviet aid followed by Cuban economic problems when the Soviet Union collapsed.
10. Economic reforms helped stabilize Latin American exporters such as Brazil and Chile, but in some countries the reforms caused hardships. For example, Argentina's attempts at reform led to a deep depression. People in Argentina faced hard times until the economy began to recover. In many nations one-third of the population remained in poverty and the gap between the rich and poor grew.
11. Supporters of globalization say the process benefits both developing and developed nations. As benefits for developed nations, supporters list new markets for goods and services produced in developed nations. They say developed nations also gain from outsourcing, which provides lower production costs. Supporters of globalization say developing nations benefit from the jobs and wealth created as a result of outsourcing. Opponents of globalization say the process does not raise the standard of living in places where outsourced jobs are performed, and that developed nations lose jobs due to outsourcing. Opponents also claim that globalization makes rich people richer and poor people poorer, and that globalization encourages practices that exploit workers and damage the environment.
12. One environmental issue affecting West Africa today is desertification. This is caused partly by drought and partly by human activity, such as farming in areas that have poor soil. Another human cause of desertification is allowing animals to overgraze. Eventually the soil may dry out to the point that grasses cannot grow. Without plant life to act as anchors, the rich soil erodes. As the spread of desert-like conditions continues, so do cycles of drought and famine that plague many African countries today. Another environmental issue that affects all areas is pollution.
13. During the seven-month period shown on the maps, the areas controlled by North and South Korea changed dramatically. First North Korea took control of most of the peninsula. Later, roles reversed and South Korea controlled almost all of Korea. Then China entered the war, and by January 1951 the boundaries were nearly back to where they were in June 1950, with South Korea controlling slightly more than it did at that time.

Unit 10: Issues in the Contemporary World

Unit Test, Form A

1. g
2. m
3. a
4. l
5. b
6. f
7. h
8. e
9. i
10. j
11. Labor
12. African National Congress
13. Mexico
14. United States
15. special economic zones
16. joint ventures
17. United Nations
18. market
19. General Assembly
20. veto

21. F
22. T
23. T
24. T
25. F
26. F
27. T
28. T
29. T
30. F
31. b
32. c
33. a
34. a
35. d
36. c
37. d
38. c
39. d
40. a
41. d
42. d
43. b
44. c
45. b
46. b
47. c
48. a
49. b
50. a

Unit Test, Form B

Possible responses:

1. Civic participation is a range of activities aimed at influencing government policies. Civic participation is more than voting. It includes contacting elected representatives, staging protests, and building coalitions.
2. Since it was elected in 1997, the Labor government has sought to reform the country's democratic institutions. These reforms have been made in part to help reverse the declining voter turnout in the United Kingdom. One reform was devolution, the redistribution of power from a central governments to local governments. This has happened in the U.K. countries of Wales and Scotland.
3. In 1978, China began moving away from its traditional communist economy. It began allowing free market trade in some areas. They also started allowing some foreign investment. Encouraged by the positive results, China expanded the program in the 1990s to create a socialist market economy. By 1999, China became the second largest economy in the world. Since 1980, China has doubled its share of world trade every five years. China joined the WTO in 2001 and became an attractive site for offshoring. China still emphasizes manufacturing and today supplies one-fifth of the world's clothing and one-third of all mobile phones. India's emphasis is on new service industries provided via the Internet, such as tax preparation and computer technical support. In the 1990s, India embraced capitalism and began moving towards a market economy. Privatization was allowed; foreign investments through joint ventures were welcome.
4. In its constitution, Ireland had recognized the "special position" of the Catholic Church in society, but this clause was removed in 1972. The church had influenced laws, such as the prohibition of divorce. As recently as the 1970s, women were not guaranteed the right to hold jobs outside of the home if they were married. When Ireland joined the EEC (the forerunner to the EU), it needed to conform to EU standards on the treatment of women. Turkey began as a secular country. Women's rights were written into law. In 2002 the elected party in Turkey had Islamic ties. This may be part of an interesting trend. Younger Turkish women identify themselves as Muslim first and a Turkish citizen second. In older Turkish women that is reversed.
5. There are four main goals included in the United Nations charter. The first goal is to maintain international peace and security. The second goal is to develop friendly relations between nations. The third goal of the UN is to cooperate in solving international problems and to promote respect for human rights. And finally, it strives to be a center for harmonizing the actions of nations.
6. As of 2000, 16.3% of Brazil's population lives in São Paolo and Rio de Janeiro. Megacities often house very wealth people and the poorest people. In many it is extremely dangerous. Megacities deal with violence, political instability, and environmental destruction.

End-of-Year Test

1. a
2. a
3. c
4. b
5. c
6. d
7. c
8. a
9. b
10. c
11. c
12. d
13. a
14. a
15. b
16. d
17. a
18. c
19. d
20. c
21. b
22. b
23. a
24. a
25. b
26. d
27. c
28. d
29. d
30. b
31. c
32. a
33. d
34. b
35. b
36. c
37. d
38. d
39. a
40. a
41. a
42. c
43. b
44. c
45. b
46. d
47. d
48. b
49. a
50. b
51. b
52. d
53. a
54. b
55. c
56. c
57. d
58. c
59. a
60. d
61. d
62. a
63. d
64. b
65. b
66. c
67. a
68. c
69. d
70. c
71. b
72. a
73. d
74. c
75. b
76. d
77. c
78. a
79. c
80. c
81. b
82. b
83. d
84. b
85. d
86. b
87. a
88. b
89. d
90. c
91. b
92. d
93. c
94. b
95. c
96. a
97. b
98. c
99. d
100. d